BARRON'S

ESSENTIAL WORDS FOR THE

GRE®

THIRD EDITION

Philip Geer, Ed.M.

P9-ARS-130

BARRON'S

About the Author

Philip Geer (Ed.M.) has been teaching English and preparing students for the GRE and SAT for over thirty years in high schools and colleges in the United States and abroad. He is the author of a number of test preparation books, including Barron's *GRE Verbal Workbook* and *6 SAT Practice Tests*, and is the director of Mentaurs Educational Consultants, which helps students around the world through Internet instruction. Students can visit *www.mentaurs.com* for free GRE vocabulary-building exercises and send an e-mail to *essay@mentaurs.com* for guidance in their GRE writing preparation.

All inquiries should be addressed to:
Barron's Educational Series, Inc.
250 Wireless Boulevard
Hauppauge, NY 11788
www.barronseduc.com

ISBN: 978-1-4380-0221-7
Library of Congress Catalog Card No.: 2013930314

PRINTED IN THE UNITED STATES OF AMERICA
9 8 7 6 5 4 3 2 1

10%
POST-CONSUMER
WASTE
Paper contains a minimum
of 10% post-consumer
waste (PCW). Paper used
in this book was derived
from certified, sustainable
forestlands.

CONTENTS

ACKNOWLEDGMENTS

I would like to thank Susan Geer for her invaluable assistance in the preparation of this book.

I am grateful to the following for permission to reproduce copyright material:

Singapore Press Holdings for the article "Delving into the Mind of a Great Thinker, Chomsky" from *The Straits Times Guide to Good English and Greater Knowledge,* © copyright 2005.

Harper San Francisco for an extract from *The Historical Jesus, The Life of a Mediterranean Jewish Peasant,* John Dominic Crossan, © copyright 1992 by John Dominic Crossan. Reprinted by permission of HarperCollins publishers.

Introduction:
Mastering Advanced
Vocabulary for the GRE

The Educational Testing Service (ETS) changed the format of the Graduate Record Exam (GRE) General Test in August 2011. The new Verbal Reasoning section of the GRE features more advanced reading passages with more demanding questions, as well as longer, more complex sentence-completion questions. The section no longer includes analogy or antonyms questions.

This is how ETS describes the new Verbal Reasoning section:

- Measure of ability to analyze and evaluate written material and synthesize information obtained from it, analyze relationships among component parts of sentences, and recognize relationships between words and concepts
- Emphasis on skills related to graduate work, such as complex reasoning

    - Greater emphasis on higher cognitive skills and less dependence on vocabulary knowledge alone
    - More text-based materials, such as reading passages
    - A broader selection of reading passages
    - Expansion of computer-enabled tasks (e.g., highlighting a sentence in a passage that serves the function described in the question)

What does this mean for you as a student preparing for the new Verbal Reasoning section of the GRE? It means that you have to practice the skills of analyzing information in a passage, understanding the relationships among parts of a sentence, and comprehending relationships between words and concepts that are specified by ETS. To do this you should work through the skills section and practice tests in a reputable GRE General Test guidebook, such as *Barron's GRE Verbal Workbook*. You also need to read widely, thinking critically about what you read. Read good books and periodicals such as *The New York Times*, the *Christian Science Monitor*, *The Atlantic*, *The New Yorker*, *Time*, *The Economist*, and *Scientific American*. Besides reading these, you should also read some material at an even higher level. This will improve your ability to understand complex sentence structure and follow a sophisticated line of reasoning. If, as you read, you look up words you do not know in a good dictionary, you will also improve your vocabulary.

Speaking of vocabulary, does the change in the GRE Verbal Reasoning section really mean that you no longer need to have a good vocabulary to do well on the test?

The answer is no. Look at what ETS says about the new test: "*Greater* emphasis on higher cognitive skills and *less* dependence on vocabulary knowledge *alone*" (italics). This means that having a good vocabulary is still very important. Although antonym and analogy questions emphasizing knowledge of vocabulary alone have been dropped, the revamped test does place a considerable emphasis on advanced vocabulary, especially in the new sentence equivalence and text completion questions that have been introduced. Let's examine some of these types of questions and answer choices to see how important vocabulary is on the revised GRE.

SENTENCE-EQUIVALENCE AND TEXT-COMPLETION QUESTIONS

In the sentence-equivalence question below, you must choose *two* answers that could correctly complete the sentence.

It would be difficult to imagine two more different personalities—Liz is shy and taciturn, while Stan is outgoing and _____

- A salubrious
- B laconic
- C specious
- D loquacious
- E doctrinaire
- F talkative

Can you arrive at the correct answers to this question without knowing the meaning of the advanced word in the sentence, *taciturn* (incommunicative, not inclined to speak much), and the meanings of the five advanced words that appear in the answer choices? If you don't know the meanings of *salubrious, laconic, specious, loquacious,* and *doctrinaire*, you will be forced to guess one of the correct answers to this question, (D) *loquacious*, which means (F) *talkative*, the second correct answer. Not all sentence-equivalence questions are so vocabulary dependent but you can expect quite a few to require knowledge of very advanced words.

Let's take a look at another type of question that requires knowledge of advanced words. In the first text-completion question below, you must choose *one* answer to fill in the blank.

In most industrial countries, government intervenes in the economy by changing fiscal and monetary policy to _____ the negative effects of the business cycle, despite the fact that there exists no theory supported by conclusive evidence to explain the underlying cause of the business cycle.

remonstrate
exacerbate
understand
establish
mitigate

If you don't know the definition of *mitigate* (to cause to become less harsh, severe, or painful), you will not be able to answer this question correctly. Also, the more words you know in the other answer choices, the more confident you can be in answering the question.

Here's a question that requires you to choose words to fill in *two* blanks.

Some scholars deny that there is a direct correlation between the scientific theory of relativity and intellectual fashions in the arts, pointing out that many important modernist works such as Igor Stravinsky's (i) _____ symphony *The Rites of Spring* (ii) _____ the theory of relativity.

Blank (i)	Blank (ii)
seminal	presage
syllogistic	antecede
ephemeral	subsume

In this question, all of the answer choices are advanced words. It is not possible to answer this question correctly without knowing the meanings of these advanced words, especially the meanings of the correct answer choices (i) *seminal* (containing the seeds of later development) and (ii) *antecede* (precede).

The final question below requires you to fill in *three* blanks.

The phrase "It's a matter of (i) _____" is often used to indicate that the real meaning of a statement is being lost in verbiage, often with the implication that there is (ii) _____ or (iii) _____.

Blank (i)	Blank (ii)	Blank (iii)
definition	exculpation	peculation
semantics	meritriciousness	equivocation
debate	obfuscation	vacillation

Two key words in the sentence—*verbiage* and *implication*—are advanced words. It would be impossible to figure out the central meaning of the sentence without knowing the meaning of *verbiage* (an excess of words for the purpose)—and if you don't know the meaning of *implication* (that which is hinted or suggested) you will be hard-pressed to follow the logic of the sentence.

Advanced vocabulary also plays a central part in the answer choices given for this question. Once again, this question would be impossible to answer without knowledge of the meanings of these difficult words. If you know that answer choice (i) *semantics* means "the meaning and interpretation of words," answer choice (ii) *obfuscation* means "the act of confusing or obscuring," and answer choice (iii) *equivocation* means "the intentional use of vague language," the sentence makes good sense.

READING QUESTIONS

Next, let's consider a GRE-level reading passage and questions. It uses quite a lot of advanced vocabulary. Do you know the difficult words in the passage and in the questions that follow it?

> To chop a stick, to catch a fly, to pile a heap of sand, is a satisfying action; for the sand stays for a while in its novel arrangement, proclaiming to the surrounding level that we have made it our instrument, while the fly will never stir nor the stick grow together
> (5) again in all eternity. If the impulse that has thus left its indelible mark on things is constant in our own bosom, the world will have been permanently improved and humanized by our action. Nature cannot but be more favorable to those ideas which have once found an efficacious champion.
> (10) Plastic impulses find in this way an immediate sanction in the sense of victory and dominion which they carry with them; it is

so evident a proof of power in ourselves to see things and animals bent out of their habitual form and obedient instead to our idea. But a far weightier sanction immediately follows. Man depends on (15) things for his experience, yet by automatic action he changes these very things so that it becomes possible that by his action he should promote his welfare. He may, of course, no less readily precipitate his ruin. The animal is more subject to vicissitudes than the plant, which makes no effort to escape them or to give chase to what it (20) feeds upon. The greater perils of action, however, are in animals covered partly by fertility, partly by adaptability, partly by success. The mere possibility of success, in a world governed by natural selection, is an earnest of progress. Sometimes, in impressing the environment, a man will improve it: which is merely to say that a (25) change may sometimes fortify the impulse which brought it about. As soon as this retroaction is perceived and the act is done with knowledge of its ensuing benefits, plastic impulse becomes art, and the world begins actually to change in obedience to reason.

—George Santayana (1906)

The first question requires you to select the best answer choice.

1. According to the author

   (A) whenever nature is shaped by a human being, art is produced

   (B) art can only come into existence when the plastic impulse ceases to exist in a person

   (C) art is created when a human being acts on a plastic impulse with awareness of its effect on the world

   (D) a human creation can only be called art when it is in accord with nature

   (E) actions prompted by the plastic impulse are always beneficial to human beings

The second question asks you to consider each of the three choices separately and select all that apply.

2. Based on the information in the passage, which of the following statements would the author be likely to agree with?

   (A) Art is an inherently irrational process.

   (B) Any viable theory of aesthetics must take into account man's relationship to nature.

   (C) All living things are subject to the process of natural selection.

The third question asks you to identify a sentence in the passage that best meets the description given in the question.

3. Select the sentence that provides examples of the plastic impulse at work in human beings.

The passage uses a lot of fairly advanced vocabulary (*indelible, dominion, retroaction, ensuing*) as well as some very advanced vocabulary (*efficacious, plastic, sanction, precipitate, vicissitudes*). You might already be familiar with the first group of words, while you may not know the more advanced words. Not knowing any of these words would make it difficult to understand this passage. The word *plastic* is especially important because it expresses one of the central concepts discussed by the author—the human ability to consciously shape nature.

How did you do on the questions? The correct answer to Question 1 is C. To answer this question correctly you must understand the meaning of the final sentence of the passage: "As soon as . . . obedience to reason" (lines 26–28). And to comprehend this sentence, you must understand the meaning of that key word in the passage, *plastic*, which was discussed above.

The correct answer to Question 2 is B and C. Here, it is necessary to know advanced vocabulary in the answer choices: *inherently, viable, aesthetics.*

Finally, the correct answer to Question 3 is "To chop a . . . in all eternity" (lines 1–5). As with Question 1, you must know the meaning of the word *plastic* to answer this question correctly.

From our analysis, it is clear that vocabulary plays a critical part in answering GRE verbal reasoning questions. Therefore, what it boils down to is that to give yourself a good chance to correctly answer questions with a lot of advanced vocabulary you should learn the words that are most likely to appear in such questions.

You may say that you can figure out words from context and use elimination. This is true, but only to an extent. Also, guessing words from context and using a process of elimination consumes valuable test time that would better be used for figuring out tricky reading comprehension and other questions.

LEARN THE MOST FREQUENTLY TESTED GRE WORDS

Let's look at the following list of advanced words that appeared in sample verbal sections of the GRE published recently by the Educational Testing Service. As a college graduate (or soon to be college graduate), you should already be familiar with many of these words. However, there are some with which you are probably not familiar. Soon, you will have a chance to take a test to tell you exactly what your vocabulary situation is for the GRE.

Look through the list. How many of these advanced words do you know? You probably know some of them, while others look familiar but you are not sure what they mean. Words that appear in **bold** are words that have appeared with the most frequency on the GRE over the past 10 years.

Turn to the list of 300 High-Frequency GRE Words on pages 26–28 and check to see if it contains the boldface advanced words from the list on the next page. Yes, these words, or one of their important forms, are all on the list of the 300 words that appear with the most frequency on the GRE and thus can be learned specifically for the test. These 300 words, as well as an additional 500 important GRE words, will be taught to you in *Essential Words for the GRE*. The 300 High-Frequency GRE Words appear with asterisks on pages 29–277.

Let's summarize the situation:

1. You need to know a lot of advanced words to do well on the GRE verbal test.

2. You may not know all the words you need to know to do well on the GRE verbal test.

3. If you don't know a lot of important GRE words, you need to learn them as quickly and efficiently as possible.

aberrant	**dogmatism**	**juxtapose**
acerbic	**ebullient**	**laconic**
aesthetics	eccentric	**laudable**
ahistorical	**eclectic**	**loquacious**
alleviated	**empirical**	**meticulous**
ambiguity	**emulated**	misnomer
ambivalence	enigmatic	**obdurate**
ameliorated	**equivocate**	**obsequious**
anachronism	euphonic	obtuse
anomaly	**exacerbated**	**obviate**
antithetical	**exacting**	oracular
apathy	**exculpate**	orthodox
arbitrary	**exigency**	panache
arcane	explicate	paradigm
arduous	explicit	**pellucid**
attenuation	**extraneous**	penitential
austerity	fastidiousness	pithy
belies	**fatuous**	polemical
caprice	**fractious**	**pragmatism**
capricious	**frugality**	**probity**
causality	**garrulous**	**prodigality**
circumscribed	**guilelessly**	profligate
commensurate	**gullible**	**profundity**
complaisant	heterogeneous	prolixity
confounds	**iconoclasm**	prosaic
contentious	**ideological**	quixotic
conventional	idiosyncrasy	**rarefied**
cynicism	**idolatry**	**recalcitrant**
delineate	**igneous**	**resolute**
demur	immured	**resolved**
derivative	**immutable**	**reverence**
desultory	impetuously	**sartorial**
didactic	**inadvertent**	scrupulous
diffidence	inalienable	**stigma**
diffuse	**incongruous**	synoptic
disapprobation	**indecorous**	syntactical
discrepancy	**inherent**	**taciturn**
disingenuously	inimical	tendentious
disinterested	**innocuous**	**unequivocal**
dismiss	**insipid**	**vapid**
disparaged	**intractable**	**verbose**
disparate	**intransigent**	vociferous
dispassionate	intrinsic	volubility
disseminate	**irresolute**	**whimsical**

HOW ESSENTIAL WORDS WILL HELP YOU
DO WELL ON THE GRE

Essential Words for the GRE teaches 800 advanced words that frequently appear on the GRE. Each word has been carefully selected through reference to published GRE lists and on the basis of my many years of experience in preparing students for the test. These 800 words also appear in Barron's *GRE Master Word List* and *High-Frequency Word List*. The principle behind this book is that the best way to learn new words for the GRE is to see how these words are used in complex sentences and practice on exercise material that is similar in content, structure, and level of difficulty to that which appears on the actual test. Practicing on such material will improve your skills in understanding complex sentences and arguments and increase your familiarity with important ideas that appear on the GRE.

THE SYSTEMATIC STUDY OF GRE WORDS

Essential Words for the GRE teaches the important words you need to know. Words are taught in units of ten words each, along with their parts of speech, most commonly used definitions on the GRE, and illustrative sentences showing how words are used. The content, style, and tone of the example sentences are consistent with that of sentences appearing in the actual GRE and generally deal with topics in the arts, sciences, and social sciences. Comprehensive exercises at the end of each unit ensure that you know the words and provide practice in their correct use. Many of the words taught in a given unit reappear in subsequent units, both in illustrative sentences and in exercises, providing systematic reinforcement of learning.

To further build your knowledge for the GRE, definitions and background information on important terms mentioned in the illustrative sentences appear in highlighted boxes labeled "Terms from the Arts, Sciences, and Social Sciences." The example below shows how this works. In the example, the illustrative sentence for the word *literati* refers to two important terms, the *First Amendment* and *Philistines*. These two important terms are explained in the highlighted box, helping you to gain a firm understanding of the context in which the word *literati* is used and expanding your knowledge of important terms.

literati *n.* scholarly or learned persons

"Any test that turns on what is offensive to the community's standards is too loose, too capricious, too destructive of freedom of expression to be squared with the *First Amendment*. Under that test, juries can censor, suppress, and punish what they don't like, provided the matter relates to 'sexual impurity' or has a tendency 'to excite lustful thoughts.' This is community censorship in one of its worst forms. It creates a regime where in the battle between the **literati** and the *Philistines*, the Philistines are certain to win."

—*U.S. Supreme Court Justice William O. Douglas, dissenting in the case of* Roth v. United States, *1957.*

Terms from the Arts, Sciences, and Social Sciences

First Amendment: A part of the United States Bill of Rights prohibiting the federal legislature from making laws that establish a state religion or prefer a certain religion, prevent free exercise of religion, infringe the freedom of speech; infringe the freedom of the press; limit the right to assemble peaceably; limit the right to petition the government for a redress of grievances.

Philistines: People considered to be ignorant of the value of cultures and smug and conventional in their thinking.

It is recommended that you keep a good college dictionary handy as you work through this book. This will allow you to explore additional meanings of words you learn and fine-tune your understanding of nuances in meaning between similar words. Two of the best college dictionaries are *The American Heritage College Dictionary* (Fourth Edition) and *Merriam-Webster's Collegiate Dictionary* (Eleventh Edition). If you prefer to use an online dictionary, the excellent *American Heritage Dictionary of the English Language* (Fourth Edition) is available for free at Bartelby.com.

MASTERING HIGH-FREQUENCY WORD ROOTS

Other than learning the difficult words likely to appear on the GRE, how can you improve your chances of doing well on the GRE Verbal Reasoning test? The answer is simple: learning important word roots. *Essential Words for the GRE* features extensive information on word roots, prefixes, and suffixes in the High-Frequency Word Roots section. This section contains a list of the 300 most important Latin and Greek roots that commonly appear in English words. It also gives you hundreds of derivative words, and includes exercises to improve your ability to make use of roots in remembering words you have learned in this book and in deciphering the meaning of unknown words. In addition to being useful for students taking the GRE, a knowledge of word roots provides a great foundation for the student embarking on a career in fields such as law, science, and medicine that use many specialized terms based on Latin and Greek.

GETTING STARTED

So, what do you do now? First, take the Pretest on the following pages. This will tell you how well prepared you are to deal with the advanced vocabulary that appears on the GRE. After that you should make a study plan based on how many words you have to learn and how much time you have to do it before the test.

On pages 22–25 you will find some suggestions to help you plan how to use this book [most] effectively. It is best to study regularly for a relatively short amount of time (30 minutes, for example) rather than intermittently for longer amounts of time.

Pretest

It's time to test your readiness for graduate-level reading. Don't worry. If you aren't familiar with the GRE words in this test, you can be sure you will learn them in Essential Words for the GRE.

Fill in the blank in each sentence by selecting *two* answer choices that fit the overall meaning of the sentence and produce completed sentences that are equivalent in meaning. Answers that are not fully correct will receive no credit.

1. The belief that music is the _____ for the other arts and best exemplifies the power of art to express subtle feelings, was expressed by the critic Walter Pater: "All art constantly aspires towards the condition of music."

   A aesthetic
   B precursor
   C paradigm
   D tome
   E sensitivity
   F model

2. Some scholars believe that the impetus for the building of the Great Pyramid of Giza was for reasons other than the purely functional one of providing imposing and secure burial chambers for pharaohs; these experts see _____ meaning behind its design.

   A an arcane
   B an insipid
   C a nefarious
   D a sportive
   E an obscure
   F a desultory

3. Many statements are not true unless they are _____ by the use of words and phrases such as *sometimes, frequently, in many cases*, and *most*.

    A sanctioned
    B limited
    C superseded
    D embellished
    E qualified
    F supported

4. In the final stage in the impeachment process of an American president, the chief justice of the Supreme Court presides over the Senate, which sits as a body _____ to a jury to decide whether to convict the president.

    A comparable
    B commensurate
    C inherent
    D analogous
    E extraneous
    F impermeable

Fill in the blank in each sentence by selecting *one* entry from the corresponding column of choices in the way that best completes the text.

5. _____, law can be used either to tyrannize the populace, denying them liberty, or to protect their rights, enabling them to live as free citizens expressing their views and doing as they wish.

Enigmatically
Paradoxically
Purportedly
Felicitously
Preternaturally

6. Steeped in mysticism and allegory, alchemy has been a favorite subject of people speculating about the existence of an occult tradition concealed behind _____ facade.

a hermetic
a sedulous
an ephemeral
a mundane
an iconoclastic

7. In 1787, when the U.S. Constitution was being framed, it was proposed that slavery be abolished, but opponents of the measure forced a compromise whereby slavery would not be _____ until early in the next century.

disparaged
stipulated
proscribed
allowed
exculpated

Fill in all of the blanks in the sentences by selecting *one* entry from the corresponding column of choices in the way that best completes the text. Answers that are not fully correct will not receive any credit.

8. The statement "India has recently made great progress in
(i) _____ poverty" should be seen in the context of India's vast population of one billion, of which 320 million remain in
(ii) _____ poverty.

Blank (i)	Blank (ii)
satiating	equivocal
vitiating	abject
alleviating	intransigent

9. Language purists pounce on errors as though they were ghastly offenses against the natural order; however, it is wise to remember that language is a wonderfully (i) _____ tool that is sometimes at its best when it is most (ii) _____ .

Blank (i)	Blank (ii)
malleable	limpid
labile	compliant
demotic	unfettered

10. According to the view of the nineteenth-century apologist for capitalism, (i) _____ was an unfortunate but unavoidable (ii) _____ of both capitalism and of the natural order of the world.

Blank (i)	Blank (ii)
misogyny	concomitant
abnegation	transgression
indigence	miscellany

11. It is interesting to (i) _____ the bromide* "Haste makes waste" and the (ii) _____ "Better safe than sorry."

Blank (i)	Blank (ii)
juxtapose	homily
delineate	platitude
belie	epithet

*A bromide is a commonplace remark or idea.

12. Quantum theory (i) _____ that waves and particles possess a dual nature, with one aspect (ii) _____ in some situations and the other becoming (iii) _____ in other situations.

Blank (i)	Blank (ii)	Blank (iii)
refutes	vacillating	pellucid
queries	vitiating	salient
postulates	predominating	obtuse

13. Dr. Gupta's hundreds of hoaxes (i) _____ the valid research of many of the scientists with whom he had collaborated; fortunately, such (ii) _____ behavior as Dr. Gupta's is (iii) _____ in the history of science.

Blank (i)	Blank (ii)	Blank (iii)
honed	obsequious	an anomaly
tainted	edifying	a paragon
substantiated	unconscionable	a metamorphosis

14. The sociologist Stanley Milgram theorized that the rise of mass society has made it easy for individuals to ignore moral responsibility because the individual is frequently "an intermediate link in a chain of evil," making it possible for a person to (i) _____ his actions by saying, "I was only carrying out my social responsibilities as given in the orders of my superiors; it is not for me to decide the ultimate morality of socially (ii) _____ actions, even if they appear (iii) _____ ."

Blank (i)	Blank (ii)	Blank (iii)
rationalize	maligned	execrable
stipulate	venerated	Machiavellian
repudiate	sanctioned	sycophantic

Read the passages below, and then answer the questions that follow them based on the information in the passages themselves and in any introductory material or notes. The correct answer may be either stated or merely suggested in the passages.

The term "the arts," when used to classify a group of academic disciplines at schools and universities, subsumes the study of languages, history, and literature, while universities use the term "fine arts" to refer to painting and sculpture as an object of study. Else-
(5) where the term "the arts" includes painting and sculpture (usually grouped together as "the plastic arts"), music, and literature, and is often extended to embrace dance, mime, and cinema (the word "artist" is used to refer to a practitioner of any of these). Art is commonly opposed to science (as "subjective," whereas science
(10) is "objective") and its sense is distinguished from etymologically related words such as "artifact," "artificial," and "artisan."

Select one answer choice for each of the following questions.

15. The word "subsumes" as it is used in line 2 most nearly means

 (A) assumes to be true
 (B) makes inferior to
 (C) undermines
 (D) includes in a less comprehensive category
 (E) incorporates in a more comprehensive category

16. Based on the information in lines 8–11 ("Art . . . artisan"), which statement would the author be most likely to agree with?

 (A) Two words can be related etymologically but have different meanings.
 (B) The word "art" has only an accidental and tangential similarity to the words "artifact," "artificial," and "artisan," because it originated from a different word.
 (C) Artifacts can only be studied subjectively.
 (D) "Artisan" is an older word than the modern word "artist" is.
 (E) The words "artifact," "artificial," and "artisan" are not cognate.

The following is a review of the book *Understanding Power: The Indispensable Chomsky* by Noam Chomsky.

You may have heard the cynic's version of the golden rule, namely, he who has the gold makes the rules. That is the thrust of this treatise on power by 75-year-old Noam Chomsky, a professor of linguistics at the Massachusetts Institute of Technology (MIT).
(5) He has written more than 30 books on linguistics and current affairs, including the best-selling *Language and Politics* (1990), *Manufacturing Consent* (1994) and *911* (2001). Once called "arguably the most important intellectual alive" by *The New York Times*, this very politically incorrect academic has taught at MIT since
(10) 1955, immediately after graduating with a PhD in linguistics from the University of Pennsylvania. He is currently one of MIT's institute professors, which means he can teach in any department of the university. But, as he notes wryly in this book: "If I even get near Political Science, you can feel the bad vibes starting."
(15) The book is an edited collection of his lectures and tutorials from 1989 to 1999. Published as a book for the first time, his talks offer high-definition snapshots of the ills of the twentieth century, even as he slices through history to serve up unpalatable truths—like how America's founding fathers actually loathed the idea of democ-
(20) racy, why the United States hires rogue states to fight its wars and why nation-states are the wrong political model for a post-modern world.

He reserves one of his biggest knives for the media, which he takes methodical stabs at for being dictated by the desires of the
(25) elite. With the same vigor, the gleeful iconoclast tells his students why there is not only no such thing as a free lunch, but also no such thing as a free market. As he puts it: "Of course, the 'free market' ideology is very useful—it's a weapon against the general population (in the U.S.), because it's an argument against social
(30) spending, and it's a weapon against poor people abroad, because we can hold it up to them and say, 'You guys have to follow these rules,' then just go ahead and rob them."

He also sees the world's current economic star, China, and its people as "brutal," and so finds no profit in cozying up to either.
(35) Still, conceding that its ascendance to power is unstoppable, he says: "I don't think we should be asking the question, 'How do we improve relations with China?' We should be asking other questions like, What kind of relations do we want to have with China?'"

The saddest cautionary tale in this book is that of Princeton
(40) University graduate Norman Finkelstein, a bright young man who committed career suicide by exposing best-selling historian Joan Peters—whose book *From Time Immemorial* said Palestinians never

existed—as a charlatan. The problem was that her work had been embraced by most of America's finest intellectuals—including (45) writer Saul Bellow and historian Barbara Tuchman—so Mr. Finkelstein's expose was akin to calling them frauds.

Eyebrow-raisers aside, the question-and-answer format of this book captures the rhythm of intellectual repartee between Chomsky and his audience but, more importantly, breaks the monotony (50) of what would otherwise be his marathon soliloquy on the world's ills. Indeed, his mind is such a ragbag of ideas that it is not above pondering such things as the validation of vegetarianism. Yet, in the end, his brilliance falls prey to a certain kind of intellectual snobbery, the sort which asserts that heroes are not to be found (55) "mentioned in the newspapers." As he puts it: "If they're there, you know probably they're not heroes, they're anti-heroes."

Still, love him or hate him, there are not many thinkers around who can proffer credible alternative perspectives on how power corrupts today. This book is as much an antidote to apathy as it is (60) a counterweight to elitist thought. As in this paradox he surfaces: "You'll see that so long as power remains privately concentrated, everybody, everybody, has to be committed to one overriding goal: To make sure that the rich folk are happy—because unless they are, nobody else is going to get anything.

(65) "So, if you're a homeless person sleeping in the streets of Manhattan, let's say, your first concern must be that the guys in the mansions are happy—because if they're happy, then they'll invest, and the economy will work, and things will function, and then maybe something will trickle down to you somewhere along (70) the line. But if they're not happy, everything's going to grind to a halt . . . basically, that's a metaphor for the whole society."

Select one answer choice for each of the following questions.

17. The phrase *unpalatable truths* as it is used in line 18 most nearly means

- (A) theories that have not been conclusively proven
- (B) facts that many people don't like to accept as true
- (C) facts that are not accepted as true by experts
- (D) facts about a wide range of topics
- (E) information that is not widely disseminated

18. Based on the information in the passage, which of the following terms would Noam Chomsky be most likely to apply to the present American economic-political system?

(A) socialistic

(B) anarchic

(C) bureaucratic

(D) plutocratic

(E) theocratic

Consider each of the three choices separately and select all that apply.

19. Which of the following are reasons that the author describes Noam Chomsky as an "iconoclast" (line 25)?

A Noam Chomsky does not accept the presupposition of most historians and political scientists that social phenomena are subject to objective scientific analysis.

B Noam Chomsky is a maverick among intellectuals because of his view that the media does not play a major role in American society.

C Noam Chomsky frequently attacks widely held cherished beliefs.

Identify the sentence by writing its first three words and last three words on the line below.

Select the sentence that gives the author's opinion of the validity of Noam Chomsky's political views.

20. _____

End of Pretest

PRETEST ANSWERS

1. C, F
2. A, E
3. B, E
4. A, D
5. Paradoxically
6. a mundane
7. proscribed
8. alleviating/abject
9. malleable/unfettered
10. indigence/concomitant
11. juxtapose/platitude
12. postulates/predominating/salient
13. tainted/an anomaly/unconscionable
14. rationalize/sanctioned/execrable
15. E
16. A
17. B
18. D
19. C
20. "Still, love him . . . power corrupts today" (lines 57–59).

YOUR PRETEST SCORE

1–2   CORRECT ANSWERS: **VERY POOR**

3–5   CORRECT ANSWERS: **POOR**

6–9   CORRECT ANSWERS: **BELOW AVERAGE**

10–13 CORRECT ANSWERS: **AVERAGE**

14–16 CORRECT ANSWERS: **GOOD**

17–18 CORRECT ANSWERS: **VERY GOOD**

19–20 CORRECT ANSWERS: **EXCELLENT**

Suggested Study Plans

PRETEST SCORE 1 TO 9
(VERY POOR TO BELOW AVERAGE)

ONE-MONTH (4 WEEKS) STUDY PLAN

▶ 3 Weeks

Learn the 300 High-Frequency GRE Words listed on pages 26–28 and asterisked on pages 29–277.

Study about 100 words per week.

▶ 1 Week

Go over all 300 High-Frequency GRE Words, concentrating on words you have trouble with.

Do the Review: 300 High-Frequency GRE Words on pages 278–282.

THREE-MONTHS (12 WEEKS) STUDY PLAN

▶ 10 Weeks

Learn all of the Essential Words for the GRE on pages 29–277 by carefully reading all the material and doing all the exercises.

Do about eight units (80 words) per week.

▶ 1 Week

Go over all of the Essential Words for the GRE, concentrating on words you have trouble with.

Do the Review: Essential Words for the GRE on pages 283–290 and the Posttest on pages 382–391.

▶ 1 Week

Study the 300 High-Frequency GRE Words listed on pages 26–28 and asterisked on pages 29–277.

Do the Review: 300 High-Frequency GRE Words on pages 278–282.

SIX-MONTHS (26 WEEKS) STUDY PLAN

▶ 20 Weeks

Learn all of the Essential Words for the GRE on pages 29–277 by carefully reading all the material and doing all the exercises.

Do about four units (40 words) per week.

▶ 3 Weeks
Go over all of the Essential Words for the GRE, concentrating on words you have trouble with.

▶ 1 Week
Do the Review: Essential Words for the GRE on pages 283–290 and the Posttest on pages 382–391.

▶ 2 Weeks
Study the 300 High-Frequency GRE Words listed on pages 26–28 and asterisked on pages 29–277.

Do the Review: 300 High-Frequency GRE Words on pages 278–282.

PRETEST SCORE 10 TO 16 (AVERAGE TO GOOD)

ONE-MONTH (4 WEEKS) STUDY PLAN

▶ 2 Weeks
Learn the 300 High-Frequency GRE Words listed on pages 26–28 and asterisked on pages 29–277. Study about 150 words per week.

▶ 1 Week
Do as much of the Essential Words for the GRE on pages 29–277 as you can.

▶ 1 Week
Go over the 300 High-Frequency GRE Words, concentrating on words you have trouble with.

Do the Review: 300 High-Frequency Words on pages 278–282.

Do the Review: Essential Words for the GRE on pages 283–290, learning as many additional new words as possible by referring to the main text for words you don't know.

THREE-MONTHS (12 WEEKS) STUDY PLAN

▶ 8 Weeks
Learn all of the Essential Words for the GRE on pages 29–277 by carefully reading all the material and doing all the exercises.

Do about ten units (100 words) per week.

▶ 2 Weeks
Go over all of the Essential Words for the GRE, concentrating on words you have trouble with.

▶ 1 Week
Do as many as possible of the 300 High-Frequency Word Roots on pages 291–378.

▶ 1 Week

Do the Review: Essential Words for the GRE on pages 283–290 and the Posttest on pages 382–391.

Go over the 300 High-Frequency GRE Words and do the Review: 300 High-Frequency GRE Words on pages 278–282.

SIX-MONTHS (26 WEEKS) STUDY PLAN

▶ 20 Weeks

Learn the Essential Words for the GRE on pages 29–277 by carefully reading all the material and doing all the exercises.

Do about four units (40 words) per week.

▶ 2 Weeks

Go over all the Essential Words for the GRE, concentrating on words you have trouble with.

▶ 2 Weeks

Do the 300 High-Frequency Word Roots on pages 291–378.

▶ 1 Week

Do the Review: Essential Words for the GRE on pages 283–290 and the Posttest on pages 382–391.

▶ 1 Week

Go through the 300 High-Frequency GRE Words listed on pages 26–28 and asterisked on pages 29–277 and do the Review: 300 High-Frequency GRE Words on pages 278–282.

PRETEST SCORE 17 TO 20 (VERY GOOD TO EXCELLENT)

ONE-MONTH (4 WEEKS) STUDY PLAN

▶ 1 Week

Go through the 300 High-Frequency GRE Words listed on pages 26–28.

Study words you don't know by referring to pages 29–277 in which the high-frequency words are asterisked.

Do the Review: 300 High-Frequency GRE Words on pages 278–282.

▶ 2 Weeks

Go through the Essential Words for the GRE on pages 29–277, concentrating on words you don't know.

▶ 1 Week

Do the Review: Essential Words for the GRE on pages 283–290.

Do as much of the 300 High-Frequency Word Roots on pages 291–378 as possible.

THREE-MONTHS (12 WEEKS) STUDY PLAN

▶ 8 Weeks

Learn the Essential Words for the GRE on pages 29–277 by carefully reading all the material and doing all the exercises.

Do about ten units (80 words) per week.

▶ 2 Weeks

Do the 300 High-Frequency Word Roots on pages 291–378.

▶ 2 Weeks

Go over the Essential Words for the GRE, concentrating on words you have trouble with.

Do the Review: Essential Words for the GRE on pages 283–290.

Go over the 300 High-Frequency GRE Words listed on pages 26–28 and asterisked on pages 29–277 and do the Review: 300 High-Frequency GRE Words on pages 278–282.

SIX-MONTHS (26 WEEKS) STUDY PLAN

▶ 10 Weeks

Learn the Essential Words for the GRE on pages 29–277 by carefully reading all the material and doing all the exercises.

Do about eight units (80 words) per week.

▶ 6 Weeks

Go over all of the Essential Words for the GRE, concentrating on words you have trouble with.

▶ 6 Weeks

Do the 300 High-Frequency Word Roots on pages 291–378.

▶ 1 Week

Do the Review: Essential Words for the GRE on pages 283–290 and the Posttest on pages 382–391.

▶ 2 Weeks

Go through the 300 High-Frequency GRE Words asterisked on pages 29–277, making sure you know them all.

▶ 1 Week

Do the Review: 300 High-Frequency GRE Words on pages 278–282.

300 High-Frequency GRE Words

The following words appear with the most frequency on the GRE and are asterisked on pages 29–277 of this book.

aberrant	boorish	desiccate
abeyance	burgeon	desultory
abstemious	burnish	diatribe
aesthetic	buttress	dichotomy
alacrity	cacophonous	diffidence
alleviate	cant	diffuse
amalgamate	capricious	disabuse
ambiguous	castigation	discordant
ambivalence	catalyst	discrepancy
ameliorate	causality	discrete
anachronism	chicanery	disingenuous
analogous	coagulate	disinterested
anarchy	commensurate	dismiss
anomalous	compendium	disparage
antipathy	complaisant	disparate
apathy	conciliatory	dissemble
apprise	concomitant	disseminate
approbation	confound	dissolution
appropriate	contentious	dissonance
arcane	conundrum	doctrinaire
arduous	conventional	dogmatic
artless	convoluted	ebullient
ascetic	cosmology	eclectic
aspersion	craven	effete
assiduous	credence	efficacy
attenuate	decorum	effrontery
audacious	deference	elegy
austere	delineate	elicit
aver	demotic	embellish
banal	demur	empirical
belie	denigrate	emulate
beneficent	denouement	endemic
bombastic	derivative	enervate

ephemeral
equanimity
equivocate
erudite
esoteric
euphemism
exacerbate
exacting
exculpate
execrable
exigency
existential
extant
extraneous
extrapolation
facetious
fallacious
fatuous
felicitous
fledgling
foment
forestall
fractious
frugality
fulminate
gainsay
garrulous
grandiloquent
gregarious
guileless
gullible
harangue
heterodox
histrionic
homily
homogeneous
hyperbole
iconoclastic
ideological
idolatry
igneous

immutable
impassive
impermeable
imperturbable
impervious
implacable
implicit
inadvertently
inchoate
incongruity
indeterminate
indigence
indolent
ineluctable
inert
ingenuous
inherent
innocuous
insensible
insinuate
insipid
insularity
intractable
intransigence
inundate
inured
invective
irascible
irresolute
juxtapose
laconic
lassitude
laud
lethargic
levity
limpid
loquacious
lucid
magnanimity
malinger
malleable

maverick
mendacious
meretricious
metamorphosis
metaphysical
meticulous
misanthrope
misogynist
mitigate
mollify
morose
mundane
neophyte
obdurate
obsequious
obviate
occlude
officious
onerous
opprobrium
oscillate
ostentatious
paragon
partisan
pathological
paucity
pedantic
pellucid
penchant
penury
perfidious
perfunctory
permeable
pervasive
phlegmatic
piety
placate
plasticity
platitude
plethora
pragmatic

precarious
precipitate
precursor
presumptuous
prevaricate
pristine
probity
problematic
prodigal
profound
proliferate
propensity
propitiate
propriety
proscribe
qualified
quiescent
rarefied
recalcitrant
recant
recondite
refractory
refute
relegate
reproach
reprobate

repudiate
rescind
resolute
resolved
reticent
reverence
sage
salubrious
salutary
sanction
sartorial
satiate
sensual
sensuous
sentient
skeptic
solicitous
soporific
specious
sporadic
stigma
stipulate
stolid
striated
substantiate
subsume

supersede
supposition
tacit
taciturn
tangential
tenuous
tirade
torpor
tortuous
tractable
transgression
truculence
turgid
untenable
vacillate
vapid
venerate
veracious
verbose
viable
viscous
vitiate
vituperative
volatile
whimsical
zealot

Essential Words for the GRE

UNIT 1

abate *v.* to decrease; reduce

> *NASA announced that it would delay the launch of the manned spacecraft until the radiation from the solar flares **abated**.*

abdicate *v.* to give up a position, right, or power

> *Romulus Augustus, the last Western Roman emperor, was forced to **abdicate** the throne in 476 A.D., and the Germanic chieftain Odovacar became the de facto ruler of Italy.*

> *The appeals judge has **abdicated** his responsibility to review the findings of the high court.*

Terms from the Arts, Sciences, and Social Sciences

de facto: in fact, whether by right or not; exercising power without being legally established (Latin: *from the fact*)

---

*aberrant *adj.* deviating from what is normal

> *When a person's behavior becomes **aberrant**, his or her peers may become concerned that the individual is becoming a deviant.*

Aberration is a noun meaning something different from the usual or normal.

> *For centuries, solar eclipses were regarded as serious **aberrations** in the natural order.*

Terms from the Arts, Sciences, and Social Sciences

deviant: a person whose behavior differs from the accepted standards of society

---

*abeyance *n.* temporary suppression or suspension

> *A good judge must hold his or her judgment in* **abeyance** *until all the facts in a case have been presented.*

abject *adj.* miserable; pitiful

> *John Steinbeck's novel* The Grapes of Wrath *portrays the* **abject** *poverty of many people during the Great Depression.*

abjure *v.* to reject; abandon formally

> *Most members of the Religious Society of Friends (commonly known as the Quakers or Friends)* **abjure** *the use of violence to settle disputes between nations.*

> *For a foreigner to become a U.S. citizen, he or she must take an oath* **abjuring** *allegiance to any other country and pledging to take up arms to defend the United States.*

abscission *n.* the act of cutting; the natural separation of a leaf or other part of a plant

> *Two scientists, Alan G. Williams and Thomas G. Whitham, have* hypothesized *that premature leaf* **abscission** *is an* adaptive *plant response to* herbivorous *attack.*

The verb *abscise* means to cut off or away.

> *The surgeon* **abscised** *a small growth on the patient's hand.*

Terms from the Arts, Sciences, and Social Sciences

hypothesized: form a hypothesis, that is a proposition put forward as a starting point for further investigation

adaptive: relating to adaptation, an alteration in structure or habits by which a species improves its condition in relationship to its environment

herbivorous: feeding mainly on plants

---

abscond *v.* to depart secretly

> *A warrant is out for the arrest of a person believed to have* **absconded** *with three million dollars.*

*abstemious *adj.* moderate in appetite

> *Some research suggests that people with an* **abstemious** *lifestyle tend to live longer than people who indulge their appetites.*

abstinence *n.* the giving up of certain pleasures

The monk's vow of **abstinence** *includes all intoxicating substances.*

REVIEW 1

Matching
Match each word with its definition.

1. abate	(A)	to abandon formally
2. abdicate	(B)	temporary suppression
3. aberrant	(C)	to give up a position or power
4. abeyance	(D)	giving up of certain pleasures
5. abject	(E)	to depart secretly
6. abjure	(F)	miserable; pitiful
7. abscission	(G)	to decrease
8. abscond	(H)	moderate in appetite
9. abstemious	(I)	the act of cutting
10. abstinence	(J)	deviating from what is normal

Fill-ins
Choose the best word to fill in the blank in each sentence.

abate	abdicated	aberrations	abeyance	abject
abjured	absconded	abscission	abstemious	abstinence

1. The 90-year-old monarch _____ the throne to allow his son to become king.
2. Psychotherapy relies on psychological rather than physiological approaches to curing mental _____ .
3. Implementation of the new plan has been held in _____ pending an investigation of its effectiveness to date.
4. Ms. Johnson's _____ lifestyle helped her to amass a fortune.
5. The crew of the vessel waited for the storm to _____ before going on deck to make repairs.
6. The alcoholic's physician recommended total _____ from liquor for her patient.
7. The documentary filmmaker was accused of using misleading footage to make it appear that nearly everyone in the country lived in _____ conditions.
8. The judge said he would reduce the convicted woman's sentence if she _____ all association with those convicted of treason.

9. The senior surgeon performed the difficult _____ .
10. The audit of the bank's financial records led investigators to suspect that someone had _____ with $100,000.

Sense or Nonsense
Indicate whether each sentence makes good sense or not.
Put S (SENSE) if it does, and put N (NONSENSE) if it does not.

1. The doctor decided to let her patient's fever abate before ordering further clinical tests. _____
2. The university's plans for expansion have been put in abeyance until the economic outlook is more favorable. _____
3. Ruth's abstemious appetite has caused her to put on ten pounds in the last month. _____
4. The senator announced that he formally accepted and abjured all of his past statements on the issue. _____
5. The judge instructed the members of the jury that they would be abdicating their responsibilities if they did not reach a verdict in the case. _____

UNIT 2

abysmal *adj.* very bad

*The **abysmal** failure of the free market system in Russia has led some people to argue that the planned economy of the Soviet Union, while not perfect, was better suited to Russia's history and culture than Western-style capitalism.*

Terms from the Arts, Sciences, and Social Sciences

free market: an economic market in which the demand and supply of goods and services is either not regulated or is slightly regulated

planned economy: an economic system in which the production, allocation, and consumption of goods and services is planned in advance. Another term for planned economy is "command economy."

capitalism: an economic and political system in which a country's industry and trade are controlled by private owners rather than the government

---

accretion *n.* growth in size or increase in amount

  *In the 1960s, the American geophysicist Harry Hess conceived the idea of sea-floor spreading, a process in which the new crust in the ocean is continually generated by igneous processes at the crests of the mid-oceanic ridges, causing a steady **accretion** of the crust.*

Terms from the Arts, Sciences, and Social Sciences

geophysicist: one who specializes in the physics of the earth and its environment

igneous: in geology, relating to the formation of rocks by solidification from a molten state. The word *igneous* is from Latin *ignis* (fire).

---

accrue *v.* to accumulate; grow by additions

  Regulating the growth of large companies when they begin to become monopolistic *is a difficult task for government in a capitalist country; if it limits monopolies too much, the nation's firms could become less competitive than foreign companies that enjoy the advantages **accruing** from greater monopolies.*

Terms from the Arts, Sciences, and Social Sciences

monopolistic: having exclusive control over a commercial activity

---

adamant *adj.* uncompromising; unyielding

  *Despite widespread opposition to his plan, the political party's leader is **adamant** that the party must move to the center to appeal to moderate voters.*

adjunct *n.* something added, attached, or joined

  *Speed walking, cross-country running, and marathons are normally regarded as **adjuncts** of track and field athletics since races in these sports are not normally held on a track.*

admonish *v.* to caution or reprimand

  *The judge **admonished** the jury to discount testimony that had been ruled inadmissible.*

adulterate *v.* to corrupt or make impure

The unscrupulous company sells an **adulterated** *version of the drug, and doesn't inform consumers that they are getting a less efficacious drug than they think they are getting.*

*aesthetic *adj.* relating to beauty or art

Members of the English **aesthetic** *movement, such as Oscar Wilde, were proponents of the doctrine of art for art's sake, which is the belief that art cannot and should not be useful for any purpose other than that of creating beauty.*

Aesthetic is also a noun that means a conception of what is artistically beautiful.

The Gothic **aesthetic** *dominated European art and architecture from approximately the twelfth to the fifteenth century.*

Aesthetics is the conception of what is beautiful; it is also a branch of philosophy dealing with beauty and art, and standards in judging them.

An *aesthete* is someone who cultivates a special sensitivity to beauty; often the word refers to a person whose interest in beauty and art is regarded as excessive or superficial.

Terms from the Arts, Sciences, and Social Sciences

Gothic: a style of architecture that was very popular in the late Middle Ages characterized by such features as pointed arches, soaring spaces, and light. In literature the term refers to a genre of fiction that was popular in the eighteenth and early nineteenth centuries. Gothic novels have an atmosphere of gloom, mystery, and horror.

---

affected *adj.* pretentious, phony

It has been argued that the emphasis on so-called "proper English" leads to unnatural and **affected** *speech.*

affinity *n.* fondness; liking; similarity

The female students in the class felt an **affinity** *for the ancient Greek playwright Euripides because he sympathized with women, slaves, and other despised members of his society.*

REVIEW 2

Matching
Match each word with its definition.

1. abysmal		(A)	grow by additions
2. accretion		(B)	very bad
3. accrue		(C)	relating to beauty or art
4. adamant		(D)	something added
5. adjunct		(E)	to corrupt or make impure
6. admonish		(F)	increase in amount
7. adulterate		(G)	pretentious
8. aesthetic		(H)	fondness
9. affected		(I)	uncompromising
10. affinity		(J)	to caution

Fill-ins
Choose the best word to fill in the blank in each sentence.

abysmal	**accretion**	**accrued**	**adamant**	**adjunct**
admonished	**adulterated**	**aesthetic**	**affected**	**affinity**

1. The film is marred by the actor's _____ English accent.
2. In Emily Brontë's *Wuthering Heights* the characters Heathcliff and Catherine feel such an _____ for each other that they almost literally cannot live without each other.
3. Over the years the university's computer system has grown so much by _____ that no one person has a complete understanding of it.
4. The committee on education reform recommended that the school introduce more art courses to develop students' _____ awareness.
5. The poet _____ the critic for failing to appreciate the subtle changes in his poem's meter.
6. Tom's savings account has _____ $3,000 in interest over the last ten years.
7. The band's playing was so _____ that they were booed off stage.
8. The English teacher is _____ about one thing: students must correct all the errors in written work that she returns to them.
9. Over the last 20 years or so consumers have increasingly demanded food that is not _____ with additives.
10. Nearly half of the college courses in America are taught by _____ professors.

Sense or Nonsense

Indicate whether each sentence makes good sense or not.
Put S (SENSE) if it does, and put N (NONSENSE) if it does not.

1. In many ways Aristotle's aesthetic dictums have never been surpassed. _____
2. Beth is so adamant about the plan that she is willing to give it up at the first opportunity. _____
3. The waiters in the expensive restaurant were told to affect a French accent to impress customers. _____
4. Most students love to be admonished for their good work. _____
5. State law requires that whole milk be 100 percent adulterated. _____

UNIT 3

aggrandize *v.* to make larger or greater

> *One of the concerns of the framers of the U.S. Constitution was that one branch of government would try to **aggrandize** itself at the expense of the others.*

aggregate *adj.* amounting to a whole; total

> *The **aggregate** wealth of a country includes private as well as public resources and possessions.*

Aggregate is also a verb meaning to collect into a mass.

> *Portals are Web sites designed to **aggregate** information and are used as a starting point on the Web.*

Aggregate is also a noun meaning collective mass or sum.

*alacrity *n.* cheerful willingness; eagerness; speed

> *The football coach was pleased to see the team get to work on the task of improving its tackling skills with **alacrity**.*

alchemy *n.* medieval chemical philosophy based on changing metal into gold; a seemingly magical power or process of transmutation.

> ***Alchemy** was the forerunner of the modern science of chemistry.*

> *None of their friends could understand the mysterious **alchemy** that caused two people as different from one another as Rob and Barbara to fall in love.*

> ### Terms from the Arts, Sciences, and Social Sciences
>
> *alchemy:* Modern scientists believe alchemy was not a true science since there's no evidence that anyone succeeded in turning a base metal into gold. Interestingly, however, the word for the modern science of "chemistry" is derived directly from the word "alchemy."

allay *v.* to lessen; ease; soothe

   *Improvements in antivirus software have **allayed** many people's fears of having their computers "infected" with malicious software.*

*alleviate *v.* to relieve; improve partially

   *According to some commentators, one of the weaknesses of capitalism is that, although it is very efficient at increasing absolute wealth, it is not as successful at **alleviating** relative poverty; thus, a person living in a slum in America may be reasonably well off by historical standards, but he might perceive himself to be poor compared to members of the* bourgeoisie, *whom he sees regularly buying luxury goods that he is not able to afford.*

> ### Terms from the Arts, Sciences, and Social Sciences
>
> *bourgeoisie:* the social order dominated by the property-owning class. The term is associated with Marxism, the political and economic philosophy of Karl Marx and Friedrich Engels, but today it is often used disparagingly to suggest materialism and philistinism (an unenlightened and smug attitude toward culture).

alloy *n.* a combination; a mixture of two or more metals

   *Scientists formulate **alloys** to create properties that are not possessed by natural metals or other substances.*

allure *n.* the power to entice by charm

   *Political groups in the United States often lobby Congress to use the **allure** of America's vast market as an incentive for countries to pursue policies in accordance with American policies.*

> ### Terms from the Arts, Sciences, and Social Sciences
>
> *lobby:* a group whose members share certain goals and work to bring about the passage, modification, or defeat of laws that affect these goals

Allure is also a verb meaning to entice by charm. The adjective is *alluring.*

> *The idea of a* clockwork universe *is very* **alluring** *to some people because it explains how the universe was created, yet allows human beings to live in it without believing in supernatural intervention.*

> ### Terms from the Arts, Sciences, and Social Sciences
>
> *clockwork universe:* a theory of the origin of the universe that compares the universe to a mechanical clock created by God. According to this theory, once created, the universe continues to run according to the laws of nature and does not require further Divine intervention. This idea was very popular in the Enlightenment, an eighteenth-century philosophical movement that emphasized the use of reason to examine accepted beliefs and traditions.

amalgamate v. to combine into a unified whole

> *In early 1999, six municipalities were* **amalgamated** *into an enlarged city of Toronto, Canada.*

ambiguous adj. unclear or doubtful in meaning

> *The gender of the* Mahayana Buddhist *deity Avalokitesuara, the god of infinite mercy, is* **ambiguous** *in both China and Japan, where the god is sometimes called a goddess.*

> ### Terms from the Arts, Sciences, and Social Sciences
>
> *Mahayana Buddhist:* one of the three major traditions of Buddhism. It regards the historical Buddha as a manifestation of the celestial Buddha.

REVIEW 3

Matching
Match each word with its definition.

1. aggrandize	(A) cheerful willingness
2. aggregate	(B) a combination
3. alacrity	(C) the power to entice by charm
4. alchemy	(D) to make larger or greater
5. allay	(E) to combine into a unified whole
6. alleviate	(F) to lessen; ease
7. alloy	(G) amounting to a whole
8. allure	(H) to relieve; improve partially
9. amalgamate	(I) unclear or doubtful in meaning
10. ambiguous	(J) medieval chemical philosophy

Fill-ins
Choose the best word to fill in the blank in each sentence.

aggrandize	aggregate	alacrity	alchemy	allay
alleviate	alloys	allure	amalgamate	ambiguous

1. The _____ of France is great; millions of people around the world study its language and culture.
2. With the organic chemistry test coming up soon, Maria knew she had to start studying for it with _____ .
3. The computer manufacturer donated one hundred computers to the inner-city school to _____ the problem of children not having access to the Internet.
4. The corporation's CEO claimed that his purchase of a personal jet airplane was not meant to personally _____ him.
5. By what remarkable artistic _____ did the interior decorator transform the drab living room into a room of vibrant color and light?
6. John's role in the affair is _____ ; it is not clear whether he took an active part in it or was merely an advisor.
7. The final plan is an _____ of the ideas of everyone in the class.
8. Modern _____ have helped make cars lighter and more resistant to corrosion.
9. To _____ the public's fears that his health was failing, the prime minister played tennis every day and invited reporters to be present.

10. Now separate entities, the twelve colleges will _____ to create a single university.

Sense or Nonsense
Indicate whether each sentence makes good sense or not.
Put S (SENSE) if it does, and put N (NONSENSE) if it does not.

1. The allure of gold is so great that hardly anyone is buying it. _____
2. The governor is concerned that one agency of government is aggrandizing itself at the expense of other agencies. _____
3. The judge instructed the witness to make an ambiguous statement so that everyone could be clear about what she meant. _____
4. The alacrity of John Milton's *Paradise Lost* makes it one of the great epic poems in English. _____
5. The charity was set up to alleviate the suffering of the poor. _____

UNIT 4

*ambivalence *n.* the state of having conflicting emotional attitudes.

> *John felt some* **ambivalence** *about getting married before finishing college.*

The adjective is *ambivalent.*

> *In public opinion surveys in the United States, scientists rank second only to physicians in public esteem, yet much of the public is increasingly* **ambivalent** *about some of the implications for society of "Big Science" and its related technology.*

ambrosia *n.* something delicious; the food of the gods

> *The combination of flavors in the Moroccan baked eggplant was pure* **ambrosia***.*

The adjective is *ambrosial.*

> *The food critic praised the chef for preparing what he called an* **"ambrosial** *meal."*

Terms from the Arts, Sciences, and Social Sciences

In Greek mythology, *ambrosia* and *nektar* were the delicious and fragrant food and drink of the gods that gave them immortality. The English word *nectar* (from Greek *nektar*) means a sweet liquid secreted by flowers, or a delicious drink.

---

*ameliorate *v.* to improve

*Knowing they could not stop the spread of a contagion in a few days, health authorities worked to inhibit its spread and to **ameliorate** its effects by issuing warnings to the public and initiating immunization programs.*

amenable *adj.* agreeable; cooperative; suited

*The young writer is **amenable** to suggestions for improving her prose style to make it more interesting.*

amenity *n.* something that increases comfort

*Many **amenities** considered normal and necessary by people in developed countries, such as indoor plumbing, were luxuries only a few generations ago.*

amulet *n.* ornament worn as a charm against evil spirits

*The early Christian Church forbade the use of **amulets**, which had become common in the Roman Empire at the time the Christian Church began to develop.*

*anachronism *n.* something out of the proper time

*Some experts regard the retirement age of 65 as an **anachronism** at a time when people in the developed world have much longer life expectancies than previously.*

analgesic *n.* medication that reduces or eliminates pain

*Aspirin (the trademark of the drug acetylsalicylic acid) is a powerful **analgesic** that was introduced in 1899 and is still one of the most effective medicines available to alleviate pain, fever, and inflammation.*

*analogous *adj.* comparable

*The psychology researcher's experiment postulates that the brain is **analogous** to a digital computer.*

Analogy is a noun meaning a similarity in some ways between things that are otherwise dissimilar.

*The idea of evolution in nature is sometimes misconstrued and applied by **analogy** to other areas in which there is scant evidence for its existence; a notable example of this is Social Darwinism, in which it is argued that society is like nature, and thus people, like animals, are competing for survival, with those who are genetically superior at surviving and reproducing.*

Analog is a noun meaning something that is comparable to something else.

> *Some commentators have posited the existence of an* **analog** *to the* Protestant work ethic *in Chinese culture, which they call the "Confucian work ethic," to explain the economic success of some countries with large Chinese populations.*

Terms from the Arts, Sciences, and Social Sciences

Social Darwinism: a theory in sociology that individuals or groups achieve advantage over others as the result of genetic or biological superiority

Protestant work ethic: a view of life that encourages hard work and a rational view of the world as a way to achieve material success

Confucian: a system or ethics based on the teachings of the ancient Chinese sage Confucius. It places a high value on family relationships.

---

*anarchy *n.* absence of government; state of disorder

> *The American philosopher Robert Nozick does not advocate* **anarchy***; rather, he argues for the merits of a minimal state that would not violate the natural rights of individuals.*

The adjective *anarchic* means lacking order or control.

> *The student of mythology speculated that Dionysos was created as a projection of the pleasure-loving,* **anarchic** *aspect of human nature.*

Terms from the Arts, Sciences, and Social Sciences

Dionysos: known as Bacchus to the Romans, Dionysos was the son of Zeus and Selene. He was the Greek god of agriculture, fertility, wine, and ecstasy, and later regarded as a patron of the arts. Dionysos was worshipped by an emotional cult that held secret rites called *Bacchanalia*—wild orgies of frenzied revelry, drunkenness, and debauchery.

The noun *anarchism* refers to the theory that all forms of government are oppressive and should be abolished. It also means the advocacy of this theory or the attempt to bring about anarchism.

> *Most political scientists do not believe* **anarchism** *to be a tenable theory of government.*

REVIEW 4

Matching
Match each word with its definition.

1. ambivalence	(A) agreeable; cooperative
2. ambrosia	(B) medication that reduces pain
3. ameliorate	(C) the state of having conflicting emotional attitudes
4. amenable	(D) absence of government
5. amenity	(E) ornament worn as a charm against evil spirits
6. amulet	(F) something out of the proper time
7. anachronism	(G) to improve
8. analgesic	(H) comparable
9. analogous	(I) something delicious
10. anarchy	(J) something that increases comfort

Fill-ins
Choose the best word to fill in the blank in each sentence.

ambivalent	ambrosia	ameliorate	amenable	amenities
amulet	anachronism	analgesic	analogy	anarchy

1. Many people have an _____ attitude to war: it causes great suffering, yet appears at times to be the only solution to a serious problem.
2. During the revolution the country began to slip toward _____ .
3. The soldier attributed his survival through three battles to an _____ he had found in Borneo.
4. After fasting for 24 hours, Wayne said that his first bite of steak tasted like _____ .
5. "I'm afraid all I can do for your headache is prescribe an _____ to relieve the pain," the doctor told her patient.
6. The governor drew an _____ between a family and society, pointing out that both need a leader if they are to function smoothly.
7. The antithesis of the principle of art for art's sake is social realism, which feels a heavy responsibility to identify, and even _____ , social ills.
8. The history professor is _____ to student suggestions for the topic of the term paper.

9. The editor discovered an _____ in the script; set in 1944, it contained a reference to the atomic bombing of Hiroshima in 1945.
10. Many modern tourists like to have all the _____ of home when they travel.

Sense or Nonsense
Indicate whether each sentence makes good sense or not.
Put S (SENSE) if it does, and put N (NONSENSE) if it does not.

1. Amulets have been used for centuries to generate electric power. _____
2. The economist drew an analogy between a family spending beyond its means and a government running a deficit. _____
3. Although the government program was intended to help the poor, in reality it has only ameliorated their situation. _____
4. John is ambivalent about whether to apply to graduate school or look for a job after receiving his degree. _____
5. A group of anarchists called for the overthrow of the government. _____

UNIT 5

anodyne *n.* something that calms or soothes pain

> *Some people use alcohol as an* **anodyne** *to numb their emotional pain.*

Anodyne is an adjective that means relaxing, or capable of soothing pain.

> *The public relations officer is remarkably* **anodyne***; all he does is mouth comforting, politically correct platitudes, saying nothing of substance.*

*anomalous *adj.* irregular; deviating from the norm

> *The psychologist discounted the* **anomalous** *behavior of the soldier, saying it was merely a short-term effect of the stress of battle.*

The noun is *anomaly*.

> *A moral dilemma that arises with humanity's ability to clone is posed in the following hypothetical scenario: a pig that produces much more meat than a normal pig can be cloned, but the pig's life span would be cut in half because of* **anomalies** *in the cloning process: Is it right to clone such an animal?*

antecedent *n.* something that comes before

> *Historical factors, such as the increased emphasis on the individual, the invention of printing, and the rise of the bourgeoisie, contributed to make the* Reformation, *which had its* **antecedents** *in the reform movement within the Roman Catholic Church, into a much broader phenomenon that created powerful churches that grew to rival the original church.*

Terms from the Arts, Sciences, and Social Sciences

Reformation: a sixteenth-century movement aimed at reforming abuses in the Roman Catholic Church. It led to the establishment of new churches.

---

antediluvian *adj.* prehistoric

> *Most of our knowledge of* **antediluvian** *times has been built up as a result of one of humanity's grandest collaborative endeavors—the gathering, identification, dating, and categorization of fossils as they are discovered.*

*antipathy *n.* dislike; hostility

> *Heathcliff, the protagonist of Emily Brontë's novel* Wuthering Heights, *feels great* **antipathy** *for Edgar Linton, the man who marries the woman he loves.*

Terms from the Arts, Sciences, and Social Sciences

protagonist: the main character in a work of literature

---

*apathy *n.* indifference

> **Apathy** *was high in the election because there was no major controversy or issue to arouse voter interest.*

The adjective is *apathetic.*

> *One criticism of the* welfare state *is that it makes people overly reliant on government, with the result that democracy is gradually weakened as citizens take a more* **apathetic** *and detached view of politics.*

Terms from the Arts, Sciences, and Social Sciences

welfare state: the provision of welfare services by the state (that is, the government)

---

apex *n.* the highest point

In English literature, classicism *reached its* ***apex*** *in the poetry of Alexander Pope and the other* Augustans.

Terms from the Arts, Sciences, and Social Sciences

classicism: an aesthetic tradition that values simplicity, elegance, restraint, and order

Augustans: a period of English literature from around 1700 to 1789. Satire was a feature of the writing of many authors of this period. Two notable authors of the Augustan Age were Alexander Pope and Jonathan Swift.

---

apogee *n.* the point in an orbit most distant from the body being orbited; the highest point

The Ottoman Empire *reached its* ***apogee*** *in the seventeenth century, when it controlled a territory running from Budapest to North Africa.*

Terms from the Arts, Sciences, and Social Sciences

Ottoman Empire: an empire that arose in Anatolia (which corresponds to the Asian portion of modern Turkey) in the fourteenth century, destroying the Byzantine Empire. By the early sixteenth century it controlled much of Persia, Arabia, Hungary, the Balkans, Syria, and Egypt.

---

apothegm *n.* a terse, witty saying (pronounced AP-uh-them and also spelled *apophthegm*)

One of the best-known political **apothegms** was written by the British historian Lord Acton: "Power tends to corrupt and absolute power corrupts absolutely."

appease *v.* to calm; pacify; placate

Many historians have criticized British Prime Minister Neville Chamberlain for trying to **appease** Adolf Hitler in the 1930s.

REVIEW 5

Matching
Match each word with its definition.

1. anodyne
2. anomalous
3. antecedent
4. antediluvian
5. antipathy
6. apathy
7. apex
8. apogee
9. apothegm
10. appease

(A) indifference
(B) prehistoric
(C) something that comes before
(D) to pacify
(E) hostility
(F) point in orbit most distant from body being orbited
(G) something that soothes pain
(H) the highest point
(I) irregular
(J) terse, witty saying

Fill-ins
Choose the best word to fill in the blank in each sentence.

anodyne	anomalous	antecedents	antediluvian	antipathy
apathy	apex	apogee	apothegms	appease

1. The transistor was the result of a collaborative effort by research-ers at Bell Laboratories in New Jersey, one of the world's most advanced scientific and technological laboratories, which had its _____ in the great laboratories created in the late nineteenth century by people like Thomas Edison.
2. In "Strange Meeting," one of Wilfred Owen's poems about World War I, the speaker says that he has no _____ for the foe he killed in battle.
3. The students are trying to overcome public _____ on the issue by setting up exhibitions about it in shopping centers.
4. The scientist asked the lab technician to check the _____ results again.
5. To _____ angry voters the legislature approved a tax cut.
6. The English teacher showed his class the classic film *On the Beach*, but many of the students had trouble appreciating it because of what one student called its "_____ black and white film technology."

7. The eighteenth-century British writer Samuel Johnson is famous for his sage _____ , such as "If you are idle, be not solitary; if you are solitary, be not idle."
8. The pastor's comforting words at the child's funeral were an _____ for the grieving family.
9. When the spacecraft reaches its _____ in its orbit around Earth, another craft will be launched from it on a voyage to Mars.
10. Many religions view human beings as standing at the _____ of creation.

Sense or Nonsense
Indicate whether each sentence makes good sense or not.
Put S (SENSE) if it does, and put N (NONSENSE) if it does not.

1. The simple electric circuit consists of a battery and an anodyne. _____
2. Although the scientist's career as a researcher had long since reached its apex, she continued to give valuable guidance to younger scientists. _____
3. The gun is capable of firing deadly apothegms that can rip enemy soldiers apart. _____
4. The anomalous test results mean that the rocket is ready to launch. _____
5. Anthropologists believe that the tribe used animal sacrifice to appease the angry gods. _____

UNIT 6

appellation *n.* name

> The discovery of the bones of a person with the **appellation** Kennewick Man in the state of Washington in 1996 has raised important questions about who the earliest people to populate America were.

apposite *adj.* strikingly appropriate and relevant

> The writer searched two dictionaries and a thesaurus before finding the perfectly **apposite** word he was looking for.

*apprise *v.* to inform

> Nadine Cohodas's biography of the blues singer Dinah Washington keeps the reader **apprised** of the racism black Americans had to endure.

*approbation *n.* praise; approval

> *The Congressional Medal of Honor is the highest* **approbation** *an American soldier can receive.*

*appropriate *v.* to take possession for one's own use; confiscate

> *The pronunciation is uh-PROH-pree-ayt. The adjective appropriate is pronounced uh-PROH-pree-it.*

The invading army **appropriated** supplies from the houses of the local people.

apropos *adj.* relevant

> **Apropos** *of nothing, the speaker declared that the purpose of life is to love.*

arabesque *n.* ornate design featuring intertwined curves; a ballet position in which one leg is extended in back while the other supports the weight of the body

> *The ballerina stunned the audience with her perfectly executed* **arabesque**.

archeology *n.* the study of material evidence of past human life

> Carbon-14 dating *is of great use in* **archeology** *because it can determine the age of specimens as old as 35,000 years, but it is of less use in geology because most of the processes studied in this field occurred millions of years ago.*

Terms from the Arts, Sciences, and Social Sciences

Carbon-14 dating: determining the actual or relative age of an object, of a natural phenomenon, or of a series of events through the use of the isotope carbon-14, which occurs naturally

---

ardor *n.* great emotion or passion

> *The twentieth-century American poet Wallace Stevens said, "It is the unknown that excites the* **ardor** *of scholars, who, in the known alone, would shrivel up with boredom."*

*arduous *adj.* extremely difficult; laborious

> *The task of writing a research paper is* **arduous**, *but if it is broken down into logical steps it becomes less daunting.*

REVIEW 6

Matching
Match each word with its definition.

1.	appellation	(A)	relevant
2.	apposite	(B)	confiscate
3.	apprise	(C)	great emotion or passion
4.	approbation	(D)	ornate design
5.	appropriate	(E)	name
6.	apropos	(F)	laborious
7.	arabesque	(G)	strikingly appropriate and relevant
8.	archeology	(H)	praise
9.	ardor	(I)	the study of material evidence of past human life
10.	arduous	(J)	to inform

Fill-ins
Choose the best word to fill in the blank in each sentence.

appellation	apposite	apprised	approbation	appropriated
apropos	arabesque	archeology	ardor	arduous

1. Some people felt the remarks were out of place, but others thought they were perfectly _____ .
2. The president ordered his chief of staff to keep him _____ of any changes in the situation.
3. The English professor has started on the _____ task of writing book-length commentaries on all thirty-seven of William Shakespeare's plays.
4. During an economic "bubble" there is a great _____ for speculative investing.
5. _____ provides anthropologists with important information about prehistoric cultures.
6. The city _____ private land to build low-cost housing.
7. The _____ is one of the fundamental ballet poses.
8. Former U.S Supreme Court justice Byron White was given the _____ "Whizzer" when he played football in college.
9. The fashion book contains the perfect, _____ image to represent one hundred famous designers.
10. The young scientist is working 80 hours a week to gain the _____ of her peers.

Sense or Nonsense
Indicate whether each sentence makes good sense or not.
Put S (SENSE) if it does, and put N (NONSENSE) if it does not.

1. The judge rejected the witness' testimony because nothing in it was apropos to the case. _____
2. One of the major questions in modern archaeology is whether God exists or not. _____
3. A comet with the appellation Shoemaker-Levy 9 collided spectacularly with Jupiter in July 1994. _____
4. The group plans to make the arduous ascent of Mt. Everest without oxygen supplies. _____
5. "Jack hit Jim" has an apposite meaning from "Jim was hit by Jack." _____

UNIT 7

argot *n.* a specialized vocabulary used by a group

*Writers of crime fiction often use the **argot** of criminals and detectives to create a realistic atmosphere.*

arrest *v.* to stop; to seize

*Temporary **arrest** of the patient's respiration made it easier for the doctor to perform surgery on him.*

artifact *n.* item made by human craft

*Marxists contend that appreciation of art has declined because capitalism has trained people to perceive human **artifacts** as commodities, and has alienated people from nature, their true humanity, and their creations.*

Terms from the Arts, Sciences, and Social Sciences

Marxist: a follower of Marxism, the political and economic philosophy of Karl Marx and Friedrich Engels. In Marxism the concept of class struggle plays a central role in understanding society's inevitable development from bourgeois oppression under capitalism to a socialist and ultimately classless society.

---

*artless *adj.* guileless; natural

*The source of the meaning of **artless** as guileless is the poet John Dryden, who wrote of William Shakespeare in 1672: "Such artless beauty lies in Shakespeare's wit. . . ."*

*ascetic *n.* one who practices self-denial

*Muslim **ascetics** consider the internal battle against human passions a greater* jihad *than the struggle against infidels.*

Ascetic is also an adjective meaning self-denying or austere.

*The writer's **ascetic** lifestyle helped her to concentrate on finishing her novel.*

The noun is *asceticism*.

*One tradition of **asceticism** derives from the belief that the body is fundamentally bad and must be subjugated to the soul.*

Terms from the Arts, Sciences, and Social Sciences

jihad: the religious duty of Muslims to defend their religion (Islam) by war or spiritual struggle against nonbelievers

---

asperity *n.* severity; harshness; irritability

*In his autobiography Gerald Trywhitt, the British writer, composer, artist, and aesthete, recounts a humorous incident: "Many years later, when I was sketching in Rome, a grim-looking Englishwoman came up to me and said with some **asperity**, 'I see you are painting MY view.'"*

*aspersion *n.* slander; false rumor

*The Republic of Singapore is a young democracy, and its leaders often respond strongly to journalists and others who cast **aspersions** on their integrity.*

*assiduous *adj.* diligent; hard-working

*The **assiduous** people of Hong Kong live in a territory with one of the highest per capita incomes in the world.*

assuage *v.* to make less severe

*On November 21, 1864, during the Civil War, President Abraham Lincoln wrote the following in a letter to Mrs. Bixby of Boston, who had lost five sons in battle: "I pray that our Heavenly Father may **assuage** the anguish of your bereavement and leave you only the cherished memory of the loved and lost, and the solemn pride that must be yours to have laid so costly a sacrifice upon the altar of freedom."*

astringent *adj.* harsh; severe

*Bob tends to nick himself when he shaves, so he uses an **astringent** aftershave to stop the bleeding.*

REVIEW 7

Matching

Match each word with its definition.

1.	argot	(A)	guileless; natural
2.	arrest	(B)	slander
3.	artifact	(C)	item made by human craft
4.	artless	(D)	to make less severe
5.	ascetic	(E)	to stop; seize
6.	asperity	(F)	hard-working
7.	aspersion	(G)	harshness
8.	assiduous	(H)	specialized vocabulary used by a group
9.	assuage	(I)	harsh; severe
10.	astringent	(J)	one who practices self-denial

Fill-ins

Choose the best word to fill in the blank in each sentence.

argot	arrest	artifact	artless	ascetic
asperity	aspersions	assiduously	assuage	astringent

1. The young actor's brilliant portrayal of the _____ young boy was the result, paradoxically, of many hours of careful rehearsal.
2. Considering that the two men had been such good friends for so long, we were surprised by the _____ of their attacks on each other.
3. In his book *Confessions*, Saint Augustine tells of his sinful life before he was converted to Christianity and began to live an _____ and virtuous life.
4. *Mate*, a popular beverage in South America, is similar to tea but is less _____ and often contains more caffeine.
5. Some scholars have argued that the idea of romantic love is an _____ of culture, unique to the West, with its origin in the European tradition of courtly love; however, sociological research has shown that romantic love exists in most cultures.
6. The new drug is able to _____ the development of cancerous cells.
7. China's leaders talked with a group of American congressional representatives to _____ fears that China plans to threaten American military preeminence.

8. The study's conclusion is that more females attend college than males because girls tend to apply themselves more _____ to their studies than boys.

9. Much of the _____ from the field of information technology that previously was familiar only to experts in the field is now used in everyday conversation ("Internet Service Provider," for example).

10. The report in the newspaper cast _____ on the candidate.

Sense or Nonsense

Indicate whether each sentence makes good sense or not.
Put S (SENSE) if it does, and put N (NONSENSE) if it does not.

1. The hungry people gratefully received the aspersions from the charity. _____

2. The crew of the submarine bid their families farewell before setting off on their long argot. _____

3. The poet Walt Whitman quotes John Burroughs's comment on the writer Henry David Thoreau: "He improves with age—in fact, it requires age to take off a little of his asperity, and fully ripen him." _____

4. "My comments on your book were merely astringent, not venomous," the critic said to the author. _____

5. The writer James Boswell is so famous for his assiduous recording of Samuel Johnson's words that the word "Boswell" now refers to a person who admires another so greatly that he or she records their words and deeds. _____

UNIT 8

asylum *n.* place of refuge or shelter

> The Stoic, *accused of seeking* **asylum** *in the consolations of philosophy, rebutted this charge, saying that Stoicism is simply the most prudent and realistic philosophy to follow.*

Terms from the Arts, Sciences, and Social Sciences

Stoic: follower of Stoicism, a pantheistic philosophy emphasizing submission to divine will and freedom from emotion

---

atavism *n.* in biology, the reappearance of a characteristic in an organism after several generations of absence; individual or a part that exhibits atavism; return of a trait after a period of absence

> *Some modern political theorists reject nationalism as a tribal* **atavism.**

54

*attenuate *v.* to weaken

Modern digital radio equipment allows even signals that have been greatly **attenuated** to be transmitted by one station and received by another station.

*audacious *adj.* bold; daring

The German army commander Erwin Rommel was known as the "Desert Fox" as a result of his **audacious** surprise attacks on Allied forces in World War II.

*austere *adj.* stern; unadorned

Deism is an **austere** belief that reflects the predominant philosophy of the Age of Enlightenment: a universe symmetrical and governed by rationality.

Terms from the Arts, Sciences, and Social Sciences

Deism: the belief in a God who created the universe and then abandoned it, assuming no control over life or natural phenomena, and giving no supernatural revelation

Age of Enlightenment: a period in European philosophy during the eighteenth century that emphasized reason

---

autonomous *adj.* self-governing; independent

Some biologists have theorized that our belief in our ability to act as **autonomous** agents is in conformity with the theory of evolution because it gives us a sense of meaning and purpose in our lives that helps us to survive.

Terms from the Arts, Sciences, and Social Sciences

theory of evolution: the theory that living things originate from other similar organisms and that differences between types of organisms are due to modifications in successive generations. A central tenet of Darwinian evolution is that surviving individuals of a species vary in a way that enables them to live longer and reproduce, thus passing this advantage to future generations (Natural Selection).

---

avarice *n.* greed

Successful investment bankers are sometimes accused of **avarice**; their defenders, however, say that they are simply very good at what they do and should be rewarded accordingly.

*aver *v.* to affirm; declare to be true

Yogis **aver** *that everyone has a* guru, *whether it be a person, God, or the experiences of the world, that helps him or her practice the* yoga *that is in accordance with his or her nature, and assists on the path toward enlightenment.*

Terms from the Arts, Sciences, and Social Sciences

yogis: a yogi is the Sanskrit (an ancient Indian language) name for a man who practices yoga. A woman who practices yoga is a *yogini.*

guru: a personal spiritual teacher. The term is also used to refer to a trusted advisor or an authority.

yoga: spiritual practices in the Hindu and Buddhist religions that are believed to help one to attain higher awareness and union with God.

---

avocation *n.* secondary occupation

Dan became so proficient at his **avocation**—*computer programming—that he is thinking of giving up his job as a teacher to do it full time.*

avuncular *adj.* like an uncle, benevolent and tolerant

Walter Cronkite, who was the anchorman of CBS News during much of the 1970s and 1980s, had an **avuncular** *manner that made him one of America's most trusted personalities.*

REVIEW 8

Matching
Match each word with its definition.

1.	asylum	(A)	stern; unadorned
2.	atavism	(B)	return of a trait after a period of absence
3.	attenuate	(C)	greed
4.	audacious	(D)	secondary occupation
5.	austere	(E)	bold; daring
6.	autonomous	(F)	like an uncle
7.	avarice	(G)	self-governing; independent
8.	aver	(H)	place of refuge
9.	avocation	(I)	to affirm
10.	avuncular	(J)	to weaken

Fill-ins

Choose the best word to fill in the blank in each sentence.

asylum	atavism	attenuate	audacious	austere
autonomous	avarice	avers	avocation	avuncular

1. It is important to have an _____ judiciary so that laws can be interpreted free of political influence and considerations.
2. The monks live in _____ quarters.
3. Scientists examining the whale discovered an _____ : it had two legs.
4. The _____ teacher is popular with students.
5. Many people prefer to pursue an _____ that is very different from their occupation.
6. The United States and Britain have long histories of offering _____ to victims of persecution.
7. The plan to eliminate hunger in the world is an _____ one, but it can be achieved if all the nations of the world cooperate.
8. A criticism that has been made of capitalism is that it encourages _____ .
9. Materialism is a philosophy that _____ that matter is the only reality and denies the existence of idealism and spiritualism.
10. Aspirin has the power to _____ a fever.

Sense or Nonsense

Indicate whether each sentence makes good sense or not.
Put S (SENSE) if it does, and put N (NONSENSE) if it does not.

1. The doctor is considering surgery because of the atavism in the patient's left eye. _____
2. Before giving testimony at a trial, each witness must solemnly aver that he or she is telling the truth. _____
3. Shortly after taking office in 1977, President Jimmy Carter fulfilled his campaign promise to pardon young men who had sought asylum in Canada because of their opposition to the war in Vietnam and to the military draft. _____
4. There is a strong tradition that physicians should practice medicine to ease human suffering rather than be motivated by avarice. _____
5. The singer's voice was so attenuated by the PA system that she could be heard even outside the stadium. _____

UNIT 9

axiomatic *adj.* taken for granted

> *In nineteenth-century geology,* uniformitarianism *was the antithesis of* catastrophism, *asserting that it was* **axiomatic** *that natural law and processes do not fundamentally change, and that what we observe now is essentially the same as what occurred in the past.*

Terms from the Arts, Sciences, and Social Sciences

uniformitarianism: a geological theory popular in the nineteenth century. Uniformitarianism holds that geological processes have slowly shaped the Earth and continue to do so.

catastrophism: a theory that was a rival to uniformitarianism. It postulates an Earth formed in a series of unique, catastrophic events.

---

bacchanalian *adj.* pertaining to riotous or drunken festivity; pertaining to revelry.

> *For some people New Year's Eve is an occasion for* **bacchanalian** *revelry.*

Terms from the Arts, Sciences, and Social Sciences

Bacchus: known as Dionysos to the ancient Greeks, Bacchus was the god of agriculture, fertility, and wine. He was worshipped by an emotional cult that held secret rites called *Bacchanalia*—wild orgies of frenzied revelry, drunkenness, and debauchery. Bacchanalian is derived from *Bacchanalia.*

---

*banal *adj.* commonplace; trite

> *The writer has a gift for making even the most* **banal** *observation seem important and original.*

banter *n.* playful conversation

> *The governor engaged in some* **banter** *with reporters before getting to the serious business of the news conference.*

bard *n.* poet

> *The great* **bards** *of English literature have all been masters of the techniques of verse.*

bawdy *adj.* obscene

Geoffrey Chaucer's Canterbury Tales *is the story of a group of Christian pilgrims who entertain one another with stories, ranging from the holy to the **bawdy**, on their journey to Canterbury Cathedral.*

beatify *v.* to sanctify; to bless; to ascribe a virtue to

*In the year 2000 Pope John Paul II traveled to Fatima in Portugal to **beatify** two of the three children who said they saw the appearance of the Virgin Mary there in 1917.*

Beatification is the noun.

***Beatification** is the second and next to last step on the path to sainthood.*

bedizen *v.* to dress in a vulgar, showy manner

*Paul went to the costume party **bedizened** as a seventeenth-century French aristocrat.*

behemoth *n.* huge creature; anything very large and powerful

*In the 1980s and 1990s, the trend in American business was toward increased privatization of government industries (such as power generation), partly because it was believed that private industry is more efficient and partly because foreign private companies were becoming commercial **behemoths**, outstripping government-owned companies in competitiveness.*

*belie *v.* to contradict; misrepresent; give a false impression

*The boxer's childlike face **belies** the ferocity with which he can attack opponents in the ring.*

REVIEW 9

Matching
Match each word with its definition.

1. axiomatic	(A) playful conversation
2. bacchanalian	(B) give a false impression
3. banal	(C) pertaining to riotous or drunken activity
4. banter	(D) dress in a vulgar, showy manner
5. bard	(E) obscene
6. bawdy	(F) commonplace
7. beatify	(G) huge creature
8. bedizen	(H) taken for granted
9. behemoth	(I) poet
10. belie	(J) to bless; sanctify

Fill-ins
Choose the best word to fill in the blank in each sentence.

axiomatic	bacchanalian	banal	banter	bard
bawdy	beatification	bedizen	behemoths	belie

1. The comedian dropped the _____ jokes from his routine for his appearance on national television.
2. The _____ Ted Hughes was appointed Britain's Poet Laureate in 1984.
3. In Jack London's novel *The Sea Wolf*, one of the characters says, "The sacredness of life I had accepted as _____ ."
4. At first, college seemed to _____ all the good things Steve had heard about it in high school; gradually, however, he came to like it.
5. First IBM, next Microsoft and then Google became the _____ of the computer industry.
6. The TV show's producer tries to steer a middle path between making a typical _____ program and being so original that much of the audience is lost.
7. The queen decided to _____ herself with expensive jewelry for the ball.
8. In the Roman Catholic Church, the final stage in the path to sainthood is canonization, which occurs after _____ .
9. The college's annual spring break party in Florida is a/an _____ affair.

10. The world leaders enjoyed some friendly _____ before getting down to the serious business of the negotiations.

Sense or Nonsense

Indicate whether each sentence makes good sense or not.
Put S (SENSE) if it does, and put N (NONSENSE) if it does not.

1. The prisoner was beatified by the jury and sentenced to ten years imprisonment. _____
2. The band's backstage crew often exchange banter during long rehearsals. _____
3. The principle that every person has certain fundamental rights is regarded by most people as axiomatic. _____
4. The ascetic monks regularly hold bacchanalian parties. _____
5. The question of whether the Greek bard Homer was a single individual or the name given to several authors is still hotly debated by scholars. _____

UNIT 10

*beneficent *adj.* kindly; doing good

   *The theologian discussed the question of why a **beneficent** and omnipotent God allows bad things to happen to good people.*

bifurcate *v.* to divide into two parts

   *Contemporary physicists generally **bifurcate** their discipline into two parts—classical physics and modern physics; the former are the fields of study that were already well developed before the momentous breakthroughs of the early twentieth century by scientists such as Albert Einstein, Niels Bohr, and Werner Heisenberg, which inaugurated the age of modern physics.*

Bifurcation is the noun.

   *Some people regard the Hindu-Buddhist philosophy on animals as more in accordance with the modern scientific view than the traditional Western view, since it does not posit a radical **bifurcation** of man and nature.*

blandishment *n.* flattery

   *Despite the salesperson's **blandishments**, Donna did not buy the car.*

Blandish is the verb, meaning to coax with flattery.

blasé *adj.* bored because of frequent indulgence; unconcerned

> *We were amazed by John's **blasé** attitude toward school; he seems to have made it a rule never to open a book.*

bolster *v.* to give a boost to; prop up; support

> *The president has visited the state several times to **bolster** his sagging popularity there.*

*bombastic *adj.* pompous; using inflated language

> *Nearly lost in the senator's long, **bombastic** speech were several sensible ideas.*

*boorish *adj.* rude; insensitive

> *Bob apologized for his **boorish** behavior at the party, saying he hadn't realized that it was such a formal occasion.*

bovine *adj.* cowlike

> *Following the slow-moving group of students up the long path to the school's entrance, the word "**bovine**" popped into the English teacher's mind.*

brazen *adj.* bold; shameless

> *The **brazen** student irritated his teacher by saying that he could learn more from a day spent "surfing" the World Wide Web than a day spent in school.*

broach *v.* to mention for the first time

> *Steve's boss knew that she couldn't put off warning him about his poor performance and decided to **broach** the subject the next time she saw him.*

REVIEW 10

Matching
Match each word with its definition.

1. beneficent	(A)	flattery
2. bifurcate	(B)	cowlike
3. blandishment	(C)	kindly; doing good
4. blasé	(D)	bold
5. bolster	(E)	bored because of frequent indulgence
6. bombastic	(F)	mention for the first time
7. boorish	(G)	give a boost to
8. bovine	(H)	rude; insensitive
9. brazen	(I)	divide into two parts
10. broach	(J)	pompous; using inflated language

Fill-ins
Choose the best word to fill in the blank in each sentence.

beneficence	**bifurcation**	**blandishments**	**blasé**	**bolstered**
bombastic	**boorish**	**bovine**	**brazen**	**broached**

1. The coach warned the lacrosse team not to become _____ even though they had won a school record twenty matches the previous season.
2. There is a _____ in American politics between a tradition that believes that interference in the affairs of other countries is imprudent, and an idealistic streak that seeks to use American power to help other countries.
3. Bill Gates showed his _____ by setting up with his wife Melinda a foundation to provide financial help to, among other things, fight disease in the third world.
4. Amanda went out with her boyfriend for two years before she _____ the subject of marriage.
5. The audience listened to the boring speech with _____ expressions on their faces.
6. Russian historians have shown how the Soviet leader Joseph Stalin used a mixture of arguments, _____ , and threats to overcome resistance to his repressive policies among his fellow Politburo members.
7. The small company startled investors by its _____ takeover of a company with three times its assets.

8. Many people in the audience were annoyed at the _____ behavior of the two men who talked loudly to each other through the entire movie.

9. The president's speechwriter told him that she was doing her best to write a speech that was serious and solemn but not

_____ .

10. The prosecutor's case was _____ by the new testimony of a credible witness.

Sense or Nonsense
Indicate whether each sentence makes good sense or not.
Put S (SENSE) if it does, and put N (NONSENSE) if it does not.

1. Satan is often portrayed as the embodiment of malevolence and beneficence. _____

2. The actor is admired by everyone for her boorish behavior. _____

3. The brazen student demanded that the teacher postpone the test so she would have more time to study for it. _____

4. The general visited the troops to bolster their morale before the crucial battle. _____

5. Jim is so blasé about the upcoming GRE test that he is studying six hours a day for it. _____

UNIT 11

bucolic *adj.* characteristic of the countryside; rustic; pastoral

> The south end of Toronto's beautiful High Park is a **bucolic** expanse of land that is perfect for anyone wanting a quiet walk.

*burgeon *v.* to flourish

> After World War II, the increased speed of industrialization and the **burgeoning** world population resulted in such an increase in pollution that it began to be recognized by some people as a threat to the human habitat, Earth.

*burnish *v.* to polish

> The poet T. S. Eliot **burnished** his reputation as one of the master poets of the twentieth century with Four Quartets, four long poems published between 1936 and 1942.

*buttress *v.* to reinforce; support

> Some critics of the American legal system argue that the requirement of proving guilt "beyond a reasonable doubt" is too difficult a criterion to use, and **buttress** their case by citing the fact that objec-

tive studies suggest that only a very small number of criminals are successfully prosecuted.

*cacophonous *adj.* unpleasant or harsh-sounding

*The dissonant harmonies of the great jazz pianist and composer Thelonious Monk might seem **cacophonous** to some listeners, but to many jazz aficionados they are sublime.*

A *cacophony* is a jarring, unpleasant noise.

Terms from the Arts, Sciences, and Social Sciences

aficionados: people who are enthusiastic admirers or followers

---

cadge *v.* to beg; sponge

*An enduring image of the Great Depression in America is the out-of-work man **cadging** money with the line, "Hey, mister, can you spare a dime for a cup of coffee?"*

Terms from the Arts, Sciences, and Social Sciences

Great Depression: a very large economic decline that began in 1929. Major industrial nations such as Great Britain, Japan, and the United States were greatly affected by declines in nearly all measures of economic prosperity (such as employment and profits).

---

callous *adj.* thick-skinned; insensitive

*Jim's terrible experiences in the war have made him **callous** about the suffering of others.*

calumny *n.* false and malicious accusation; slander

"Be thou chaste as ice, as pure as snow, thou shalt not escape **calumny**.*"*
> —William Shakespeare, *Hamlet* Act III, Scene 1
> (Hamlet addressing Ophelia)

canard *n.* false, deliberately misleading story

*Most politicians do not want to be associated with the old **canard** that big government in Washington can solve all of America's problems.*

canon *n.* an established principle; a basis or standard for judgment; a group of literary works

> *Canons of aesthetic taste vary over the years; the* Rococo *period, for example, valued ornate art.*

> *The sixty-volume* Great Books of the Western World *is an attempt to gather the central* **canon** *of Western civilization into one collection.*

Canon is also an adjective.

> *The system of civil law originated in the Roman Empire and was kept alive in the Middle Ages in the* **canon** *law of the Church.*

Canonical is an adjective meaning belonging to a group of literary works.

> *The English professor is trying to persuade the chairperson of her department to let her teach some writers that are not* **canonical***.*

Terms from the Arts, Sciences, and Social Sciences

Rococo: refers to a style of architecture in eighteenth-century Europe that made use of elaborate curved forms. The word is often used to refer to something that is excessively ornate.

REVIEW 11

Matching
Match each word with its definition.

1.	bucolic	(A)	to polish
2.	burgeon	(B)	to reinforce
3.	burnish	(C)	to beg
4.	buttress	(D)	false, misleading story
5.	cacophonous	(E)	established principle
6.	cadge	(F)	characteristic of the countryside
7.	callous	(G)	insensitive
8.	calumny	(H)	to flourish
9.	canard	(I)	unpleasant or harsh-sounding
10.	canon	(J)	false, malicious accusation

Fill-ins

Choose the best word to fill in the blank in each sentence.

bucolic	burgeoning	burnish	buttress	cacophonous
cadge	callous	calumny	canard	canon

1. The _____ of modern communications has made fiber optics nearly indispensable because of its ability to transmit vast amounts of information.
2. The link between economic boom and war is used by Marxists to _____ their view that capitalism thrives on war, and to some degree, encourages it in periods of low economic activity.
3. How many times have you heard the old _____ "Those who can, do; those who can't, teach"?
4. A traditional olive farm is a _____ sight: big trees spaced fairly far apart providing good cover for grass and grazing animals.
5. The student is well known for his tendency to _____ money from his friends.
6. The company's new advertising campaign is intended to _____ its image as a dynamic, forward-looking firm.
7. The movie star sued the newspaper for printing _____ about him.
8. The task the poultry farm worker looked forward to the least was going into the _____ hen yard at feeding time.
9. The public relations director's comments that the inmates had hanged themselves as a public relations stunt was widely regarded as showing a _____ disregard for life.
10. The nineteenth-century French composer Hector Berlioz has become a central figure in the Western musical _____ .

Sense or Nonsense

Indicate whether each sentence makes good sense or not.
Put S (SENSE) if it does, and put N (NONSENSE) if it does not.

1. It may sound odd, but I actually enjoy the cacophonous sound of an orchestra tuning up. _____
2. The artist is painting a bucolic rush hour scene in Manhattan. _____
3. We sailed our canard around the world last year. _____
4. Government officials in China are concerned about the burgeoning numbers of old people in their country. _____
5. Steve buttressed his position in the pharmaceutical company by earning a Ph.D. in chemistry. _____

UNIT 12

*cant *n.* insincere talk; language of a particular group

*Many of the beat artists of the 1950s reacted against what they regarded as the **cant** of bourgeois society.*

Terms from the Arts, Sciences, and Social Sciences

bourgeois: both *bourgeois* and *bourgeoisie* come from Old French *burgeis*, citizen of a *bourg* (town). *Bourgeois* refers to a person who belongs to the middle class or has middle-class attitudes. It can be used in a neutral way. However, it is frequently used to suggest that someone is not sophisticated.

---

cantankerous *adj.* irritable; ill-humored

*Many of us have in our mind the stereotype of the **cantankerous** old man who is constantly complaining about something or other.*

*capricious *adj.* fickle

*The rule of law is regarded by many historians as one of humanity's great achievements because since its inception citizens are no longer subject to **capricious** decisions and penalties of rulers.*

Caprice is a noun meaning an inclination to change one's mind compulsively.

*Styles in high fashion seem governed by **caprice** as much as anything else.*

captious *adj.* faultfinding; intended to entrap, as in an argument

*The pedantic and **captious** critic seems incapable of appreciating the merits of even the most highly regarded books.*

cardinal *adj.* of foremost importance

*The **cardinal** rule of any weight-loss diet must be limiting the intake of calories.*

carnal *adj.* of the flesh or body; related to physical appetites

*The yogi's goal is to achieve nirvana through, among other things, the overcoming of **carnal** desires.*

> **Terms from the Arts, Sciences, and Social Sciences**
>
> *nirvana:* ideal condition of rest, harmony, or joy. Nirvana is from Sanskrit *nirvanam* (a blowing out), as in the blowing out of a flame. According to Buddhism and Hinduism, in order to reach nirvana one must extinguish the fire fueled by the ego, which causes suffering, ignorance, delusion, and greed.

carping *v.* to find fault; complain

> Cost-benefit analysis *owes much of its origin to* utilitarian *thought; despite the* **carping** *of critics that such analysis is based on faulty premises, the technique has proved useful in many areas.*

> **Terms from the Arts, Sciences, and Social Sciences**
>
> *Cost-benefit analysis:* the process of weighing the total expected costs against the total expected benefits of one or more actions in order to choose the best option
>
> *utilitarian:* the ethical philosophy that human activity should be aimed at achieving the greatest good for the greatest number. Jeremy Bentham was the founder of the theory and his student John Stuart Mill was its most famous proponent. Mill used the theory to argue for social reform and increased democracy.

cartography *n.* science of making maps

> *Satellites in Earth orbit take pictures of topography that have greatly aided* **cartography**.

caste *n.* any of the hereditary social classes of Hindu society; social stratification

> *The dalits, formerly known as untouchables, are at the bottom of the thousands of* **castes** *that make up Indian society.*

Caste is also an adjective.

> *Most modern corporations employ a sort of* **caste** *system, with senior executives at the top and ordinary workers at the bottom.*

Terms from the Arts, Sciences, and Social Sciences

There are four main *castes* or heredity groups (and thousands of subcastes) in Hindu society that restrict the occupations of members and limit their interaction with members of other castes. There are four main castes:

Brahmans (priests and teachers)
Ksatriyas (noblemen)
Vaisyas (merchants and traders)
Sudras (laborers)

A fifth group, called "Harijans" or "untouchables" are considered impure and are discriminated against. They toil in lowly occupations such as cleaning up waste and leatherworking.

---

*castigation *n.* punishment; chastisement; criticism

Many British writers recall with loathing the **castigation** *they received at school.*

REVIEW 12

Matching
Match each word with its definition.

1. cant
2. cantankerous
3. capricious
4. captious
5. cardinal
6. carnal
7. carping
8. cartography
9. caste
10. castigation

(A) of foremost importance
(B) fickle
(C) science of making maps
(D) insincere talk
(E) of the flesh or body
(F) hereditary social class
(G) complaining
(H) punishment
(I) irritable
(J) faultfinding

Fill-ins

Choose the best word to fill in the blank in each sentence.

cant	cantankerous	capricious	captious	cardinal
carnal	carping	cartography	caste	castigated

1. The military employs a type of _____ system with generals at the top and privates at the bottom.
2. Commentators dismissed the speech as the mere _____ of someone desperately trying to be reelected.
3. The English teacher is so pedantic and _____ in her marking that her students have become discouraged.
4. It is a postulate of science that the laws of nature are not _____ and that the universe is not chaotic.
5. According to this book the _____ rule of good writing is to be clear.
6. Rococo painting often reflects the great pleasure the French aristocracy took in all things _____ .
7. The ability of modern _____ to produce very accurate maps of the Earth's surface has been a boon to navigators.
8. The boss _____ the worker for losing the important client's file.
9. The band decided to continue to play in their new style despite the _____ of critics who said it was a sell-out to commercial interests.
10. The _____ old woman is always getting into arguments with people.

Sense or Nonsense

Indicate whether each sentence makes good sense or not.
Put S (SENSE) if it does, and put N (NONSENSE) if it does not.

1. The judge is respected by legal scholars for her capricious rulings. _____
2. The cantankerous old man seems to like nothing better than arguing with the checkout clerk in the supermarket. _____
3. Cartography has helped scientists gain a good understanding of the fundamental workings of the human brain. _____
4. A cardinal rule of hiking is to never hike alone. _____
5. The painting's caste gives it the mood of a Rembrandt. _____

UNIT 13

cataclysm *n.* a violent upheaval that causes great destruction and change

>*The French Revolution of 1789 was a **cataclysm** whose effects are still felt today.*

*catalyst *n.* something causing change

>*Among the catalysts of the Romantic movement were the libertarian ideals of the French Revolution.*

Terms from the Arts, Sciences, and Social Sciences

Romantic movement: a late eighteenth- and nineteenth-century movement in literature and the arts. The movement was a very varied one, and so is not easily described in a few words. Romanticism was a revolt against classicism and reason and emphasized the individual and the emotional. The Romantics also stressed the inherent goodness of man and nature and valued freedom highly. Important Romantic poets in England include William Blake, John Keats, William Wordsworth, and P. B. Shelley. Famous Romantic composers include Hector Berlioz, Franz Liszt, and Frederic Chopin.

libertarian: libertarians place great importance on individual freedom. They believe that no limitations should be placed on a person's freedom unless that person's actions limit the freedom of others.

French Revolution: a crucial period (1789–1799) in French, and more generally, Western civilization. France's absolute monarchy was replaced by republicanism. It is regarded by most historians as a major turning point in Western civilization, ushering in the era of citizens as the major force in politics.

---

categorical *adj.* absolute; without exception

>*Although incest is **categorically** forbidden by every state, recent evidence that marriage between cousins is no more likely to produce abnormal offspring than "normal" marriages may allow the constitutionality of bans on marriage between cousins to be challenged.*

caucus *n.* smaller group within an organization

>*The workers formed an informal **caucus** to discuss their difficulties.*

causal *adj.* involving a cause

>*The philosopher Plato believed there is a **causal** relationship between income inequality, on the one hand, and political discontent and crime, on the other hand: in his Laws he quantified his argument, contending that the income of the rich should be no more than five*

times that of the poor, and he proposed policies to limit extremes of wealth and poverty.

caustic *adj.* sarcastically biting; burning

*The columnist's **caustic** comments on government policy did not win her any friends among government officials.*

celestial *adj.* concerning the sky or heavens; sublime

*Astronomers make use of the Doppler effect to measure the velocities and distance from Earth of stars and other **celestial** objects.*

Terms from the Arts, Sciences, and Social Sciences

Doppler effect: change in the wavelength and frequency of a wave as a result of the motion of either the source or receiver of the waves

---

centrifugal *adj.* moving away from a center

*As the empire expanded, there was an ever-increasing **centrifugal** stress as remote colonies sought autonomy.*

centripetal *adj.* moving or directed toward a center

*Astronomers calculate that the **centripetal** force exerted by the Earth's gravity on the Moon will keep the Moon in orbit around the Earth for billions of years.*

champion *v.* to defend or support

*Robin Hood is famous for **championing** the underdogs of England.*

REVIEW 13

Matching
Match each word with its definition.

1. cataclysm	(A)	involving a cause
2. catalyst	(B)	absolute
3. categorical	(C)	concerning the sky or heavens
4. caucus	(D)	moving toward a center
5. causal	(E)	violent upheaval
6. caustic	(F)	moving away from a center
7. celestial	(G)	defend or support
8. centrifugal	(H)	something causing change
9. centripetal	(I)	sarcastically biting
10. champion	(J)	smaller group within an organization

Fill-ins
Choose the best word to fill in the blank in each sentence.

cataclysm	catalysts	categorical	caucus	causal
caustic	celestial	centrifugal	centripetal	championed

1. Since its founding in 1966, the National Organization for Women (NOW) has _____ the rights of women.

2. A study finds that people who exercise more tend to be healthier: Its authors raise the question, "Are these individuals healthier because they exercise—a _____ link—or do they exercise more because they are healthier to begin with?"

3. "My position is _____ ," the CEO said. "I will not allow this company to be bought out."

4. Biochemical _____ , called enzymes, occur naturally in cells, changing one molecule into another.

5. Scientists say that the impact of a large meteor with the Earth would cause a _____ that might end all life on our planet.

6. Japanese sociologists are studying the _____ effects of a homogenous population on society.

7. Theoretically, a space station could be rotated to create artificial gravity as a result of _____ force.

8. Gothic cathedrals place a great importance on light and a sense of space that seems to lift one toward the _____ .

9. The parliament's minority _____ issued a report condemning government policy.

10. Wear protective gloves when working with _____ substances in the laboratory.

Sense or Nonsense
Indicate whether each sentence makes good sense or not.
Put S (SENSE) if it does, and put N (NONSENSE) if it does not.

1. Laboratory centrifuges make use of centrifugal force to separate substances according to their relative masses. _____

2. A study in Western Australia established a causal relationship between talking on a cell phone while driving and an increased likelihood of having an accident. _____

3. Catalysts for change on the school board blocked attempts to implement reforms. _____

4. In 1054, ancient Chinese astronomers recorded their observation of many important celestial events, such as the supernova that created the Crab Nebula. _____

5. The newly discovered species of caucus is remarkable for its ability to survive for months with almost no water. _____

UNIT 14

chasten *v.* to correct by punishment or reproof; to restrain or subdue

*The child's behavior improved after she had been **chastened** by punishment.*

***chicanery** *n.* trickery; fraud

*The governor ordered an audit to investigate alleged financial **chicanery**.*

chivalry *n.* the qualities idealized by knighthood such as bravery and gallantry toward women

*   ***Chivalry** was rooted in Christian values, and the knight was bound to be loyal to Christian ideals; the* Crusades *enhanced this idea, as knights vowed to uphold Christianity against heathens.*

Terms from the Arts, Sciences, and Social Sciences

chivalry: The code of chivalry dictated how a knight should act; this code enjoined the knight to defend the Church, make war against infidels, perform scrupulously feudal duties, and in general champion virtue against evil.

Crusades: military expeditions by Christians in the Middle Ages to win the Holy Land from the Muslims

---

churlish *adj.* rude; boorish

*According to the chivalric code, a knight was never supposed to be **churlish**, especially toward noble ladies, to whom he was supposed to be unfailingly gentle and courteous.*

circuitous *adj.* roundabout

*According to Hindu philosophy, some souls take a **circuitous** path through many births to reach God.*

clairvoyant *n.* one who can predict the future; psychic

*Edgar Cayce was a famous **clairvoyant** who some people believe was able to go into a trance during which he was in touch with a spiritual realm.*

clamor *n.* noisy outcry

> *Over the past 12 years or so the* **clamor** *for better protection of the Earth's rain forests has increased dramatically.*

Clamor is also a verb meaning to cry out noisily.

> *The crowd* **clamored** *their disapproval of the plan.*

clique *n.* a small, exclusive group

> *The principal of the high school is concerned that one* **clique** *of students is dominating the student council.*

cloister *v.* to confine; seclude

> *The writer* **cloistered** *herself in a country house to finish her novel.*

The adjective *cloistered* means shut away from the world.

> *The journalist described the large American philanthropic foundations as arrogant, elitist, and* **cloistered.**

The noun *cloister* means a monastery or convent.

*coagulate *v.* thicken; congeal

> *In normal individuals, blood begins to* **coagulate** *about 20 seconds after a wound is sustained, thus preventing further bleeding.*

REVIEW 14

Matching
Match each word with its definition.

1. chasten	(A)	rude; boorish
2. chicanery	(B)	to confine
3. chivalry	(C)	trickery; fraud
4. churlish	(D)	roundabout
5. circuitous	(E)	correct by punishment
6. clairvoyant	(F)	noisy outcry
7. clamor	(G)	thicken; congeal
8. clique	(H)	qualities idealized by knighthood
9. cloister	(I)	small, exclusive group
10. coagulate	(J)	psychic

'ill-ins

Choose the best word to fill in the blank in each sentence.

chastened	chicanery	chivalric	churlish	circuitous
clairvoyant	clamor	clique	cloistered	coagulates

1. The idea of the gentleman is derived from the _____ ideal that a man should be honorable, courteous, brave, and loyal, especially to women.
2. Egg white _____ when heated.
3. The college newspaper is dominated by a _____ of students who seem to be interested mainly in sports.
4. Over the last few years there has been a _____ in the media about increased global warming.
5. After robbing the store, the thief took a _____ route back to his house in case anyone was following him.
6. Mr. Jones tends to be _____ before he has had breakfast.
7. The government's budget deficit was covered up by _____ ; several items were moved off-budget and unrealistically high revenues were projected.
8. The dictator of the small country was _____ by the great power's show of naval strength in the harbor of his country's capital city.
9. We all said that Claire must be _____ after she predicted the exact score of the football game.
0. The scholar lives a _____ life among his books.

;ense or Nonsense

ndicate whether each sentence makes good sense or not.
'ut S (SENSE) if it does, and put N (NONSENSE) if it does not.

1. The chivalric code commanded knights to be brave, generous, and faithful. _____
2. Blood is coagulating around the wound. _____
3. The United States is an open, cloistered society that prides itself on being tolerant of a wide range of views. _____
4. Herb's boss chastened him with a raise of $10,000 dollars a year. _____
5. Stage magicians often use clever tricks to make it appear that they are clairvoyant. _____

UNIT 15

coalesce *v.* to cause to become one

> *President John F. Kennedy said that Americans must be vigilant s* *that the interests of business and the military do not* **coalesce** *and thus undermine those of society as a whole.*

coda *n.* concluding part of a literary or musical composition; something that summarizes or concludes

> *The* **coda** *of the Danish composer Per Norgard's Sixth Symphony seems to return to the serene sounds of the opening.*

codify *v.* to systematize

> *The state legislature voted to* **codify** *regulations governing banking fraud.*

Codification is the noun.

> *The most influential* **codification** *of civil law was the Napoleonic Code in France, which became the paradigm for law in the non-English-speaking countries of Europe and had a generally civilizing influence on most of the countries in which it was enacted.*

Codified is the adjective.

> *Common law is the system of laws that originated in England; it is based on court decisions and on customs rather than on* **codified** *written laws.*

Terms from the Arts, Sciences, and Social Sciences

civil law: a system of law developed from Roman law that is used in continental Europe, the U.S. state of Louisiana, and several other places. The basis of civil law is statute rather than custom and precedent, which are the basis of common law.

Napoleonic Code: French legal code enacted by Napoleon in 1804. It made uniform the private law of France.

common law: body of law that includes many nonstatutory laws based on many years of precedent derived from rulings by judges

---

cognizant *adj.* informed; conscious; aware

> *O. Henry's "The Gift of the Magi" is a simple evocation of a young couple's love for one another, a story in which a husband and wife in straitened circumstances each sacrifices to buy a Christmas present for the other, not* **cognizant** *of what the other is doing.*

collage *n.* artistic composition of materials pasted over a surface; an assemblage of diverse elements

> The cubist *Juan Gris is noted for his use of* **collage** *to create* trompe l'oeil *effects—the illusion of photographic reality.*

Terms from the Arts, Sciences, and Social Sciences

cubist: a movement in art in the twentieth century that represented subjects from several points of view rather than from a single perspective. Pablo Picasso and Georges Braques were the two most influential cubist artists.

trompe l'oeil: a French term meaning "deceive the eye." It refers to a style of portraying objects in a way that deceives the observer into believing it is the object itself.

---

commensurate *adj.* proportional

> In the United States, malpractice suits have raised the cost of medicine because doctors must pay more for insurance, and thus increase their fees **commensurately**.

compendium *n.* brief, comprehensive summary

> The Mozart **Compendium**: A Guide to Mozart's Life and Music *by H. C. Robbins Landon is a convenient reference for finding information about the life and music of Wolfgang Amadeus Mozart.*

complacent *adj.* self-satisfied

> Although Tom received an "A" on his midterm exam, Professor Donovan warned him not to become **complacent** since the work in the second term would be harder.

complaisant *adj.* overly polite; willing to please; obliging

> Although France and Germany have a close relationship, neither would consider the other a **complaisant** ally.

complement *n.* something that completes or makes up a whole

> Some people envision chess developing into a game between teams of humans and computers, each **complementing** the other and providing investigators with insight into the cognitive processes of each.

REVIEW 15

Matching
Match each word with its definition.

1. coalesce	(A) to systematize
2. coda	(B) cause to become one
3. codify	(C) assemblage of diverse elements
4. cognizant	(D) overly polite
5. collage	(E) proportional
6. commensurate	(F) self-satisfied
7. compendium	(G) something that makes up a whole
8. complacent	(H) something that summarizes
9. complaisant	(I) brief, comprehensive summary
10. complement	(J) informed; conscious

Fill-ins
Choose the best word to fill in the blank in each sentence.

coalesced	coda	codification	cognizant
collage	commensurate	compendium	complacent
complaisant	complement		

1. The final chapter of the scientist's book is a _____ in which the author reflects on her life and the important role science played in it.
2. The former chain-smoker describes herself as "Now a _____ passive nonsmoker."
3. A recent theory of how the Earth got its moon is that a very large object collided with the Earth about 4.5 billion years ago, producing iron-free material that gradually _____ into the Moon.
4. One of the cornerstones of capitalism is the conviction that a worker's rewards should be _____ with his or her contribution.
5. Another important _____ of modern civil law in addition to the Napoleonic Code is the German Civil Code (German *Bürgerliche. Gesetzbuch*) that went into effect in the German Empire in 1900.
6. When one is studying a complex novel, it is helpful to have a _____ that gives information about characters, setting, plot, etc.
7. Traditionally, white wine is considered a good _____ to fish, whereas red wine is considered to be more suitable for meat.
8. The company's CEO is worried that this quarter's record profits will make his employees _____ .

9. It is important that a person accused of a crime be _____ of his or her legal rights.
10. Modern Singapore is a multiethnic _____ of Malays, Indians, Chinese, and many other groups.

Sense or Nonsense
Indicate whether each sentence makes good sense or not.
Put S (SENSE) if it does, and put N (NONSENSE) if it does not.

1. After three months of training, the battalion coalesced into a formidable fighting force. _____
2. The collage portrays the university's history since its founding in 1766. _____
3. A widely held belief is that an employee's pay should be commensurate with his or her qualifications and experience. _____
4. It is unwise to become complaisant and assume you will do well on the GRE just because you did well on the SAT or ACT. _____
5. During World War II German naval commanders radioed codas to their submarines containing the location of Allied ships. _____

UNIT 16

compliant *adj.* yielding
> The young negotiator is trying to learn the skill of being open to proposals by the other side without seeming too **compliant**.

compunction *n.* uneasiness caused by guilt
> The American psychiatrist Frank Pittman said, "Men who have been raised violently have every reason to believe it is appropriate for them to control others through violence; they feel no **compunction** over being violent to women, children, and one another."

concave *adj.* curving inward
> **Concave** lenses are used in glasses to compensate for myopia (nearsightedness).

***conciliatory** *adj.* overcoming distrust or hostility
> The leader of the country made **conciliatory** statements assuring the world that his country did not intend to acquire nuclear weapons.

concoct *v.* to invent
> The various human cultures have **concocted** a great many explanations to describe the beginning of the Earth, life, and humanity.

*concomitant *n.* existing concurrently

*A rebuttal of the argument that homo sapiens's higher cognitive functions could not be the result solely of evolution is that such abilities arose as **concomitants** of language, which gave early hominids a tremendous advantage over other species.*

Terms from the Arts, Sciences, and Social Sciences

hominids: a hominid is any member of the biological family Hominidae (the "great apes"), which include, chimpanzees, gorillas, orangutans, and humans.

---

condone *v.* to overlook voluntarily; forgive

Mahatma Gandhi believed in the principle of ahimsa and refused to condone violence of any kind, even if used in a just cause.

Terms from the Arts, Sciences, and Social Sciences

Mahatma Gandi: twentieth-century Indian political leader who was instrumental in India's gaining independence. Gandi is widely revered for his championing of nonviolence.

ahimsa: a belief in Hinduism, Jainism, and Buddhism that advocates noninjury to all living beings

---

*confound *v.* to baffle; perplex; mix up

*Everyone but astrophysicists seems to be **confounded** by the question, "What happened before the Big Bang?"*

Terms from the Arts, Sciences, and Social Sciences

Big Bang: a model of the origin of the universe stating that it began as infinitely compressed and has been expanding since then

---

congenial *adj.* similar in tastes and habits; friendly; suited to

*The physicist Freeman Dyson has expressed his awe at how **congenial** the universe is to intelligent life and consciousness.*

conjugal *adj.* pertaining to marriage agreement

*The goal of the Bennett sisters in Jane Austen's Pride and Prejudice is to find a suitable man to marry with whom they can live in **conjugal** happiness.*

REVIEW 16

Matching
Match each word with its definition.

1. compliant		(A)	curving inward
2. compunction		(B)	yielding
3. concave		(C)	baffle; perplex
4. conciliatory		(D)	to invent
5. concoct		(E)	to overlook voluntarily
6. concomitant		(F)	pertaining to marriage agreement
7. condone		(G)	overcoming distrust or hostility
8. confound		(H)	similar in tastes or habits
9. congenial		(I)	uneasiness caused by guilt
10. conjugal		(J)	existing concurrently

Fill-ins
Choose the best word to fill in the blank in each sentence.

compliant	compunction	concave	conciliatory	concocted
concomitant	condoned		confounded	congenial	conjugal

1. It appears that bureaucracies are today a necessary evil, a _____ of modern society.
2. Amateur radio operators must be _____ with federal laws as administered by the Federal Communications Commission.
3. The novel's plot centers around a woman's search for _____ bliss.
4. One of the main goals of military training is to train soldiers to kill without _____ .
5. The dating service matches men and women with _____ interests.
6. For centuries, Fermat's last theorem _____ mathematicians.
7. The story Bud _____ about having been abducted by Veg- ans in search of Earth's greatest knowledge was not deemed by his professor an acceptable excuse for not handing in his term paper.
8. A lens with two _____ surfaces is called a biconcave lens.
9. Some people believe that the use of nuclear weapons should never be _____ .
10. After ten years of feuding with her neighbor, Mrs. Clampett decided enough was enough: as a _____ gesture, she baked a cake and brought it over to her neighbor.

Sense or Nonsense

Indicate whether each sentence makes good sense or not.
Put S (SENSE) if it does, and put N (NONSENSE) if it does not.

1. Since the enemy had made a number of conciliatory gestures, we had no option but to attack them in return. _____
2. The prison allows conjugal visits on weekends. _____
3. This amateur radio transceiver's complex menu system has me completely confounded. _____
4. How the mind concocts new ideas is still a mystery to both psychologists and philosophers. _____
5. The optical telescope's complex system of lenses contains both concave and convex lenses. _____

UNIT 17

connoisseur *n.* a person possessing expert knowledge or training; a person of informed and discriminating taste

> *The art connoisseur selected works by Van Gogh, Rembrandt, and Picasso for the exhibition.*

conscript *n.* person compulsorily enrolled for military service

> *The position of NOW (The National Organization for Women) is that having male-only conscripts violates the principle of gender equality.*

Conscript is also a verb meaning to enroll a person for military service

> *The French writer Andre Breton was conscripted into the artillery and had to put his medical studies in abeyance for the duration of World War I.*

Conscription is the noun.

> *During the War of 1812, American political leaders considered national conscription to augment state militias, but Daniel Webster successfully argued before Congress that such a measure would be unconstitutional and thus the proposal was rejected.*

Terms from the Arts, Sciences, and Social Sciences

War of 1812: a war fought between the British Empire and the United States from 1812 to 1815. The war ended in a stalemate.

conscription: forced enlistment of people in the military. Modern conscription originated during the French Revolution.

Daniel Webster: American lawyer and political leader during the period before the Civil War, which he tried to avert

---

consecrate *v.* to declare sacred

> *In his Gettysburg Address, President Abraham Lincoln said of the soldiers who died in the Battle of Gettysburg in July, 1863: "We have come to dedicate a portion of that field, as a final resting place for those who here gave their lives that that nation might live...But, in a larger sense, we cannot dedicate—we cannot **consecrate**—we cannot hallow—this ground. The brave men, living and dead, who struggled here, have **consecrated** it, far above our poor power to add or detract."*

contend *v.* to assert

> *One of the most famous philosophers to argue for* ethical relativism *was the German* Friedrich Nietzsche, *who contended that the rightness of a particular action is dependent on the circumstances of the time and culture in which it occurs.*

Contention is a noun meaning an assertion.

> *The study's **contention** is that obesity is America's biggest health problem.*

Terms from the Arts, Sciences, and Social Sciences

ethical relativism: the view that there is no objective truth in issues of what is right or wrong

Friedrich Nietzsche: nineteenth-century German philosopher. Nietzsche is best known for his doctrine of "the Superman," which held that superior people should reject the "slave morality" of traditional Christianity in favor of a new morality centered on the individual.

---

*contentious *adj.* quarrelsome; causing quarrels

> *When genetic engineering began in the 1970s, there was a **contentious**, and sometimes acrimonious, debate among scientists themselves about its dangers.*

Terms from the Arts, Sciences, and Social Sciences

genetic engineering: the use of various methods to manipulate the DNA (genetic material) of cells to change hereditary traits or produce biological products

---

contiguous *adj.* touching; neighboring; connecting without a break

*There are forty-eight **contiguous** states in the United States of America.*

continence *n.* self-control; abstention from sexual activity

*Saint Augustine's famous line "Give me chastity and **continence**, but not just now" is sometimes used to highlight the idea that action is desirable at some point, but not at present.*

contrite *adj.* very sorrowful for a wrong

*In sentencing the convicted man to a life sentence, the judge took into consideration the fact that he did not seem to be at all **contrite** about his crime.*

contumacious *adj.* disobedient; rebellious

*In the late eighteenth century, Great Britain tried unsuccessfully to put down the uprising against their rule by **contumacious** Americans, leading eventually to the establishment of a separate nation.*

*conundrum *n.* riddle; puzzle with no solution

*The paradoxical statement "This statement is false" presents us with a **conundrum**.*

REVIEW 17

Matching
Match each word with its definition.

1.	connoisseur	(A)	self-control
2.	conscript	(B)	to declare sacred
3.	consecrate	(C)	touching; neighboring
4.	contend	(D)	disobedient; rebellious
5.	contentious	(E)	person compulsorily enrolled for military service
6.	contiguous	(F)	quarrelsome
7.	continence	(G)	person of informed and discriminating taste
8.	contrite	(H)	puzzle with no solution
9.	contumacious	(I)	very sorry for a wrong
10.	conundrum	(J)	to assert

Fill-ins
Choose the best word to fill in the blank in each sentence.

connoisseur	conscripted	consecrated	contends
contentious	contiguous	continence	contrite
contumacious	conundrums		

1. The appropriate function of literary criticism is a _____ issue, even among critics themselves.
2. The art critic _____ that the art of what are called less sophisticated cultures has an immediacy that is often lacking in civilized art, perhaps because it is less self-conscious, intellectual, and stylized.
3. In Israel, women as well as men are _____ into the armed forces; however, men can be made to serve in combat, whereas women serve in a noncombat capacity.
4. One of the great _____ in economics is how to achieve full employment without high inflation.
5. The monk pledged himself to a life of _____ .
6. The dream holiday of the wine _____ is a trip to France to visit famous chateaux in the region of Bordeaux.
7. The king ordered his army to quell the rebellion by his _____ subject.
8. The landowner had the abandoned house _____ to his house torn down.
9. The Cardinal _____ the cathedral in 1676.
10. The _____ sinner prayed every day for God to forgive her.

Sense or Nonsense
Indicate whether each sentence makes good sense or not.
Put S (SENSE) if it does, and put N (NONSENSE) if it does not.

1. There is nothing that a connoisseur of fine cigars hates more than smoking the finest Cuban cigars. _____
2. Conscription is seen by many people as a last resort to be used when an army must absolutely be raised and sufficient forces cannot be provided by a volunteer army. _____
3. Canada and the United States are contiguous. _____
4. The meeting was so contentious that the proposal was passed in a few minutes and without objection. _____
5. Cynthia contends that jogging is the best way to keep physically fit. _____

UNIT 18

convention *n.* practice widely observed in a group; custom; accepted technique or device

> *The work of French artist Henri Rousseau demonstrates a naiveté that many people find more attractive than the sophistication of highly complex works that make use of all the **conventions** of their genre.*

Conventional is an adjective meaning customary or commonplace

> *Guerrilla war presents a dilemma for framers of rules of war: should guerrilla fighters be subject to the same rules as those imposed on soldiers who fight *conventional wars?*

Terms from the Arts, Sciences, and Social Sciences

Henri Rousseau: French painter (1844–1910) famous for his paintings, often of jungles, done in a Primitive manner

guerrilla war: a war involving small groups of soldiers that are flexible and mobile. In guerrilla war there is no front line as there is in conventional war.

---

converge *v.* to approach; come together; tend to meet

> *Although the People's Republic of China and India are rivals in many ways, in certain areas their interests **converge**.*

convex *adj.* curved outward

> *The term for a lens with one **convex** and one concave side is "convex-concave."*

convivial *adj.* sociable

> *One of the jobs of an ambassador is to provide a **convivial** atmosphere for diplomats to meet.*

*convoluted *adj.* twisted; complicated

> *Unraveling the **convoluted** genetic code is one of the great achievements of modern science.*

copious *adj.* abundant; plentiful

> *The **copious** rainfall was welcomed by farmers in the parched land.*

coquette *n.* woman who flirts

*After she had played the part of a **coquette** in the college play, Pam's boyfriend felt that he needed to remind her that real life was quite different from the theater.*

cornucopia *n.* horn overflowing with fruit and grain; state of abundance

*The U.S. economy has produced a **cornucopia** of employment opportunities.*

*****cosmology** *n.* study of the universe as a totality; theory of the origin and structure of the universe

*Albert Einstein downplayed the strength of the evidence for quantum theory because a universe governed by laws that are inconsistent in their application was not congruent with his personal **cosmology**.*

Cosmos is a noun meaning the physical universe regarded as a totality.

*Shakespeare embodies the incredible confidence and vitality of Renaissance artists and writers, depicting the entire **cosmos**, not intimidated by its vastness.*

Cosmic is an adjective meaning relating to the physical universe, especially as distinct from Earth, and suggests infinite vastness.

*The gods of ancient Greece were concerned not only with **cosmic** events, but also with the ordinary events of everyday life.*

Terms from the Arts, Sciences, and Social Sciences

quantum theory: a theory in physics based on the principle that matter and energy have the properties of both particles and waves

Renaissance: the period of revival in art and learning that occurred in Europe during the fourteenth to the seventeenth century

---

covert *adj.* hidden; secret

*The CIA gathers information about foreign intelligence through many means, including **covert** ones.*

REVIEW 18

Matching
Match each word with its definition.

1. convention	(A) complicated
2. converge	(B) curved outward
3. convex	(C) study of the universe
4. convivial	(D) to approach; come together
5. convoluted	(E) horn overflowing with fruit and grain
6. copious	(F) practice widely observed in a group
7. coquette	(G) abundant
8. cornucopia	(H) woman who flirts
9. cosmology	(I) hidden; secret
10. covert	(J) sociable

Fill-ins
Choose the best word to fill in the blank in each sentence.

conventions	converges	convex	convivial	convoluted
copious	coquette	cornucopia	cosmology	covert

1. One need not know anything of medieval Christian _____ to appreciate the great Gothic cathedrals, edifices that are a supreme legacy of that age.
2. A work of art may seem contrived to a person who is unfamiliar with the _____ of the form of art he is observing.
3. Fyodor Dostoevsky's *The Possessed* has a fascinating, though _____ , plot.
4. _____ lenses are used to correct farsightedness.
5. Politicians are often _____ individuals who are comfortable with a wide variety of people.
6. Stella takes _____ notes in all of her classes.
7. In Robert Frost's famous poem "The Road Not Taken" the speaker must choose which path to take after the one he is on _____ with another.
8. The plainclothes detective took part in a _____ operation.
9. Sarah has a reputation as a bit of a _____ .
10. Tropical rain forests contain a _____ of plant substances that have proven to be effective medicines.

Sense or Nonsense
Indicate whether each sentence makes good sense or not.
Put S (SENSE) if it does, and put N (NONSENSE) if it does not.

1. Every Sunday morning Steve buys half a dozen fresh coquettes at the corner bakery. _____
2. After the technician replaced the damaged convex lens in my 5″ reflector telescope, it worked fine. _____
3. The government launched the covert operation amid great fanfare. _____
4. The convivial host helped make sure everyone enjoyed the party. _____
5. Cosmology has helped poetry to become more popular among the public. _____

UNIT 19

covetous *adj.* desiring something owned by another

*The astronomer is **covetous** of the time that his colleague gets for research using the Hubble Space Telescope.*

Covet is the verb.

*The latest model cell phone is designed to make people **covet** it so much that they go out and buy it even though their present phone is perfectly adequate.*

cozen *v.* to mislead by trick or fraud; deceive

*The writer H. L. Mencken pointed out that a common strategy of politicians is to **cozen** the people by exaggerating the seriousness of a problem and then offering a solution that, conveniently, only they can provide.*

*craven *adj.* cowardly

In the Hindu epic poem the Bhagavad-Gita, *Lord Krishna warns the hero, who is reluctant to fight, that refusing to fight would be a **craven** act.*

*credence *n.* acceptance of something as true

*One of the lessons in Aesop's fable "The Shepherd Boy and the Wolf" is that if a person "cries wolf" too many times without real danger being present (that is, raises too many false alarms) people will be less likely to give **credence** to future alarms raised by that person.*

credo *n.* statement of belief or principle; creed

> *The **credo** of Google is "Don't be evil."*

daunt *v.* to discourage; intimidate; dishearten

> *Do not let the difficulty of learning the 800 words in* Essential Words for the GRE ***daunt** you.*

Daunting is an adjective that means discouraging or disheartening.

> *Earning a Ph.D. is a **daunting** task, but it can be done.*

The adjective *dauntless* means fearless.

dearth *n.* scarcity

> *In his book* The Affluent Society, *published in 1958, the economist J. K. Galbraith pointed out that in America affluence is located disproportionately in the private sector, leaving a **dearth** of resources available for the public sector.*

debauchery *n.* corruption

> *The prince lived a life of **debauchery** until he discovered a spiritual dimension to life.*

*decorum *n.* proper behavior

> *When addressing the nation, the president generally has an air of **decorum**.*

The adjective is *decorous*.

defame *v.* to malign; harm someone's reputation

> *The ancient Greek philosopher Socrates was **defamed** as a teacher who corrupted the morals of his students.*

REVIEW 19

Matching
Match each word with its definition.

1. covetous		(A)	cowardly
2. cozen		(B)	scarcity
3. craven		(C)	to intimidate; discourage
4. credence		(D)	desiring something owned by another
5. credo		(E)	acceptance of something as true
6. daunt		(F)	to harm someone's reputation
7. dearth		(G)	corruption
8. debauchery		(H)	to mislead by trick or fraud
9. decorum		(I)	statement of belief or principle; creed
10. defame		(J)	proper behavior

Fill-ins
Choose the best word to fill in the blank in each sentence.

covets	cozens	craven	credence	credo
daunting	dearth	debauchery	decorum	defaming

1. Because so many young men were killed in the war, there is a _____ of potential husbands for the young women of the village.
2. The general called his advisor's suggestion that he surrender "the _____ proposal of a coward."
3. The sales pitch _____ potential customers by omitting the fact that the product has been superseded by far superior products available at the same price.
4. To make the task of writing the book less _____ , the author broke the task into a number of small tasks he could do one at a time.
5. I admit that the professor's statement is baffling; however, it should be given some _____ because of his towering reputation in the field.
6. The principal reminded the students to conduct themselves with _____ during the guests' visit.
7. The amateur radio operator _____ a new ICOM 7800 high-frequency transceiver costing more than $10,000, but his wife says he can afford only the Kenwood 570D costing about $1,000.
8. The novelist follows the _____ that plot proceeds from character.
9. The students went to Fort Lauderdale for a week of _____ .

10. The journalist was sued for _____ a police officer in his
    article.

Sense or Nonsense
Indicate whether each sentence makes good sense or not.
Put S (SENSE) if it does, and put N (NONSENSE) if it does not.

1. The unscrupulous newspaper regularly defames public figures to
   boost circulation. _____
2. The candidate was elected governor on a platform of moral purity
   and debauchery. _____
3. The company's credo is "The buyer is king." _____
4. No one called the boxer craven after he asked the referee to stop
   the bout; he had been knocked down six times and was bleeding
   profusely. _____
5. A trial should be conducted with decorum. _____

UNIT 20

default *v.* to fail to act

> *Economists have pointed out the danger of using government
> money to help banks in danger of **defaulting** on a loan: such help
> might encourage banks to take excessive risks on the future, knowing
> they will be "bailed out" by the government.*

*deference *n.* respect; regard for another's wish

> *There was a movement to condemn slavery among some of the
> writers of the* Declaration of Independence, *but despite many misgiv-
> ings, the proposal was dropped in **deference** to the objections of a
> number of people.*

The verb *defer* means to submit to the wishes of another due to
respect or recognition of the person's authority or knowledge.

> *The young lawyer **deferred** to the view of the senior partner in the
> law firm.*

defunct *adj.* no longer existing

> *Skeptics have been prognosticating that Moore's Law, which says
> computer processing power doubles every 18 months, will soon
> become **defunct**, but the ingenuity of engineers, coupled with com-
> mercial incentives, has so far succeeded in preventing the law from
> being invalidated.*

*delineate *v.* to represent or depict

*Quantum theory led to the formulation of the uncertainty principle, which was **delineated** in 1937 by Werner Heisenberg.*

Terms from the Arts, Sciences, and Social Sciences

uncertainty principle: the statement in quantum mechanics stating that it is impossible to measure accurately two properties of a quantum object, such as its position and momentum

---

demographic *adj.* related to population balance

***Demographic** trends in many European countries indicate that in the next generation there will be relatively fewer working people to support retired people.*

Demography is the study of human population.

***Demography** makes use of the knowledge of other fields such as geography and statistics.*

A *demographer* is one who studies human population.

*If, beginning in the mid-twentieth century, many governments in the world had not taken steps to promote birth control among their citizens, causing a diminution in the birth rate, **demographers** say the world would now have a much greater population than it does.*

*demotic *adj.* pertaining to people

*Walt Whitman is considered by many to be a quintessentially American poet, a poet who celebrated the glory of the ordinary person; one critic praised him as a poet who was able to "make the **demotic** sing."*

*demur *v.* to express doubt

*The Supreme Court's decision was not unanimous; one justice **demurred**, saying that the majority decision used specious reasoning.*

*denigrate *v.* to slur someone's reputation

*According to a recent biography of Napoleon Bonaparte, the famous leader felt a need to **denigrate** women.*

denizen *n.* an inhabitant; a regular visitor

*The U.S. Census Bureau has the responsibility of collecting information about the **denizens** of the United States.*

*denouement *n.* outcome; unraveling of the plot of a play or work of literature

> *The book tells the story of what was for Europe a rather embarrassing **denouement** to the Crusades.*

REVIEW 20

Matching
Match each word with its definition.

1. default	(A) to express doubt
2. deference	(B) respect; regard for another's wish
3. defunct	(C) an inhabitant
4. delineate	(D) relating to the study of human population
5. demographic	(E) to slur someone's reputation
6. demotic	(F) failure to act
7. demur	(G) to represent or depict
8. denigrate	(H) outcome
9. denizen	(I) pertaining to people
10. denouement	(J) no longer existing

Fill-ins
Choose the best word to fill in the blank in each sentence.

default	deference	defunct	delineated	demographic
demotic	demurred	denigrated	denizens	denouement

1. The _____ of a novel by crime writer Mickey Spillane is generally very violent.
2. Data gathered in the census provides planners with important _____ information.
3. On his first scuba dive, Kenny was happy to find that the _____ of the sea did not appear to be hostile.
4. Solid-state electronic equipment has made vacuum tube equipment _____ in most areas other than very specialized applications.
5. The political science professor _____ a plan to reorganize the United Nations to make it better reflect the realities of the contemporary world.

6. The chairperson asked for a vote on the proposal; since no one _____ , it passed unanimously.
7. The professor never watches movies, which he calls "_____ entertainment for the semiliterate."
8. Rather than _____ on her car loan payments after losing her job, Ruth worked out an agreement that allowed her to make lower monthly payments.
9. In Victorian times servants were expected to show great _____ to their employers.
10. In many societies women have been _____ as inferior to men.

Sense or Nonsense

Indicate whether each sentence makes good sense or not.
Put S (SENSE) if it does, and put N (NONSENSE) if it does not.

1. The denouement at the beginning of the story really caught my interest. _____
2. The book delineates the characters clearly. _____
3. The demotic king was deposed in the popular uprising. _____
4. Demographic trends in Japan show that the proportion of old people to young people is increasing. _____
5. Since Singapore became an independent country in 1965, its denizens have become among the wealthiest in the world. _____

UNIT 21

deride *v.* to mock

*Innovation often requires challenges to orthodox thinking; for example, in the late 1960s, scientists from the U.S. Department of Defense's Advanced Research Projects Agency presented their idea of a vast network of computers to leading scientists from IBM and AT&T—companies with innumerable research breakthroughs to their credit—and were **derided** as impractical visionaries.*

*derivative *n.* something derived; unoriginal

*The drug morphine—considered by doctors to be one of the most effective analgesics—is the principal **derivative** of opium, which is the juice in the unripe seed pods of the opium poppy.*

Derivative is also an adjective.

*The critic dismissed the new novel as dull and **derivative**.*

The verb *derive* means obtained from another source.

One of the attempts to create a lingua franca *resulted in Esperanto, a synthetic language whose vocabulary is created by adding various* affixes *to individual roots and is* **derived** *from Latin and Greek, as well as Germanic and* Romance languages.

Terms from the Arts, Sciences, and Social Sciences

lingua franca: a language used as a medium of communication between peoples of different languages

affixes: word elements that are affixed to the beginning (prefixes) or the end (suffixes) of words to refine the meaning or change the word's grammatical form

Romance languages: the Romance languages, or Indo-European languages that descended from Vulgar Latin, include Italian, Romanian, Spanish, Portuguese, French, their many dialects, and the pidgins and creoles (mixed languages) that developed from them.

The term "Romance" is from Vulgar Latin *romanice loqui* (vulgar languages derived from Latin).

---

*desiccate *v.* to dry completely

The dry desert air caused the bodies of the dead animals to **desiccate** *quickly.*

desuetude *n.* state of disuse

NASA is considering a plan to refurbish booster rockets from the Apollo Program that have fallen into **desuetude***.*

*desultory *adj.* random; disconnected; rambling

The jury had difficulty following the witnesses' **desultory** *testimony.*

deterrent *n.* something that discourages or hinders

During the Cold War, the United States maintained a large number of nuclear weapons as a **deterrent** *to aggression by the Soviet Union and its allies.*

detraction *n.* the act of taking away; derogatory comment on a person's character

The writer responded in a letter to the critic's long list of **detractions** *about his book.*

diaphanous *adj.* transparent; fine-textured; insubstantial; vague

In World War II, many soldiers went to war with **diaphanous** *dreams of glory, but found instead horror and death.*

diatribe n. bitter verbal attack

The speaker launched into a **diatribe** against what he called "the evils of technology."

dichotomy n. division into two usually contradictory parts

The philosopher is a dualist who argues that there is a **dichotomy** between the mind and physical phenomena.

Terms from the Arts, Sciences, and Social Sciences

dualist: one who believes in dualism, the theory that two basic entities constitute reality (such as mind and matter or good and evil)

REVIEW 21

Matching
Match each word with its definition.

1. deride
2. derivative
3. desiccate
4. desuetude
5. desultory
6. deterrent
7. detraction
8. diaphanous
9. diatribe
10. dichotomy

(A) something that discourages
(B) bitter verbal attack
(C) to dry completely
(D) random; disconnected
(E) the act of taking away
(F) unoriginal
(G) division into two contradictory parts
(H) state of disuse
(I) transparent; fine-textured
(J) to mock

Fill-ins
Choose the best word to fill in the blank in each sentence.

| derided | derivative | desiccated | desuetude | desultory |
| deterrent | detraction | diaphanous | diatribe | dichotomy |

1. In his book *Supernature* the British biologist Lyell Watson argues that the _____ between nature and the supernatural exists more in the human mind than in reality.
2. The two areas of the room are separated only by a _____ curtain.

3. Scientists are studying the _____ bones to see if they are the remains of a person.

4. Some studies suggest that capital punishment is a _____ against murder.

5. The critics _____ the movie as "a waste of $100 million dollars."

6. The poet describes his work as _____ because it draws on the work of many other poets.

7. The two men walked along the beach, engaged in _____ conversation.

8. The rise of Irish nationalism has probably helped bring the Irish language back from the _____ it was falling into in the nineteenth century.

9. The prime minister's _____ against foreign influence in the country lasted three hours.

10. The only _____ from the excellence of the climate is the rainy winter.

Sense or Nonsense
Indicate whether each sentence makes good sense or not.
Put S (SENSE) if it does, and put N (NONSENSE) if it does not.

1. In many traditional societies women wear diaphanous clothing to hide their bodies. _____

2. Early attempts to communicate by the use of electromagnetic waves were derided by many people as ridiculous. _____

3. The book is a long, desultory narrative recounting its author's life. _____

4. The senator's speech was a diatribe against the increasing influence of government in everyday life. _____

5. South Korea maintains a large military force as a deterrent against North Korean aggression. _____

UNIT 22

*diffidence n. shyness; lack of confidence

As a result of the strength of his opposition to the Vietnam War Senator Eugene McCarthy overcame his diffidence and ran against President Lyndon Johnson for the Democratic nomination for president.

*diffuse *v.* to spread out

> *The idea of equality and liberty **diffused** through society after the French Revolution.*

Diffuse is also an adjective meaning wordy; rambling; spread out.

> *This essay is so **diffuse** it is difficult to follow its central argument.*

digression *n.* act of straying from the main point

> *The novel* Zen and the Art of Motorcycle Maintenance *by Robert M. Pirsig contains many fascinating **digressions** from the main story that discuss topics such as* Platonic *philosophy.*

Terms from the Arts, Sciences, and Social Sciences

Platonic: refers to the philosophy of Plato, an ancient Greek philosopher who held that both actual things and ideas such as beauty and truth are copies of transcendent ideas

The adjective *platonic* (with a small "p") means spiritual, without sensual desire, or theoretical.

---

dirge *n.* funeral hymn

> *The music critic described the movement of the symphony portraying the hero's last days as "**dirge**like."*

*disabuse *v.* to free from a misconception

> *The chairman of the Federal Reserve used his testimony before Congress to **disabuse** his audience of the idea that the business cycle had been eliminated by the unprecedented period of prosperity.*

discerning *adj.* perceptive; exhibiting keen insight and good judgment

> ***Discerning** movie critics have praised the work of producer Stanley Kubrick, who produced such excellent films as 2001, Dr. Strangelove, A Clockwork Orange, and Lolita.*

Discern is a verb that means to perceive something obscure.

> *Superficially, expressionism can appear to be unrealistic because of its extreme distortion of reality, but upon closer examination, an inner psychological reality can often be **discerned**.*

Terms from the Arts, Sciences, and Social Sciences

expressionism: an artistic style in which the artist expresses emotional experience as opposed to his or her view of the external world. Expressionists often use distortion and exaggeration. El Greco, Van Gogh, and Edward Munch are examples of expressionist artists.

---

discomfit *v.* to make uneasy; disconcert

> The young man was **discomfited** being the only male in the play.

*discordant *adj.* not in tune

> In a pluralistic society there exists a cacophony of **discordant** voices, each shouting to be heard.

discredit *v.* to dishonor; disgrace; cause to be doubted

> The candidate's attempt to **discredit** his opponent by spreading damaging rumors about him failed.

*discrepancy *n.* difference between

> The book studies the **discrepancy** in values and outlook between men who fought in the war, whether voluntarily or not, and those who remained civilians.

REVIEW 22

Matching
Match each word with its definition.

1.	diffidence	(A)	to free from a misconception
2.	diffuse	(B)	to spread out
3.	digression	(C)	to make uneasy
4.	dirge	(D)	act of straying from the main point
5.	disabuse	(E)	difference between
6.	discerning	(F)	shyness
7.	discomfit	(G)	not in tune
8.	discordant	(H)	funeral hymn
9.	discredit	(I)	to dishonor; disgrace
10.	discrepancy	(J)	exhibiting keen insight and good judgment

Fill-ins
Choose the best word to fill in the blank in each sentence.

diffidence	diffuse	digressions	dirge	disabuse
discerning	discomfited	discordant	discredited	discrepancy

1. One year of medical school was enough to _____ Steve of the idea that medical school is a "piece of cake."
2. Auditors are investigating the _____ between the company's stated earnings and its projected earnings based on sales.
3. The band played a _____ at the soldier's funeral.
4. Some readers are annoyed by the long _____ on geology and other scientific subjects in Kim Stanley Robinson's Mars trilogy; other readers, however, find them fascinating, illuminating and beautifully written.
5. Historians of science study theories that have become accepted by modern science as well as those that have been _____ .
6. One of the aims of the English literature course is to help students become _____ readers.
7. The study suggests that women do not find _____ in men to be an attractive quality.
8. The intravenous drug will _____ through the patient's body in about 20 minutes.
9. Many people are _____ by the idea of their own death.
10. The governor traveled around the state listening to the _____ views on the controversial issue.

Sense or Nonsense
Indicate whether each sentence makes good sense or not.
Put S (SENSE) if it does, and put N (NONSENSE) if it does not.

1. A woman of discerning taste in literature, Jane mainly reads works by William Shakespeare, William Blake, Henry James, and Willa Cather. _____
2. There is a great discrepancy between the performance of the best student in the class and the worst student. _____
3. Good writers often use digression to help keep their discussion on the main topic. _____
4. The opposition party tried to discredit the leadership of the ruling party by charging it with corruption. _____
5. A week doing the house cleaner's chores disabused Cindy of the idea that the house cleaner has an easy job. _____

UNIT 23

*discrete *adj.* constituting a separate thing; distinct

> *Like the physicist, the abstract artist strives to identify the* **discrete** *elements of reality and to understand how they interact.*

discretion *n.* quality of showing self-restraint in speech or actions; circumspection; freedom to act on one's own

> *In nineteenth-century Britain gentlemen were expected to behave with* **discretion**.

*disingenuous *adj.* not candid; crafty

> *When a person starts a sentence, "I don't mean to appear* **disingenuous**," *one might be tempted to suspect that the person is being just that.*

*disinterested *adj.* unprejudiced; objective

> *The newspaper reporter looked for* **disinterested** *witnesses to the events so that she could get an objective account of what had happened.*

disjointed *adj.* lacking order or coherence; dislocated

> *The technique of telling a story through a* **disjointed** *narrative is a technique best left to masters of the modern novel such as James Joyce and William Faulkner.*

*dismiss *v.* put away from consideration; reject

> *Investigators* **dismissed** *the man's account of a visit to another planet aboard an alien spacecraft as the product of an overactive imagination.*

*disparage *v.* to belittle

> *Though sometimes* **disparaged** *as merely an intellectual game, philosophy provides us with a method for inquiring systematically into problems that arise in areas such as medicine, science, and technology.*

*disparate *adj.* dissimilar

> *Many technological projects are interdisciplinary, requiring a knowledge of fields as* **disparate** *as physics and biology.*

Disparity is a noun meaning the condition of being unequal or unlike.

> *The huge income* **disparity** *in the world is clearly illustrated by the fact that the assets of the world's two hundred richest people exceed the combined income of 41 percent of the world's population.*

*dissemble *v.* to pretend; disguise one's motives

"Miss," the prosecutor said, "I believe you are **dissembling**. I want you to tell me the whole truth about what happened that night."

*disseminate *v.* to spread; scatter; disperse

While belief in reincarnation appeared as doctrine first in India and was **disseminated** throughout Asia by Buddhism, it is interesting that it was accepted by the most influential philosophy of the West, Platonism, and by some important early Christian thinkers, such as the theologian Origen.

Terms from the Arts, Sciences, and Social Sciences

Platonism: the philosophy of Plato, which holds that both actual things and ideas such as beauty and truth are copies of transcendent ideas

---

REVIEW 23

Matching
Match each word with its definition.

1. discrete	(A)	lacking order or coherence
2. discretion	(B)	unprejudiced; objective
3. disingenuous	(C)	dissimilar
4. disinterested	(D)	to belittle
5. disjointed	(E)	to spread; disperse
6. dismiss	(F)	circumspection
7. disparage	(G)	to pretend
8. disparate	(H)	not candid; crafty
9. dissemble	(I)	constituting a separate thing; distinct
10. disseminate	(J)	to reject

Fill-ins
Choose the best word to fill in the blank in each sentence.

discrete	discretion	disingenuous	disinterested	disjointed
dismissed	disparaged	disparate	dissembled	disseminated

1. The historian tries to take a _____ view of how the United States got involved in the Vietnam War.

2. The great increase in travel in modern times makes it difficult to determine how and where a disease originated, as well as how it was _____ , so that measures can be taken to mitigate its effects.

3. The novel's narrative is so _____ that many readers have trouble following it.

4. Scientific laws identify a common fundamental element in seemingly _____ phenomena.

5. The historian describes her method as "not so much the study of _____ events but rather the study of relationships between those events."

6. The judge _____ the evidence as not relevant to the case at hand.

7. The school lets its teachers use considerable _____ in designing lessons for students.

8. The investigating committee ruled that the governor "had been _____" in not providing important information to them.

9. The noted director Stanley Kubrick, who turned down the chance to go to college when he was seventeen, _____ formal education, saying, "I never learned anything at all at school."

10. The girl _____ when her date asked if she had ever been kissed.

Sense or Nonsense

Indicate whether each sentence makes good sense or not.
Put S (SENSE) if it does, and put N (NONSENSE) if it does not.

1. The technician dissembled the computer to find out what was wrong with it. _____

2. The battalion's commander told his men to use their own discretion in selecting enemy targets. _____

3. Diplomats must be discrete to do their job effectively. _____

4. The disingenuous student must work harder than other students to make up for his lack of ability. _____

5. The writer was proud to have her work disparaged by leading critics. _____

UNIT 24

dissident *n.* person who disagrees about beliefs, etc.

Some of the most notorious concentration camps in history were the Gulag *camps used by the Soviet Union to control* **dissidents**.

Terms from the Arts, Sciences, and Social Sciences

Gulag: forced-labor prison camps in the Soviet Union. Established in the 1920s, the Gulag system had 476 camps throughout the country used to imprison people considered a threat to the state.

---

*dissolution *n.* disintegration; debauchery

Some philosophers maintain that the **dissolution** *of the body does not mean the destruction of the mind.*

*dissonance *n.* discord; lack of harmony

In psychology, the term "cognitive **dissonance**" *refers to a conflict resulting from inconsistency between one's beliefs and one's actions. For example, a soldier who believes that all killing is immoral but is forced to kill by his superiors might experience cognitive dissonance.*

distend *v.* to expand; swell out

People in an advanced stage of starvation often have **distended** *bellies.*

distill *v.* extract the essential elements

In his book Men of Ideas: Some Creators of Contemporary Philosophy, *Bryan Magee manages to* **distill** *the essence of leading thinkers such as W. V. Quine, John Searle, Iris Murdoch, and Noam Chomsky.*

distrait *adj.* inattentive; preoccupied

The chairperson became **distrait** *because his secretary was not sitting in her usual position on his right.*

diverge *v.* to vary; go in different directions from the same point

A famous line in American poetry is from Robert Frost's "The Road Not Taken":

> *Two roads* **diverged** *in a wood, and I—*
> *I took the one less traveled by ....*

Divergence is the noun.

Psychological tests show that there is a wide **divergence** *between citizens of different countries in how much importance they place on the virtue of justice, on the one hand, and the virtue of mercy, on the other hand.*

divest *v.* to strip; deprive; rid

> The candidate for secretary of defense pledged to **divest** himself of the shares he held in defense-related companies.

divulge *v.* to make known something that is secret

> Under the Geneva Conventions, prisoners of war cannot be tortured and forced to **divulge** information.

*doctrinaire *adj.* relating to a person who cannot compromise about points of a theory or doctrine; dogmatic; unyielding

> The **doctrinaire** Marxists say that capitalism is merely a temporary phenomenon on the road to socialism.

REVIEW 24

Matching
Match each word with its definition.

1. dissident
2. dissolution
3. dissonance
4. distend
5. distill
6. distrait
7. diverge
8. divest
9. divulge
10. doctrinaire

(A) unyielding; dogmatic
(B) to extract the essential elements
(C) disintegration
(D) to strip; deprive
(E) to expand; swell out
(F) to go in different directions from the same point
(G) inattentive; preoccupied
(H) to make known something secret
(I) person who disagrees about beliefs
(J) lack of harmony

Fill-ins
Choose the best word to fill in the blank in each sentence.

| dissidents | dissolution | dissonance | distended | distill |
| distrait | diverged | divested | divulge | doctrinaire |

1. How the poet John Keats was able to _____ so much beauty and wisdom into his poetry remains a mystery.
2. The members' vote of no confidence in the ruling government led to the _____ of parliament.
3. The man who ate more than fifty hot dogs to win the hot dog eating competition gained seven pounds and had a _____ belly for a few days.

4. According to the child psychologist, _____ between family and school is normal.
5. The psychologist's patient _____ himself of the secrets he had been carrying within for 30 years.
6. During World War I many people in the United States considered conscientious objectors to be radical _____ .
7. Pam's life _____ from Bob's after they graduated from college in 1971; he was drafted and sent to fight in Vietnam and she went to Paris to do a Ph.D. in French literature.
8. The guest seemed to be melancholy and _____ , so I asked him what was troubling him.
9. Companies that are not publicly listed and have no major debt normally do not need to _____ much about their sales and other matters to financial markets.
10. "If the world is lucky enough to enjoy peace, it may even one day make the discovery, to the horror of _____ free-enterprisers and doctrinaire planners alike, that what is called capitalism and what is called socialism are both capable of working quite well." (J. K. Galbraith, American economist)

Sense or Nonsense
Indicate whether each sentence makes good sense or not. Put S (SENSE) if it does, and put N (NONSENSE) if it does not.

1. Peter and Paul disagree on most political issues, but their views diverge on religion. _____
2. During the holiday season the story distends its opening hours to accommodate customers. _____
3. The *Bhagavad-Gita,* one of the holy books of the Hindus, is a long poem that distills much of the teachings of Hinduism. _____
4. The foreign government gave dissidents in the country support in the hope of destabilizing the country. _____
5. The moderate urged her political party to adopt a less doctrinaire position on the issue. _____

UNIT 25

document *v.* to provide with written evidence to support

> *The insurance company asked Debbie to **document** her claim with letters from the doctors who treated her for her condition.*

doggerel *n.* poor verse

> In his book Poetic Meter and Poetic Form, *the literary critic Paul Fussell quotes this bit of **doggerel** from a U.S. Army latrine during World War II:*
>> *Soldiers who wish to be a hero*
>> *Are practically zero.*
>> *But those who wish to be civilians,*
>> *Jesus, they run into millions.*

*dogmatic *adj.* stating opinions without proof

> *Since every case is unique, jurists must not be **dogmatic** in applying precedents to make their decision, but instead must base their decision on a combination of such precedents and the facts of the case at hand.*

Dogma is a noun meaning a belief asserted on authority without evidence.

> *Religions whose **dogma** specifies a time of the creation of the world have found difficulty in reconciling their view of creation with that of modern science.*

Terms from the Arts, Sciences, and Social Sciences

The original meaning of *dogma* was "that which seems good." In Christian theology it came to mean truths known by divine revelation and taught by the Church.

---

dormant *adj.* inactive

> *There is a considerable body of evidence showing that many diseases, such as ulcers, asthma, and hypertension have a large psychological component; the working hypothesis is that they represent manifestations of **dormant** emotional disturbances.*

dross *n.* waste; worthless matter; trivial matter

> *One of the ways the **dross** among blogs on the Internet are filtered out from the worthwhile ones is through links good blogs provide to other good blogs.*

Terms from the Arts, Sciences, and Social Sciences

blog: short for weblog, an online journal

---

dupe *v.* to deceive; trick

*"In friendship, as well as in love, the mind is often **duped** by the heart." (Philip Dormer Stanhope)*

*ebullient *adj.* exhilarated; enthusiastic

*The **ebullient** candidate for president appeared before his supporters to announce that he had won in a landslide.*

*eclectic *adj.* selecting from various sources

*Neo-Platonism—an **eclectic** third-century synthesis of Platonic, Pythagorean, Aristotelian, Stoic, and Jewish philosophy—was an essentially mystical belief that a person can achieve spiritual emancipation through union of the soul with the ultimate source of existence.*

Terms from the Arts, Sciences, and Social Sciences

Platonic: refers to the philosophy of Plato, an ancient Greek philosopher who held that both actual things and ideas such as beauty and truth are copies of transcendent ideas

Pythagorean: refers to the philosophy of Pythagoras, a sixth-century B.C. philosopher and mathematician. Pythagoras described reality in terms of arithmetical relationships.

Aristotelian: refers to the philosophy of Aristotle, an ancient Greek scientist and philosopher whose teaching had a great influence on Western thought, especially in the areas of logic, metaphysics, and science

Stoic: refers to Stoicism, a philosophy of ancient Greece that taught that the highest good is virtue, which is based on knowledge. The Stoics believed that the wise live in harmony with Divine Reason that governs nature and are indifferent to suffering and the changing fortunes of life.

mystical: related to mysticism, the practice of putting oneself into direct relation with God, the absolute, or any unifying principle of life

---

effervescence *n.* state of high spirits or liveliness; the process of bubbling as gas escapes

*olive **Effervescence** occurs when hydrochloric acid is added to a block of limestone.*

The adjective is *effervescent.*

*A person who believes himself to be physically unattractive might develop an **effervescent** personality as a compensation for his perceived deficiency.*

*effete *adj.* depleted of vitality; overrefined; decadent

> In 1969, U.S. Vice President Spiro T. Agnew denounced people protesting against the Vietnam War: "A spirit of national masochism prevails, encouraged by an **effete** corps of impudent snobs who characterize themselves as intellectuals."

REVIEW 25

Matching
Match each word with its definition.

1.	document	(A)	to deceive
2.	doggerel	(B)	poor verse
3.	dogmatic	(C)	provide with written evidence to support
4.	dormant	(D)	state of high spirits
5.	dross	(E)	selecting from various sources
6.	dupe	(F)	stating opinions without proof
7.	ebullient	(G)	exhilarated
8.	eclectic	(H)	inactive
9.	effervescence	(I)	depleted of vitality
10.	effete	(J)	worthless matter

Fill-ins
Choose the best word to fill in the blank in each sentence.

documented	doggerel	dogmatic	dormant	dross
duped	ebullient	eclectic	effervescent	effete

1. Clinical psychologists provide treatment for psychological disorders, and today can choose from an array of psychotherapies; often they are _____ , choosing elements of therapies best suited to each particular case.
2. Police investigators _____ the case with photographs and recorded interviews.
3. The country's leaders _____ the people into thinking it was necessary to declare war.
4. Even the _____ of a great poet like John Milton is interesting.
5. It is interesting to observe how some traditions remain strong, while others gradually become _____ .
6. The philosopher Bertrand Russell once observed that people are often most _____ about things that it is least possible to be certain about.

7. Julia's _____ personality makes her one of the college's most popular students.
8. The doctor suspected that the patient had once contracted malaria, but that the disease was now _____ .
9. One of the traditional functions of literary critics is to help separate the _____ from the worthwhile among the many books published every year.
10. Oregon State baseball fans were _____ after their team captured the College World Series in June 2006.

Sense or Nonsense

Indicate whether each sentence makes good sense or not.
Put S (SENSE) if it does, and put N (NONSENSE) if it does not.

1. The poet's sonnets are superb, but it is his doggerel that has made him immortal. _____
2. The student duped the teacher into thinking she had written the paper herself. _____
3. The historian was happy to find several sources documenting the same event. _____
4. The bride and groom looked ebullient after the priest pronounced them man and wife. _____
5. The dogmatic philosopher has a well-deserved reputation for being open-minded. _____

UNIT 26

efficacy n. efficiency; effectiveness

> *A cardinal rule of medicine is that the **efficacy** of a treatment should be measured against the seriousness of its side effects.*

The adjective is *efficacious*.

> *In a situation where some subjects are benefiting while others are not, a researcher is likely to have ambivalent feelings, since he or she is in a "no-win" situation. In such a situation, the experimenter must choose between, on the one hand, getting more conclusive results by continuing the experiment and, on the other hand, stopping it and administering the drug that has proven **efficacious** to those who have not received it.*

113

*effrontery *n.* shameless boldness; presumptuousness

*In her essay the student had the **effrontery** to argue that school is largely a waste of time.*

egoism *n.* the tendency to see things in relation to oneself; self-centeredness

*The beginning of philosophy has been described as a moving away from **egoism** to an understanding of the larger world.*

egotistical *adj.* excessively self-centered; conceited

*The critics accused the writer of being **egotistical** since she wrote only about herself.*

*elegy *n.* poem or song expressing lamentation

*Adonais is a pastoral **elegy** written by Percy Bysshe Shelley in the spring of 1821 after he learned of the death of his friend and fellow poet John Keats.*

*elicit *v.* to provoke; draw out

*The Socratic method is designed to **elicit** responses that guide the student toward understanding.*

Terms from the Arts, Sciences, and Social Sciences

Socratic method: a method of seeking the truth about a subject through systematic questioning. Often it results in the questioning of assumptions. The Socratic method is attributed to the ancient Greek philosopher Socrates.

---

elixir *n.* a substance believed to have the power to cure ills

*The doctor said that her prescription would help to alleviate my condition but that I could not expect it to be an **elixir**.*

Elysian *adj.* blissful; delightful

*In Book VI of Virgil's Aeneid, the hero Aeneas descends to the Underworld where he meets the soul of his dead father, Anchises, in the **Elysian** fields and learns from him the future of the Roman race.*

Terms from the Arts, Sciences, and Social Sciences

Elysian fields or Elysium: in Greek and Roman mythology this refers to an otherworld where the spirits of the virtuous and heroic dwell after being transported there without experiencing death

Elysium is described in Homer's *Odyssey* as a place of eternal spring where the souls of heroes and others who are blessed by the gods wander blissfully. Homer placed Elysium at the western edge of the Earth near the stream of Oceanus, while other ancient Greek poets, such as Hesiod and Pindar, placed it in the Isles of the Blessed, or the Fortunate Islands, of the Western Ocean. Later, in the *Aeneid*, Virgil describes it as being located in the realms of the dead under the Earth.

---

emaciated *adj.* thin and wasted

> The prisoner was **emaciated** after being fed only bread and water for three months.

*embellish *v.* to adorn; decorate; enhance; make more attractive by adding details

> The story he had been told was so powerful that the writer felt no need to **embellish** it.

REVIEW 26

Matching
Match each word with its definition.

1. efficacy	(A) blissful; delightful
2. effrontery	(B) song expressing lamentation
3. egoism	(C) substance that cures ills
4. egotistical	(D) seeing things in relation to oneself
5. elegy	(E) shameless boldness
6. elicit	(F) excessively self-centered
7. elixir	(G) thin and wasted
8. Elysian	(H) to provoke; draw out
9. emaciated	(I) efficiency
10. embellish	(J) to adorn; enhance

Fill-ins
Choose the best word to fill in the blank in each sentence.

efficacious	effrontery	egoism	egotistical	elegy
elicit	elixirs	Elysian	emaciated	embellish

1. In the nineteenth century, snake oil salesmen traveled around America selling _____ to gullible people.
2. One theory of child development is that the infant moves from _____ to an increased ability to understand the viewpoint of other people.
3. Nothing the teacher could say was able to _____ a response from the bored students.
4. The aid program provides emergency food to feed the _____ people of the drought-stricken country.
5. Some critics consider the artist _____ because he does only self-portraits.
6. It seems to be almost a natural human trait to _____ a good story to make it an even better story.
7. The politician has found a grassroots approach to garnering support to be most _____ .
8. The teachers were shocked when the student council had the _____ to pass a motion stating that teachers were using outdated methods of instruction.
9. The novel portrays an _____ world in which suffering and death have been eliminated.
10. The poet wrote an _____ for the soldiers who had given their lives for their country.

Sense or Nonsense
Indicate whether each sentence makes good sense or not.
Put S (SENSE) if it does, and put N (NONSENSE) if it does not.

1. No one could solve the efficacious math problem. _____
2. In her second account of events, the witness emaciated her story. _____
3. Some people are considered egotistical simply because they are not conceited. _____
4. The poem contains an allusion to an elixir that was believed to make a person immortal. _____
5. The scientist embellished the results of his experiment with data that had not been subjected to rigorous testing. _____

UNIT 27

emollient *adj.* soothing; mollifying

> *The politician's speech is filled with* **emollient** *phrases to make his message more palatable.*

Emollient is also a noun that means an agent that soothes or makes more acceptable.

empirical *adj.* derived from observation or experiment

> *Some people erroneously cite the theory of relativity as support for ethical relativism, whereas in reality the former is a scientific theory, while the latter is a moral issue, and thus by its nature is not subject to* **empirical** *verification.*

Empiricism is a noun meaning the view that experience is the only source of knowledge. It can also mean the employment of empirical methods, as in science.

Terms from the Arts, Sciences, and Social Sciences

theory of relativity: the theory of the relative as opposed to the absolute character of motion and mass, and the interdependence of matter, space, and time

---

emulate *v.* to imitate; copy

> *Bionics uses technology to* **emulate** *nature, but sometimes a similar process occurs in reverse, in which scientists use technology as a heuristic tool to better understand natural processes.*

Terms from the Arts, Sciences, and Social Sciences

Bionics: the application of biological principles to the design of electrical or engineering systems

heuristic: relating to a speculative formulation guiding the investigation or solution of a problem; educational method in which students learn from their own investigations

---

encomium *n.* a formal expression of praise

> *The prime minister asked her speechwriter to compose an* **encomium** *for the retiring general.*

*endemic *adj.* inherent; belonging to an area

*Malaria, once **endemic** to the area, has now been largely eradicated.*

*enervate *v.* to weaken

*During World War II Russian commanders counted on the bitter cold to **enervate** German soldiers invading their country.*

engender *v.* to cause; produce

*Freudians believe that the traumatic events of infancy often **engender** repression that creates neuroses.*

Terms from the Arts, Sciences, and Social Sciences

Freudians: followers of Sigmund Freud, the nineteenth-century physician who pioneered the study of the unconscious mind. Some central ideas of Freudian psychology are given below.

repression: a psychological process by which desires and impulses are kept out of the conscious mind and kept in the subconscious mind

neuroses: a mental disease that causes distress but does not interfere with a person's ability to function in everyday life. In Freudian psychology, a neurosis results from an ineffectual strategy adopted by the *Ego to resolve conflict between the *Id and the *Superego.

*Ego: in Freudian psychology, the part of the mind that tries to match the desires of the Id with what is required by reality

*Id: in Freudian psychology, the part of the mind that is the source of psychic energy that comes from instinctual drives and needs

*Superego: in Freudian psychology, the part of the mind that opposes the desires of the Id. It is based on the childhood process by which a person makes the values of society part of his or her personality.

---

enhance *v.* to increase; improve

*Although it is widely believed that the primary objective of the researchers developing the Internet was to secure the American nuclear missile system, in fact their main goal was to foster science by **enhancing** the ability of technology to disseminate information among scientists.*

entomology *n.* the scientific study of insects

*Considering that there are approximately 925,000 species of insects (more than all other species combined), **entomology** is a vast field of study.*

enunciate *v.* to pronounce clearly

*In everyday speech the sounds of many words are not **enunciated** clearly.*

REVIEW 27

Matching
Match each word with its definition.

1. emollient
2. empirical
3. emulate
4. encomium
5. endemic
6. enervate
7. engender
8. enhance
9. entomology
10. enunciate

(A) to increase; improve
(B) inherent; belonging to an area
(C) agent that soothes or makes more acceptable
(D) scientific study of insects
(E) derived from observation or experiment
(F) to cause; produce
(G) to pronounce clearly
(H) to weaken
(I) to imitate; copy
(J) formal expression of praise

Fill-ins
Choose the best word to fill in the blank in each sentence.

emollient	empirical	emulated	encomiums	endemic
enervating	engendered	enhance	entomologist	enunciate

1. As technology developed at a prodigious rate in the nineteenth and twentieth centuries, technologists increasingly _____ the professionalization and methodology of science by establishing, for example, professional associations and publications that published peer-reviewed articles.
2. The dream of many Internet users is the building of a network connected entirely by optical cable, which would greatly _____ the ability of the system to cope with the vast amount of data that it carries.

3. It has been said that Charles Darwin, virtually single-handedly, emancipated science from the ideologies of philosophy and religion by being fiercely independent in his thinking, rejecting all prevailing dogmas as to the immutability of species, and relying solely on _____ evidence.

4. Many people who travel to tropical countries find the heat _____ .

5. There is a tendency in casual conversation for speakers to not _____ each word clearly.

6. Faced with _____ high unemployment, the government lowered taxes on foreign investment to encourage economic growth.

7. Much of the tragedy of the Holocaust can be attributed to the fanatical racism _____ by the Nazis.

8. _____ to Pope Paul II began to be published in newspapers around the world shortly after his death in 2005.

9. The veteran mediator is famous for his _____ approach that rarely fails to find a way to bring opposing sides together.

10. The eminent Harvard biologist Edward O. Wilson is an _____ specializing in ants.

Sense or Nonsense
Indicate whether each sentence makes good sense or not.
Put S (SENSE) if it does, and put N (NONSENSE) if it does not.

1. Knowing the entomology of a difficult word can help you remember it. _____

2. Carrying the fifty-pound pack in the 95° Fahrenheit heat enervated the infantryman. _____

3. The Supreme Court ruling has engendered new debate on the controversial issue. _____

4. When learning to speak a new language, it is a good idea to enunciate words clearly. _____

5. It is advisable to see a doctor before traveling to countries in which malaria or other infectious diseases are endemic. _____

UNIT 28

*ephemeral *adj.* short-lived; fleeting

Impressionist *painters such as Claude Monet share with the Romantics an affinity for nature, but the Impressionists took a more scientific interest in it, attempting to accurately depict* **ephemeral** *phenomena such as the play of light on water.*

Terms from the Arts, Sciences, and Social Sciences

Impressionist: refers to Impressionism, a movement in art that began in France in the late nineteenth century. Impressionism seeks to portray the visual effects of light reflected on subjects. Claude Monet is one of the most famous Impressionist painters. The term can also be used to refer to literature that tries to convey a general impression of a subject rather than a detailed one and to musical compositions that create impressions and moods.

---

epistemology *n.* branch of philosophy that examines the nature of knowledge

> *A major question in* **epistemology** *is whether the mind can ever gain objective knowledge, limited as it is by its narrow range of sense experience.*

equable *adj.* steady; unvarying; serene

> *Throughout the crisis the president remained* **equable**.

Do not confuse *equable* with *equitable*, which means fair, or just, or impartial.

> *Much of modern economic history can be seen as a* dialectic *between advocates of* laissez-faire *policies, who want to leave the market free to create wealth untrammeled by restrictions (believing it will "trickle down" to all members of the society), and exponents of redistribution of wealth, who want to ensure that the fruits of capitalism are shared* **equitably**.

Terms from the Arts, Sciences, and Social Sciences

dialectic: in this context, dialectic refers to the action of opposing forces in society

laissez-faire: in economics and politics, doctrine that an economic system functions best when there is no interference by government. It is based on the belief that the natural economic order tends, when undisturbed by artificial stimulus or regulation, to secure the maximum well-being for the individual and therefore for the community as a whole.

---

*equanimity *n.* composure; calmness

> *Emergency room doctors and nurses are trained to maintain their* **equanimity** *when treating patients.*

*equivocate *v.* to intentionally use vague language

> *The businessperson has earned a reputation as someone who never* **equivocates** *and can be trusted to do exactly what he promises.*

The noun is *equivocation.*

> *The saying "It's a matter of semantics" is often used to indicate that the real meaning of something is being lost in verbiage, often with the implication that there is obfuscation or* **equivocation.**

Terms from the Arts, Sciences, and Social Sciences

semantics: interpretation of a word, sentence, or other language form

---

errant *adj.* mistaken; straying from the proper course

> *The pitcher's* **errant** *fastball struck the batter on the shoulder.*

*erudite *adj.* learned; scholarly

> *Frederick Copleston, author of the nine-volume* History of Philosophy, *was undoubtedly one of the most* **erudite** *people who ever lived.*

The noun is *erudition.*

> *Great* **erudition** *does not necessarily mean that a person is sagacious.*

*esoteric *adj.* hard to understand; known only to a few

> Epidemiologists, *using* **esoteric** *statistical analyses, field investigations, and complex laboratory techniques, investigate the cause of a disease, its distribution (geographic, ecological, and ethnic), method of spread, and measures for preventing or controlling it.*

Terms from the Arts, Sciences, and Social Sciences

Epidemiologists: experts in the branch of medicine that deals with the study of the causes, distribution, and control of disease in populations

---

essay *v.* to make an attempt; subject to a test

> *The composer began work on a sonata, a form she had not previously* **essayed**.

estimable *adj.* admirable; possible to estimate

Alistair Cooke's book Six Men *contains character studies of esti-*
mable *modern figures including H. L. Mencken, Humphrey Bogart, and Adlai Stevenson.*

REVIEW 28

Matching
Match each word with its definition.

1. ephemeral	(A) admirable
2. epistemology	(B) branch of philosophy that examines the nature of knowledge
3. equable	(C) hard to understand
4. equanimity	(D) steady; unvarying; serene
5. equivocate	(E) to intentionally use vague language
6. errant	(F) mistaken
7. erudite	(G) to make an attempt
8. esoteric	(H) short-lived; fleeting
9. essay	(I) learned
10. estimable	(J) composure; calmness

Fill-ins
Choose the best word to fill in the blank in each sentence.

ephemeral	epistemology	equable	equanimity	equivocate
errant	erudition	esoteric	essayed	estimable

1. Much slang originates in a specific group as a sort of argot that allows that group to share something _____ .
2. Although most slang is _____ , there are many examples of slang that endures and even comes to be accepted as legitimate.
3. Swami Vivekananda, the founder of the Ramakrishna Math, an Indian order of monks, counseled that one should try to maintain one's _____ , even in trying circumstances.
4. The _____ missile had to be destroyed after it veered off course.
5. Members of the Society of Jesus (often called Jesuits), are famous for their _____ , which they believe should be used in the service of God.
6. The cognitive sciences are providing _____ with new insights into how the mind acquires knowledge.

7. "Don't _____ ; tell me if you want to marry me or not," Ruth said to Seth.
8. The infant _____ walking up a stairs for the first time in her life.
9. Perth, Australia is often cited as a pleasant place to live because of its _____ climate.
10. Chris Evert was an _____ tennis player who won three Wimbledon titles.

Sense or Nonsense
Indicate whether each sentence makes good sense or not.
Put S (SENSE) if it does, and put N (NONSENSE) if it does not.

1. One of the important disciplines that a doctor must master to become a brain surgeon is epistemology. _____
2. The young history Ph.D. candidate is not as erudite as his supervising professor, who appears to know just about everything that happened in history. _____
3. The literary critic essayed the new novel in her review. _____
4. In view of the fact that journalism is so often ephemeral, the reporter was pleased when some of her work was published in book form. _____
5. The logic of the argument is so errant we cannot help but agree with it. _____

UNIT 29

ethnocentric *adj.* based on the attitude that one's group is superior

  The words "primitive" and "savage" reflect an **ethnocentric** *bias in Western culture that regards societies that do not have Western science and technology as inferior because they have not achieved as much material success as Western societies.*

The noun is *ethnocentrism.*

  During certain periods of Chinese history, foreigners were considered to be "barbarians"; perhaps this **ethnocentrism** *made it difficult for the Chinese to accept innovations from other countries.*

etiology *n.* causes or origins

  The **etiology** *of mental illness is complex because of the diversity of factors—social, biological, genetic, and psychological—that contribute to many disorders.*

etymology *n.* origin and history of a word

> The origin of the word "barbarian" reflects the ethnocentrism of the ancient Greeks; its **etymology** is that it comes (through Latin and French words) from the Greek word barbaros, meaning non-Greek, foreign.

eugenics *n.* study of factors that influence the hereditary qualities of the human race and ways to improve these qualities

> The science fiction novel describes a military **eugenics** program designed to create a race of "super-soldiers" possessing intelligence, strength, and other qualities far in advance of the ordinary person.

eulogy *n.* high praise, especially of a person who has recently died

> After the death of Abraham Lincoln, many **eulogies** of him appeared in newspapers throughout America.

*euphemism *n.* use of agreeable or inoffensive language in place of unpleasant or offensive language

> An illustration of the tendency toward **euphemism** is the change (reflecting the political concerns of the day) in the accepted appellation of poor countries from the unambiguous poor, to undeveloped, to underdeveloped, to less developed, to developing.

euphoria *n.* a feeling of extreme happiness

> There was **euphoria** in the professor's house after it was learned that she had received the Nobel Prize for Chemistry.

euthanasia *n.* mercy killing

> Modern medicine's ability to prolong life has raised ethical questions, such as "Is **euthanasia** ever morally justifiable?"

evince *v.* to show plainly; be an indication of

> The student's response to the teacher's question **evinced** his ignorance of the subject.

evocative *adj.* tending to call to mind or produce a reaction

> Somerset Maugham's short stories are often **evocative** of exotic places such as Pago-Pago and Gibraltar.

Evocation is the noun.

> Some literary critics believe that Charles Dickens' use of caricature makes his characters one-dimensional, but others see these characters as **evocations** of universal human types that resonate powerfully with readers' experiences of real people.

The verb is *evoke*.

> *The terms "loaded language" and "charged language" are used to specify language that has so many connotations for most readers that it is difficult for a writer to use it without **evoking** myriad associations, which will distract attention from the topic under discussion.*

Terms from the Arts, Sciences, and Social Sciences

one-dimensional: relating to a portrayal of a character that lacks depth

---

REVIEW 29

Matching
Match each word with its definition.

1. ethnocentric	(A)	origins
2. etiology	(B)	high praise
3. etymology	(C)	based on attitude that a person or group is superior
4. eugenics	(D)	feeling of extreme happiness
5. eulogy	(E)	tending to produce a reaction
6. euphemism	(F)	use of inoffensive language in place of unpleasant language
7. euphoria	(G)	origin and history of a word
8. euthanasia	(H)	mercy killing
9. evince	(I)	study of factors that influence hereditary qualities
10. evocative	(J)	to show plainly

Fill-ins
Choose the best word to fill in the blank in each sentence.

ethnocentrism	**etiology**	**etymology**	**eugenics**	**eulogy**
euphemisms	**euphoria**	**euthanasia**	**evinces**	**evocative**

1. "Folk _____ " is the term used by linguists to refer to popular theories of how words originated or changed their meaning.
2. The book describes the _____ among Allied soldiers after Japan surrendered in 1945.

3. The Oxford Dictionary of the English Language _____ the scholarship of a large team of dedicated scholars.
4. The diversity of factors involved in triggering cancers makes it difficult to be certain of the _____ of a particular case of cancer.
5. Alexander Graham Bell advocated a form of _____ ; from his research, he concluded that deafness was hereditary and in 1881 he recommended that deaf people be prohibited from getting married.
6. The novel includes many descriptions _____ of New England in winter.
7. The captain's _____ of the dead soldier described his bravery in battle.
8. In order to discourage _____ the college requires students to take three courses dealing with other cultures.
9. Advances in medical technology have made the question of whether _____ is morally justifiable an important issue in many countries.
10. Modern warfare has produced _____ such as *antipersonnel mines* for mines that rip soldiers' bodies into shreds with bits of metal and *collateral damage* for noncombatants killed as a result of war.

Sense or Nonsense
Indicate whether each sentence makes good sense or not.
Put S (SENSE) if it does, and put N (NONSENSE) if it does not.

1. The phrase "domestic helper" can be considered a euphemism for "maid." _____
2. The patient was given euthanasia before undergoing major surgery. _____
3. The euphoria in the stadium rose to a fever pitch as the seconds ticked down on the college football team's 12th straight victory. _____
4. The eulogy talked only about the many flaws in the dead man's character. _____
5. The ethnocentric villagers have no interest in anything outside their own little world. _____

UNIT 30

*exacerbate *v.* to aggravate; make worse

*The release of carbon dioxide from the burning of fossil fuels has increased the amount of this gas in the atmosphere, **exacerbating** the naturally occurring "greenhouse effect" that has predominated in Earth's recent past.*

Terms from the Arts, Sciences, and Social Sciences

greenhouse effect: the process by which a planet's atmosphere warms the planet

---

exact *v.* to force the payment of; demand and obtain by authority

*The conquering rulers **exacted** a tax of 10% from every adult male in the country.*

The adjective *exacting* means extremely demanding.

*Early in his career the English writer Aldous Huxley made this comment: "What occupation is pleasanter, what less ***exacting**, than the absorption of curious literary information?"*

*exculpate *v.* to clear of blame; vindicate

*The report **exculpated** the FBI of any wrongdoing in its handling of the investigation.*

*execrable *adj.* detestable; abhorrent

*When folk artists such as Bob Dylan began to use rock instruments, many folk music traditionalists considered it an **execrable** travesty.*

exhort *v.* to urge by strong appeals

*In 1943 U.S. General George S. Patton **exhorted** American troops about to invade Hitler's Europe, saying that victory was assured because American soldiers were more virile and courageous than their German counterparts.*

*exigency *n.* crisis; urgent requirements

*Astronauts must be prepared for **exigencies** such as damage to their spacecraft's life support system.*

existential *adj.* having to do with existence; based on experience; having to do with the philosophy of *existentialism*

> *Existential* *writers such as Jean-Paul Sartre have argued that human beings are free, but that this freedom entails a burden of responsibility that makes them anxious.*

Terms from the Arts, Sciences, and Social Sciences

Existentialism is a philosophical movement that stresses individual experience in relation to the world. Existential thought is very varied, but often concerns itself with the ideas of freedom, responsibility, and the isolation of the individual self.

---

exorcise *v.* to expel evil spirits; free from bad influences

> *A modern parallel to the* shaman *is the psychiatrist, who helps the patient* **exorcise** *personal demons and guides him toward mental wholeness.*

Terms from the Arts, Sciences, and Social Sciences

shaman: a tribal healer who is believed to be able to enter the world of good and evil spirits. Shamans often enter a trance and practice divination.

---

expatiate *v.* to speak or write at length

> *Every year the book club invites a famous author to come to* **expatiate** *on the art of writing.*

expatriate *v.* to send into exile
The pronunciation is **ek-SPAY-tree-ayt**.

> *People seeking asylum in another country are sometimes* **expatriated**.

Expatriate is also a noun meaning a person living outside his or her own land.

The pronunciation is **ek-SPAY-tree-it**.

The adjective is also *expatriate*.

REVIEW 30

Matching
Match each word with its definition.

1. exacerbate		(A)	crisis; urgent requirements
2. exact		(B)	to clear of blame
3. exculpate		(C)	relating to existence
4. execrable		(D)	to make worse
5. exhort		(E)	speak or write at length
6. exigency		(F)	to urge by strong appeals
7. existential		(G)	to force the payment of
8. exorcise		(H)	to send into exile
9. expatiate		(I)	to free from bad influences
10. expatriate		(J)	detestable

Fill-ins
Choose the best word to fill in the blank in each sentence.

exacerbating	**exacting**	**exculpated**	**execrable**	**exhorted**
exigency	**existential**	**exorcises**	**expatiate**	**expatriate**

1. The Boy Scouts motto, "Be Prepared," is a concise reminder to be ready for any _____ .
2. In E. M. Forster's *A Passage to India*, Miss Quested, one of the novel's important characters, _____ what she calls her psychological "bothers" by coming to terms with their underlying cause.
3. In India, small farmers are increasingly abandoning their farms to live in urban centers, _____ the problems faced by already overcrowded cities with insufficient infrastructure and services.
4. Amateur radio equipment generally is not built to the _____ standards that professional and military radio equipment is.
5. The eminent poet T. S. Eliot was born in the United States in 1888 and lived in England as an _____ from 1914 until 1927, when he became a British subject.
6. The principal _____ the students to study hard for the final exams.
7. The literature student was amazed that the professor could _____ for an hour on a poem containing only twelve words.
8. The people living in the slums of Mexico City live in _____ conditions.

9. _____ writers such as Albert Camus and Jean-Paul Sartre tend to focus on the individual human condition as opposed to human social interaction.
10. The defendant's attorney brought forward new evidence that _____ her of the crime.

Sense or Nonsense
Indicate whether each sentence makes good sense or not.
Put S (SENSE) if it does, and put N (NONSENSE) if it does not.

1. The builder exculpated the ground to build a foundation for the house. _____
2. The football fans exhorted their team's defense to keep the opposition from scoring a touchdown. _____
3. The expedition to Antarctica brought equipment to help deal with any exigency. _____
4. The philosopher's existential approach stresses an objective, rational approach to seeking truth. _____
5. The expatriate loves her country so much that she has never set foot on foreign soil. _____

UNIT 31

expiate *v.* to atone for

> *The pilgrims undertook their long journey to **expiate** their sins.*

Expiation is the noun.

explicate *v.* to explain; interpret; clarify

> *The literature exam requires students to **explicate** three poems they studied in class and one they have not studied.*

Explication is the noun.

expository *adj.* explanatory

> *There is no one model of **expository** prose that a student can emulate, since each piece of good writing is unique.*

*extant *adj.* in existence; not lost

> *Unfortunately for Bible scholars, there are no **extant** writings of Jesus Christ.*

extemporaneous *adj.* unrehearsed

*I enjoyed the speaker's **extemporaneous** remarks more than her prepared speech, because they gave me insight into her personality that helped me understand the decisions she made during her time as a federal judge.*

extirpate *v.* to root up; to destroy

*The new federal prosecutor promised voters that he would **extirpate** corruption in the state.*

*extraneous *adj.* not essential

*The encyclopedia editors worked hard to cut out **extraneous** material so that readers could find information easily on a given subject.*

*extrapolation *n.* the act of estimation by projecting known information

*The economist's **extrapolation** suggests that the economy will grow by 4 percent next year.*

The verb is *extrapolate*.

*Strict determinists believe that it is possible, at least theoretically, to **extrapolate** the future movement of every atom in the universe based on present conditions.*

Terms from the Arts, Sciences, and Social Sciences

determinists: followers of the belief that all events are determined by causes external to the will

---

extrinsic *adj.* not inherent or essential

*The experiment is designed to exclude factors that are **extrinsic** to the phenomenon.*

*facetious *adj.* humorous

*The comedian's **facetious** comments about prominent politicians kept the audience amused.*

REVIEW 31

Matching
Match each word with its definition.

1. expiate	(A)	unrehearsed
2. explicate	(B)	act of estimation by projecting known information
3. expository	(C)	to root up; to destroy
4. extant	(D)	in existence; not lost
5. extemporaneous	(E)	humorous
6. extirpate	(F)	to explain; interpret
7. extraneous	(G)	not inherent or essential
8. extrapolation	(H)	explanatory
9. extrinsic	(I)	to atone for
10. facetious	(J)	not essential

Fill-ins
Choose the best word to fill in the blank in each sentence.

expiate	explication	expository	extant	extemporaneous
extirpate	extraneous	extrapolating	extrinsic	facetious

1. Joan's comments are so subtle some of us have trouble telling whether she is being _____ or not.
2. If you would like to read a profound _____ of English Romantic poetry, a good book to read is Harold Bloom's *The Visionary Company.*
3. To solve the mystery of who had committed the crime, the detective systematically eliminated _____ evidence.
4. Three modern masters of _____ writing are Bertrand Russell, C. S. Lewis, and Lewis Thomas.
5. The book contains all the _____ writings of Edgar Allan Poe.
6. The students were assigned to give a/an _____ talk on a subject of their choice.
7. Many of the comic book heroes of the 1950s pledged to _____ evil wherever they found it.
8. Being born to a wealthy family can be considered a/an _____ advantage to a person.
9. The priest advised the man to perform penance to _____ his sins.
10. _____ from present trends, scientists predict that the star will explode 100 million years from now.

Sense or Nonsense
Indicate whether each sentence makes good sense or not.
Put S (SENSE) if it does, and put N (NONSENSE) if it does not.

1. Upon investigation, we found that the extant of the problem was not as great as we had feared. _____
2. The two events that occurred in 1969 were extemporaneous. _____
3. Using complex mathematical extrapolations, astronomers predict that the asteroid will pass by the Earth at a distance of 400,000 miles. _____
4. The book contains clear explications of twenty difficult poems. _____
5. The new ruler made it a priority to extirpate gangs of criminals. _____

UNIT 32

facilitate *v.* to make less difficult

*The Internet—together with the availability of relatively inexpensive personal computers—has greatly **facilitated** the ability of ordinary people to conveniently exchange information with one another and with large computer systems.*

factotum *n.* a person who does all sorts of work; a handyman

In Shakespeare's play Twelfth Night, *the character Malvolio aspires to become more than merely a **factotum** in the house of Lady Olivia.*

*fallacious *adj.* based on a false idea or fact; misleading

*The belief of the Nazis that they could create a "master race" was based on the **fallacious** premise that some races are inherently superior to others.*

The noun *fallacy* means an incorrect idea.

*Critics of the "strong" anthropic principle argue that its proponents are guilty of a logical **fallacy**: on the basis of one known case of intelligent life, they extrapolate the existence of a multitude of such cases.*

Terms from the Arts, Sciences, and Social Sciences

anthropic principle: the theory that only a limited number of possible universes are favorable to the creation of life and that of these only some have intelligent observers. Since humankind exists, it follows that the universe is suited to the evolution of intelligence.

fallow *adj.* plowed but not sowed; uncultivated

*At the beginning of each school year the teacher looks out at the new students and thinks of a **fallow** field, ready to be cultivated.*

*fatuous *adj.* foolishly self-satisfied

*The student could not understand why no one took seriously his **fatuous** comments.*

fauna *n.* animals of a period or region

*When humans introduce **fauna** from one habitat into another habitat, the ecological balance is upset.*

fawning *adj.* seeking favor by flattering

*The boss has a reputation for hiring **fawning** employees.*

*felicitous *adj.* suitably expressed; appropriate; well-chosen

*The Gettysburg Address is full of **felicitous** phrases such as "government of the people, by the people, and for the people."*

feral *adj.* existing in a wild or untamed state

***Feral** dogs returning to an untamed state after domestication sometimes form packs, becoming a threat to humans.*

fervor *n.* warmth and intensity of emotion

*American soldiers were welcomed back to the United States with **fervor** after the end of World War II.*

The adjective *fervent* means full of strong emotion, or impassioned.

*The **fervent** libertarian believed that government is a necessary evil that should be constrained from excessive interference in the affairs of individuals.*

REVIEW 32

Matching
Match each word with its definition.

1. facilitate	(A) foolishly self-satisfied
2. factotum	(B) existing in a wild state
3. fallacious	(C) to make less difficult
4. fallow	(D) suitably expressed
5. fatuous	(E) based on a false idea or fact
6. fauna	(F) plowed but not sowed
7. fawning	(G) person who does all sorts of work
8. felicitous	(H) seeking favor
9. feral	(I) animals of a period or region
10. fervor	(J) warmth and intensity of emotion

Fill-ins
Choose the best word to fill in the blank in each sentence.

facilitate	factotum	fallacious	fallow	fatuous
fauna	fawning	felicitous	feral	fervor

1. The _____ of Australia includes quite a number of species introduced from Europe.
2. The bishop's secretary tries to be respectful of his superior's office without being _____ .
3. _____ dogs have become a problem in the more rural areas of Hong Kong, where people buy dogs as pets only to later abandon them.
4. The general's aide-de-camp functions as the general's _____ .
5. President John F. Kennedy expressed the idea of duty to the country in these _____ words: "Ask not what your country can do for you; ask what you can do for your country."
6. Carbon-14 dating is predicated on the assumption that the amount of carbon-14 in the atmosphere remains constant, but recently this has been proved _____ .
7. The football team's leading running back blocks and runs with equal _____ .
8. The teacher was becoming tired of her students' _____ response to literature.

9. The black box on commercial airliners, which records flight and engineering data, is usually painted a bright color to _____ finding it after a crash.
10. The farmer could not afford to let any of his fields lie _____ .

Sense or Nonsense

Indicate whether each sentence makes good sense or not.
Put S (SENSE) if it does, and put N (NONSENSE) if it does not.

1. The chairperson of the investigative committee announced, "I will not make a decision until all the factotums in the case have been discovered. _____
2. Vegetarians eat only fauna. _____
3. The president's chief speechwriter is admired for his felicitous style. _____
4. The statement "George Washington was the first president of the United States" is fallacious. _____
5. The farmer let his field lie fallow for three years. _____

UNIT 33

fetid *adj.* having a bad smell
   Many people find the smell of Limburger cheese fetid.

fetter *v.* to bind; confine
   The poet William Blake believed that each person creates "mind-forged manacles," fettering his or her natural instincts and spirit.

The noun *fetter* means something that restricts or restrains.

The adjective *fettered* means bound or confined.

fiat *n.* arbitrary order; authorization
   The dictator rules almost entirely by fiat.

fidelity *n.* loyalty; exact correspondence
   Monks joining the Franciscan Order pledge fidelity to the ideals and rules of the Order.

filibuster *n.* use of obstructive tactics in a legislature to block passage of a law
   The senator threatened that his filibuster would include a full reading of his eight-volume autobiography.

finesse *v.* to handle with a deceptive or evasive strategy; to use finesse, that is, refinement in performance

*Engineers decided that the problem could be **finessed** by using lighter materials.*

fissure *n.* crevice

*Geologists measure the width of the **fissure** regularly to monitor movement of the Earth's plates in the area.*

flag *v.* to droop; grow weak

*Noticing that the students' attention was **flagging**, the professor gave them a short break.*

*fledgling *n.* beginner; novice

*The coach said that some of the team's **fledglings** would play in Saturday's game.*

The adjective *fledgling* means immature or inexperienced.

flora *n.* plants of a region or era

*Singapore's Botanical Gardens contain an extensive collection of the **flora** of Southeast Asia.*

REVIEW 33

Matching
Match each word with its definition.

1.	fetid	(A)	use of obstructive tactics in a legislature to block passage of a law
2.	fetter	(B)	crevice
3.	fiat	(C)	arbitrary order
4.	fidelity	(D)	to droop; grow weak
5.	filibuster	(E)	loyalty
6.	finesse	(F)	to bind; confine
7.	fissure	(G)	plants of a region or era
8.	flag	(H)	to handle with deceptive strategy
9.	fledgling	(I)	having a bad smell
10.	flora	(J)	beginner; novice

Fill-ins
Choose the best word to fill in the blank in each sentence.

fetid	fettered	fiat	fidelity	filibuster
finesse	fissures	flag	fledgling	flora

1. In the U.S. Senate, a two-thirds vote is required to break a
   _____ .
2. Mosquitoes are breeding in the _____ pond.
3. _____ to one's spouse is one of the most important requirements for a successful marriage.
4. The country's prime minister reflected how much easier it would
   be to rule by _____ than by seeking consensus.
5. The marathon runner began to _____ about two miles from
   the finish line.
6. The _____ reporter was assigned to cover mundane events
   such as school board meetings.
7. Botanists at the university have carried out a comprehensive survey of the _____ of the region.
8. He refused to be _____ by the conventions of society.
9. The boxer is known for relying more on _____ than
   strength.
10. The appearance of _____ in the rock suggested to geologists
    a movement in the Earth's crust.

Sense or Nonsense
Indicate whether each sentence makes good sense or not.
Put S (SENSE) if it does, and put N (NONSENSE) if it does not.

1. We all enjoyed the fetid smell of the meal being cooked. _____
2. Members of the minority party in the Senate were so much against
   the legislation that they threatened to filibuster. _____
3. The libertarian believes that modern democratic governments
   place unacceptable fetters on individual liberty. _____
4. The president gave a speech to rally flagging public support for the
   war. _____
5. The fledgling soldiers gradually became accustomed to army
   life. _____

UNIT 34

florid *adj.* ruddy; reddish; flowery

*As he grew older, the novelist eschewed the **florid**, ostentatious style of his youth in favor of a more direct and sparse style.*

flourish *n.* an embellishment or ornamentation

*The Sophists often gave interminable speeches full of rhetorical **flourishes**.*

Flourish is also a verb meaning to grow vigorously, or to thrive.

*Capitalism **flourished** in the eighteenth century in Europe and the United States as the industrial revolution created a prodigious amount of wealth that, for the first time in history, was in the hands of land-owners.*

Terms from the Arts, Sciences, and Social Sciences

Sophists: fifth-century B.C. Greek philosophers (*Sophistes* meant expert or deviser) who speculated on theology, science, and metaphysics. Many people came to dislike the Sophists, accusing them of dishonest reasoning. The word *sophistry* means reasoning that is subtle and seemingly true but is actually incorrect.

---

flout *v.* to treat scornfully

In his book Poetic Meter and Poetic Form *the distinguished literary critic Paul Fussel discusses the dangers poets face when they **flout** poetic conventions.*

flux *n.* flowing; a continuous moving

*In some cultures time is conceptualized as a **flux** moving in one direction.*

*foment *v.* to incite; arouse

*The government accused the newspaper of **fomenting** unrest in the country.*

forbearance *n.* patience

*The president warned that great courage and **forbearance** would be required to see the war through to a successful conclusion.*

*forestall *v.* to prevent; delay

*The government took steps to **forestall** an economic downturn by increasing government spending.*

formidable *adj.* menacing; threatening

> By the middle of the nineteenth century the United States had become a **formidable** economic and military power.

forswear *v.* renounce; repudiate

> When she became a U.S. citizen, Julia **forswore** allegiance to all other countries and pledged to defend the United States if called upon to do so.

founder *v.* to sink; fail; collapse

> Most attempts to create advanced new technology by government fiat **founder**, probably because of the difficulty in anticipating changes in the fluid world of high technology.

REVIEW 34

Matching
Match each word with its definition.

1. florid	(A)	an embellishment or ornamentation
2. flourish	(B)	menacing; threatening
3. flout	(C)	patience
4. flux	(D)	a continuous moving
5. foment	(E)	fail; collapse
6. forbearance	(F)	to treat scornfully
7. forestall	(G)	to renounce; repudiate
8. formidable	(H)	to prevent; delay
9. forswear	(I)	ruddy; reddish
10. founder	(J)	to incite; arouse

Fill-ins
Choose the best word to fill in the blank in each sentence.

florid	flourishes	flouts	flux	foment
forbearance	forestall	formidable	forswear	foundered

1. Rhetorical _____ are generally frowned upon under the canons of modern English.
2. The negotiations _____ when agreement could not be reached on the central issue.

3. The head football coach and his staff spent the week devising a way to break down the _____ defense of the next week's opponent.
4. Peace activists are working to get governments to _____ the use of nuclear weapons.
5. The education system is in a state of _____ , as administra-tors struggle to keep up with changes in society.
6. Negotiators worked frantically to _____ the outbreak of hostilities.
7. The country accused the neighboring country of employing agents to _____ revolution.
8. The student's essay _____ the rules of written English.
9. The governor urged the people of the state to show _____ during the crisis.
10. A _____ style is generally best avoided when one is writing a business letter or report.

Sense or Nonsense
Indicate whether each sentence makes good sense or not.
Put S (SENSE) if it does, and put N (NONSENSE) if it does not.

1. Good Scottish whiskey must be fomented for at least 12 years. _____
2. The company was foundered by a Scot who came to America in 1828. _____
3. "If you insist on flouting the law," the warden told the prisoner, "you'll be spending a lot more time behind bars." _____
4. The U.S. Navy's Seventh Fleet, with its more than 50 ships and 350 aircraft, possesses a formidable amount of firepower. _____
5. The teacher took steps on the first day of school to forestall discipline problems in the class. _____

UNIT 35

fracas *n.* a loud quarrel; brawl

> *The police were called in to break up a **fracas** that had erupted in the bar.*

*fractious *adj.* quarrelsome; unruly; rebellious

> *In an effort to unify their divided party, its leaders decided to first placate the party's most **fractious** elements.*

fresco *n.* a painting done on plaster

> *The Italian Renaissance was the greatest period of **fresco** painting, as seen in the work of artists such as Michelangelo, Raphael, and Giotto.*

frieze *n.* ornamental band on a wall

> *One of the best-known **friezes**, on the outer wall of the Parthenon in Athens, is a 525-foot depiction of the Panathenaic procession honoring Athena.*

Terms from the Arts, Sciences, and Social Sciences

Parthenon: the chief temple of the goddess Athena on the Acropolis in Athens

Panathenaic: relating to the Panathenaea, an Athenian festival held in honor of the Greek goddess Athena, the patron goddess of Athens

---

froward *adj.* stubbornly contrary; obstinately disobedient

> *The teacher had no choice but to send the **froward** child to the vice-principal for disciplining.*

*frugality *n.* thrift

> *In these days of credit card and installment plan buying, **frugality** seems to have become a rarely practiced virtue.*

*fulminate *v.* to attack loudly; denounce

> *The senator **fulminated** against what he termed "foreign meddling in America's business."*

fulsome *adj.* so excessive as to be disgusting

> *The actor was embarrassed by the **fulsome** praise he received after winning the Academy Award for best actor.*

fusion *adj.* union; synthesis

> *A hydrogen bomb requires tremendous heat to trigger the **fusion** reaction, which is provided by the detonation of a fission bomb.*

Terms from the Arts, Sciences, and Social Sciences

fusion: In physics, nuclear fusion is the process by which multiple nuclei join together to form a heavier nucleus, resulting in the release of energy.

fission: splitting into two parts. In physics, nuclear fission is a process where a large nucleus is split into two smaller nuclei. In biology, binary fission refers to the process whereby a prokaryote (a single-celled organism lacking a membrane-bound nucleus) reproduces by cell division

---

futile *adj.* ineffective; useless; fruitless

*To some non-philosophers, the discipline seems frivolous and **futile** because it produces no tangible benefits.*

REVIEW 35

Matching
Match each word with its definition.

1. fracas	(A)	painting done on plaster
2. fractious	(B)	so excessive as to be disgusting
3. fresco	(C)	stubbornly contrary
4. frieze	(D)	useless
5. froward	(E)	quarrelsome; unruly
6. frugality	(F)	ornamental band on a wall
7. fulminate	(G)	to denounce
8. fulsome	(H)	synthesis
9. fusion	(I)	loud quarrel
10. futile	(J)	thrift

Fill-ins
Choose the best word to fill in the blank in each sentence.

fracas	fractious	fresco	frieze	froward
frugality	fulminated	fulsome	fusion	futile

1. The philosopher's conclusion is that it is _____ to try to understand the ultimate meaning of existence.
2. The genesis of the computer revolution lay, to a large extent, in a _____ of science and technology.

3. A _____ broke out on the field after the pitcher hit a third batter in a row.
4. Many people find _____ a difficult virtue to practice.
5. The _____ horse resisted every effort of its rider to make it follow the path.
6. Archaeologists are studying the _____ , which they hope will give them a better understanding of life in ancient Greece.
7. The guest of honor at the banquet warned her hosts that she would leave if speakers began to heap _____ praise on her for her work for the poor.
8. _____ elements within the party have prevented a consensus from being reached on the issue.
9. The reformer _____ against a society in which wealth is distributed so unequally.
10. The earliest form of _____ in history was Egyptian wall paintings in tombs.

Sense or Nonsense
Indicate whether each sentence makes good sense or not.
Put S (SENSE) if it does, and put N (NONSENSE) if it does not.

1. The development of modern friezing techniques allows us to enjoy foods from all over the world. _____
2. We had to fulminate the house to kill the insects that had infested it. _____
3. The froward child refuses to go to bed when he's told to. _____
4. The country's leader urged citizens to practice frugality to help reduce private debt. _____
5. There were quite a few futile attempts at manned flight before the Wright brothers. _____

UNIT 36

*gainsay v. to deny; dispute; oppose

   *No one can **gainsay** the fact that she put great effort into the project.*

gambol v. to frolic; leap playfully

   *The children **gamboled** on the lawn while their parents ate lunch.*

The noun *gambol* means frolicking about.

*garrulous *adj.* very talkative; wordy

The **garrulous** houseguest made it difficult for us to get much work done on the project.

gauche *adj.* coarse and uncouth; clumsy

What is considered **gauche** in one culture might not be considered gauche in another culture; for example, burping is considered rude in America but is acceptable in China.

geniality *n.* cheerfulness; kindliness; sociability

Hosts of television talk shows are generally people who possess a great deal of **geniality**.

The adjective *genial* means having a pleasant or friendly disposition.

gerrymander *v.* to divide an area into voting districts in a way that favors a political party

An argument against the practice of **gerrymandering** is that it tends to make it difficult for the party that is out of power to regain power.

glib *adj.* fluent in an insincere way; offhand

Sharon's parents were not satisfied by her **glib** explanation of why she had not been able to study for the exam.

goad *v.* to prod; urge on

Goaded by his friends into trying out for the football team as a walk-on, Jeff went on to become an all-American linebacker.

gossamer *adj.* sheer; light and delicate, like cobwebs

Some experts in NASA believe that what they call a gigantic "**gossamer** spacecraft" could be constructed in space using extremely lightweight materials.

gouge *v.* to tear out; scoop out; overcharge

The store is able to **gouge** its customers because it is the only store in the area that carries that particular line of merchandise.

REVIEW 36

Matching
Match each word with its definition.

1. gainsay	(A) to tear out; overcharge
2. gambol	(B) to prod; urge on
3. garrulous	(C) to deny; dispute
4. gauche	(D) very talkative
5. geniality	(E) sheer; light and delicate, like cobwebs
6. gerrymander	(F) to frolic; leap playfully
7. glib	(G) fluent in an insincere way
8. goad	(H) cheerfulness; kindliness
9. gossamer	(I) coarse and uncouth
10. gouge	(J) to divide into voting districts so that a political party is favored

Fill-ins
Choose the best word to fill in the blank in each sentence.

gainsay	gambol	garrulous	gauche	geniality
gouged	glib	goaded	gossamer	gerrymandering

1. The _____ witness keeps digressing from his account of the incident to tell amusing anecdotes.
2. Semi-tame deer _____ in the lush green field.
3. The host's _____ impressed everyone at the party.
4. The suspect's explanation sounded suspiciously _____ to the detective.
5. The political scientist suggested that _____ be prohibited so that political districts would remain the same over the years.
6. Jim's friends _____ him into joining the Marines.
7. The pilot assured me that the glider's _____ wings would support the aircraft just fine, but I still had my doubts.
8. The protagonist of the novel is a shy woman who becomes flustered and _____ in formal social situations.
9. Engineers _____ a new channel for the stream to follow.
10. No one can _____ the fact that China has made great progress in improving the lives of its people over the past half century.

Sense or Nonsense

Indicate whether each sentence makes good sense or not.
Put S (SENSE) if it does, and put N (NONSENSE) if it does not.

1. Ted gamboled away his savings in Atlantic City. _____
2. The river gerrymanders through Ocean County. _____
3. After goading on the problem for several days, the mathematician hit on a solution. _____
4. The garrulous baseball announcer told a record twenty-six anecdotes in the course of a single game. _____
5. The dean applauded the students for their gauche, decorous behavior. _____

UNIT 37

*grandiloquent *adj.* pompous; bombastic

> The orator abandoned **grandiloquent** phrases and instead uses simple and direct language.

*gregarious *adj.* sociable

> A recent anthropological theory is that human beings are **gregarious** creatures that are comfortable living in groups of around 150 individuals.

grouse *v.* to complain

> Instead of **grousing** about the policy, do something about it: write to your congressional representative.

Grouse is also a noun.

> The lieutenant told his men "If you have any **grouses**, take them to the captain."

*guileless *adj.* free of cunning or deceit; artless

> One of the charms of the novel is that the **guileless** hero manages to defeat the scheming villain.

Guile is a noun meaning deception or trickery.

> Playing poker well requires **guile** as well as skill.

guise *n.* outward appearance; false appearance; pretense

> In Greek mythology, the god Zeus often appeared to mortal women to whom he was attracted in strange **guises**: as a swan, he made love to Leda of Sparta; with other women he took on the form of a shower of gold, or a bull, or thunder and lightning.

> **Terms from the Arts, Sciences, and Social Sciences**
>
> *Zeus*, known to the Romans as Jupiter, was the head of the Olympian pantheon and the god of weather. An amorous god, his liaisons with goddesses, nymphs, and mortal women produced many offspring, including Perseus, Heracles, Hermes, Ares, the Fates, and the Muses.
>
> *Leda* was the wife of King Tyndareus of Sparta. Her union with Zeus produced Helen and Polydeuces.

*gullible *adj.* easily deceived

> *Gullible members of the audience believed the young performer's claim that he had composed "Hey, Jude."*

gustatory *adj.* affecting the sense of taste

> *According to scientists, our **gustatory** sense depends to a large extent on our olfactory sense.*

halcyon *adj.* calm and peaceful; happy; golden; prosperous

> *The movie evokes the **halcyon** years immediately after World War II when America was at peace and the economy was booming.*

As a noun, *halcyon* is a genus of kingfisher. It also is the name of a mythological bird identified with the kingfisher that symbolizes life and renewal.

> **Terms from the Arts, Sciences, and Social Sciences**
>
> In folklore the *halcyon* (kingfisher) is a bird that brings peace and calm to the ocean waves for several days around the time of winter solstice, when it builds its nest on the sea and lays its eggs there. The expressions *halcyon days* and *halcyon years* describes periods of time that are tranquil and happy.
>
> The origins of the halcyon myth can be traced back to ancient Greece and the story of the queen Alcyone (Halcyone) who threw herself into the sea when she saw the dead body of her husband Ceyx, the King of Thessaly, who had drowned in a shipwreck. Pitying Alcyone, the gods transformed both her and Ceyx into kingfishers (halcyon), and they remained in the sea where they mated and had young. While Alcyone laid her eggs and brooded over the nest on the sea, Aeolus, keeper of the sea winds, restrained these winds so that the ocean surface would remain calm and peaceful.

hallowed *adj.* holy; sacred

> *The questioning of scientific and religious orthodoxy by scientists such as Charles Lyell and Charles Darwin led to stupendous advances in both geology and biology, as these fields freed themselves from the fetters of **hallowed**, but fallacious, assumptions about the age and development of the Earth and life.*

*harangue *n.* long, pompous speech; tirade

> *The football team sat silently listening to their coach's half-time **harangue** about poor tackling, dropped passes, and lost opportunities to score.*

REVIEW 37

Matching
Match each word with its definition.

1. grandiloquent	(A) free of deceit
2. gregarious	(B) affecting the sense of taste
3. grouse	(C) long, pompous speech
4. guileless	(D) easily deceived
5. guise	(E) calm and peaceful
6. gullible	(F) pompous; bombastic
7. gustatory	(G) outward appearance
8. halcyon	(H) to complain
9. hallowed	(I) holy; sacred
10. harangue	(J) sociable

Fill-ins
Choose the best word to fill in the blank in each sentence.

grandiloquent	**gregarious**	**grouse**	**guileless**	**guises**
gullible	**gustatory**	**halcyon**	**hallowed**	**harangue**

1. "Anyone with a _____ about my marking can see me in my office after class," the law professor told her class.
2. Researchers have found that many primates—such as chimpanzees and humans, for example—are _____ , while others, like the orangutan, live largely solitary lives.
3. The field in France is _____ by the graves of the brave soldiers who fought and died for their country.

4. Abraham Lincoln's famous adage—"You can fool some of the people all the time, and all of the people some of the time, but you cannot fool all of the people all the time."—can be paraphrased: "There are a lot of _____ people in the electorate, but there are also some people who insist on knowing the truth."
5. The president governs with the adage " _____ phrases don't house the homeless" always in mind.
6. The restaurant critic called the dish "a _____ triumph."
7. According to Hindu belief, God appears throughout history in many _____ .
8. In Somerset Maugham's story "The Facts of Life" a _____ young man triumphs over a crafty, worldly-wise young woman who tries to steal his money.
9. In retrospect, the prosperous 1950s seem like _____ years to many Americans.
10. The professor finished his _____ about student tardiness with the words, "The next time any of you are late, don't bother coming to my class."

Sense or Nonsense
Indicate whether each sentence makes good sense or not.
Put S (SENSE) if it does, and put N (NONSENSE) if it does not.

1. Gustatory winds made it difficult to sail the yacht back to port. _____
2. The con man is always on the lookout for guileless individuals. _____
3. The poem harkens back to an imagined halcyon Golden Age. _____
4. Many of America's greatest thinkers and leaders have passed through the hallowed halls of Harvard University. _____
5. The computer dating service helps people too gregarious to mingle with others at social functions to find a partner. _____

UNIT 38

harrowing *adj.* extremely distressing; terrifying

*The journey "inward" to explore the unconscious mind has been described as more **harrowing** than the most dangerous voyage to explore the Earth.*

herbivorous *adj.* relating to a herbivore, an animal that feeds mainly on plants

*Most researchers now believe that the common ancestor of apes and humans was a strongly **herbivorous** animal.*

hermetic *adj.* tightly sealed; magical

Scholars have traced many of the **hermetic** traditions of ancient Greece to Egypt.

*heterodox *adj.* unorthodox; not widely accepted

The orthodox view among scientists is that the ancestors of the great apes and humans evolved solely in Africa; however, recently a competing, **heterodox** view has arisen theorizing that they also may have evolved in Euroasia.

hieroglyphics *n.* a system of writing in which pictorial symbols represent meaning or sounds; writing or symbols that are difficult to decipher; the symbols used in advanced mathematics

The deciphering of **hieroglyphics** on the Rosetta Stone in 1822 was a great step forward in understanding hieroglyphics.

Terms from the Arts, Sciences, and Social Sciences

Rosetta Stone: a granite stone inscribed with the same passage of writing in two Egyptian languages and one in classical Greek. Comparative translation helped scholars to gain a much better understanding of hieroglyphics.

---

hirsute *adj.* covered with hair

One of the most obvious differences between humans and closely related species such as chimpanzees is that the latter are **hirsute**, while the former have relatively little hair.

*histrionic *adj.* relating to exaggerated emotional behavior calculated for effect; theatrical arts or performances

Whenever the star of the movie does not get her way on the set, she flies into a **histrionic** fit.

The noun *histrionics* means emotional behavior done for effect.

"Cut the **histrionics** and tell me how you really feel," the woman said to her angry husband.

homeostasis *n.* automatic maintenance by an organism of normal temperature, chemical balance, etc. within itself

An example of **homeostasis** in mammals is the regulation of glucose levels in the blood, which is done mainly by the liver and insulin secreted by the pancreas.

*homily *n.* sermon; tedious moralizing lecture; platitude

The pastor's **homilies** have been published in an anthology.

*homogeneous *adj.* composed of identical parts; uniform in composition

    Pluralists in America argue that the country's institutions can withstand great diversity, and even be strengthened by it, while those who argue for a more **homogeneous** *society believe that such a situation results in unhealthy contention and animosity between groups.*

Terms from the Arts, Sciences, and Social Sciences

Pluralists: followers of pluralism, the belief that it is beneficial to have a variety of distinct ethnic and cultural groups in society

---

REVIEW 38

Matching
Match each word with its definition.

1.	harrowing	(A)	unorthodox
2.	herbivorous	(B)	extremely distressing
3.	hermetic	(C)	relating to exaggerated emotional behavior calculated for effect
4.	heterodox	(D)	composed of identical parts
5.	hieroglyphic	(E)	tightly sealed; magical
6.	hirsute	(F)	covered with hair
7.	histrionic	(G)	sermon
8.	homeostasis	(H)	ability of a cell to maintain its internal equilibrium
9.	homily	(I)	relating to a herbivore, an animal that feeds on plants
10.	homogeneous	(J)	relating to a system of writing using pictorial symbols

Fill-ins
Choose the best word to fill in the blank in each sentence.

harrowing	**herbivorous**	**hermetic**	**heterodox**	**hieroglyphics**
hirsute	**histrionic**	**homeostatic**	**homily**	**homogeneous**

1. This Sunday's _____ deals with the parable of the Good Samaritan.
2. The " _____ tradition" refers to a number of interrelated subjects such as alchemy, magic, and astrology.

3. The theologian's _____ conclusions were censured by the Church.
4. Many primatologists believe that early human beings were _____, living on fruit, seeds, and nuts.
5. J. R. R. Tolkien's story *The Lord of the Rings* recounts Frodo Baggin's _____ journey to carry the One Ring from Rivendell to the Crack of Doom and destroy it before the evil Sauron could get his hands on it.
6. Some educators believe it is best to group students according to their ability, while others prefer _____ grouping.
7. Anthropologists believe that early human beings were _____ .
8. The removal of waste products by excretory organs such as the lungs and kidneys is an important _____ process in mammals.
9. The UFO researcher claims to have found writings inscribed on the side of an alien craft that resemble _____ .
10. Most mothers are astute at judging whether their child's tears are genuine or merely _____ .

Sense or Nonsense

Indicate whether each sentence makes good sense or not.
Put S (SENSE) if it does, and put N (NONSENSE) if it does not.

1. Stan's herbivorous diet consists mainly of hamburgers and steaks. _____
2. In the seventeenth century, a voyage by ship from London to New York was a harrowing experience. _____
3. Many patients are turning to homeostasis as an alternative to traditional medicine. _____
4. The heterodox pastor teaches only doctrines approved by his church. _____
5. Hieroglyphics on the Egyptian pot indicate it was used to store records of the pharaoh's accounts. _____

UNIT 39

hyperbole n. purposeful exaggeration for effect

> The American tradition of the tall tale uses **hyperbole** to depict a world in which the inhabitants and their deeds are larger than life, as befitting a people inhabiting a vast landscape.

iconoclastic adj. attacking cherished traditions

> The linguist and political commentator Noam Chomsky has been described as gleefully **iconoclastic** because of the zeal with which he attacks many of the central beliefs of American society.

An *icon* is an image or representation.

> *The internal combustion engine is a ubiquitous feature of modern industrial society, helping the automobile to become an **icon** of the twentieth century, loved by many people but loathed by environmentalists.*

Terms from the Arts, Sciences, and Social Sciences

The *icons* of the Eastern Orthodox Church are usually portraits of holy men and women that worshipers use as a help to focus their prayers. A person who smashes such an object is an *iconoclast*, which comes from the Greek word *eikonoklastes* meaning "breaking of an image." *Iconoclastic* has come to be used more generally to refer to an attack on any cherished belief.

---

*ideological *adj.* relating to ideology, the set of ideas that form the basis of a political or economic system

> *Recent social science research suggests that a person's psychological makeup plays a large part in determining his or her **ideological** leanings.*

*idolatry *n.* idol worship; blind or excessive devotion

> *During the Protestant Reformation images in churches were felt to be a form of **idolatry** and were banned and destroyed.*

*igneous *adj.* produced by fire; volcanic

> *The presence of **igneous** rocks on the beach suggests that there was a volcanic eruption in the area millions of years ago.*

imbroglio *n.* complicated situation; an entanglement

> *The plot of many of Somerset Maugham's stories consists of an unraveling of an **imbroglio** in which the main character finds himself.*

*immutable *adj.* unchangeable

> *If humanity colonizes Mars, it will become a tabula rasa on which we will inscribe our **immutable** values and beliefs in a new environment.*

Terms from the Arts, Sciences, and Social Sciences

tabula rasa: something that is new and not marked by external influence. Tabula rasa is from Latin, meaning "scraped tablet" (a tablet from which the writing has been erased).

The noun is *immutability.*

> *The dogma of creation and the* **immutability** *of species was endorsed virtually unanimously by the leading anatomists, botanists, and zoologists of Charles Darwin's day.*

*impassive *adj.* showing no emotion

> *The judge sat,* **impassive***, listening to the man's emotional account of the crime.*

impecunious *adj.* poor; having no money

> *The businessman's biography tells how he went from being an* **impecunious** *student in the 1980s to one of the richest people in America.*

impede *v.* to hinder; block

> *The development of the western region of China has been* **impeded** *by a lack of trained workers.*

REVIEW 39

Matching
Match each word with its definition.

1. hyperbole		(A)	complicated situation
2. iconoclastic		(B)	relating to the set of ideas that form the basis of a political or economic system
3. ideological			
4. idolatry		(C)	purposeful exaggeration for effect
5. igneous		(D)	worshipping idols
6. imbroglio		(E)	to hinder
7. immutable		(F)	unchangeable
8. impassive		(G)	attacking cherished traditions
9. impecunious		(H)	poor
10. impede		(I)	volcanic
		(J)	showing no emotion

Fill-ins
Choose the best word to fill in the blank in each sentence.

hyperbole	iconoclastic	ideological	igneous	imbroglio
immutable	idolatry	impassive	impecunious	impeded

1. It would be _____ to say that scientists have gained a perfect understanding of the process of human evolution; however, it is fair to say that over the last century and a half a reasonably clear idea of it has emerged.

2. The _____ artist is applying for a grant so that she can continue painting full-time.
3. Anthropologists, mindful of the danger of ethnocentrism, avoid the use of emotionally charged words such as " _____ ."
4. The president warned Congress that the United States should not become involved in the diplomatic _____ .
5. This week's essay topic is "War has _____ human progress."
6. The philosopher searches for _____ truths, striving to gain a comprehensive view of reality.
7. _____ rocks are formed when molten rock cools and solidifies.
8. The _____ book debunks the belief that all of America's Founding Fathers believed fervently in democracy.
9. The judge sat _____ through the entire murder trial, carefully considering the evidence presented.
10. The leader of the political party urged members to stop their endless _____ debates and concentrate instead on achieving realistic goals.

Sense or Nonsense
Indicate whether each sentence makes good sense or not.
Put S (SENSE) if it does, and put N (NONSENSE) if it does not.

1. Politicians often use hyperbole to embellish their achievement so that the electorate will vote for them. _____
2. Modern biologists regard evolution to be an immutable law of nature. _____
3. Gorillas are an igneous species in which a single male usually dominates a family unit. _____
4. The doctor warned her patient that alcohol would impede the action of the antibiotics that she had prescribed. _____
5. Since he regularly questioned conventional wisdom, the philosopher Socrates can be described as an iconoclast. _____

UNIT 40

impermeable adj. impossible to penetrate

> The virus protection software is said to be **impermeable** to attacks by malicious software sent over the Internet.

imperturbable adj. not easily disturbed

> Buddha counseled that one should try to remain **imperturbable** through life's vicissitudes.

*impervious *adj.* impossible to penetrate; incapable of being affected

*We were amazed how Laura could sit at the noisy party studying organic chemistry, **impervious** to the noise around her.*

impinge *v.* to strike; encroach

*Scientists have found chimpanzees to be a territorial species; individuals that are not members of a group **impinging** on the territory of that group are normally met with aggression.*

*implacable *adj.* inflexible; incapable of being pleased

*Once an **implacable** foe of capitalism, the People's Republic of China in recent years seems, in practice if not in principle, to have embraced it.*

implausible *adj.* unlikely; unbelievable

To say that Napoleon Bonaparte achieved what he did merely because he was compensating for his shortness is simplistic, reductionistic, *and **implausible**.*

Terms from the Arts, Sciences, and Social Sciences

reductionistic: attempting to explain complex phenomena by simple principles

---

*implicit *adj.* implied; understood but not stated

***Implicit** in the review is the idea that the writing of serious literature is a moral undertaking.*

An *implication* is that which is hinted at or suggested.

*The guiding principle of common law is that decisions of previous courts should be followed unless there are compelling reasons for ruling differently, which by **implication** would invalidate the earlier rulings.*

implode *v.* collapse inward violently

*The building was **imploded** in order to make way for the construction of a new apartment complex.*

The noun is *implosion*.

imprecation *n.* curse

*The convicted man was taken away by court officers, uttering **imprecations** against the jury that had found him guilty.*

impute *v.* to relate to a particular cause or source; attribute the fault to; assign as a characteristic

> *Primatologists generally* **impute** *relatively high intelligence to chimpanzees based on, among other things, the ability of chimpanzees to recognize themselves in a mirror.*

REVIEW 40

Matching
Match each word with its definition.

1. impermeable	(A) unlikely
2. imperturbable	(B) to encroach
3. impervious	(C) curse
4. impinge	(D) to collapse inward violently
5. implacable	(E) implied
6. implausible	(F) impossible to penetrate
7. implicit	(G) to attribute the fault to
8. implode	(H) incapable of being affected
9. imprecation	(I) inflexible
10. impute	(J) not easily disturbed

Fill-ins
Choose the best word to fill in the blank in each sentence.

impermeable	implicit	impinging	implacable
implausible	impervious	imprecations	impute
imperturbable	implosions		

1. It seems _____ to some people that a complex organ such as the human eye developed purely as a result of the process of evolution through natural selection.
2. Sometimes seen as _____ foes of science, many theologians are working to reconcile divergent views of science and religion.
3. _____ in the idea of democracy is the notion of individual liberty.
4. Submarines are pressurized to prevent catastrophic _____ due to the pressure of water on the hull.
5. When you look at a star that is 50 light-years away, the light that is _____ on your retina forms an image of the star as it was 50 years in the past.
6. The plastic coating on the table's surface makes it _____ to water.
7. Joe, _____ to reason, insisted on trying to swim to the island alone.

8. An important attribute of a leader is the ability to remain
_____ in a crisis.
9. People often _____ great cleverness to cats.
10. Frustrated by his inability to gain revenge on his enemies, all
George could do was hurl _____ at them.

Sense or Nonsense

Indicate whether each sentence makes good sense or not.
Put S (SENSE) if it does, and put N (NONSENSE) if it does not.

1. The young soldiers were amazed how their captain sat, imperturbable, through the heavy enemy bombardment, chatting and playing cards. _____
2. Cornered by the police, the fleeing suspect began to utter
imprecations. _____
3. Before the development of radio, the idea that people could speak
to each other over thousands of miles was generally regarded as
implausible. _____
4. Everyone in the class likes Professor Wilson because of her fair,
flexible, and implacable marking. _____
5. The first mate warned the captain of the submarine that implosion
was imminent. _____

UNIT 41

*inadvertently *adv.* carelessly; unintentionally
- *The songwriter says that it is easy to **inadvertently** use the mel-
ody of another song when composing.*

incarnate *adj.* having bodily form
*Christians believe that Jesus Christ was God **incarnate**.*

*inchoate *adj.* imperfectly formed or formulated
In his book Chronicles, *Bob Dylan describes the process of how
some of his songs went from an **inchoate** state to finished, well-
produced songs.*

*incongruity *n.* state of not fitting
*There is an **incongruity** between the poem's solemn tone and its
light-hearted theme.*

The adjective is *incongruous*.
*The assumptions underlying Jonathan Swift's definition of liter-
ary style—"The proper words in the proper order"—recognize that*

there are many effective styles, but that the effectiveness of each is dependent on the context within which it is found: for example, the rambling, exuberant style of Walt Whitman's poem "Song of Myself" would be **incongruous** in Alexander Pope's The Rape of the Lock, with its dependence on sustained wit and irony.

Terms from the Arts, Sciences, and Social Sciences

Jonathan Swift: Anglo-Irish writer (1667–1745) known today mainly for his prose satires such as *Gulliver's Travels*

Walt Whitman: American poet (1819–1892) widely regarded as one of the nation's greatest writers. His most famous work is *Leaves of Grass*

Alexander Pope: English poet (1688–1744) known today mainly for his satirical poetry, most notably *The Rape of the Lock*

---

inconsequential *adj.* insignificant; unimportant

*The meeting of the two women seemed **inconsequential** at the time, but in retrospect it led to one of literature's great collaborations.*

incorporate *v.* introduce something into another thing already in existence; combine

According to Bob Dylan in his autobiography, Chronicles, *he systematically tried to **incorporate** what he learned about life and music into the songs he wrote.*

incursion *n.* sudden invasion

*At first, the Native Americans were not too concerned about the **incursions** of European settlers, but their anxiety grew with the relentless flow of people, until, finally, calamitous wars were fought between the two sides.*

*indeterminate *adj.* uncertain; indefinite

*The novel describes the main character as "being of an **indeterminate** age, somewhere between 50 and 60."*

*indigence *n.* poverty

*Most economists believe that the best way to prevent **indigence** is to expand employment opportunities.*

The adjective is *indigent.*

*For approximately 20 percent of the world's population, nearly all of whom are **indigent**, malnutrition is the main impediment to achieving good health.*

*indolent *adj.* habitually lazy; idle

> *An argument against welfare is that it encourages people to be* **indolent**.

REVIEW 41

Matching
Match each word with its definition.

1.	inadvertently	(A)	imperfectly formed
2.	incarnate	(B)	to introduce something into another thing already in existence; combine
3.	inchoate	(C)	insignificant; unimportant
4.	incongruity	(D)	sudden invasion
5.	inconsequential	(E)	habitually lazy; idle
6.	incorporate	(F)	carelessly; unintentionally
7.	incursion	(G)	poverty
8.	indeterminate	(H)	having bodily form
9.	indigence	(I)	uncertain; indefinite
10.	indolent	(J)	state of not fitting

Fill-ins
Choose the best word to fill in the blank in each sentence.

inadvertently	incarnate	inchoate	incongruous
inconsequential	incorporates	incursions	indeterminate
indigent	indolent		

1. In view of the fact that in most elections fewer than half the eligible voters cast their ballot, it would appear that many citizens consider their vote to be _____ .
2. In societies that place a high value on hard work, people who spend most of the day sitting around chatting are often considered to be _____ .
3. During an ice age, the polar ice caps make _____ into regions that are temperate at other times.
4. The study of human evolution _____ the latest research from primatology, anthropology, and related fields.
5. The writer is approaching that _____ age at which one cannot accurately be described either as young or middle-aged.
6. In retrospect, it seems _____ that a country founded on the principle of liberty condoned slavery.

7. Astronomers believe that the solar system formed out of an
_____ mass of dust and gas.
8. The typesetter _____ omitted a line from the poem.
9. Many people consider Adolf Hitler to have been evil _____ .
10. The new welfare program is targeted to help the truly _____
in the population.

Sense or Nonsense

Indicate whether each sentence makes good sense or not.
Put S (SENSE) if it does, and put N (NONSENSE) if it does not.

1. "The method you use to memorize the information is inconsequential," the teacher told her class, "as long as it works." _____
2. The book *The Historical Jesus* by John Dominic Crossan incorporates the methodology of and insights of a number of fields,
including anthropology, history, and theology. _____
3. Military intelligence indicates that the enemy has been making
incursions into our territory. _____
4. The president hailed the unprecedented economic growth as
"ushering in a new era of industry and indigence." _____
5. The poem is the writer's attempt to articulate an inchoate vision of
the future that was beginning to form in her mind. _____

UNIT 42

ineluctable adj. not to be avoided or escaped; inevitable

> *No one can escape the **ineluctable** truth that every creature that is
> born will one day die.*

inert adj. unable to move; sluggish

> *The teacher was frustrated by his inability to get an answer to his
> question from his **inert** class.*

The noun is *inertia*, meaning disinclination to action or change.

> *The fact that industrialization occurred in Europe hundreds of
> years before it did in China, which had reached a similar level
> of technology, is perhaps attributable to cultural factors such as
> bureaucratic **inertia** in China and a culture that placed a high
> value on the* status quo.

Terms from the Arts, Sciences, and Social Sciences

status quo: the existing state of affairs (Latin, *state in which*)

---

*ingenuous *adj.* naive and trusting; lacking sophistication

The conman could not bring himself to take advantage of the **ingenuous** *boy.*

*inherent *adj.* firmly established by nature or habit

Some studies of random numbers generated by computers suggest that an **inherent** *order exists in nature, since certain patterns appear that one would not expect in a random system, but skeptics dismiss such patterns as either artifacts of imperfectly designed experiments, or as the attempt of the human mind to impose a pattern where there is no intrinsic order.*

*innocuous *adj.* harmless

The bodyguard looked **innocuous** *enough, but under his jacket were several weapons that could kill an attacker in seconds.*

*insensible *adj.* unconscious; unresponsive

The gas is intended to render enemy soldiers **insensible**.

*insinuate *v.* to suggest; say indirectly; imply

If you read his speech carefully you will see that the senator is **insinuating** *that his party has taken the wrong path.*

*insipid *adj.* lacking in flavor; dull

Ironically, the book about how to write lively, engaging prose is an **insipid** *piece of writing.*

insouciant *adj.* indifferent; lacking concern or care

Considering the gravity of the situation, Nancy's colleagues could not understand her **insouciant** *attitude.*

*insularity *n.* narrow-mindedness; isolation

The **insularity** *of many tribes in New Guinea allows anthropologists to study cultures that have been relatively uninfluenced by the modern world.*

REVIEW 42

Matching
Match each word with its definition.

1.	ineluctable	(A)	to suggest; say indirectly
2.	inert	(B)	indifferent; lacking concern
3.	ingenuous	(C)	unable to move
4.	inherent	(D)	unconscious; unresponsive
5.	innocuous	(E)	lacking in flavor; dull
6.	insensible	(F)	not to be avoided or escaped
7.	insinuate	(G)	firmly established by nature or habit
8.	insipid	(H)	narrow-mindedness; isolation
9.	insouciant	(I)	naive and trusting
10.	insularity	(J)	harmless

Fill-ins
Choose the best word to fill in the blank in each sentence.

ineluctable	inert	ingenuous	inherent	innocuous
insensible	insinuating	insipid	insouciance	insularity

1. The referee stopped the bout after one boxer was rendered
   _____ .
2. The country's _____ makes it difficult for its people to
   accept ideas from different cultures.
3. Indonesians who travel to America sometimes find the food so
   _____ that they add chili to it.
4. The Internet "scam" relies on _____ people to sign up and
   spend money for which they get essentially nothing in return.
5. Scientists are still studying the question of how life arose from
   _____ matter.
6. The lawyer apologized to the judge for _____ that she was
   biased.
7. The "cool" look that many fashion models affect seems meant to
   convey a look of _____ .
8. The judicious doctor knows that sometimes the best therapy is not
   physical but emotional, reassuring the patient that the illness will
   run its course as a result of the body's _____ powers of
   self-healing.
9. We cannot escape the _____ truth that someone in the
   group has betrayed our cause.
10. The toxic chemical is present in the drug in such minute amounts
    that it is _____ .

Sense or Nonsense

Indicate whether each sentence makes good sense or not.
Put S (SENSE) if it does, and put N (NONSENSE) if it does not.

1. The mathematician has devised an ingenuous solution to the problem. _____
2. Innocuous weapons such as the hydrogen bomb are capable of killing millions of people in an instant. _____
3. The professor's comment on the student's essay read, "An insensible and incoherent piece of writing." _____
4. Spicy, insipid dishes are popular throughout Southeast Asia. _____
5. In today's interconnected world, countries that remain insular face the risk of falling behind technologically. _____

UNIT 43

insuperable *adj.* insurmountable; unconquerable

Attempts by the United States to develop an antiballistic missile system have met with limited success because of the almost **insuperable** *difficulties presented by the speed of the approaching warhead that must be intercepted.*

intangible *adj.* not material

When considering what occupation to pursue it is prudent to consider **intangible** *rewards as well as financial ones.*

interdict *v.* to forbid; prohibit; to confront and halt the activities, advance, or entry of

Under U.S. law, **interdicted** *goods can be seized by customs officials.*

internecine *adj.* deadly to both sides

The U.S. Civil War (1861–1865) was an **internecine** *conflict that lead to the deaths of 620,000 soldiers out of the 2.4 million who fought in the war.*

interpolate *v.* to insert; change by adding new words or material

The book The Five Gospels *was produced by having leading Bible scholars vote on which sayings of Jesus they believe to be authentic and which they believe to have been* **interpolated** *by other writers.*

interregnum *n.* interval between reigns; gap in continuity

> *Those who believe that Western culture represents the culmination of history are not disheartened by considering the fall of previous dominant civilizations, believing that these were merely **interregnums** in the march of humanity from the cave to a united world founded on Western principles.*

intimate *adj.* marked by close acquaintance

Intimate is pronounced **IN-tuh-mit**.

> *During the 1990s Bob Dylan and Jerry Garcia became good, though not **intimate**, friends.*

The noun is *intimacy*.

> *The American artist Grandma Moses, although considered by art experts to be deficient in technique, achieved an admirable **intimacy** with her subject matter.*

The verb *intimate* means to make known subtly and indirectly. It is pronounced **IN-tuh-mayt**.

> *The editor **intimated** that substantial changes would have to be made in the book.*

*intractable *adj.* not easily managed

> *General practitioners are equipped to deal with most* psychosomatic disorders, *but in **intractable** cases a psychiatrist is consulted.*

Terms from the Arts, Sciences, and Social Sciences

psychosomatic disorder: a disease with physical symptoms believed to be caused by emotional or psychological factors

---

*intransigence *n.* stubbornness; refusal to compromise

> *Each side in the negotiations accused the other of **intransigence**, so talks broke down.*

introspective *adj.* contemplating one's own thoughts and feelings

> *In many ways William Wordsworth's great poem* The Prelude *is an **introspective** work, retrospectively exploring his thoughts and feelings as he matured.*

REVIEW 43

Matching
Match each word with its definition.

1. insuperable	(A) stubbornness
2. intangible	(B) insurmountable
3. interdict	(C) not easily managed
4. internecine	(D) not material
5. interpolate	(E) deadly to both sides
6. interregnum	(F) marked by close acquaintance
7. intimate	(G) interval between reigns
8. intractable	(H) contemplating one's own thoughts and feelings
9. intransigence	(I) to forbid
10. introspective	(J) to insert

Fill-ins
Choose the best word to fill in the blank in each sentence.

insuperable	intangible	interdicting	internecine	interpolated
interregnum	intimate	intractable	intransigence	introspection

1. The _____ of both sides means that there will be no progress in the peace talks.
2. Over the years the boss and her assistant have become _____ friends as well as colleagues.
3. Since, according to the theory of relativity, an object traveling at the speed of light would have infinite mass, astronauts traveling at that speed would, presumably, face _____ difficulties.
4. Military intelligence officers played a major role in _____ spies attempting to pass top-secret intelligence to the enemy.
5. In addition to providing a salary, a job often provides _____ benefits such as camaraderie with colleagues.
6. Scholars disagree on whether the text is entirely the work of the original author or contains passages _____ by later writers.
7. The book analyzes the _____ struggles within Christianity throughout its history.
8. The injunction "Know Thy Self," which was inscribed over the sanctuary of Apollo at Delphi, suggests that for spiritual advancement it is necessary to engage in _____ .
9. The _____ between the two empires was a period of near anarchy.

10. Although the majority of Americans are members of what has been called the "affluent society," poverty remains an _____ problem, with a sizable minority of people living below what is considered to be an acceptable standard of living.

Sense or Nonsense
Indicate whether each sentence makes good sense or not.
Put S (SENSE) if it does, and put N (NONSENSE) if it does not.

1. The king's interregnum lasted 22 years, during which time he presided over a happy and peaceful kingdom. _____
2. Greater intransigence on the part of both sides will increase the chance of an agreement. _____
3. The problem seemed intractable at first, but after we analyzed it as being the result of a number of smaller problems, we were able to solve it. _____
4. The old text contains a number of interpolations by a rival group seeking to justify their views. _____
5. Many African countries are beset by internecine conflict between rival tribes. _____

UNIT 44

*inundate *v.* to cover with water; overwhelm

> *Farmers in the arid areas called for the government to build a dam to provide water to irrigate their crops and provide hydroelectric power; however, this plan was opposed by environmentalists, who dislike **inundation** of land because it would have an adverse effect on wildlife.*

*inured *v.* hardened; accustomed; used to

> *After 20 years in the army, the chaplain had not become **inured** to the sight of men dying on the battlefield.*

*invective *n.* verbal abuse

> *The debate judge cautioned participants not to engage in **invective**, but rather in reasoned and decorous discourse.*

inveigh *v.* to disapprove; protest vehemently

> *The conservative writer **inveighed** against the school board's decision to exclude moral education from the curriculum.*

inveigle *v.* to win over by flattery or coaxing

> The students **inveigled** their professor into postponing the test for a week.

inveterate *adj.* confirmed; long-standing; deeply rooted

> The columnist is an **inveterate** iconoclast who continually questions conventional wisdom.

invidious *adj.* likely to provoke ill will; offensive

> Most publications in the United States prohibit their writers from making **invidious** comparisons between racial groups.

*irascible *adj.* easily angered

> The **irascible** old man complains every time someone makes a little noise.

*irresolute *adj.* unsure of how to act; weak

> The president admonished Congress, saying that although it faced difficult choices it must not be **irresolute**.

itinerant *adj.* wandering from place to place; unsettled

> According to state law, companies hiring **itinerant** workers must provide adequate housing for them.

REVIEW 44

Matching
Match each word with its definition.

1. inundate	(A)	to disapprove; protest vehemently
2. inured	(B)	hardened; accustomed
3. invective	(C)	wandering from place to place
4. inveigh	(D)	to overwhelm
5. inveigle	(E)	verbal abuse
6. inveterate	(F)	confirmed; long-standing
7. invidious	(G)	unsure of how to act; weak
8. irascible	(H)	likely to provoke ill will
9. irresolute	(I)	easily angered
10. itinerant	(J)	to win over by flattery

Fill-ins

Choose the best word to fill in the blank in each sentence.

inundated	inured	invective	inveigh	inveigle
inveterate	invidious	irascible	irresolute	itinerant

1. The talk show host uses _____ to anger his guests so that they say things they ordinarily would not.
2. The _____ young man gets into a fight practically every weekend.
3. The book makes _____ comparisons between French and American culture.
4. The writer spent his twenties as a/an _____ salesperson traveling throughout the Midwest.
5. The country's leaders regularly _____ against "the corrupting influence of Western decadence."
6. Some developing countries argue that they lack the capacity to compete in a completely free world market, and that in such a situation their domestic market would be _____ with foreign goods to the detriment of local manufacturers.
7. An _____ gambler, every year Tom offers his family a choice of two vacation destinations—Las Vegas, Nevada, or Atlantic City, New Jersey.
8. War has raged for so long in the country that people have become _____ to violence.
9. The president warned the nation that we must not be _____ in our determination to prevent terrorism.
10. I was amazed how Charlie, Doris, and Marcia managed to _____ Fred into playing bridge, a game he finds completely boring.

Sense or Nonsense

Indicate whether each sentence makes good sense or not.
Put S (SENSE) if it does, and put N (NONSENSE) if it does not.

1. Sam inured himself for one million dollars before going on the dangerous expedition. _____
2. Every summer, the apple orchard hires itinerant workers to pick the apples. _____
3. The educators are concerned that students are being inundated with so much information that they have trouble making sense of it. _____

4. Medical researchers are working on a cure for various types of invective. _____

5. The pastor warned his congregation that they must not be irresolute in facing evil. _____

UNIT 45

itinerary *n.* route of a traveler's journey

> We planned our **itinerary** to be flexible, so that if we especially enjoyed a particular place we could stay there longer.

jaundiced *adj.* having a yellowish discoloration of the skin; affected by envy, resentment, or hostility

> Norman's experience as an infantryman during the war has given him a **jaundiced** view of human nature.

The noun *jaundice* refers to a medical condition often due to liver disease and characterized by yellowness of the skin.

jibe *v.* to be in agreement

> The auditor checked the company's account books to make sure that they **jibed** with the tax return it filed.

jocose *adj.* fond of joking; jocular; playful

> The English words **jocose**, jocular, and joke all come from derivatives of the Latin noun jocus, which means "jest" or "joke," but the etymology of the word jocund is unrelated to these. Jocose (fond of joking; jocular; playful) is from Latin jocosus (humorous, merry, sportive), from jocus. Jocular (fond of joking; playful; speaking in jest) is from Latin jocularis (jocular; laughable), also from jocus. Jocund (mirthful; merry; light-hearted; delightful) is from jocundus (pleasant, agreeable), from juvare (to delight).

juggernaut *n.* huge force destroying everything in its path

> Some people in Britain regard American English as a **juggernaut** sweeping through the British Isles, destroying British English.

junta *n.* group of people united in political intrigue

> The country's ruling **junta** consists of a general, an admiral, and the mayor of the capital city.

*juxtapose *v.* place side by side

> To illustrate their case, opponents of functionalism **juxtapose** the products of modern architecture and those of classical architecture, such as the Parthenon, or those of medieval architecture, such as the Cathedral of Notre-Dame.

The noun *juxtaposition* means a side-by-side placement.

Terms from the Arts, Sciences, and Social Sciences

functionalism: twentieth-century aesthetic doctrine in architecture. Functionalists believe that the outward form of a structure should follow its interior function.

---

kudos *n.* fame; glory; honor

> **Kudos** won by Bob Dylan include an honorary doctorate in music from Princeton University.

labile *adj.* likely to change

> Blood pressure in human beings is, to varying degrees, **labile**.

*laconic *adj.* using few words

> The **laconic** actor seemed to be a good choice to play the strong, silent hero in the western.

REVIEW 45

Matching
Match each word with its definition.

1.	itinerary	(A)	to be in agreement
2.	jaundiced	(B)	to place side by side
3.	jibe	(C)	fond of joking; jocular
4.	jocose	(D)	likely to change
5.	juggernaut	(E)	having a yellowish discoloration of the skin
6.	junta	(F)	fame; glory
7.	juxtapose	(G)	group of people united in political intrigue
8.	kudos	(H)	route of a traveler's journey
9.	labile	(I)	using few words
10.	laconic	(J)	huge force destroying everything in its path

Fill-ins

Choose the best word to fill in the blank in each sentence.

itinerary	jaundiced	jibe	jocose	juggernaut
junta	juxtaposed	kudos	labile	laconic

1. During the first several years of World War II, the German army was a/an _____ , easily defeating any force that tried to stop it.
2. A military _____ seized power in the country in 1988.
3. Dr. Taylor's considerable girth and _____ manner made him the obvious choice to play Santa Claus in the faculty Christmas play.
4. The _____ for our visit to Edinburgh, Scotland included a visit to Edinburgh University and Edinburgh Castle.
5. The psychologist's diagnosis was that Eric was emotionally _____ .
6. The textual scholar _____ the two translations in order to compare them.
7. Infectious hepatitis is a viral form of hepatitis that causes fever and makes a person's skin _____ .
8. Most scientists regard the Noble Prize as the highest _____ they can receive.
9. It is difficult for a person who tends to be _____ to learn how to speak a new language.
10. Listening to the witness' testimony, the judge discovered that it did not _____ with the account of the incident he had given to the police.

Sense or Nonsense

Indicate whether each sentence makes good sense or not.
Put S (SENSE) if it does, and put N (NONSENSE) if it does not.

1. The young jazz trumpeter decided he should learn to "talk the jibe." _____
2. The juggernauts performed amazing feats of legerdemain that had the children laughing all afternoon. _____
3. In a healthy individual body temperature is not labile. _____
4. The host has decided to seat people at the formal dinner so that people who tend to be laconic sit next to individuals that are more garrulous. _____
5. Thirty years on the police force has given Captain Lucas a jaundiced view of life. _____

UNIT 46

lambaste *v.* to thrash verbally or physically

*The critic **lambasted** the movie in her column, calling it "the most insipid, jejune film made in our generation."*

lascivious *adj.* lustful

*The court ruled that the movie could be censored because its sole aim was to promote **lascivious** thoughts.*

*lassitude *n.* lethargy; sluggishness

*After the death of his wife, Steven suffered a three-month period of **lassitude** and depression.*

latent *adj.* present but hidden; potential

*Some experts in human psychology believe that we are just beginning to explore the **latent** powers of the human mind.*

*laud *v.* to praise

*The literary critic **lauded** Jane Austen's Pride and Prejudice, calling it a novel that "explores the tension between a person's life as a social being and his or her individual consciousness."*

*lethargic *adj.* inactive

*After the 18-hour flight from New York to Singapore, the passengers were **lethargic**.*

levee *n.* an embankment that prevents a river from overflowing

*An extensive system of **levees** is the only way to prevent the river from flooding the area during periods of heavy rain.*

*levity *n.* light manner or attitude

*The comedian has a gift for finding an element of **levity** in the most serious of subjects.*

liberal *adj.* tolerant; broad-minded; generous; lavish

*Bankruptcy laws should not be too stringent, or not enough people will venture their capital; on the other hand, they should not be too **liberal**, or entrepreneurs will take unreasonable risks and waste capital.*

libertine *n.* one without moral restraint

*Don Juan is a legendary, archetypal **libertine** whose story has been told by many poets, such as Lord Byron.*

REVIEW 46

Matching
Match each word with its definition.

1. lambaste		(A)	embankment that prevents a river from overflowing
2. lascivious		(B)	to thrash verbally or physically
3. lassitude		(C)	to praise
4. latent		(D)	lustful
5. laud		(E)	inactive
6. lethargic		(F)	tolerant
7. levee		(G)	present but hidden; potential
8. levity		(H)	light manner or attitude
9. liberal		(I)	person without moral restraint
10. libertine		(J)	lethargy; sluggishness

Fill-ins
Choose the best word to fill in the blank in each sentence.

lambasted	**lascivious**	**lassitude**	**latent**	**lauded**
lethargic	**levee**	**levity**	**liberal**	**libertine**

1. Engineers worked to reinforce the _____ after the prediction of an unprecedented amount of rain.
2. To everyone's surprise, the 14-point underdog _____ the reigning champions 42–0.
3. Suddenly overcome by _____ in the afternoon, Jill decided to take a nap.
4. The former president was _____ for his indefatigable efforts to bring peace to the war-torn area.
5. In the view of some commentators, a paradox of modern _____ democracy is that although people have more freedom than ever, they often are unable to use this freedom to find meaningful values and goals.
6. The goal of the course is to help people develop their _____ abilities.
7. After the long winter layoff, many of the baseball players were _____ at the first day of spring training.
8. The bikini-clad young woman attracted _____ stares from a group of men.
9. The speaker decided to tell a joke to introduce some _____ into the solemn occasion.

10. James Boswell, the eighteenth-century Scottish writer best remembered for his biography of the eminent literary figure Samuel Johnson, was a heavy drinker and a _____ .

Sense or Nonsense

Indicate whether each sentence makes good sense or not.
Put S (SENSE) if it does, and put N (NONSENSE) if it does not.

1. The captain lauded his troops into battle. _____
2. The psychologist suggested that the patient take life less seriously and try to introduce some levity into her life every day. _____
3. The picnickers were overcome by lassitude after eating a heavy lunch. _____
4. Carol discovered late in life that she had a latent ability for mathematics. _____
5. The women's rights group condemned the swimsuit part of the Miss Galaxy contest "designed solely to appeal to men's lascivious impulses." _____

UNIT 47

libido *n.* sexual desire

   *According to psychologists, the **libido** of human males peaks at around the age of 18.*

Lilliputian *adj.* extremely small

   *Microbiologists study **Lilliputian** organisms.*

limn *v.* to draw; describe

   *The artist based his painting on a sketch he had **limned** several years earlier.*

*limpid *adj.* clear; transparent

   *At the bottom of the **limpid** pond we could see hundreds of fish swimming.*

linguistic *adj.* pertaining to language

   *Humans are at the acme of their **linguistic** proficiency in the first several years of life, during which they master thousands of complex grammatical operations.*

Linguistics is the scientific study of language.

A *linguist* is someone who studies language.

Linguists such as Noam Chomsky believe that what people come to know and believe depends on experiences that evoke a part of the cognitive system that is latent in the mind.

litany *n.* lengthy recitation; repetitive chant

*The student listened intently to his teacher's **litany** of the grammatical errors committed by the class.*

literati *n.* scholarly or learned persons

"Any test that turns on what is offensive to the community's standards is too loose, too capricious, too destructive of freedom of expression to be squared with the First Amendment. *Under that test, juries can censor, suppress, and punish what they don't like, provided the matter relates to 'sexual impurity' or has a tendency 'to excite lustful thoughts.' This is community censorship in one of its worst forms. It creates a regime where in the battle between the **literati** and the* Philistines, *the Philistines are certain to win."*

—U.S. Supreme Court justice William O. Douglas,
dissenting in the case of *Roth v. United States,* 1957.

Terms from the Arts, Sciences, and Social Sciences

First Amendment: a part of the United States Bill of Rights prohibiting the federal legislature from making laws that establish a state religion or prefer a certain religion, prevent free exercise of religion, infringe the freedom of speech; infringe the freedom of the press; limit the right to assemble peaceably; limit the right to petition the government for a redress of grievances

Philistines: people considered to be ignorant of the value of cultures and smug and conventional in their thinking

---

litigation *n.* legal proceedings

*The radio amateur's neighbor resorted to **litigation** in an attempt to have her neighbor dismantle his 100-foot-high antenna tower.*

log *n.* record of a voyage; record of daily activities

*Although no longer required to do so by the Federal Communications Commission, many amateur radio operators nevertheless keep a meticulous record of stations they communicate with, **logging** the details of each contact.*

*loquacious *adj.* talkative

> *Eighty meters is a portion of the radio spectrum where a shortwave listener can often hear* **loquacious** *"hams" chatting ("chewing the rag" in amateur radio parlance) for hours.*

REVIEW 47

Matching
Match each word with its definition.

1. libido	(A) transparent
2. Lilliputian	(B) sexual desire
3. limn	(C) legal proceedings
4. limpid	(D) to draw; describe
5. linguistic	(E) talkative
6. litany	(F) extremely small
7. literati	(G) lengthy recitation
8. litigation	(H) scholarly or learned persons
9. log	(I) record of a voyage
10. loquacious	(J) pertaining to language

Fill-ins
Choose the best word to fill in the blank in each sentence.

libido	Lilliputian	limning	limpid	linguistics
litany	literati	litigation	logs	loquacious

1. The study's hypothesis is that the low birthrate is a result of a reduction in many people's _____ .
2. According to the historian Richard J. Hofstadter, there has been a strong feeling of suspicion of the _____ throughout American history.
3. The _____ of the eighteenth-century ships' captains provide an interesting perspective on that time.
4. The judge warned the _____ attorney to stop digressing and "cut to the chase."
5. The critic praised the novel for its _____ prose and original characters.
6. The United Nations Human Rights Commission outlined a _____ of the rights regularly being abused in the country.
7. The threat of _____ was enough to induce the company to settle the claim against it.

8. The writer Somerset Maugham had a gift for _____ a character perfectly in a few paragraphs.
9. Applied _____ takes the findings of theoretical linguistics and applies them to such areas as language learning.
10. After his experiences in the war, the problems Howard encountered in civilian life seemed positively _____ .

Sense or Nonsense
Indicate whether each sentence makes good sense or not.
Put S (SENSE) if it does, and put N (NONSENSE) if it does not.

1. If ants can perceive human beings, we must appear Lilliputian to them. _____
2. Exhaustive litigation has proven that gravity exists throughout the universe. _____
3. To the unaided eye the liquid appears limpid, but in reality it contains millions of microscopic organisms. _____
4. Magazines read regularly by most members of the New York literati include *The New Yorker* and the *New York Review of Books*. _____
5. The judge warned the witness not to use the occasion to give a litany of his personal grievances. _____

UNIT 48

*lucid *adj.* bright; clear; intelligible

> *The eminent surgeon Dr. Christian Barnard, who performed the first human heart-transplant operation in 1967, made his views on euthanasia clear in this* **lucid** *injunction: "The prime goal is to alleviate suffering, and not to prolong life. And if your treatment does not alleviate suffering, but only prolongs life, that treatment should be stopped."*

lucre *n.* money or profits

> *Many religions regard the pursuit of* **lucre** *for what it can do to help others as laudable.*

luminous *adj.* bright; brilliant; glowing

> *The Moon is the most* **luminous** *object in the night sky.*

The noun is *luminosity.*

> *A supernova can suddenly increase its* **luminosity** *to as much as a billion times its normal brightness.*

Terms from the Arts, Sciences, and Social Sciences

supernova: a rare astronomical event in which most of the material in a star explodes, resulting in the emission of vast amounts of energy for a short period of time

---

lustrous *adj.* shining

> On the clear night we gazed up in awe at the **lustrous** stars.

Machiavellian *adj.* crafty; double-dealing

> One theory of the evolution of high intelligence in primates is that it evolved largely as a result of **Machiavellian** calculations on the part of apes.

Terms from the Arts, Sciences, and Social Sciences

Machiavelli: Niccolo Machiavelli (1469–1527) was an Italian philosopher known for his writings on how a ruler should govern, notably by favoring expediency over principles.

---

machinations *n.* plots or schemes

> The mayor resorted to behind-the-scenes **machinations** to try to win his party's nomination for governor.

maelstrom *n.* whirlpool; turmoil

> Nearly everyone in Europe was caught up in the **maelstrom** that was World War II.

*magnanimity *n.* generosity; nobility

> The senator showed his **magnanimity** when he conceded defeat to his opponent in the disputed election, saying that further uncertainty would be harmful to public confidence in the political system.

malign *v.* to speak evil of

> Lawyers are sometimes **maligned** as greedy and dishonest.

*malinger *v.* to feign illness to escape duty

> In order to discourage **malingering**, the company decided to require employees taking sick leave to produce a doctor's certification of their illness.

REVIEW 48

Matching
Match each word with its definition.

1. lucid	(A) bright; brilliant; glowing
2. lucre	(B) money or profits
3. luminous	(C) generosity; nobility
4. lustrous	(D) plots or schemes
5. Machiavellian	(E) to feign illness to escape duty
6. machinations	(F) whirlpool; turmoil
7. maelstrom	(G) clear; intelligible
8. magnanimity	(H) to speak evil of
9. malign	(I) crafty; double-dealing
10. malinger	(J) shining

Fill-ins
Choose the best word to fill in the blank in each sentence.

lucid	**lucre**	**luminous**	**lustrous**	**Machiavellian**
machinations	**maelstrom**	**magnanimity**	**maligned**	**malingering**

1. The magazine *Scientific American* can be relied on to provide _____ discussions of complex scientific topics.
2. We could only imagine the _____ maneuvering that allowed Stan to replace his boss as the company's manager.
3. The Sun is by far the most _____ object in the daytime sky.
4. Tired of being _____ as a coach who "can't win the big games," Coach Butler resolved that his team would be ready for the Super Bowl.
5. The lure of _____ draws many people to speculate in the stock market.
6. Harriet Beecher Stowe described saintliness as "a certain quality of _____ and greatness of soul that brings life within the circle of the heroic."
7. The soldiers marched toward battle under the _____ Moon.
8. The book tells the story of a young British soldier thrust into the _____ of the Napoleonic Wars.
9. One of a military commander's most difficult tasks is to separate soldiers who are seriously battle-stressed from those who are merely _____ .

10. No one outside a few powerful party leaders could say by what
_____ they had managed to have their crony nominated to
run for governor.

Sense or Nonsense
Indicate whether each sentence makes good sense or not.
Put S (SENSE) if it does, and put N (NONSENSE) if it does not.

1. Several of us malingered late at the party, discussing politics. _____
2. The dual pursuits of lucre and adventure have been the motivation of many explorers throughout history. _____
3. The mechanic maligned my tires, so I took my car to another mechanic. _____
4. Most offices seem to have at least one Machiavellian schemer, ready to do almost anything to get ahead. _____
5. Eric proposed to Wendy, calling her eyes "as lustrous as this diamond that will soon be on your finger." _____

UNIT 49

**malleable* adj. capable of being shaped by pounding; impressionable

> Behaviorists *such as B. F. Skinner believe that human nature is* **malleable**, *and that people's behavior can be changed by changing their environment.*

Terms from the Arts, Sciences, and Social Sciences

Behaviorists: followers of behaviorism, the school of psychology that seeks to explain behavior entirely in terms of observable responses to environmental stimuli

---

**maverick* n. dissenter

> *Bernie Sanders of Vermont has a reputation as a* **maverick**; *he is one of only two members of the United States Congress who is independent (that is, not a member of the Republican or Democratic Party).*

megalomania n. delusions of power or importance

> *In his farewell speech the retiring trial judge warned his colleagues to beware of* **megalomania** *as they exercise their power in the courtroom.*

menagerie *n.* a variety of animals kept together

> *Linda seems to take home every abandoned pet in the town; she now has an incredible **menagerie** of dogs, cats, turtles, rabbits, and other animals.*

*mendacious *adj.* dishonest

> *The judge ruled the testimony inadmissible because he considered it **mendacious**.*

mendicant *n.* beggar

> *In Thailand it is traditional for young men to become monks for a year, a period during which they become **mendicants**.*

*meretricious *adj.* gaudy; plausible but false; specious

> *One of the allures of jargon is that it can make a poor idea appear worthwhile, or something **meretricious** easier to accept because it is dressed in fancy language.*

mesmerize *v.* to hypnotize

> *The audience sat, **mesmerized**, listening to the retired soldier's account of hand-to-hand combat against the Japanese in New Guinea during World War II.*

*metamorphosis *n.* change; transformation

> *In recent years, many areas of China have been undergoing a **metamorphosis**, transforming themselves from predominantly agricultural areas to industrial ones.*

metaphysics *n.* a branch of philosophy that investigates the ultimate nature of reality

> *To skeptics, **metaphysics** is an arbitrary search for a chimerical truth.*

Metaphysical is an adjective meaning pertaining to metaphysics.

> *Some critics of evolution object to its implication that human thought is reduced to a peripheral phenomenon; they find it implausible that the ability to conceptualize—to write a sonnet, a symphony, a ***metaphysical** treatise—would have evolved in early hominids solely as a secondary effect.*

Metaphysician is a noun meaning a person who is an expert in metaphysics.

> *Whether we are aware of it or not, we are all **metaphysicians** in the sense that we all have beliefs about what things are the most real; for example, a person who believes in God may believe that God is the "ultimate reality."*

REVIEW 49

Matching
Match each word with its definition.

1. malleable	(A)	dissenter
2. maverick	(B)	variety of animals kept together
3. megalomania	(C)	transformation
4. menagerie	(D)	beggar
5. mendacious	(E)	delusions of power
6. mendicant	(F)	branch of philosophy that examines the nature of reality
7. meretricious	(G)	hypnotize
8. mesmerize	(H)	impressionable
9. metamorphosis	(I)	gaudy
10. metaphysics	(J)	dishonest

Fill-ins
Choose the best word to fill in the blank in each sentence.

malleable	mavericks	megalomania	menagerie
mendacious	mendicant	meretricious	mesmerized
metamorphosed	metaphysical		

1. Realist novelists such as Charles Dickens seem to have had little interest in _____ questions; rather, they seem to have been interested mainly in analyzing social and psychological reality.
2. We were amazed when we saw Lionel after ten years; he had _____ from a lazy, carefree young man into a hard-working and responsible member of the community.
3. Tom spent one year as a _____ monk before becoming a priest.
4. It is hard to escape the feeling that it requires at least a touch of _____ to run for the office of President of the United States.
5. For many years the prevailing view among social scientists was that human nature is essentially _____ ; however, recent thinking in the field has placed more emphasis on the part played by genes in human nature.
6. The World Wide Web has made it easier for _____ to have their views on controversial issues heard.
7. The judge ruled that the defendant's argument was rejected as disingenuous and _____ .
8. The students, _____ by the professor's fascinating lecture, did not realize the class had run overtime.

9. The writer's biographer could not escape the conclusion that her subject had given _____ testimony on various occasions.

10. The local SPCA shelter has a _____ of animals—parrots, cats, dogs, and many others.

Sense or Nonsense

Indicate whether each sentence makes good sense or not.
Put S (SENSE) if it does, and put N (NONSENSE) if it does not.

1. One thing that no one disputes is that metaphysics does more than any other area of human pursuit to put food on the table. _____

2. Many people consider it unfair that approximately two hundred super-wealthy mendicants control 60 percent of the country's wealth. _____

3. In four years, Leonard Rice has metamorphosed from a gangling 140-pound freshman third-string football player into a 210-pound All-State tailback. _____

4. The party leader can always count on the vote of a group of loyal party mavericks. _____

5. The teacher regards her students as malleable clay that she can mold into fine, intelligent young people. _____

UNIT 50

meteorological *adj.* concerned with the weather

> *Some experts believe that reports of UFOs are attributable to natural astronomical or **meteorological** phenomena.*

Meteorology is a science that deals with weather and atmospheric phenomena.

Meteorologists are those who study meteorology or forecast weather conditions.

> *The term "butterfly effect" to refer to the process driving chaotic systems was first used in 1979 by **meteorologist** E. M. Lorenz in an address entitled, "Predictability: Does the Flap of a Butterfly's Wings in Brazil Set Off a Tornado in Texas?"*

*meticulous *adj.* very careful; fastidious

> *Science is an empirical field of study based on the belief that the laws of nature can best be discovered by **meticulous** observation and experimentation.*

mettle *n.* courage; endurance

In many cultures, young men are expected to test their **mettle** by performing difficult and dangerous tasks.

mettlesome *adj.* full of courage and fortitude; spirited

The **mettlesome** young officer was well regarded by all the senior officers.

Do not confuse *mettlesome* with *meddlesome*, which means "inclined to interfere."

microcosm *n.* a small system having analogies to a larger system; small world

For many years the atom was seen as a sort of **microcosm** of the larger universe, with electrons—analogous to the planets of a solar system—orbiting the nucleus, or "sun."

militate *v.* to work against

The manager asked all of his employees to think of any factors that might **militate** against the project's success.

minatory *adj.* threatening; menacing

Intelligence information suggests **minatory** troop concentrations on the border.

minuscule *adj.* very small

Ancient geological processes are beyond the scope of carbon-14 dating (which is at most 120,000 years) because the amount of carbon-14 in material from such processes that has not decayed is **minuscule**.

minutia *n.* petty details

President Ronald Reagan said that a president should concentrate on the formulation and execution of broad policy and leave the **minutia** of running the country to subordinates.

***misanthrope** *n.* one who hates humanity

One of the most famous **misanthropes** in literature is the protagonist of the seventeenth century French writer Moliere's play Le Misanthrope (The Misanthrope).

REVIEW 50

Matching
Match each word with its definition.

1.	meteorological	(A)	courage; endurance
2.	meticulous	(B)	very small
3.	mettle	(C)	very careful; fastidious
4.	mettlesome	(D)	to work against
5.	microcosm	(E)	one who hates humanity
6.	militate	(F)	a small system having analogies to a larger system
7.	minatory	(G)	full of courage and fortitude; spirited
8.	minuscule	(H)	concerned with the weather
9.	minutia	(I)	threatening
10.	misanthrope	(J)	petty details

Fill-ins
Choose the best word to fill in the blank in each sentence.

meteorological	**meticulous**	**mettle**	**mettlesome**
microcosm	**militates**	**minatory**	**minuscule**
minutia	**misanthropic**		

1. After a month of inter-squad scrimmage, the members of the football team were eager to test their _____ against another team.
2. _____ data collected from around the world helps scientists to get an accurate picture of the world's weather patterns.
3. In many of Arthur Conan Doyle's Sherlock Holmes stories the detective reveals quite strong _____ tendencies.
4. The student's laziness _____ strongly against the likelihood of his success.
5. In the retired general's memoirs, he says that most of the battles he fought were won through a combination of courage on the part of soldiers, _____ planning, and luck.
6. The student stood silent as the teacher scolded him, her hand making _____ gestures.
7. Political pollsters keep a close watch on the town because they view it as a representative _____ of American society.
8. The _____ horse can only be controlled by a very skillful rider.
9. Engineers decided that the anomaly was so _____ that it could safely be ignored.

10. The general's factotum deals with the _____ of everyday life, leaving him free to do his job as commander of the Third Division.

Sense or Nonsense

Indicate whether each sentence makes good sense or not.
Put S (SENSE) if it does, and put N (NONSENSE) if it does not.

1. The poison is so powerful that even minuscule amounts of it can cause harm. _____
2. The diary contains a meticulous record of the events of the poet's life when she traveled to France in 1888. _____
3. "Stop being mettlesome and mind your own business," we told the busybody. _____
4. "Not only do I not like human beings in the abstract, I don't like even one individual member of the human race," the misanthrope declared. _____
5. The scientist's meteorological record deals exclusively with meteors and comets in orbit around the Sun. _____

UNIT 51

miscellany n. mixture of writings on various subjects

*The book is a fascinating **miscellany** collected from the writer's life work.*

miscreant n. villain; criminal

*The public execution of **miscreants** was common in Great Britain in the eighteenth century.*

*misogynist n. one who hates women

*Some people have called the philosopher Freidrich Nietzsche a **misogynist** because of the numerous negative comments he made about women.*

*mitigate v. to cause to become less harsh, severe, or painful; alleviate

*Although the Supreme Court under the leadership of Chief Justice Warren Burger did not rescind any of the fundamental rulings of the Warren Court that preceded it, its decisions did **mitigate** the effects of some of the rulings of the Warren Court.*

Terms from the Arts, Sciences, and Social Sciences

Warren Court: Earl Warren was named chief justice of the Supreme Court in 1953, and served on the Court until 1969. Under his leadership the Supreme Court tended to interpret the Constitution boldly, frequently with the result that disadvantaged people were helped.

Mitigation is a noun meaning the act of reducing the severity or painfulness of something.

> *Before sentencing the woman, the judge asked if she had anything to say in* **mitigation**.

mnemonic *adj.* related to memory; assisting memory

> *In the introduction to a collection of poetry,* By Heart, *the British poet Ted Hughes says that "the more absurd, exaggerated, grotesque" the images used as a* **mnemonic** *device to help remember a poem, the easier it will be to recall.*

Mnemonics is a system that develops and improves the memory.

> *Symbolic languages—the second generation of computer languages—were developed in the early 1950s, making use of* **mnemonics** *such as "M" for "multiply," which are translated into machine language by a computer program.*

modicum *n.* limited quantity

> *The scientist Carl Sagan wrote about astronomy and other scientific subjects in a way that enabled a reader with even a* **modicum** *of knowledge of science to understand what he was saying.*

*mollify *v.* to soothe

> *The prime minister tried to* **mollify** *people protesting the tax increase with a promise that she would order a study of other means to raise revenue.*

monolithic *adj.* solid and uniform; constituting a single, unified whole

> *In the fifteenth century, there was a significant movement to revitalize the Church from within; however, it had become so* **monolithic** *over the centuries and contained so many vested interests that piecemeal reform was difficult and ineffective.*

*morose *adj.* ill-humored; sullen

> *The assessment of some skeptical critics of existentialism is that it is generally a view of life created by a group of thinkers whose distinguishing characteristic is that they are* **morose**.

motley *adj.* many colored; made up of many parts

> *The new political party is made up of a* **motley** *group of people who are unhappy with the existing parties.*

REVIEW 51

Matching
Match each word with its definition.

1. miscellany	(A) solid and uniform
2. miscreant	(B) villain
3. misogynist	(C) limited quantity
4. mitigate	(D) ill humored; sullen
5. mnemonic	(E) mixture of writings on various subjects
6. modicum	(F) one who hates women
7. mollify	(G) related to memory
8. monolithic	(H) many colored; made up of many parts
9. morose	(I) to alleviate
10. motley	(J) to soothe

Fill-ins
Choose the best word to fill in the blank in each sentence.

miscellany	miscreant	misogynist	mitigate	mnemonic
modicum	mollify	monolithic	morose	motley

1. The writer was able to offer constructive criticism of the feminist movement without being called a _____ .
2. To _____ war "hawks," the president ordered a one-week bombing campaign against the country.
3. Socialists tend to view big business as _____ ; however, many large corporations are in direct competition with one another, and thus collusion is usually not to their advantage.
4. Many people find it useful to use _____ devices to memorize information.
5. The volume contains a _____ of the writings of Walt Whitman.
6. Mr. Samuels was _____ for over a month following the death of his beloved wife.
7. In the nineteenth century, accurate prognosis based on the history of disease began to be possible, but it was not until the twentieth century that doctors were able to actually cure a number of diseases rather than merely _____ their effects.
8. "I'm not looking for adulation, just a _____ of respect," the angry teacher told his class.

9. The judge said she had no alternative but to sentence the
_____ to 20 years imprisonment.
10. The protest began with a _____ group of people from virtually all occupations.

Sense or Nonsense
Indicate whether each sentence makes good sense or not.
Put S (SENSE) if it does, and put N (NONSENSE) if it does not.

1. Mnemonic devices currently supply nearly 20 percent of the country's electric power. _____
2. Anyone with even a modicum of common sense could see that the plan had little chance of success. _____
3. Hindus believe that one should not be morose as one approaches death, since physical death means only the death of the body and not the soul. _____
4. The speaker's misogynist comments drew the ire of several women's rights groups. _____
5. The president ordered the creation of a commission to study ways to mitigate the effects of unemployment on the poor. _____

UNIT 52

multifarious *adj.* diverse

> *Modern technology is so complex and **multifarious** that it requires thousands of specialists to devise and operate; thus, even a brilliant engineer could not by himself fabricate a sophisticated radio or computer without the help of existing black boxes and expertise.*

*mundane *adj.* worldly as opposed to spiritual; concerned with the ordinary

> *Fundamentalists contend that the Bible's account of the creation is literally true, while others believe that it is the retelling of a powerful myth current in the Middle East that sought to explain the **mundane** in spiritual language.*

Terms from the Arts, Sciences, and Social Sciences

Fundamentalists: those who stress adherence to a set of basic beliefs, especially in religion. Specifically, fundamentalism refers to the movement in Protestantism stressing a literal interpretation of the Bible.

---

necromancy *n.* black magic

> *Television might seem like **necromancy** to a time traveler from the fifteenth century.*

negate *v.* to cancel out; nullify

> *The soldiers' poor treatment of the prisoners **negated** the goodwill they had built up among the population.*

neologism *n.* new word or expression

> *The word "anesthesia" was the **neologism** of the American physician and poet Oliver Wendell Holmes, who used it in 1846 in a letter to Dr. William Morton, who had recently demonstrated the use of ether; the word is derived from the Latin word* anaisthesia, *meaning "lack of sensation."*

*neophyte *n.* novice; beginner

> *The school provides extensive support and guidance for **neophyte** teachers.*

nexus *n.* a means of connection; a connected group or series; a center

> *Wall Street is the **nexus** of America's financial system.*

nonplussed *adj.* bewildered

> *The members of the football team were **nonplussed** by the presence of a female reporter in the locker room.*

nostalgia *n.* sentimental longing for a past time

> *The product's marketing is centered on **nostalgia** for the 1950s.*

The adjective is *nostalgic*.

> *The idea of an extended family existing in nineteenth-century America consisting of loving uncles and doting aunts has been shown to be largely a product of a **nostalgic** and romanticized view of the past.*

nostrum *n.* medicine or remedy of doubtful effectiveness; supposed cure

> *Although there are many **nostrums** urged on obese consumers, the only effective remedy for this condition is prosaic but nonetheless valid: eat less and exercise more.*

REVIEW 52

Matching
Match each word with its definition.

1. multifarious	(A) to cancel out
2. mundane	(B) novice
3. necromancy	(C) black magic
4. negate	(D) diverse
5. neologism	(E) sentimental longing for a past time
6. neophyte	(F) new word or expression
7. nexus	(G) bewildered
8. nonplussed	(H) remedy of doubtful effectiveness
9. nostalgia	(I) a connected group or series
10. nostrum	(J) worldly as opposed to spiritual

Fill-ins
Choose the best word to fill in the blank in each sentence.

multifarious	**mundane**	**necromancy**	**negated**	**neologisms**
neophyte	**nexus**	**nonplussed**	**nostalgia**	**nostrums**

1. A number of commentators have argued that the benefits offered by television are _____ by its narcotic effect on viewers.
2. Some theologians regard attempts to prove God's existence logically valuable largely as pointers toward God, helping to turn a person's attention from the _____ to the spiritual.
3. Even the normally unflappable police officer was _____ when confronted by the armed suspect.
4. Many _____ for "correcting" English to make it more consistent and "rational" have been proposed, but the language is robust and has survived such attempts.
5. Although intelligence agents have identified parts of the terrorist organization around the world, they are still working to locate its _____ .
6. Dr. Robert Burchfield, chief editor of the *Oxford English Dictionary*, has estimated that approximately 90 percent of English _____ originate in the United States.
7. The head football coach at a Division I college has _____ duties, such as supervising the coaching staff, recruiting players, and talking to the media.
8. The advertisement is based on _____ for an America that probably never existed.

9. The _____ novelist was fortunate to have the advice of an established older writer.
10. A colorful term used to belittle something regarded as nonsense is "voodoo"; another one is "_____ ."

Sense or Nonsense

Indicate whether each sentence makes good sense or not.
Put S (SENSE) if it does, and put N (NONSENSE) if it does not.

1. Mrs. Morrison was nonplussed when she discovered that her husband was a humanoid creature from the planet Varga, a small planet in a nearby galaxy. _____
2. After suffering through ten losing football seasons in a row, the president of the college's alumni association suggested—somewhat sarcastically, no doubt—hiring a necromancer to replace the current head coach. _____
3. It is generally advisable to avoid neologisms such as "like" and "and" when writing. _____
4. After running the giant corporation for 30 years, the retiring CEO found himself looking forward to a simple life doing mundane tasks around his house. _____
5. The speaker mounted the nostrum to give the keynote speech of the convention. _____

UNIT 53

nugatory *adj.* trifling; invalid

> *The historian has a knack for focusing on information that appears nugatory but that, upon examination, illuminates the central issue.*

*obdurate *adj.* stubborn

> *Coach Knight is obdurate about one thing: the offensive line is the heart of his football team.*

*obsequious *adj.* overly submissive

> *Tom's tendency to submit meekly to any bullying authority is so great that his wife suggested he overcome this obsequiousness by taking an assertiveness training course.*

obsequy *n.* funeral ceremony (often used in the plural, obsequies)

> *Solemn obsequies were held for President John F. Kennedy following his assassination on November 22, 1963.*

*obviate *v.* to make unnecessary; to anticipate and prevent

*An experienced physician can often discern if a patient's symptoms are psychosomatic, thus **obviating** the need for expensive medical tests.*

*occlude *v.* to shut; block

*One of the primary uses of solar cells is in spacecraft to provide electric power; this is because space is an environment uniquely suited to these devices since it has no weather to **occlude** the Sun and it is not susceptible to interruptions in sunlight caused by the rotation of the Earth.*

occult *adj.* relating to practices connected with supernatural phenomena

In his book Supernature *the biologist Lyell Watson explores what he regards as phenomena on the border between natural and **occult** phenomena.*

odyssey *n.* a long, adventurous voyage; a quest

*Steve's quest for enlightenment took him on a spiritual **odyssey** that helped him to gain an understanding of many philosophers and religions.*

*officious *adj.* too helpful; meddlesome

*Some of us on the tour found the guide **officious**, but others thought she was helpful and courteous.*

olfactory *adj.* concerning the sense of smell

*Wine connoisseurs say that the **olfactory** senses play as important a part in appreciating good wine as the sense of taste.*

REVIEW 53

Matching
Match each word with its definition.

1. nugatory	(A)	too helpful
2. obdurate	(B)	overly submissive
3. obsequious	(C)	stubborn
4. obsequy	(D)	a long voyage
5. obviate	(E)	to shut; block
6. occlude	(F)	funeral ceremony
7. occult	(G)	trifling; invalid
8. odyssey	(H)	practices connected with supernatural phenomena
9. officious	(I)	concerning the sense of smell
10. olfactory	(J)	to make unnecessary

Fill-ins
Choose the best word to fill in the blank in each sentence.

nugatory	**obdurate**	**obsequious**	**obsequies**	**obviated**
occludes	**occult**	**odyssey**	**officious**	**olfactory**

1. The assertiveness-training course helped Jeremy go from being _____ to being assertive and confident.
2. Nuclear power has _____ the needs for submarines to refuel frequently, allowing long undersea voyages.
3. Sometimes a/an _____ stimulus can trigger a memory associated with that particular smell.
4. The director of the government agency encouraged workers to provide efficient service without being _____ .
5. The _____ has been described as what does not fit into a rationalistic view of the world.
6. Astronomers welcome an eclipse of the Sun because when the Moon _____ the light of the Sun, observation of that body becomes easier.
7. The president is _____ about the issue; he will not negotiate with terrorists.
8. In the television show *Star Trek: The Next Generation*, the *Enterprise* embarks on a/an _____ to explore the Universe.
9. After the judge ruled the evidence he had presented to the court to be _____ , the lawyer muttered jocularly to his partner, "Negatory."

10. Solemn _____ were held for Pope John Paul II after his death in 2005.

Sense or Nonsense

Indicate whether each sentence makes good sense or not.
Put S (SENSE) if it does, and put N (NONSENSE) if it does not.

1. Modern refinement in olfactory processes have made it possible to mass-produce complex electronic circuits. _____
2. Since the Sun was occluded by clouds, the sailor could not use it to determine his position. _____
3. After the couple retired they went on an odyssey around the world. _____
4. Science is concerned primarily with the study of occult phenomena. _____
5. The obdurate student refused to study despite repeated warnings that he would fail if he did not start to work in the course. _____

UNIT 54

oligarchy n. form of government in which power belongs to only a few leaders

> In 411 B.C., democratic government was overthrown in Athens and a conservative **oligarchy** called the Four Hundred came to power.

*onerous adj. burdensome

> The duty the judge considers most **onerous** is sentencing convicted criminals.

onomatopoeia n. formation or use of words that imitate sounds of the actions they refer to

> One theory of the origin of language is that it began as a sort of **onomatopoeia** as early humans imitated sounds they heard.

*opprobrium n. disgrace; contempt

> It is difficult to imagine the **opprobrium** heaped on a person who is a traitor to his or her group.

ornithologist n. scientist who studies birds

> **Ornithologists** believe that there currently exist only about twenty individuals of a bird called the Balinese sparrow.

*oscillate *v.* to move back and forth

 *The teacher **oscillates** between a student-centered approach to teaching and a subject-centered approach.*

*ostentatious *adj.* showy; trying to attract attention; pretentious

 *A member of the bourgeoisie might purchase a vacation home on Maui or Cape Cod that some would regard as an **ostentatious** display of wealth, but that the person regards as simply a pleasant place to go on vacation.*

overweening *adj.* presumptuous; arrogant; overbearing

 *The ancient Greeks believed that **overweening** pride—what they called* hubris—*would be punished, eventually, by the gods.*

paean *n.* song of joy or triumph; a fervent expression of joy

 *Fundamentally, the poem is a **paean** of joy, celebrating the coming of democracy to the country.*

paleontology *n.* study of past geological eras through fossil remains

 *Primatology, together with anthropology, **paleontology**, and several other fields, has given scientists a fairly accurate picture of the evolution of* homo sapiens.

A *paleontologist* is an expert in the field of paleontology.

 *The attempts of the Jesuit priest and **paleontologist** Teilhard de Chardin to reconcile evolution and the Catholic dogma of original sin were regarded by Church authorities as nearly heretical, and he had to abandon his position in 1926.*

Terms from the Arts, Sciences, and Social Sciences

Primatology: the branch of zoology that deals with the study of primates (that is, mammals belonging to any of the suborders of primates: Anthropoides (humans, great apes, and several others), Prosimi (lemurs and several others), and Tarsiodea. Primates are characterized by a high level of social interaction, flexible behavior, and use of hands.

REVIEW 54

Matching
Match each word with its definition.

1.	oligarchy	(A)	disgrace; contempt
2.	onerous	(B)	showy
3.	onomatopoeia	(C)	burdensome
4.	opprobrium	(D)	song of joy or triumph
5.	ornithologist	(E)	government by a few leaders
6.	oscillate	(F)	to move back and forth
7.	ostentatious	(G)	presumptuous; arrogant
8.	overweening	(H)	scientist who studies birds
9.	paean	(I)	study of past geological eras through fossil remains
10.	paleontology	(J)	formation of words that imitate sounds of actions they refer to

Fill-ins
Choose the best word to fill in the blank in each sentence.

oligarchy	onerous	onomatopoeia	opprobrium
ornithologists	oscillating	ostentatious	overweening
paeans	paleontologists		

1. After the end of the war, churches across the country rang out _____ of joy.
2. The country is ruled by an _____ consisting of senior military officers.
3. Over the last few days, the weather has been _____ between sunny and cloudy.
4. _____ are studying a bird that can fly without stopping from Scotland to Africa.
5. The physician faced the _____ task of telling the patient that the disease was terminal.
6. The system of gathering, identifying, dating, and categorizing fossils allows _____ to place newly discovered fossils in their proper place, making their picture of the past progressively more accurate.
7. An argument for the wearing of school uniforms is that it discourages _____ displays of wealth through the wearing of expensive jewelry and clothing.

8. The manager's _____ ambition led her to do something she regretted for the rest of her life: she told a lie about a vice-president to help her get his job.
9. The country incurred global _____ for its poor treatment of prisoners of war.
10. The word "ping-pong" arose from _____ ; the sound of the words is similar to the sound of a table tennis ball hitting first one paddle and then another.

Sense or Nonsense
Indicate whether each sentence makes good sense or not.
Put S (SENSE) if it does, and put N (NONSENSE) if it does not.

1. Onomatopoeia helps scientists to understand the nature of the atom. _____
2. The paeans live a basic existence, subsisting mostly on rice and vegetables. _____
3. Ornithologists are concerned that Canadian geese migrating south no longer have enough places to rest and feed along the way. _____
4. Geologists called in a paleontologist to examine fossils they had uncovered. _____
5. When it was discovered that the scientist had published a paper based on data he knew was falsified, he received the opprobrium of the scientific community. _____

UNIT 55

pallid *adj.* lacking color or liveliness

*Archeological evidence indicates that women have been using makeup to give color to a **pallid** face for millennia.*

panegyric *n.* elaborate praise; formal hymn of praise

*Many **panegyrics** were written to Abraham Lincoln in the years after his death, and he has become one of the most revered figures in American history.*

*paragon *n.* model of excellence or perfection

*The epic poet Homer was regarded by the ancient Greeks as a **paragon** of literary excellence.*

*partisan *adj.* one-sided; committed to a party, group, or cause; prejudiced

Supporters of constitutional monarchy believe that while in this system, as it is generally practiced today, virtually all power is vested in popularly elected assemblies, the institution of the monarchy continues to serve a purpose as a focus of national unity above the furor of **partisan** politics.

*pathological *adj.* departing from normal condition

People sometimes confound psychology and psychiatry: the former is the science that studies cognitive and affective functions, both normal and **pathological**, in human beings and other animals, whereas the latter is a branch of medicine that deals with mental disorders.

Pathology is the noun.

Some of the most spectacular examples of spin-off in the twentieth century are the advances that have been made in medicine as an unforeseen result of pure biological research; an example of this is diagnostic testing for defective genes that predispose a person to certain **pathologies**.

Pathos is a quality that causes a feeling of pity or sorrow. It is pronounced **PAY-thahs**.

patois *n.* a regional dialect; nonstandard speech; jargon

In Singapore the lingua franca is increasingly becoming Singapore English, widely regarded as a **patois**.

*paucity *n.* scarcity

An argument sometimes advanced for euthanasia is that the amount of money spent on prolonging a person's life for several months is exorbitant in relation to the **paucity** of funds available for preventive health programs and child health, both of which are highly cost-effective.

*pedantic *adj.* showing off learning

The Sophists have acquired a reputation as being learned but rather **pedantic** entertainers who gave didactic talks on every subject under the Sun; the truth, however, is that some of the Sophist philosophers (notably Protagoras) were very able thinkers.

The noun pedant means an uninspired, boring academic.

*pellucid *adj.* transparent; translucent; easily understood

> *Two writers often mentioned as having an admirably **pellucid** style are Bertrand Russell and George Orwell.*

*penchant *n.* inclination

> *Sue has a **penchant** for science, while her brother is more interested in the arts.*

REVIEW 55

Matching
Match each word with its definition.

1. pallid	(A) regional dialect; nonstandard speech	
2. panegyric	(B) one-sided	
3. paragon	(C) showing off learning	
4. partisan	(D) departing from normal condition	
5. pathological	(E) inclination	
6. patois	(F) transparent; easily understood	
7. paucity	(G) model of excellence	
8. pedantic	(H) lacking color or liveliness	
9. pellucid	(I) scarcity	
10. penchant	(J) elaborate praise	

Fill-ins
Choose the best word to fill in the blank in each sentence.

pallid	panegyric	paragons	partisan	pathology
patois	paucity	pedantic	pellucid	penchant

1. Subtle differences in symptoms between one patient and another one with a similar condition allow a competent doctor to diagnose the nature of the underlying _____ .
2. The textbook was so well written and edited that students describe it as "wonderfully _____ ."
3. Academic writing should be erudite without being _____ .
4. The job of political scientists is the objective study of government and politics; thus they are expected to be aloof from _____ politics.
5. The people of the area speak a _____ based on English, Spanish, and French.

6. According to archeologists, Roman tiles were not the _____ objects we see today; rather, they were painted a variety of vivid colors.

7. In his later years Lewis was able to indulge the _____ for performing music that he had as a young man.

8. The business professor assigned her students to select the three firms they would consider _____ for other companies to imitate.

9. No funeral _____ for the slain general was as eloquent as the looks of grief on the faces of the mourners at his funeral.

10. The historian is unable to reach a definite conclusion about when the battle began because of a _____ of evidence.

Sense or Nonsense

Indicate whether each sentence makes good sense or not.
Put S (SENSE) if it does, and put N (NONSENSE) if it does not.

1. Every weekend the Scott family has a gathering on the patois. ____

2. The museum has an exhibition of elaborately carved penchants. ____

3. There is a paucity of specialist doctors in many rural areas of the United States. ____

4. The class became bored listening to the pedantic, long-winded professor. ____

5. Steve's penchant for collecting things when he was a child led his mother to speculate that he might become a museum curate. ____

UNIT 56

*penury *n.* extreme poverty

> *The autobiography tells the story of the billionaire's journey from **penury** to riches beyond his imagining.*

peregrination *n.* a wandering from place to place

> *Swami Vivekananda's **peregrinations** took him all over India.*

peremptory *adj.* imperative; leaving no choice

> *The general's words were spoken in the **peremptory** tone of a man who is used to having his commands obeyed without question.*

perennial *adj.* present throughout the years; persistent

Perennial warfare has left most of the people of the country in poverty.

*****perfidious** *adj.* faithless; disloyal; untrustworthy

*The novel tells the story of the hero's **perfidious** lover.*

*****perfunctory** *adj.* superficial; not thorough; performed really as a duty

*The **perfunctory** inspection of the airplane failed to reveal structural faults in the wing.*

perigee *n.* point in an orbit that is closest to the Earth

*The Earth observation satellite reaches a **perigee** of 320 miles above the Earth's surface.*

*****permeable** *adj.* penetrable

*Wetsuits, used by divers in cold water, are **permeable** to water but designed to retain body heat.*

perturb *v.* to disturb greatly; make uneasy or anxious; cause a body to deviate from its regular orbit

*The findings that violence is increasing in schools greatly **perturbed** government officials.*

The noun *perturbation* means disturbance.

*Scientists believe that the Earth has undergone alternating periods of relatively cooler and warmer climate, and that this is due largely to fluctuations in the intensity of the greenhouse effect and **perturbations** in the Earth's orbit around the Sun.*

*****pervasive** *adj.* spread throughout every part

*It is a plausible hypothesis that the atheistic and materialistic philosophy of Marxism was readily accepted in China because of its similarities with Confucian views on spiritual matters, which had a **pervasive** influence in China for many centuries.*

The noun is *pervasiveness.*

*An indicator of the **pervasiveness** of psychotropic drugs in American society is the fact that approximately 50 percent of adults have used tranquilizers at some time in their lives.*

The verb is *pervade.*

REVIEW 56

Matching
Match each word with its definition.

1. penury		(A)	penetrable
2. peregrination		(B)	superficial
3. peremptory		(C)	point in an orbit closest to body being orbited
4. perennial		(D)	present throughout the years
5. perfidious		(E)	to disturb greatly
6. perfunctory		(F)	extreme poverty
7. perigee		(G)	imperative
8. permeable		(H)	spread throughout every part
9. perturb		(I)	a wandering from place to place
10. pervasive		(J)	faithless; disloyal

Fill-ins
Choose the best word to fill in the blank in each sentence.

penury	**peregrinations**	**peremptory**	**perennial**	**perfidious**
perfunctory	**perigee**		**permeable**	**perturbed** **pervasive**

1. Scientists calculate that the satellite will have a _____ of 120 miles from Earth.
2. Our well draws water from a _____ rock layer (an aquifer) in which the water is under pressure, so we generally do not have to use a pump.
3. Caricature is _____ in the work of the English novelist Charles Dickens.
4. Once again, Congress debated the _____ problem of the budget deficit.
5. While its diplomats were negotiating a peace settlement with the enemy, its _____ leaders were planning a full-scale invasion.
6. The great expense of his continual legal battles has practically reduced the man to _____ .
7. A proverb says that time heals everything; it might be commented, however, that its healing is rarely complete and is often _____ .
8. The rock band's _____ have taken it to over fifty cities around the world.

9. Military leaders were _____ by the report that important classified information had fallen into enemy hands.
10. The boss dismissed her employee's suggestion with a _____ laugh.

Sense or Nonsense

Indicate whether each sentence makes good sense or not. Put S (SENSE) if it does, and put N (NONSENSE) if it does not.

1. The consumer group accused the bank of using penury to amass vast profits. _____
2. The poet laureate wrote a perigee condemning the nation's king as an incompetent ruler. _____
3. Astronomers believe that the distant star's orbit is being perturbed by some unknown body. _____
4. The dictator was used to having his peremptory commands obeyed. _____
5. Typhoons are a perennial problem in the coastal areas of Southeast China during the late summer and early autumn. _____

UNIT 57

petulant *adj.* rude; peevish

> *The boy's father worried that his disobedient and **petulant** child would grow up to be a bitter and annoying man.*

*phlegmatic *adj.* calm in temperament; sluggish

> *"**Phlegmatic** natures can be inspired to enthusiasm only by being made into fanatics." (Friedrich Nietzsche)*

phoenix *n.* mythical, immortal bird that lives for 500 years, burns itself to death, and rises from its ashes; anything that is restored after suffering great destruction

> *The captain believed the battalion had been destroyed by the enemy and was amazed to see it arise, **phoenix**-like, its men still fighting valiantly.*

physiognomy *n.* facial features

> *The art teacher assigned her students to make drawings of people with a wide variety of **physiognomy**.*

*piety *n.* devoutness

Saint Bernard of Clairvaux was a medieval French monk revered for his **piety**.

piquant *adj.* appealingly stimulating; pleasantly pungent; attractive

Many of the guests enjoyed the **piquant** barbecue sauce, but others found it too spicy for their taste.

pique *n.* fleeting feeling of hurt pride

Sally left the restaurant in a fit of **pique** after her date called to say he couldn't come because he was working late.

As a verb, *pique* means to provoke or arouse.

The geologist's curiosity was **piqued** by the unusual appearance of the rock formation.

*placate *v.* to lessen another's anger; to pacify

After his team's third consecutive winless season, the Big State football coach opened his address to the irate alumni with a barrage of clichés and euphemisms to try to **placate** them: "Gentlemen, it is not my intention today to pull the wool over your eyes. Heaven only knows I have given my all. I have truly made the old college try. Unfortunately, however, by any reasonable criteria we have been less than completely successful in our endeavors, but I assure you that hope springs eternal in the human breast and next year we will rise to the occasion, put our noses to the grindstone and emerge triumphant in the face of adversity. I certainly admit that we have had a run of bad luck but that is nothing that can't be cured by true grit and determination."

placid *adj.* calm

We were amazed how the monk was able to remain **placid** despite the fire that was raging through the building.

plaintive *adj.* melancholy; mournful

After the battle all that could be heard was the **plaintive** cries of women who had lost their husbands.

REVIEW 57

Matching
Match each word with its definition.

1. petulant	(A)	calm
2. phlegmatic	(B)	calm in temperament; sluggish
3. phoenix	(C)	rude; peevish
4. physiognomy	(D)	art of judging character from facial features
5. piety	(E)	mournful
6. piquant	(F)	mythical, immortal bird
7. pique	(G)	fleeting feeling of hurt pride
8. placate	(H)	pleasantly pungent
9. placid	(I)	to pacify
10. plaintive	(J)	devoutness

Fill-ins
Choose the best word to fill in the blank in each sentence.

petulant	phlegmatic	phoenix	physiognomy	piety
piquant	piqued	placated	placid	plaintive

1. Rebecca is a quiet person, but beneath a _____ exterior lies a continual ferment of emotion.
2. The monk is admired for his _____ .
3. The only sound after the battle was the _____ cry of a soldier who had been disemboweled.
4. The teacher _____ the students' interest in geology by taking them on a field trip to look at rock formations.
5. Studies show that a person's _____ has an effect on his or her life; for example, people considered to have attractive features are more likely to be successful than those considered to be unattractive.
6. The _____ child will not stop complaining that he does not like the present he has been given.
7. Japan rose like a _____ from the destruction of World War II to become one of the world's leading industrial nations.
8. The restaurant manager apologized for the poor service and _____ the customer by saying that the meal was on the house.
9. The chef is known throughout Texas for his wonderfully _____ sauces.

10. The emergency room doctor trained herself to be _____ despite the great suffering she witnessed every day.

Sense or Nonsense
Indicate whether each sentence makes good sense or not.
Put S (SENSE) if it does, and put N (NONSENSE) if it does not.

1. The chef has prepared a range of plaintive desserts for our enjoyment. _____
2. People stare at the man because of his unusual physiognomy. _____
3. After being destroyed by an atomic bomb in 1945, the Japanese city of Hiroshima rose like a phoenix to become once again one of Japan's major cities. _____
4. Tom, with his phlegmatic and excitable personality, is not the person I would like to see in charge during a crisis. _____
5. The pastor urged the members of his congregation to show their piety by attending church every week. _____

UNIT 58

plasticity n. condition of being able to be shaped or formed; pliability

> The sociologist is continually amazed by the **plasticity** of social institutions.

platitude n. stale, overused expression

> Though Sarah's marriage didn't seem to be going well, she took comfort in the **platitude** that the first six months of a marriage were always the most difficult.

platonic adj. spiritual; without sensual desire; theoretical

> Gradually what had been a **platonic** relationship between Tim and Kyoko became a romantic one.

plethora n. excess; overabundance

> Because it deals with death and grieving, the funeral business has produced a plethora of **euphemisms** such as "slumber room" for the place where the corpse is placed for viewing.

plumb v. to determine the depth; to examine deeply

> A recurrent theme of mystical experience is "the dark night of the soul," in which a person **plumbs** the depths of despair before finding a transcendent reality that brings the person closer to what he or she regards as God.

The pronunciation of plumb is **PLUM**. Do not confuse plumb with the verb plume, which means to congratulate oneself in a self-satisfied way.

> John **plumed** himself on his ability to read both Sanskrit and Greek.

plummet v. to fall; plunge

> The fighter jet, struck by an enemy missile, **plummeted** to earth.

plutocracy n. society ruled by the wealthy

> It has been argued that modern democracies are **plutocracies** to the extent that wealth allows certain people to have a disproportionately large influence on political decision-making.

porous adj. full of holes; permeable to liquids

> If you go camping, make sure to spend enough money to buy a tent with a roof that is not **porous**.

poseur n. person who affects an attitude or identity to impress others

> The critic labeled the writer a **poseur** who was more interested in getting the public's attention than in writing good books.

*pragmatic adj. practical

> The cult of romantic love was a major factor in making a marriage for love, rather than for more **pragmatic** reasons, a ubiquitous phenomenon in the West by the nineteenth century.

Pragmatism means a practical way of approaching situations or solving problems.

> **Pragmatism** is similar to Positivism in rejecting lofty metaphysical conceptions and in asserting that the main role of philosophy is to help clarify phenomena experienced.

A pragmatist is someone who approaches situations in a practical way.

> The word "**pragmatist**" is often used to refer to someone who is willing to sacrifice his principles to expediency.

REVIEW 58

Matching
Match each word with its definition.

1. plasticity		(A)	overused expression
2. platitude		(B)	full of holes; permeable to liquids
3. platonic		(C)	practical
4. plethora		(D)	excess
5. plumb		(E)	to fall; plunge
6. plummet		(F)	spiritual; without sensual desire
7. plutocracy		(G)	pliability
8. porous		(H)	society ruled by the wealthy
9. poseur		(I)	to examine deeply
10. pragmatic		(J)	person who affects an identity to impress others

Fill-ins
Choose the best word to fill in the blank in each sentence.

plasticity	**platitudes**	**platonic**	**plethora**	**plumbed**
plummet	**plutocracy**	**porous**	**poseur**	**pragmatic**

1. The _____ of excellent rock bands makes it difficult for new bands to gain an audience.

2. The _____ clay allows the track to dry quickly.

3. Scholars are not certain whether Socrates' relation with his student Plato was only _____ .

4. The poet William Wordsworth _____ his own psyche in his masterpiece, *The Prelude, or Growth of a Poet's Mind.*

5. The motivational speaker is full of _____ , such as "Nothing succeeds like success."

6. The members of the stage club finally realized that Anthony was a _____ who enjoyed acting like an actor more than doing all the work necessary to be a real actor.

7. Some commentators have likened the United States more to a _____ than a democracy because of the great power held by the rich.

8. A _____ leader is not constrained by ideological preconceptions and continually adjusts his plans to conform to reality.

9. A compelling body of evidence has been built up by scientists suggesting that the _____ of human nature is more limited than was generally believed by social scientists for much of the twentieth century.
10. Scientists predict that the orbit of the satellite will decay over the next few days and it will _____ to Earth.

Sense or Nonsense
Indicate whether each sentence makes good sense or not.
Put S (SENSE) if it does, and put N (NONSENSE) if it does not.

1. Anthropologists and sociologists tend to stress the plasticity of human nature, whereas biologists emphasize the role of genes. _____
2. State law forbids platonic relationships between members of the same family. _____
3. The tennis court is designed to be porous enough to dry thoroughly in a few hours. _____
4. The coach told the press, "It might be a platitude, but I really mean it: We're taking the season one game at a time." _____
5. Some of his friends consider Morris to be a bit of a poseur: he loves to hang out at the café, sipping an espresso and acting as if he were America's most famous writer. _____

UNIT 59

prate *v.* to talk idly; chatter

> *The "talk radio" program allows people to call in and **prate** about their pet peeves.*

prattle *n.* meaningless, foolish talk

> *The sociologist theorizes that what may seem like **prattle** often has an important social function: what might be labeled "gossip" is an important means for people to communicate valuable information about themselves and others.*

preamble *n.* preliminary statement

> *Along with the opening words of the Declaration of Independence and the Gettysburg Address, the **preamble** to the Constitution of the United States contains some of the most memorable language in American history: "We the People of the United States, in order to form a more perfect Union, establish justice, insure domestic tranquility, provide for the common defense, promote the general welfare, and secure the blessings of liberty, to ourselves and our posterity, do ordain and establish this Constitution for the United States of America."*

*precarious *adj.* uncertain

> *The prime minister's **precarious** hold on power ended when she lost a vote of confidence in Parliament.*

precept *n.* principle; law

> *A good **precept** to follow in writing is to avoid redundancies such as "track record" (unless the record was set on a racecourse), "revert back," "free gift," and "general consensus."*

*precipitate *v.* to cause to happen; throw down from a height

> *Full-scale American entry into World War II remained unpopular with the vast majority of Americans until a declaration of war was **precipitated** by the Japanese attack on the naval base at Pearl Harbor, a day that President Roosevelt predicted, in a memorable phrase, would "live in infamy."*

*precipitate *adj.* rash; hasty; sudden

> *The secretary of state advised the president not to take **precipitate** action.*

Precipitous is another adjective meaning hasty; quickly with too little caution.

Precipitation is water droplets or ice particles from atmospheric water vapor that falls to Earth.

> *It would be helpful if the atmosphere could be induced to deposit its **precipitation** more evenly over the Earth's surface, so that some land areas are not inundated while others remain arid.*

*precursor *n.* forerunner; predecessor

> *The **precursor** to the theory of* plate tectonics *was the theory of* continental drift.

Terms from the Arts, Sciences, and Social Sciences

plate tectonics: geological theory stating that the outer part of the Earth's interior is composed of two layers, one of which "floats" on the other. According to this theory, which is widely accepted by scientists, ten major plates move in relation to one another, creating such phenomena as earthquakes and mountain building along the boundaries of the plates.

continental drift: the theory that the continents shift their positions over time

preempt *v.* to supersede; appropriate for oneself

*The movie was **preempted** for the president's emergency address to the nation.*

prehensile *adj.* capable of grasping

*Many more animals in South America have **prehensile** tails than those in Southeast Asia and Africa, possibly because the greater density of the forest there favored this adaptation over the ability to glide through the trees.*

REVIEW 59

Matching
Match each word with its definition.

1. prate	(A)	capable of grasping
2. prattle	(B)	talk idly
3. preamble	(C)	preliminary statement
4. precarious	(D)	cause to happen
5. precept	(E)	meaningless talk
6. precipitate (adj.)	(F)	supersede
7. precursor	(G)	principle; law
8. preempt	(H)	rash; hasty
9. prehensile	(I)	uncertain
10. precipitate (v.)	(J)	forerunner

Fill-ins
Choose the best word to fill in the blank in each sentence.

prated	**prattle**	**preamble**	**precarious**	**precepts**
precipitate	**precursor**	**preempted**	**prehensile**	**precipitated**

1. Thomas Edison's famous laboratory in Menlo Park, New Jersey, was a _____ to the great laboratories later created by corporations such as AT&T and IBM, out of which have poured a torrent of new techniques and devices.
2. Moral _____ vary from society to society, but all societies have sanctions against certain acts, such as murder.
3. _____ tails help many arboreal animals to find and eat food as they move through the trees.
4. Steve earns a _____ living as a part-time waiter.

5. Tired of the gossip's _____ , Alicia said she was late for an appointment so she could end the conversation.
6. The _____ to the bill describes the background of the legislation and explains how it relates to existing laws.
7. The increased tariffs in the 1930s _____ a collapse in world trade, exacerbating the Great Depression.
8. All TV and radio broadcasts have been _____ by an emergency announcement by the president.
9. The commander said he would not be pressured into making a _____ decision.
10. The retired couple _____ all evening about their latest trip to Europe, oblivious to the fact that no one had the slightest interest in what they were talking about.

Sense or Nonsense
Indicate whether each sentence makes good sense or not.
Put S (SENSE) if it does, and put N (NONSENSE) if it does not.

1. Scientists have shown that the precursor to birds was a flying dinosaur. _____
2. The Democrats have a precarious majority in the state senate. _____
3. The audience of distinguished scientists listened intently as the Nobel Prize-winning physicist prated eloquently about her latest discovery. _____
4. The man studied the religion's precepts so that he could be accepted as a convert. _____
5. A preamble to the official report describes its rationale and how the commission gathered its information. _____

UNIT 60

premonition *n.* forewarning; presentiment

> Shortly after his reelection in 1864, President Abraham Lincoln had a **premonition** of his impending death, and on April 14, 1865, he was shot and died the next day.

presage *v.* to foretell; indicate in advance

> The English poet William Blake believed his work **presaged** a new age in which people would achieve political, social, psychological, and spiritual freedom.

*presumptuous *adj.* rude; improperly bold; readiness to presume

*The new employee did not offer her advice to her boss because she was afraid he might consider it **presumptuous** for a recent graduate to make a suggestion to someone with 30 years experience in the field.*

The verb *presume* means assume or act with impertinent boldness.

*Proponents of the view **presume** that there exist only two antithetical positions, with no middle ground between their opponent's view and their own (eminently more reasonable) position.*

The noun is *presumption*.

*Anti-Semitism originated in the **presumption** that Jews were responsible for Jesus' crucifixion, and was responsible for periodic persecutions such as the expulsion of Jews from Spain in 1492.*

preternatural *adj.* beyond the normal course of nature; supernatural

*Most scientists believe that putative **preternatural** phenomena are outside the scope of scientific inquiry.*

*prevaricate *v.* to quibble; evade the truth

*Journalists accused government leaders of **prevaricating** about the progress of the war.*

primordial *adj.* original; existing from the beginning

*Scholars are divided as to whether polytheism represents a degeneration from a **primordial** monotheism, or was a precursor to a more sophisticated view, monotheism.*

Terms from the Arts, Sciences, and Social Sciences

polytheism: belief in the existence of more than one god

monotheism: belief in the existence of one god

---

*pristine *adj.* untouched; uncorrupted

*The bank's hermetically sealed vault has kept the manuscript in **pristine** condition for 50 years.*

*probity *n.* honesty; high-mindedness

*No one questioned the **probity** of the judge being considered for elevation to the U.S. Supreme Court; what was at issue was his controversial views on several important issues.*

*problematic *adj.* posing a problem; doubtful; unsettled

*The idea of the universe originating at a certain point in time seems **problematic** to many scientists.*

*prodigal *adj.* wasteful; extravagant; lavish

> *Betty warned her husband that he must stop his **prodigal** spending on sports cars and expensive clothing.*

REVIEW 60

Matching
Match each word with its definition,

1.	premonition	(A)	rude
2.	presage	(B)	doubtful
3.	presumptuous	(C)	beyond the normal course of nature
4.	preternatural	(D)	existing from the beginning
5.	prevaricate	(E)	forewarning
6.	primordial	(F)	honesty
7.	pristine	(G)	to foretell
8.	probity	(H)	wasteful
9.	problematic	(I)	to quibble
10.	prodigal	(J)	untouched

Fill-ins
Choose the best word to fill in the blank in each sentence.

premonition	presage	presumptuous	preternatural	prevaricating
primordial	pristine	probity	problematic	prodigal

1. Scientists are investigating Edna's claim to having a _____ ability to predict the future.
2. Air strikes against military bases _____ a full-scale invasion.
3. Ruth's dream contained a _____ that war would break out.
4. The museum exhibition allows visitors to experience what a _____ forest was like.
5. The president told the senator to stop _____ on the issue and give him her decision by Monday on whether she had his support.
6. Tom keeps his pride and joy, a 1966 Triumph, in _____ condition in his temperature-controlled garage.
7. One of the considerations that makes a return to a military draft _____ is that gender equality would almost certainly require the equal participation of males and females.
8. Bruce's _____ spending on luxuries left him nearly bankrupt.

9. The math student decided that it would be _____ of her to correct the error in the eminent mathematics professor's calculations.
10. The senator's unquestioned _____ and incisive intelligence made her a unanimous choice to lead the sub-committee investigating official misconduct.

Sense or Nonsense

Indicate whether each sentence makes good sense or not.
Put S (SENSE) if it does, and put N (NONSENSE) if it does not.

1. A primordial number is an integer divisible only by itself or one. _____
2. The premonition to the play introduces us to the main characters and the setting. _____
3. Some people believe that prevaricating helps to develop character because it encourages a person to make up his or her mind quickly. _____
4. The chairperson of the finance committee warned that the state's prodigal spending would have to stop. _____
5. The brain researcher believes that what may appear to be preternatural occurrences are actually the result of the activation of certain areas of the brain. _____

UNIT 61

*profound *adj.* deep; not superficial

> *There is an adage in philosophy that everyone is born either a Platonist or an *Aristotelian, meaning that everyone has a predisposition to believing either that reality is completely "here and now," or that there exists a more* **profound**, *hidden reality.*

The noun *profundity* means the quality of being profound.

prohibitive *adj.* so high as to prevent the purchase or use of; preventing; forbidding

> *Most people in poor countries are unable to purchase a computer because of its* **prohibitive** *price.*

Prohibition is the noun.

> *The word* taboo *was taken from Polynesia* (tabu *in Tongan*) *and broadened to mean any culture's* **prohibition** *of a particular object or activity.*

*Note: Aristotle was Plato's student; in contrast to Plato, he believed that there exist no entities separate from matter.

*proliferate *v.* to increase rapidly

*With the pervasive influence of American culture, "fast-food" restaurants are **proliferating** in many countries.*

Proliferation is the noun.

*A problem with the **proliferation** of jargon is that it impedes communication between different fields of knowledge.*

*propensity *n.* inclination; tendency

*There is a natural **propensity** to stress the importance of what one is saying by exaggerating it.*

*propitiate *v.* to win over; appease

*M.E.W. Sherwood, an author alive at the time of the U.S. Civil War, eloquently expressed the sacrifice made by soldiers on both sides of that great conflict: "But for four years there was a contagion of nobility in the land, and the best blood of North and South poured itself out a libation to **propitiate** the deities of Truth and Justice. The great sin of slavery was washed out, but at what a cost!"*

*propriety *n.* correct conduct; fitness

*Judges are expected to conduct themselves with **propriety**, especially in the courtroom.*

*proscribe *v.* to condemn; forbid; outlaw

*The expert in English believes that since the tendency to use hyperbole is natural and often enriches the language, it should not be **proscribed**.*

The adjective *proscriptive* means relating to prohibition.

*Proponents of the view that dictionaries should be **proscriptive**, dictating what correct usage is, believe that without such guides the standard of language will decline; however, advocates of descriptive dictionaries argue that dictionary makers have no mandate to dictate usage and therefore should merely record language as it is used.*

provident *adj.* providing for future needs; frugal

*Most people have heard the story of the prodigal grasshopper and the **provident** ant that spends the summer saving food for the winter.*

puissant *adj.* powerful

The article analyzes the similarities and differences between the Roman Empire and the British Empire when each was at its most ***puissant***.

The noun is *puissance*.

punctilious *adj.* careful in observing rules of behavior or ceremony.

The prime minister reminded his staff that they must be ***punctilious*** *in following protocol during the visit by the foreign head of state.*

REVIEW 61

Matching
Match each word with its definition.

1. profound
2. prohibitive
3. proliferate
4. propensity
5. propitiate
6. propriety
7. proscribe
8. provident
9. puissant
10. punctilious

(A) correct conduct
(B) powerful
(C) preventing; forbidding
(D) to condemn
(E) not superficial
(F) frugal
(G) inclination; tendency
(H) careful in observing rules of behavior
(I) to win over
(J) to increase rapidly

Fill-ins
Choose the best word to fill in the blank in each sentence.

| profound | prohibitive | proliferating | propensity | propitiated |
| propriety | proscribes | provident | puissant | punctilious |

1. In 1972, the United States Supreme Court voided all state and federal laws specifying the death penalty on the basis that they are unconstitutional, since they violate the eighth amendment of the Constitution, which _____ "cruel and unusual punishment."
2. As Russ grew older, he found his intellectual interests _____ rather than narrowing, as he had expected.

3. Sharon is _____ in doing her homework; every evening she reviews all of the day's classes and carefully completes the written tasks.

4. American cultural influence in the world has been described as a force more _____ than any army.

5. _____ in that country demands that young single women be accompanied in public by an adult female.

6. Defenders of philosophy say that, far from being a superfluous and self-indulgent activity, it is one of the most _____ of human enterprises, having given humankind such useful fields of thought as science, and conceived of such noble ideas as freedom, democracy, and human rights.

7. In her article the anthropologist suggests that *homo sapiens* is a species with an innate _____ for violence.

8. A belief in angry gods who must be _____ to prevent them from venting their wrath on human beings is pervasive in human cultures.

9. According to some scientists, the technology exists for establishing a base on Mars, but the cost of doing so would be _____ .

10. The _____ housekeeper insists on buying everything when it is on sale.

Sense or Nonsense
Indicate whether each sentence makes good sense or not.
Put S (SENSE) if it does, and put N (NONSENSE) if it does not.

1. The letter argues that the city council must take measures to control the proliferation of wild dogs. _____

2. No one could blame the passengers on the jetliner for being a bit puissant after a UFO was sighted flying off their plane's wing. _____

3. Throughout the priest's writings is a profound regard for the dignity and sanctity of human life. _____

4. The chief of protocol planned every official function so that propriety was strictly observed. _____

5. The prohibitive cost of many modern medical therapies makes them unsuitable for patients in poor countries. _____

UNIT 62

pungent *adj.* strong or sharp in smell or taste; penetrating; caustic; to the point

> *Slang frequently expresses an idea succinctly and **pungently**.*

purport *v.* to profess; suppose; claim

> *The United States is generally considered to be a secular society in which church and state are separate; however, religion plays a large role, since nearly everyone **purports** to believe in God and many people are members of churches.*

Purport is also a noun. Its definition is meaning intended or implied.

pusillanimous *adj.* cowardly

> *Traditionally, a ship captain is considered **pusillanimous** if he abandons his ship before everyone else has.*

The noun is *pusillanimity*, which means cowardice.

quagmire *n.* marsh; difficult situation

> *The federal government's antitrust suit in the 1990s against Microsoft created a legal **quagmire**.*

quail *v.* to cower; lose heart

> *The defendant **quailed** when the judge entered the room to announce the sentence.*

*qualified *adj.* limited; restricted

> *In Indian philosophy a position between monism at one extreme and dualism at the other is **qualified** nondualism, a philosophy in which reality is considered to have attributes of both dualism and monism.*

Terms from the Arts, Sciences, and Social Sciences

monism: the belief that reality is a unified whole consisting of one fundamental principle

dualism: the theory that two basic entities constitute reality (e.g. mind and matter or good and evil)

Qualification is a noun meaning limitation or restriction.

> *So many **qualifications** had been added to the agreement that Sue was now reluctant to sign it.*

The verb *qualify* means to modify or limit.

qualm *n.* sudden feeling of faintness or nausea; uneasy feeling about the rightness of actions

*The judge had no **qualms** about sentencing the thief to five years imprisonment.*

query *v.* to question

*Until widespread industrialization caused massive pollution in the nineteenth and twentieth centuries, the ability of the biosphere to dissipate and assimilate waste created by human activity was not **queried**.*

Query is also a noun meaning a question.

*The history professor answered the student's interesting **query** about the influence of Arabic thought on Western civilization.*

quibble *v.* to argue over insignificant and irrelevant details

*The lawyers spent so much time **quibbling** over details that they made little progress in reaching an agreement on the central issue.*

Quibble is also a noun.

*quiescent *adj.* inactive; still

*Although malignant tumors may remain **quiescent** for a period of time, they never become benign.*

The noun is *quiescence*.

REVIEW 62

Matching
Match each word with its definition.

1.	pungent	(A)	difficult situation
2.	purport	(B)	argument over insignificant details
3.	pusillanimous	(C)	to profess; suppose
4.	quagmire	(D)	inactive
5.	quail	(E)	strong or sharp in smell or taste
6.	qualified	(F)	limited
7.	qualm	(G)	cowardly
8.	query	(H)	to question
9.	quibble	(I)	lose heart
10.	quiescent	(J)	uneasy feeling

Fill-ins
Choose the best word to fill in the blank in each sentence.

pungent	purported	pusillanimous	quagmire	quailed
qualified	qualms	query	quibble	quiescent

1. The Nissan Patrol sank halfway into the _____ .
2. The _____ alien craft turned out to be an experimental aircraft performing unusual maneuvers.
3. During our tennis match we smelled the _____ odor of lamb curry being cooked.
4. The bank teller _____ as the masked robber threatened her with a gun.
5. The soldier said he has no _____ about killing the enemy since it was his duty.
6. The fortune-teller answered her customer's _____ with an ambiguous "It will come about if Fate wills it."
7. The student's essay asserts that "Humanity made great progress in the twentieth century"; however, when her teacher asked her what she meant by "progress" she _____ her statement by specifying that she meant that humanity made great economic and scientific progress.
8. The senator argued that it would be _____ for Congress to simply rubber-stamp every bill proposed by the president.
9. When asked by reporters which of the starting pitchers he thought was better, the manager replied, "I'm not going to _____ about which is better. They're both superb."
10. The patient's emotional disturbance appeared to be _____ , but the psychologist feared that it would manifest itself again soon.

Sense or Nonsense
Indicate whether each sentence makes good sense or not.
Put S (SENSE) if it does, and put N (NONSENSE) if it does not.

1. The discovery was purported to be the most important technological breakthrough of the modern age. _____
2. The head football coach called spring practice a qualified success because the conditioning program had gone well but there had been only limited progress in other areas. _____
3. The quiescent volcano is spewing out lava that is threatening to destroy the nearby town. _____

4. "Let's accept the report's conclusion and not quibble over inconsequential details," the manager told his workers. _____
5. U.S. military leaders are leery of becoming involved in a quagmire that would drain resources and limit their forces' effectiveness in other theatres. _____

UNIT 63

quorum *n.* number of members necessary to conduct a meeting

The U.S. Senate's majority leader asked three members of his party to be available to help form a quorum.

raconteur *n.* witty, skillful storyteller

Former president Bill Clinton is known as an accomplished raconteur who can entertain guests with amusing anecdotes about politics all evening.

rail *v.* to scold with bitter or abusive language

The critic of globalization railed against its effect on the poor people of the world.

raiment *n.* clothing

It took two hours for the princess' handmaidens to help her put on her splendid raiment for her coronation as queen.

ramification *n.* implication; outgrowth; consequence

The full ramification of the invention of the laser did not become apparent for many years; now it is used in a great variety of applications, from DVD players to surgery.

*rarefied *adj.* refined

Many scholars flourish in the rarefied intellectual atmosphere of the Institute for Advanced Studies in Princeton, New Jersey.

The verb *rarefy* means to make thinner, purer, or more refined.

rationale *n.* fundamental reason

The philosophy of "enlightened self-interest" justifies acting in one's own interest by asserting that this is not selfish or motivated by a "beggar thy neighbor" rationale, but is simply the best way to ensure the welfare of the entire community.

rebus *n.* puzzle in which pictures or symbols represent words

Egyptian writing uses the principle of the **rebus**, *substituting pictures for words.*

*recalcitrant *adj.* resisting authority or control

The officer had no choice but to recommend that the **recalcitrant** *soldier be court-martialed.*

*recant *v.* to retract a statement or opinion

The bishop told the theologian that he must **recant** *his heretical teaching or risk excommunication.*

REVIEW 63

Matching
Match each word with its definition.

1. quorum	(A) fundamental reason
2. raconteur	(B) implication
3. rail	(C) refined
4. raiment	(D) clothing
5. ramification	(E) witty, skillful storyteller
6. rarefied	(F) resisting authority or control
7. rationale	(G) to retract a statement or opinion
8. rebus	(H) to scold with bitter or abusive language
9. recalcitrant	(I) puzzle in which pictures or symbols represent words
10. recant	(J) number of members necessary to conduct a meeting

Fill-ins
Choose the best word to fill in the blank in each sentence.

quorum	**raconteur**	**rails**	**raiment**	**ramifications**
rarefied	**rationale**	**rebus**	**recalcitrant**	**recant**

1. A counselor was called in to talk to the _____ student.
2. Carl Sagan's novel *Contact* explores the _____ for humanity of contact with an advanced alien civilization.
3. The _____ offered for invading the country was that it posed a threat to peace in the region.

4. As a girl Sheila dreamed of being dressed in the golden _____ of a princess.
5. Every week the newspaper columnist _____ against what he calls the "unprecedented stupidity of our age."
6. Unable to obtain a _____ , leaders of the majority party had no choice but to postpone the vote on the legislation.
7. The _____ was the life of the party, telling hilarious jokes long into the evening.
8. Saint Thomas Aquinas combined an acute, practical intellect and the most _____ spirituality.
9. The fourth-grade class project was to design a _____ incorporating pictures of animals.
10. The company said it would drop its lawsuit for defamation if the journalist agreed to publicly _____ his false statement about its products.

Sense or Nonsense
Indicate whether each sentence makes good sense or not.
Put S (SENSE) if it does, and put N (NONSENSE) if it does not.

1. The witch cast a raiment on the man, turning him into a tree. _____
2. Scientists had to destroy the rebus because they were afraid it would break out of the lab and infect the population of the city. _____
3. The speaker railed against profligate government spending. _____
4. The raconteur has a repertoire of over three hundred jokes, all of which he can tell with perfect timing. _____
5. Fans questioned the rationale for the coach's decision to go for a risky two-point conversion after the touchdown rather than a nearly certain one-point conversion. _____

UNIT 64

recluse n. person who lives in seclusion and often in solitude

The monk spent three years of his life as a recluse, praying and meditating.

The adjective is *reclusive.*

John is a reclusive person who enjoys reading more than anything else.

*recondite *adj.* abstruse; profound

Many classical and biblical references known to educated nineteenth-century readers are now considered **recondite** by most readers.

redoubtable *adj.* formidable; arousing fear; worthy of respect

As a result of winning 95 percent of her cases, the prosecutor has earned a reputation as a **redoubtable** attorney.

*refractory *adj.* stubborn; unmanageable; resisting ordinary methods of treatment

The general practitioner called in specialists to help determine the cause of the patient's **refractory** illness.

The verb *refract* means to deflect sound or light.

Intermittently the ionosphere **refracts** radio waves of certain frequencies, allowing transmissions between distant points on the Earth.

refulgent *adj.* brightly shining; resplendent

On the queen's neck was a necklace of jewels, in the middle of which was a large, **refulgent** diamond.

*refute *v.* to contradict; disprove

The eighteenth-century English author Samuel Johnson claimed to have **refuted** the philosophy of idealism by kicking a large stone.

The noun is *refutation*.

Fundamentalism arose in Protestantism as a **refutation** of the liberal theology of the early twentieth century, which interpreted Christianity in terms of contemporary scientific theories.

Terms from the Arts, Sciences, and Social Sciences

Idealism: the belief that everything that exists is fundamentally mental in nature

---

regale *v.* to entertain

Former U.S. presidents Lyndon Johnson, Ronald Reagan, and Bill Clinton often **regaled** visitors with amusing political anecdotes.

*relegate *v.* to consign to an inferior position

Idealist *philosophers are a common target of satire; however, instead of* **relegating** *them all to the garbage can, one should reflect that thinkers such as Plato and* Kant *have given humanity some of its most profound ideas.*

Terms from the Arts, Sciences, and Social Sciences

Idealist: refers to the followers of the philosophy of Idealism, which holds that the object of external perception consists of ideas.

Immanuel Kant (1724–1804): German philosopher who held that the mind shapes the world as it perceives it and that this world takes the form of space and time

---

remonstrate *v.* to object or protest

Minority members of the committee **remonstrated** *with the majority members, saying that the proposal was unjust; nevertheless, it was approved.*

renege *v.* to go back on one's word

Generally, if one party to an agreement **reneges** *on its contractual obligations, it must provide appropriate compensation to the other party.*

REVIEW 64

Matching
Match each word with its definition.

1. recluse		(A) brightly shining
2. recondite		(B) to entertain
3. redoubtable		(C) abstruse; profound
4. refractory		(D) to object or protest
5. refulgent		(E) to contradict; disprove
6. refute		(F) person who lives in seclusion
7. regale		(G) stubborn; unmanageable
8. relegate		(H) to go back on one's word
9. remonstrate		(I) arousing fear
10. renege		(J) to consign to an inferior position

Fill-ins
Choose the best word to fill in the blank in each sentence.

recluse	recondite	redoubtable	refractory	refulgent
refute	regaled	relegated	remonstrated	reneged

1. The guest speaker _____ the audience with hilarious anecdotes from her childhood.
2. The school has announced plans to deal with the _____ students.
3. Students of religion have discerned a pattern in many religions in which some gods gradually attain prominence and others are _____ to an inferior status.
4. Tim _____ on his bet with Harry, claiming it had just been a joke.
5. Astronomers are studying the _____ object that suddenly appeared in the sky.
6. Edith's friends are concerned that she is becoming a _____ ; she does not go out with them anymore and rarely leaves her house.
7. The book *God and the New Physics* by the Australian physicist Paul Davies succeeds in making _____ areas of physics more comprehensible to the general public.
8. The prospect of being interviewed for admission by the _____ dean of the law school was a daunting one.
9. The conservative and liberal _____ with each other over the issue long into the night.
10. One way to _____ an argument is to show that one or more of the premises on which it is based is false.

Sense or Nonsense
Indicate whether each sentence makes good sense or not.
Put S (SENSE) if it does, and put N (NONSENSE) if it does not.

1. When learning a new subject, it is wise to start with straightforward, recondite topics first. _____
2. The retired football coach regaled the young coaches with stories from his playing days with the Green Bay Packers in the 1960s. _____
3. In the English professional soccer league, a team can be relegated from the "premier" division to a lower division because of poor performance. _____
4. The debate coach reminded his team to refute every argument made by the opposing team. _____
5. The recluse has many friends at his house every night. _____

UNIT 65

reparation *n.* amends; compensation

> *The judge said she would not sentence the man to jail on the condition that he pay full* **reparation** *to the family hurt by his crime.*

repine *v.* fret; complain

> *The president told the congressional representative he should stop* **repining** *over the lost opportunity and join the majority in exploring new ones.*

reprise *n.* repetition, especially of a piece of music

> *The standing ovation at the end of the set meant that the band had little choice but to* **reprise** *a few of their most popular tunes.*

The verb is also *reprise*.

*reproach *v.* to find fault with; blame

> *The speaker in Andrew Marvell's poem "To His Coy Mistress"* **reproaches** *his beloved for ignoring the passing of time and for not being willing to physically express her love for him.*

Reproach is also a noun.

*reprobate *n.* morally unprincipled person

> *The social worker refused to give up hope of reforming the criminal who was generally regarded as a* **reprobate**.

*repudiate *v.* to reject as having no authority

> *In the 1960s, many black leaders such as Malcolm X and Stokely Carmichael* **repudiated** *integration and nonviolence in favor of black separatism and passive resistance in the fight for civil rights.*

*rescind *v.* to cancel

> *The salesperson said he would* **rescind** *his offer to sell the goods at a 10 percent discount unless he received full payment within 24 hours.*

*resolution *n.* determination; resolve

> *Fred's* **resolution** *to succeed is unshaken despite the many setbacks he has suffered.*

resolve *n.* determination; firmness of purpose

President Abraham Lincoln displayed remarkable **resolve** *in preventing the Confederate states from seceding.*

The verb is also *resolve.*

reticent *adj.* not speaking freely; reserved; reluctant

Many people in the west are **reticent** *to criticize science, which in the view of many has become a* sacred cow.

Terms from the Arts, Sciences, and Social Sciences

sacred cow: something that is so greatly respected that it is beyond question, e.g., "The virtue of free trade is a sacred cow of modern economic theory."

REVIEW 65

Matching
Match each word with its definition.

1. reparation	(A) to blame
2. repine	(B) to fret
3. reprise	(C) determination
4. reproach	(D) firmness of purpose
5. reprobate	(E) to reject as having no authority
6. repudiate	(F) morally unprincipled person
7. rescind	(G) amends
8. resolution	(H) reserved
9. resolve	(I) repetition
10. reticent	(J) to cancel

Fill-ins
Choose the best word to fill in the blank in each sentence.

reparations	repine	reprise	reproached	reprobate
repudiated	rescinded	resolution	resolved	reticent

1. Janet _____ her friend for being lazy.
2. John _____ to study hard so he would get an "A" in chemistry.

3. The gangster _____ all his past associations with criminals in the city.
4. The company _____ its job offer when it was found that the candidate had provided falsified documents.
5. Every year Joanne makes a firm _____ to work harder.
6. The court ordered the convicted woman to make _____ to the family that she had done so much harm to.
7. The counselor was finally able to get the _____ boy to talk about the problems in his family.
8. The employee did not _____ at being assigned to do the arduous task, but rather, accepted it as a challenge.
9. The judge warned the convicted man that he was beginning to consider him a hopeless _____ who should be kept in prison away from innocent people.
10. The New Year's Eve revelers demanded a _____ of "Auld Lang Syne."

Sense or Nonsense
Indicate whether each sentence makes good sense or not.
Put S (SENSE) if it does, and put N (NONSENSE) if it does not.

1. The burden of war reparations plunged the country into a financial crisis. _____
2. The counselor is encouraging the reticent patient to talk about his feelings. _____
3. The teacher reproached the student for her sloppy work. _____
4. The gangster pledged to start a new life and repudiate his past involvement with criminals. _____
5. The couple's grandchildren decided to reprise them with a 30th anniversary party. _____

UNIT 66

reverent *adj.* expressing deep respect; worshipful

The biologist Loren Eisely had what could be described as a **reverent** attitude toward nature.

The verb is *revere*.

riposte *n.* a retaliatory action or retort

The commander decided that the enemy attack must be countered with a quick **riposte**.

rococo *adj.* excessively ornate; highly decorated; style of architecture in eighteenth-century Europe

> *In music, the* **Rococo** *period (1730–1780) comes between the preceding Baroque period and the subsequent Classical period. The highly ornamented style of the Rococo period created new forms of dissonance that to listeners in previous eras would have sounded cacophonous.*

The noted authors Lawrence Durrell and Vladimir Nabokov often wrote in a rich, almost **rococo** style.

Terms from the Arts, Sciences, and Social Sciences

Rococo: a style of architecture that made use of elaborate curved forms. Examples of the Rococo in architecture are the extremely ornate court and opera buildings of Mannheim and Stuttgart in Germany

---

rubric *n.* title or heading; category; established mode of procedure or conduct; protocol

> *The data from the experiment was so diverse that the scientist decided to design a new* **rubric** *to organize it.*

rue *v.* to regret

> *The judge told the convicted man that he would come to* **rue** *his decision to commit the crime.*

ruse *n.* trick; crafty stratagem; subterfuge

> *In July, 1999, a group of Christians from the United Kingdom traveled to various countries in which Crusaders had massacred people to apologize; however, many of the Moslems spurned this overture, believing it to be another Crusade in the form of a* **ruse**.

sage *adj.* wise

> *Samuel Johnson gave this* **sage**, *albeit hard, advice to writers wishing to improve their style: "Read over your compositions, and whenever you meet with a passage that you think is particularly fine, strike it out."*

Sage is also a noun meaning a wise older person.

salacious *adj.* lascivious; lustful

> *The school board decided that the book is too* **salacious** *to be in the school library.*

*salubrious *adj.* healthful

The **salubrious** *effects of exercise on both physical and mental health have been well documented.*

*salutary *adj.* expecting an improvement; favorable to health

"The system of universal education is in our age the most prominent and **salutary** feature of the spirit of enlightenment. . . ."
—President Benjamin Harrison, 1892

REVIEW 66

Matching
Match each word with its definition.

1. reverent	(A)	crafty stratagem
2. riposte	(B)	lustful
3. rococo	(C)	wise older person
4. rubric	(D)	excessively ornate
5. rue	(E)	expecting an improvement
6. ruse	(F)	expressing deep respect
7. sage	(G)	to regret
8. salacious	(H)	retaliatory action
9. salubrious	(I)	favorable to health
10. salutary	(J)	title or heading

Fill-ins
Choose the best word to fill in the blank in each sentence.

revere	riposte	rococo	rubric	rue
ruse	sage	salacious	salubrious	salutary

1. In Chinese culture children are expected to _____ their parents.
2. The talk show host is always ready with a clever _____ to the barbs of her guests.
3. The defendant told the members of the jury that they would _____ the day they had convicted him.
4. As a _____ , the president's press secretary opened the news conference with the statement that the government would guarantee everyone in America a minimum salary of $100,000 per year.

5. The ancient Greek philosopher Socrates was a _____ who believed that everyone must engage in his or her own search for truth.
6. The movie was given an "R" rating because of its _____ content.
7. Many people from the Midwest retire to Arizona because of the _____ climate.
8. Advocates of Prohibition believed that it would have a _____ effect on people who enjoyed drinking alcoholic beverages.
9. The author decided to discuss forced sterilization under the _____ of eugenics.
10. The _____ furniture seems out of place in the ultramodern building.

Sense or Nonsense
Indicate whether each sentence makes good sense or not.
Put S (SENSE) if it does, and put N (NONSENSE) if it does not.

1. The debater prepared clever ripostes for the arguments she expected her opponent to make. _____
2. Some readers find the writer's straightforward, rococo style boring. _____
3. Confucius was a Chinese sage revered for his wisdom. _____
4. The fraternity brother who came up with the best ruse was told he would get a date with the homecoming queen. _____
5. To have your article published in the chemistry journal, you must carefully follow the rubric provided by its editor. _____

UNIT 67

*sanction v. to approve; ratify; permit

> The establishment of the state of Israel from Palestinian territory in 1948 was the realization of a hallowed dream for Zionists, but for many Palestinians it meant the **sanctioning** of continued domination of their land by Europeans.

Sanction is also a noun meaning approval; ratification; permission.

> In the West, the institution of marriage is traditionally given formal **sanction** by both the Church and the State, which has the social function of reinforcing its importance and the seriousness of the duties it entails.

The noun *sanction* can also mean penalization.

> *The United Nations has the power to compel obedience to international law by **sanctions** or even war, but there must be unanimity for such action among the five permanent members of the Security Council.*

The verb *sanction* can also mean to penalize.

sardonic *adj.* cynical; scornfully mocking

> *Satire that is too **sardonic** often loses its effectiveness.*

*sartorial *adj.* pertaining to tailors

> *Off-screen, the glamorous actress' **sartorial** style runs more to jeans and T-shirts than to elaborate gowns.*

*satiate *v.* to satisfy

> *The bully **satiated** his fury by pummeling the helpless little boy.*

saturate *v.* to soak thoroughly; imbue throughout

> *The writer's recollection of her childhood is **saturated** with sunshine and laughter.*

saturnine *adj.* gloomy

> *When the long list of casualties from the battle were announced, the mood in the room was **saturnine**.*

satyr *n.* a creature that is half-man, half-beast with the horns and legs of a goat; it is a follower of Dionysos; a lecher

> *One of the best-known **satyrs** is Pan, the god of the woods in Greek mythology.*

savor *v.* to enjoy; have a distinctive flavor or smell

> *The coach gave his team a day off practice to **savor** their big victory.*

schematic *adj.* relating to or in the form of an outline or diagram

> *The engineer outlined the workings of the factory in **schematic** form.*

secrete *v.* produce and release substance into organism

> *The pancreas gland **secretes** a fluid that helps fat, carbohydrates, and protein to be digested in the small intestine.*

REVIEW 67

Matching
Match each word with its definition.

1. sanction		(A)	pertaining to tailors
2. sardonic		(B)	half-man, half-beast
3. sartorial		(C)	relating to a diagram
4. satiate		(D)	to approve; ratify
5. saturate		(E)	to produce and release substance into organism
6. saturnine		(F)	to satisfy
7. satyr		(G)	cynical
8. savor		(H)	gloomy
9. schematic		(I)	to enjoy
10. secrete		(J)	to soak thoroughly

Fill-ins
Choose the best word to fill in the blank in each sentence.

sanctions	sardonic	sartorial	satiate	saturated
saturnine	satyr	savored	schematic	secrete

1. Celebrating the end of her diet, Tina _____ every mouthful of the ice cream sundae.
2. A fried chicken dinner should be enough to _____ the hungry student's appetite.
3. June is one of those people whose mood can suddenly become _____ and then just as quickly become sunny and cheerful.
4. The company decided to try to sell another product because the market for personal computers had become _____ .
5. Economic _____ against the country have made life difficult for its people; even everyday necessities are becoming scarce.
6. The book claims to give advice that solves men's _____ problems easily and cheaply.
7. Hugh has a reputation as a bit of a _____ among the women in the office.
8. The electrical engineer made a _____ diagram of the circuit.
9. Cells in the mucous membrane of the stomach _____ hydrochloric acid to help in the digestion of food.

10. The satirist's unremittingly _____ tone left the reviewer feeling that here was a man of great talent who had, sadly, retreated to a bitterly cynical, even misanthropic attitude toward the world.

Sense or Nonsense

Indicate whether each sentence makes good sense or not.
Put S (SENSE) if it does, and put N (NONSENSE) if it does not.

1. The novel is a satyr on human nature. _____
2. We satiated our appetite for science fiction novels by reading twenty of them on summer vacation. _____
3. Not everyone appreciates the comedian's sardonic commentary on modern life. _____
4. Twelve hours of heavy rain left the field saturated. _____
5. I suggest you savor the food, not just gobble it down. _____

UNIT 68

sedition *n.* behavior prompting rebellion

> *The federal prosecutor argued that the journalist's article could be interpreted as an act of* **sedition** *since it strongly suggested that the government should be overturned.*

sedulous *adj.* diligent

> *The Nobel Prize-winning scientist attributed his success to what he termed "curiosity, a modicum of intelligence, and* **sedulous** *application."*

seismic *adj.* relating to earthquakes; earthshaking

> *The study of* **seismic** *waves enables scientists to learn about the Earth's structure.*

*sensual *adj.* relating to the senses; gratifying the physical senses, especially sexual appetites

> *The yogi teaches his students that attachment to* **sensual** *pleasure is one of the great hindrances to spiritual advancement.*

*sensuous *adj.* relating to the senses; operating through the senses

> *The American painter Georgia O'Keeffe is known especially for her* **sensuous** *paintings of plants and flowers and for her landscapes.*

*sentient *adj.* aware; conscious; able to perceive

> *Charles Darwin regarded many animals as being **sentient** and as having intelligence.*

The noun is *sentience.*

> *An analgesic relieves pain but unlike an anesthetic, does not cause loss of sensation or **sentience.***

servile *adj.* submissive; obedient

> *None of the dictator's **servile** citizens dared question his decree.*

sextant *n.* navigation tool that determines latitude and longitude

> *Because it enabled precise determination of position, the **sextant** quickly became an essential tool in navigation after its invention in 1731.*

shard *n.* a piece of broken glass or pottery

> *Archeologists were able to reconstruct the drinking vessel from **shards** found around the ancient campsite.*

sidereal *adj.* relating to the stars

> *A **sidereal** year is longer than a solar year by 20 minutes and 23 seconds.*

REVIEW 68

Matching
Match each word with its definition.

1. sedition	(A) operating through the senses
2. sedulous	(B) navigation tool
3. seismic	(C) behavior prompting rebellion
4. sensual	(D) piece of broken glass or pottery
5. sensuous	(E) gratifying the physical senses
6. sentient	(F) aware
7. servile	(G) diligent
8. sextant	(H) relating to the stars
9. shard	(I) submissive
10. sidereal	(J) relating to earthquakes

Fill-ins
Choose the best word to fill in the blank in each sentence.

sedition	sedulous	seismic	sensual	sensuous
sentient	servile	sextant	shards	sidereal

1. Most of the population of the occupied country behaved in a
   _____ manner toward the foreign soldiers.
2. _____ is treated so seriously because it is a threat to the
   very existence of the state.
3. The detective was _____ in collecting evidence to prove his
   client's innocence.
4. According to geologists, in its early history the Earth was continually shaken by massive _____ disturbances.
5. _____ found at the site suggest that there was human
   habitation in the area 5,000 years ago.
6. Because it is not dependent on electricity for power, the
   _____ is still used as a backup navigation tool on many
   ships.
7. The science fiction novel describes a _____ adventure.
8. The book explores the question of how _____ beings that
   evolved differently from humans would regard the world.
9. The book describes a society almost entirely dedicated to
   _____ delight.
10. The philosopher Plato believed that a process of reason, indepen-
    dent of _____ information, could help a man arrive at the
    true nature of reality.

Sense or Nonsense
Indicate whether each sentence makes good sense or not.
Put S (SENSE) if it does, and put N (NONSENSE) if it does not.

1. The French Revolution was a momentous event that sent seismic
   shocks through Western civilization. ____
2. Sidereal surveillance of the suspect provided police with enough
   evidence to make an arrest. ____
3. One of the goals of artificial intelligence is to produce a machine
   that an unbiased observer judges to be sentient. ____
4. The police captain warned the protesters that they were in
   danger of crossing the line between lawful public protest and
   sedition. ____
5. The invention of the magnetic compass and the sextant were two
   of the major developments in navigation. ____

UNIT 69

simian *adj.* apelike; relating to apes

Many people in the nineteenth century denied the evolutionary significance of the **simian** characteristics of human beings.

simile *n.* comparison of one thing with another using "like" or "as"

In his autobiographical book Chronicles, Volume 1, Bob Dylan uses two **similes** in succession to try to convey the experience of writing a song: "A song is like a dream, and you try to make it come true. They're like strange countries you have to enter."

sinecure *n.* well-paying job or office that requires little or no work

The company established the high-paying position of senior advisor as a **sinecure** for the man who had been instrumental in the company's success for so many years.

singular *adj.* unique; extraordinary; odd

The defendant's **singular** appearance made it easy for the witness to identify him as the person at the scene of the crime.

sinuous *adj.* winding; intricate; complex

The students had trouble following the philosopher's **sinuous** line of reasoning.

*skeptic *n.* one who doubts

Like the nihilist, a comprehensive philosophic **skeptic** can be a difficult person to debate: if you tell him you know you exist, he is likely to ask you to prove it—and that can be harder than it first appears.

The adjective is *skeptical.*

A good scientist is **skeptical** about inferences made from data; however, he must not be dogmatic about the possible implications the data might have.

Terms from the Arts, Sciences, and Social Sciences

nihilist: one who believes that existence and all traditional values are meaningless

---

sobriety *n.* seriousness

> The student approaches her studies with commendable **sobriety**.

sodden *adj.* thoroughly soaked; saturated

> The **sodden** field makes it difficult for the soccer players to move effectively.

*solicitous *adj.* concerned; attentive; eager

> The nurse is extremely **solicitous** of the health of every patient in the ward.

soliloquy *n.* literary or dramatic speech by one character, not addressed to others

> The nineteenth-century English poet Robert Browning used the dramatic monologue—which is essentially a **soliloquy** in a poem—successfully in many of his poems.

REVIEW 69

Matching
Match each word with its definition.

1. simian	(A) well-paying job requiring little work
2. simile	(B) seriousness
3. sinecure	(C) comparison of one thing with another using "like" or "as"
4. singular	(D) thoroughly soaked
5. sinuous	(E) unique
6. skeptic	(F) one who doubts
7. sobriety	(G) dramatic speech by one character
8. sodden	(H) concerned
9. solicitous	(I) apelike
10. soliloquy	(J) winding

Fill-ins
Choose the best word to fill in the blank in each sentence.

simian	**similes**	**sinecure**	**singular**	**sinuous**
skeptic	**sobriety**	**sodden**	**solicitous**	**soliloquy**

1. The judge recommended her law clerk for the position in the law firm as "a young person of probity and _____ ."
2. "Money is a _____ thing. It ranks with love as man's greatest source of joy. And with death as his greatest source of sorrow."
   —John Kenneth Galbraith

3. Mary complains that when they were young her husband was very _____ of her, but now he practically ignores her.
4. The _____ argued that the purported exhibition of occult powers was created by the use of conjurer's tricks.
5. We often use _____ in expressions like "as old as the hills" and "as sharp as a tack" without being consciously aware that they are similes.
6. The governor awarded his advisor with a _____ as a reward for 20 years of service to the party and the state.
7. The _____ road curves along the mountainside.
8. In Act III of *Hamlet*, Shakespeare has Hamlet speak a _____ on the question of "To be, or not to be."
9. Looking at the _____ field, the football coach realized he would have to adapt his game plan to wet conditions.
10. Before Charles Darwin proved the close biological relation between human beings and apes, many people saw human _____ characteristics as comical and inconsequential.

Sense or Nonsense
Indicate whether each sentence makes good sense or not.
Put S (SENSE) if it does, and put N (NONSENSE) if it does not.

1. The philosopher Bertrand Russell was skeptical of Idealist philosophies, believing they are based on false assumptions about knowledge. _____
2. The philosophy student compared following the treatise's long, subtle argument to following the path of a sinuous river for thousands of miles. _____
3. The poem's central simile is that the nation's leader is like a captain of a ship. _____
4. Italian mothers are famous for being so solicitous of their sons that they spend most of the day cooking for them. _____
5. The farmers are hoping for rain after the long period of hot and sodden weather. _____

UNIT 70

solvent *adj.* able to meet financial obligations
> *During the financial crisis several large banks had difficulty remaining **solvent**.*

somatic *adj.* relating to or affecting the body; corporeal
> *A psychosomatic disorder is a malady caused by a mental disturbance that adversely affects **somatic** functioning.*

*soporific *adj.* sleep producing

> For some people the best **soporific** is reading a boring book.

sordid *adj.* filthy; contemptible and corrupt

> The Monica Lewinsky scandal, which led to President Bill Clinton's impeachment in 1998, must certainly rank as one of the most **sordid** affairs in American history.

*specious *adj.* seeming to be logical and sound, but not really so

> The article systematically rebuts the **specious** argument advanced by the so-called expert in the field.

spectrum *n.* band of colors produced when sunlight passes through a prism; a broad range of related ideas or objects

> The political science course deals with the whole **spectrum** of political ideologies.

spendthrift *n.* person who spends money recklessly

> A Chinese proverb describes a paradox: Rich **spendthrifts** never save enough, but the poor always manage to save something.

The adjective *spendthrift* means wasteful and extravagant.

> Tom's **spendthrift** habits resulted in his accumulating a huge amount of credit card debt.

*sporadic *adj.* irregular

> Despite the ceasefire, there have been **sporadic** outbreaks of violence between the warring factions.

squalor *n.* filthy, wretched condition

> The family lives in **squalor** in the slums of Mexico City.

staccato *adj.* marked by abrupt, clear-cut sounds

> We listened to the **staccato** steps of the woman in high heels running down the street.

REVIEW 70

Matching
Match each word with its definition,

1. solvent	(A) filthy; corrupt
2. somatic	(B) broad range
3. soporific	(C) irregular
4. sordid	(D) able to meet financial obligations
5. specious	(E) person who spends recklessly
6. spectrum	(F) seeming to be logical and sound, but not so
7. spendthrift	(G) filthy, wretched condition
8. sporadic	(H) affecting the body
9. squalor	(I) marked by abrupt, clear-cut sounds
10. staccato	(J) sleep producing

Fill-ins
Choose the best word to fill in the blank in each sentence.

solvent	somatic	soporific	sordid	specious
spectrum	spendthrift	sporadic	squalor	staccato

1. Newspapers sometimes publish stories with _____ claims to increase sales.
2. A _____ most of his life, Alex has only recently begun to save for his retirement.
3. Many towns have an area where people live in _____ .
4. The salesperson has a sort of machine-gun way of speaking, fast and _____ .
5. The various portions of the electromagnetic _____ are allocated to broadcasters, commercial operators, amateur hobbyists, and other users.
6. _____ outbreaks of violence marred the ceasefire.
7. Economists are concerned that some of the poorest countries will have difficulty remaining _____ as interest rates rise and the amount of their debt repayments increase.
8. The long car ride was a _____ for the family's small children; soon they were fast asleep in the back of the car.
9. In recent years, medicine has placed greater emphasis on how psychological factors contribute to _____ disorders such as heart disease and cancer.
10. The governor issued a complete and public apology to put the _____ affair behind him.

Sense or Nonsense
Indicate whether each sentence makes good sense or not.
Put S (SENSE) if it does, and put N (NONSENSE) if it does not.

1. The novels of Mickey Spillane portray the sordid world of criminals. _____
2. In the logic class, students were asked to identify specious lines of reasoning in several arguments. _____
3. If you absolutely have to stay awake you should take a soporific. _____
4. The bank's president warned its directors that it could not remain solvent if it kept making bad loans. _____
5. What the tourist brochure described as "local color" was called "squalor" by a plain-speaking member of the tour group. _____

UNIT 71

stanch *v.* to stop or check the flow of

*The country's government has put controls on currency movement to **stanch** the flow of money out of the country.*

stentorian *adj.* extremely loud

*The **stentorian** speaker prefers not to use a microphone so that the audience can appreciate what he calls "the full effect of my powerful oratory."*

*stigma *n.* mark of disgrace or inferiority

*A problem with giving formal psychological treatment to a child who is believed to be poorly adjusted to society is that he may acquire a **stigma** as a result of officially being labeled as deviant, and he may act to corroborate society's expectation.*

The verb is *stigmatize*.

*The civil rights movement helped to **stigmatize** racism, augmenting legal efforts to desegregate American society.*

stint *v.* to be sparing

***Stinting** on funding for education strikes many people as shortsighted.*

Stint is also a noun meaning a period of time spent doing something

*Isaac Asimov did a short involuntary **stint** in the army as a conscript during the 1950s.*

*stipulate *v.* to specify as an essential condition

*The president's lawyer **stipulated** that he would appear before the investigative committee, but would answer only questions directly relevant to the issue at hand.*

The noun is *stipulation.*

***Stipulations** in a contract should be clear in order to obviate the need for parties to resort to litigation.*

*stolid *adj.* having or showing little emotion

*Behind the professor's **stolid** appearance is a fun-loving, gregarious character.*

stratified *adj.* arranged in layers

*One of the implications of an increasingly **stratified** economy for America might be increased social unrest.*

The noun *stratum* means a layer.

*In the English-speaking world many members of the upper classes historically have had a deprecatory attitude toward slang, a form of language they regard as indecorous and thus suitable only for the lowest **stratum** of society.*

The plural of stratum is *strata.*

*As it matured as a science, geology began to complement biology, a process that helped it to gain a more comprehensive view of the history of life on Earth by allowing fossils to be dated and identified (paleontology), often using knowledge gained from stratigraphy—the study of the deposition, distribution, and age of rock **strata**.*

The noun *stratification* is used in the sociological term *social stratification.* It refers to the hierarchical arrangement of individuals in a society into classes or castes.

*striated *adj.* marked with thin, narrow grooves or channels

*The **striated** surface suggested to the geologist that he was walking over an area in which there once had been a torrent of water.*

Striation is the noun.

*The geologist examined **striations** in the rock to learn about the glacier that had made them 10,000 years ago.*

stricture *n.* something that restrains; negative criticism

As professionals, lawyers are expected to abide by a set of ethical **strictures** in their practice of the law.

strident *adj.* loud; harsh; unpleasantly noisy

Calls for the prime minister's resignation became more **strident** after it was discovered that he had strong connections to organized crime.

REVIEW 71

Matching
Match each word with its definition.

1. stanch
2. stentorian
3. stigma
4. stint
5. stipulate
6. stolid
7. stratified
8. striated
9. stricture
10. strident

(A) to be sparing
(B) arranged in layers
(C) something that restrains
(D) to specify as an essential condition
(E) unpleasantly noisy
(F) showing little emotion
(G) marked with thin, narrow grooves
(H) extremely loud
(I) to stop or check the flow of
(J) mark of disgrace

Fill-ins
Choose the best word to fill in the blank in each sentence.

stanch	stentorian	stigma	stint	stipulate
stolid	stratified	striated	strictures	strident

1. The baseball stadium's ground rules _____ that a batter who hits a ball that bounces off the ground into the left field bleachers gets a double.
2. Luke was one of those _____ individuals who rarely show their feelings.
3. The geologists examined _____ rocks left by the retreating glaciers.
4. Modern societies tend to be _____ into classes determined by such factors as wealth and occupation.

5. They sat silently in the room, listening to the telephone's
   _____ ringing.
6. The medic used a tourniquet to _____ the woman's bleeding
   wound.
7. The speaker's _____ voice rang through the hall.
8. A two-year _____ in the navy allowed Janet to visit
   22 countries.
9. Perhaps the central paradox of poetry is that the _____
   imposed by form on a poet of talent can help produce works of
   great power.
10. In most societies there is a _____ attached to mental illness.

Sense or Nonsense
Indicate whether each sentence makes good sense or not.
Put S (SENSE) if it does, and put N (NONSENSE) if it does not.

1. The young doctor learned a lot about both medicine and human
   nature during her stint in the emergency room. _____
2. The contract stipulates that the agreement will remain in force
   unless both sides agree to cancel it. _____
3. The banker deliberately cultivated his image as a careful, stolid,
   conservative person. _____
4. The Greeks and Persians fought a stentorian battle at Thermopy-
   lae in 480 B.C. _____
5. Anthropologists believe that the society is stratified by occupation,
   with warriors at the top and workers at the bottom. _____

UNIT 72

strut *v.* to swagger; display to impress others
> *The star quarterback **strutted** around campus the entire week
> after he led his team to a 42–0 win over the county's top-ranked
> team.*

stultify *v.* to impair or reduce to uselessness
> *The professor of education believes that overreliance on rote learn-
> ing **stultifies** students' creativity.*

stupefy *v.* to dull the senses of; stun; astonish
> *After drinking three glasses of wine, Linda was **stupefied**.*

stygian *adj.* dark and gloomy; hellish

Wilfred Owens's famous poem "Dulce Et Decorum Est" describes an unfortunate soldier who was unable to get his gas mask on in time, seen through the stygian gloom of poison gas:

> *GAS! Gas! Quick, boys!—An ecstasy of fumbling,*
> *Fitting the clumsy helmets just in time;*
> *But someone still was yelling out and stumbling*
> *And floundering like a man in fire or lime.—*
> *Dim, through the misty panes and thick green light*
> *As under a green sea, I saw him drowning.*

subpoena *n.* notice ordering someone to appear in court

The judge issued a subpoena for the man but the prosecutor had little hope that he would appear because he was living abroad.

subside *v.* to settle down; grow quiet

Army personnel told the civilians to wait for the violence to subside before reentering the town.

*substantiate *v.* to support with proof or evidence

The validity of fossil identification is substantiated by data from geology and carbon-14 dating.

substantive *adj.* essential; pertaining to the substance

The judge cautioned the attorney to present only information that was substantive to the case at hand.

*subsume *v.* to include; incorporate

The philosopher described his work as an attempt to arrive at a final generalization that will subsume all previous generalizations about the nature of logic.

subversive *adj.* intended to undermine or overthrow, especially an established government

The verb is also *subvert.*

Anything that subverts the market mechanism is believed to cause anomalies in prices, making the economy less efficient.

Subversive is also a noun meaning a person intending to undermine something.

REVIEW 72

Matching
Match each word with its definition.

1. strut		(A)	dark and gloomy
2. stultify		(B)	to support with proof
3. stupefy		(C)	to dull the senses of
4. stygian		(D)	intended to undermine or overthrow
5. subpoena		(E)	to display to impress others
6. subside		(F)	to settle down
7. substantiate		(G)	notice ordering someone to appear in court
8. substantive		(H)	to include; incorporate
9. subsume		(I)	to impair or reduce to uselessness
10. subversive		(J)	essential

Fill-ins
Choose the best word to fill in the blank in each sentence.

strutted	stultifying	stupefied	stygian	subpoenaed
subside	substantiate	substantive	subsumes	subversive

1. Several people at the party were _____ from overdrinking.
2. The experiment provided such _____ evidence for the new theory that most scientists now accept it.
3. The drill team _____ into the stadium to perform the half-time show.
4. The scientist was able to formulate a general principle that _____ five more specific principles.
5. Businesses complained that government regulations are _____ free competition and innovation.
6. The critic called Emily Bronte's novel *Wuthering Heights* _____ because it attacks capitalist beliefs.
7. The news that the country was being invaded plunged it into a _____ gloom.
8. The prosecution _____ three witnesses it considered vital to its case.
9. The engineers waited for the floodwaters to _____ before assessing the damage.
10. Advocates of the theory that Atlantis existed more than 6,000 years ago sometimes use evidence of dubious authenticity to _____ their claims.

Sense or Nonsense
Indicate whether each sentence makes good sense or not.
Put S (SENSE) if it does, and put N (NONSENSE) if it does not.

1. Prosecutors obtained a subpoena to require the witness to testify. _____
2. The old miser is so stygian he refuses to buy his grandchildren birthday presents. _____
3. After the excitement of the election subsided, the new administration settled down to the serious business of governance. _____
4. The theory was substantiated by new evidence, so scientists were forced to abandon it. _____
5. The Army–McCarthy hearings of the 1950s investigated many citizens alleged to be engaged in subversive activities. _____

UNIT 73

succor *n.* relief; help in time of distress or want

*The woman was accused of providing **succor** to the enemy in the form of food and medical help.*

suffrage *n.* the right to vote

*The pivotal feminist goal of **suffrage** was not obtained in the United States until 1920, and in Britain not until 1928.*

sundry *adj.* various

*The main character in the novel returns home safely after his **sundry** adventures.*

*supersede *v.* to replace, especially to displace as inferior or antiquated

*Malay was the lingua franca of the Malay peninsula for centuries, but in many parts of that region it is being **superseded** in that role by a European interloper, English.*

supine *adj.* lying on the back; marked by lethargy

*The captured robbery suspects were held **supine** on the floor.*

supplant *v.* to replace; substitute

*The "Frankenstein monster" fear of some people is that AI machines will eventually **supplant** biological life forms, making such life redundant or even subservient.*

suppliant *adj.* beseeching

The worshippers raised their **suppliant** voices to God, praying for forgiveness.

supplicant *n.* one who asks humbly and earnestly

The mother of the man sentenced to be executed appeared as a **supplicant** before the governor, asking him to grant her son clemency.

*supposition *n.* the act of assuming to be true or real

Science proceeds on the **supposition** that knowledge is possible.

syllogism *n.* a form of deductive reasoning that has a major premise, a minor premise, and a conclusion

The following **syllogism** is often taught in logic courses: "All Xs are Ys, all Ys are Zs; therefore, all Xs are Zs."

REVIEW 73

Matching
Match each word with its definition.

1. succor	(A) beseeching
2. suffrage	(B) various
3. sundry	(C) lying on the back
4. supersede	(D) one who asks humbly and earnestly
5. supine	(E) to replace, especially as inferior or antiquated
6. supplant	(F) a form of deductive reasoning
7. suppliant	(G) relief
8. supplicant	(H) act of assuming to be true
9. supposition	(I) to replace; substitute
10. syllogism	(J) the right to vote

Fill-ins
Choose the best word to fill in the blank in each sentence.

succor	suffrage	sundry	superseded	supine
supplanted	suppliant	supplicants	supposition	syllogism

1. Some experts predict that books made from paper will one day be _____ by electronic books.
2. The book tells the story of the protagonist's _____ adventures in Africa over the last 20 years.

3. The _____ approached the king, begging him to forgive their offences.

4. The depressed man found _____ by going inside the church to pray.

5. After eating our picnic lunch, we all lay _____ on the ground, looking at the clouds.

6. The logic instructor asked her class to consider whether the following _____ was true: Some A are B, some B are C. Therefore, some A are C.

7. The astronomers searching for extraterrestrial life are proceeding on the _____ that life requires water.

8. The Twenty-sixth Amendment to the United States Constitution extended _____ to both men and women from the age of 18 years, largely because of the fact that many men younger than 21 were being conscripted to fight in the Vietnam War but had no vote.

9. The first generation of digital computers based on vacuum tube technology were _____ by a second generation of transistor-ized computers in the late 1950s and 1960s that could perform millions of operations a second.

10. The painter portrays a _____ sinner begging for forgiveness.

Sense or Nonsense

Indicate whether each sentence makes good sense or not.
Put S (SENSE) if it does, and put N (NONSENSE) if it does not.

1. The political scientist predicts that by the year 2050 China will supplant Japan as Asia's most powerful nation. _____

2. The president ordered a halt to the bombing to end the suffrage of the people. _____

3. The astronomer's theory makes several suppositions about the nature of the early universe that are not well supported by the evidence. _____

4. The poem makes use of sophisticated figurative language, notably syllogism. _____

5. The science fiction novel speculates that human beings will one day be superseded by a race of specially bred superintelligent cyborgs. _____

UNIT 74

sylvan *adj.* related to the woods or forest

*The house's **sylvan** setting provides the family with beauty and tranquility.*

*tacit *adj.* silently understood; implied

> *During the* Cold War, *there was a* **tacit** *assumption on the part of both the Soviet Union and the United States that neither side would launch an unprovoked nuclear attack against the other side.*

Terms from the Arts, Sciences, and Social Sciences

Cold War: the ideological, geopolitical, and economic conflict between capitalist nations (led by the United States) and communist nations (led by the Soviet Union) from around 1947 to 1991

---

*taciturn *adj,* habitually untalkative

> *The teacher couldn't get the* **taciturn** *child to tell her what activities he enjoyed during recess.*

talisman *n.* charm to bring good luck and avert misfortune

> *The soldier's mother gave him a* **talisman** *to protect him from harm during battle.*

*tangential *adj.* peripheral; digressing

> *The judge ruled that the evidence had only a* **tangential** *bearing on the case and directed the lawyer to present only a brief summary of it.*

tautology *n.* unnecessary repetition

> *Unless the phrase "repeat again" is being used to refer to something that has occurred more than twice, it is a* **tautology***.*

taxonomy *n.* science of classification; in biology, the process of classifying organisms in categories

> *In the late seventeenth century and the eighteenth century accurate observation of organisms developed, leading to the development of the sciences of* **taxonomy** *and morphology (the study of the form and structure of organisms.)*

tenet *n.* belief; doctrine

> *In his novel* Walden II, *the psychologist B. F. Skinner depicts a brave new world based on the* **tenets** *of a behavioral psychology that frees human beings from the inhibitions and preconceptions of traditional society.*

Terms from the Arts, Sciences, and Social Sciences

behavioral psychology: the school of psychology that seeks to explain behavior entirely in terms of observable responses to environmental stimuli

---

*tenuous *adj.* weak; insubstantial

Study of the historical evidence has shown that there is only a **tenuous** connection between the country Plato describes in The Republic and the legendary land of Atlantis.

theocracy *n.* government by priests representing a god

All Islamic fundamentalists are opposed to secularism, and some of them support **theocracy**.

Terms from the Arts, Sciences, and Social Sciences

secularism: a political movement that advocates making society less religious

Secularization is a process by which society gradually changes from close identification with the institutions of religion to a greater separation of religion from the rest of social life.

REVIEW 74

Matching
Match each word with its definition.

1. sylvan	(A) science of classification
2. tacit	(B) implied
3. taciturn	(C) government by priests
4. talisman	(D) weak; insubstantial
5. tangential	(E) digressing; diverting
6. tautology	(F) related to the woods or forest
7. taxonomy	(G) unnecessary repetition
8. tenet	(H) habitually untalkative
9. tenuous	(I) charm to bring good luck
10. theocracy	(J) belief; doctrine

Fill-ins

Choose the best word to fill in the blank in each sentence.

sylvan	tacit	taciturn	talismans	tangential
tautologies	taxonomy	tenet	tenuous	theocracy

1. By _____ agreement no one in the group talked about the controversial subject of the war.
2. The judge asked everyone involved in the hearing to avoid introducing information _____ to the main issue.
3. The poet lives in _____ seclusion, writing about the beauty of nature.
4. Alice is _____, whereas Amy is garrulous.
5. The aim of the revolutionaries was to establish a _____ in the country run by senior clergy.
6. Archeologists have discovered objects they believe were used as _____ by warriors to ward off death.
7. A central _____ of democracy is that the law should treat everyone equally, regardless of his or her race, gender, or social status.
8. Linnaean _____ , used in biology, classifies living things into a hierarchy, assigning each a unique place in the system.
9. The study has established a relationship, albeit a _____ one, between brain size in mammals and intelligence.
10. The English teacher asked the class to consider whether the phrases "past history" and "old adage" are _____ .

Sense or Nonsense

Indicate whether each sentence makes good sense or not. Put S (SENSE) if it does, and put N (NONSENSE) if it does not.

1. The landlord went to court to evict his tenets. _____
2. Research has demonstrated only a tenuous connection between the two phenomena. _____
3. Most successful politicians are not taciturn. _____
4. Members of the tribe believe that the talisman protects them from the evil spirits of the dead. _____
5. Religious leaders are arguing that the only way to save the country is to establish a theocracy. _____

UNIT 75

thespian *n.* an actor or actress

> *Every year the Edinburgh Festival in Scotland gives* **thespians** *from around the world the opportunity to perform before a diverse audience.*

timbre *n.* the characteristic quality of sound produced by a particular instrument or voice; tone color

> *The audience was delighted by the rich* **timbre** *of the singer's soprano.*

*tirade *n.* long, violent speech; verbal assault

> *The students had no choice but to sit and wait for the principal's* **tirade** *about poor discipline to end.*

toady *n.* flatterer; hanger-on; yes-man

> *The boss had no respect for the employee because he considered him a* **toady** *who would do anything he said.*

tome *n.* book, usually large and academic

> *Despite being an abridged edition of the twenty-volume* Oxford English Dictionary, *the* Shorter Oxford English Dictionary *consists of two* **tomes** *that define over half a million words.*

*torpor *n.* lethargy; dormancy; sluggishness

> *After returning home from his coast-to-coast trip, the truck driver sank into a peaceful* **torpor**, *watching TV and dozing.*

torque *n.* a turning or twisting force; the moment of a force; the measure of a force's tendency to produce twisting or turning and rotation around an axis

> *Internal combustion engines produce useful* **torque** *over a rather circumscribed range of rotational speeds (normally from about 1,000 rpm to 6,000 rpm).*

*tortuous *adj.* having many twists and turns; highly complex

> *Only the world's leading mathematicians are able to follow the* **tortuous** *line of reasoning used by the English mathematician Andrew Wiles to prove Fermat's Last Theorem via the Taniyama-Shimura conjecture.*

tout *v.* to promote or praise energetically

*The critic **touted** Moby Dick as the greatest book in American literature.*

*tractable *adj.* obedient; yielding

*The country's leader found that the people became more **tractable** when he made them believe there was a great threat facing them that only he could overcome.*

REVIEW 75

Matching
Match each word with its definition.

1. thespian		(A)	long, violent speech
2. timbre		(B)	a turning or twisting force
3. tirade		(C)	to promote
4. toady		(D)	actor or actress
5. tome		(E)	obedient; yielding
6. torpor		(F)	flatterer
7. torque		(G)	combination of qualities of a sound that distinguish it from others
8. tortuous		(H)	large, academic book
9. tout		(I)	having many twists and turns
10. tractable		(J)	lethargy; sluggishness

Fill-ins
Choose the best word to fill in the blank in each sentence.

thespians	timbre	tirade	toady	tome
torpor	torque	tortuous	touts	tractable

1. The musician has a special affinity for the guitar because of its beautiful _____ .
2. The college _____ plan to perform three of Shakespeare's comedies this year.
3. The café _____ its cappuccino as the best in town.
4. The violent prisoner became _____ after he was given a sedative.

5. Every day the talk show host launches into a _____ against the failings of modern society.
6. In his *Malayan Trilogy*, the British novelist Anthony Burgess describes the _____ induced by hot Malaysian afternoons.
7. The book describes the author's _____ journey from cynicism and despair to faith and hope.
8. The diesel model of the Nissan Patrol is popular in Australia because it develops sufficient _____ to drive through steep, muddy terrain.
9. This 800-page _____ called *Biology* contains most of the information students need to learn for the introductory biology course.
10. Yes, the _____ won his promotion, but at what cost to his self-respect?

Sense or Nonsense
Indicate whether each sentence makes good sense or not.
Put S (SENSE) if it does, and put N (NONSENSE) if it does not.

1. Many high church officials are interred in tomes in the cathedral. _____
2. The farmer leased 100 acres of tractable land to grow corn. _____
3. The enemy launched a tirade of artillery and missiles against our position. _____
4. Timbre in the forests of most of the developed countries is self-sustaining. _____
5. The group of experts working on the space probe includes mechanical engineers, electrical engineers, physicists, and thespians. _____

UNIT 76

*transgression *n.* act of trespassing or violating a law or rule

*The teacher made it clear on the first day of the term that she would not countenance any **transgression** of classroom rules.*

The verb is *transgress.*

*Western medicine **transgressed** Hippocrates' prescriptions for medicine when doctors debilitated patients through the administration of purges and bloodletting.*

Terms from the Arts, Sciences, and Social Sciences

Hippocrates: ancient Greek physician who is often called "the father of medicine." He believed that medicine should stress prevention rather than cure of illness and that a regimen of a good diet and a sensible lifestyle is healthy, building a person's ability to withstand disease.

---

transient *adj.* temporary; short-lived; fleeting

A hypothesis to explain the fact that American states in which the population is composed of a large number of recently settled people (California, for example) tend to have high rates of crime, suicide, divorce, and other social problems is that anomie *is higher in* **transient** *populations than in more stable populations, resulting in more antisocial behavior.*

Terms from the Arts, Sciences, and Social Sciences

anomie: a social condition marked by a breakdown of social norms

---

translucent *adj.* partially transparent

The architect decided to install a **translucent** *door in the room to allow outside light to shine in.*

travail *n.* work, especially arduous work; tribulation; anguish

America's early pioneers endured great **travail***, but persevered and eventually settled much of the vast continent.*

Travail is also a verb meaning to work strenuously.

travesty *n.* parody; exaggerated imitation; caricature

The playwright complained that the musical comedy version of his play was a **travesty** *of his work.*

treatise *n.* article treating a subject systematically and thoroughly

The thesis of the philosopher's **treatise** *is that reality is, ultimately, opaque to human understanding.*

tremulous *adj.* trembling; quivering; frugal; timid

One of the most famous poems in English literature is Matthew Arnold's "Dover Beach," in which the speaker listens to the **"tremulous** *cadence slow" of waves on the shore.*

trepidation *n.* fear and anxiety

John tried to hide his **trepidation** *when he proposed to Susie, the girl he loved.*

*truculence *n.* aggressiveness; ferocity

The principal warned the student that his **truculence** *might one day land him in jail.*

tryst *n.* agreement between lovers to meet; rendezvous

In his novel The Mayor of Casterbridge, *Thomas Hardy describes an ancient Roman amphitheater where lovers often arranged secret* **trysts**.

REVIEW 76

Matching
Match each word with its definition.

1. transgression	(A)	article treating a subject systematically
2. transient	(B)	partially transparent
3. translucent	(C)	fear and anxiety
4. travail	(D)	temporary; fleeting
5. travesty	(E)	exaggerated imitation; parody
6. treatise	(F)	aggressiveness
7. tremulous	(G)	arduous work
8. trepidation	(H)	act of violating a law
9. truculence	(I)	rendezvous
10. tryst	(J)	quivering; fearful

Fill-ins
Choose the best word to fill in the blank in each sentence.

transgressed	**transient**	**translucent**	**travails**	**travesty**
treatise	**tremulous**	**trepidation**	**truculence**	**tryst**

1. The pastor urged the members of his congregation to face life's _____ cheerfully.
2. The gang has such a reputation for _____ that even the police approach its members with great caution.
3. This afternoon's solar eclipse will be a _____ phenomenon, so make sure you are ready to observe it as soon as it begins.

4. The philosophic _____ deals with Spinoza's metaphysics.
5. The soldier, his voice _____ , begged his captor not to kill him.
6. A prism is a _____ piece of glass or crystal that creates a spectrum of light separated according to colors.
7. The judge in the most recent of the many times Dr. Jack Kervorkian was tried for murder for assisting a terminally ill person to kill himself held that the law is sacrosanct and cannot be _____ by an individual, even for reasons of conscience.
8. Bill and Sue arranged a _____ for Saturday afternoon.
9. The defense attorney called the trial of the soldier accused of war crimes a _____ of justice since the judges were all citizens of the nation that had defeated the country for which her defendant had been fighting.
10. The young scholar approached the problem with considerable _____ , knowing that it had been thoroughly discussed by many of the great thinkers through the ages.

Sense or Nonsense

Indicate whether each sentence makes good sense or not.
Put S (SENSE) if it does, and put N (NONSENSE) if it does not.

1. Beth's father said he would prefer that she wore the opaque top, but her mother said she could wear the translucent one. _____
2. The transient nature of the phenomenon makes it difficult for scientists to study. _____
3. The professor's treatise on the influence of structuralism on modern thought was published last year. _____
4. The principal congratulated the student for successfully transgressing every school regulation. _____
5. The doctor in the soap opera spends so much of her time arranging trysts with her lover one wonders how she has time left to practice medicine. _____

UNIT 77

tumid *adj.* swollen; distended

> *The prose of writers discussing lofty subjects sometimes becomes* **tumid***.*

turbid *adj.* muddy; opaque; in a state of great confusion

> *The poem captures the restless and* **turbid** *state of the soldier's mind the night before the decisive battle was set to begin.*

*turgid *adj.* swollen; bloated; pompous

> *The professor's editor advised him to change his writing style so that it was less pedantic and* **turgid** *if he wanted to appeal to a mass audience.*

tutelary *adj.* serving as a guardian or protector

> *Most of the people of ancient Rome believed in the existence of* **tutelary** *spirits.*

Terms from the Arts, Sciences, and Social Sciences

tutelary spirits: gods who are guardians of a particular area or person

---

uncanny *adj.* mysterious; strange

> *Some people believe that the psychic has an* **uncanny** *ability to accurately predict the future.*

undulating *adj.* moving in waves

> *The* **undulating** *terrain of the area has made it difficult for engineers to build roads there.*

unfeigned *adj.* not false; not made up; genuine

> *The child smiled in* **unfeigned** *delight when she opened the Christmas present.*

*untenable *adj.* indefensible

> *Skeptics are inclined to regard arguments for God's existence from design as meaningless, since they rely on a logically* **untenable** *position that assumes the conclusion of their argument—God's existence.*

Terms from the Arts, Sciences, and Social Sciences

design: The argument from design is a philosophical argument for God's existence stating that God must exist because the universe is too complex to have been created any other way.

---

untoward *adj.* not favorable; troublesome; adverse; unruly

> *Police were called in to investigate whether anything* **untoward** *had happened to the missing man.*

usury *n.* practice of lending money at exorbitant rates

*In the 1980s, Delaware Governor Pierre S. Du Pont succeeded in having the state's **usury** laws liberalized, with the result that many large New York banks set up subsidiaries in Delaware.*

The adjective is *usurious.*

*The consumer advocate's group complained about the bank's **usurious** interest rates.*

REVIEW 77

Matching
Match each word with its definition.

1. tumid
2. turbid
3. turgid
4. tutelary
5. uncanny
6. undulating
7. unfeigned
8. untenable
9. untoward
10. usury

(A) serving as a guardian
(B) moving in waves
(C) swollen; distended
(D) not made up; genuine
(E) mysterious
(F) practice of lending money at exorbitant rates
(G) muddy; opaque; in a state of great confusion
(H) not favorable; adverse; troublesome
(I) swollen; bloated; pompous
(J) indefensible

Fill-ins
Choose the best word to fill in the blank in each sentence.

tumid	turbid	turgid	tutelary	uncanny
undulating	unfeigned	untenable	untoward	usury

1. The student looked up with _____ astonishment—"You mean I got a perfect score on the GRE?"
2. The prime minister's position became _____ after he lost the support of his own party, so he resigned from office.
3. The consumer organization accused the credit card company of _____ after it raised its interest rate to 22 percent per year.
4. The head of the commission said that she did not want the report written in the _____ prose too often found in official documents.
5. The British writer George Orwell often satirized _____ political prose.

6. The commander told his troops that _____ circumstances had prevented victory, but that if they fought on valiantly, victory would be achieved eventually.

7. The orbiting spacecraft sent a manned vehicle down to the Martian surface, where it explored the area's _____ surface.

8. Steve's _____ ability to predict the outcome of college basketball games has helped him to win a lot of money on bets.

9. Many people believe that they have a guardian angel, a/an _____ being that guides and protects them.

10. After the storm the river was _____ because of all the soil that had flowed into it from the nearby stream.

Sense or Nonsense
Indicate whether each sentence makes good sense or not.
Put S (SENSE) if it does, and put N (NONSENSE) if it does not.

1. When chess grand masters find themselves in an untenable position they generally resign. _____

2. The tumid weather has made it difficult for the soccer team to train. _____

3. Despite its entertaining plot, the novel's turgid prose makes it rather difficult to enjoy. _____

4. The professor holds an extra tutelary class every Saturday morning. _____

5. The loan shark's usurious interest rates have attracted the attention of the district attorney. _____

UNIT 78

*vacillate *v.* to waver; oscillate

   *The senator's position keeps **vacillating** between remaining neutral and lending his support to the proposal.*

vacuous *adj.* empty; void; lacking intelligence; purposeless

   In Jane Austen's novel Pride and Prejudice, *the youngest of the five Bennett daughters, Lydia, is portrayed as a **vacuous** young woman with few interests other than having fun.*

valedictory *adj.* pertaining to a farewell

   *The 80-year-old actor came out of retirement to give a **valedictory** performance on Broadway.*

*vapid *adj.* tasteless; dull

*To relax in the evening the judge likes to watch **vapid** situation comedies on TV.*

variegated *adj.* varied; marked with different colors

*Botanists are still working to catalog the **variegated** species of the tropical rain forest.*

vaunt *v.* to boast; brag

*The head coach warned her players not to **vaunt** their undefeated record.*

Vaunted is an adjective meaning boasted about.

*Since every human activity depends on the integrity and proper functioning of the biological system, its destruction through pollution would cause our **vaunted** technological and economic systems to founder.*

venal *adj.* bribable; mercenary; corruptible

*The depressing though inescapable conclusion the journalist reached is that the mayor went into politics for motives that were almost entirely **venal**.*

vendetta *n.* prolonged feud marked by bitter hostility

*The judge warned both families that the **vendetta** between them had to end at once.*

*venerate *v.* to adore; honor; respect

*Mother Teresa is **venerated** for her compassion for the poor people of India.*

Venerable is an adjective meaning respected because of age, character, or position.

*In the plain-language edition of the **venerable** Merck Manual of Diagnosis and Therapy the original definition of a hangnail—"Acute or chronic inflammation of the periungual tissues"—is transmogrified into "An infection around the edge of a fingernail or toenail."*

*veracious *adj.* truthful; accurate

*The witness' testimony appeared to be **veracious** at first, but under cross-examination, several inconsistencies appeared.*

REVIEW 78

Matching
Match each word with its definition.

1. vacillate	(A) bribable; corruptible
2. vacuous	(B) varied
3. valedictory	(C) to waver; oscillate
4. vapid	(D) to boast; brag
5. variegated	(E) truthful; accurate
6. vaunt	(F) tasteless; dull
7. venal	(G) to adore; honor
8. vendetta	(H) pertaining to a farewell
9. venerate	(I) prolonged feud
10. veracious	(J) empty; lacking intelligence

Fill-ins
Choose the best word to fill in the blank in each sentence.

vacillating	**vacuous**	**valedictory**	**vapid**	**variegated**
vaunted	**venal**	**vendetta**	**venerated**	**veracious**

1. The saint is _____ for her compassion toward all living things.
2. It is a mystery to critics how the writer went from producing _____ and sentimental stories to turning out some of the best stories ever written in America.
3. The jury's decision was based largely on the testimony of a single witness they believed to be _____ .
4. The historian's book describes America's allies in Vietnam during the 1960s and 1970s as _____ and corrupt.
5. The booster club held a _____ breakfast for the football team.
6. The plot of *Romeo and Juliet* is centered around a _____ between two noble families, the Capulets and the Montagues.
7. Despite its _____ high-tech weapons, the invading army could not defeat the peasants, who were armed only with rifles.
8. The actress, a highly intelligent and well-educated young woman, plays the stereotyped part of the _____ "bimbo" in the film.
9. From odd bits of material the artist has achieved _____ effects.
10. Philip is _____ between going to medical school and law school.

Sense or Nonsense
Indicate whether each sentence makes good sense or not.
Put S (SENSE) if it does, and put N (NONSENSE) if it does not.

1. A veracious reader, Heather is planning to read five of Joseph Conrad's novels this month. _____
2. The president of the university has prepared some valedictory remarks for the Commencement ceremony. _____
3. The district attorney was elected mayor largely on his promise to prosecute venal government officials whenever possible. _____
4. The plot of the movie centers around a family's vendetta against another family that they believed had disgraced them. _____
5. The editor knew that the reporter's claim could not be true because it was clearly veracious. _____

UNIT 79

verbose *adj.* wordy

The skillful editor cut 20 percent of the words from the **verbose** manuscript without appreciably altering its meaning.

vertigo *n.* dizziness

The physician diagnosed the patient's **vertigo** as being caused by an acute anxiety attack.

vexation *n.* irritation; annoyance; confusion; puzzlement

Some people have the ability to prosper and live happily despite life's inevitable **vexations**.

viable *adj.* practicable; capable of developing

Since the early 1950s, government planners have faced a dilemma: Spend a great deal of money to keep cities **viable** by rebuilding decrepit infrastructure, or allow them to decay.

The noun is *viability*.

According to the historian Arnold Toynbee, there is a strong relationship between a society's view of itself relative to other societies and its continued **viability**.

vindictive *adj.* spiteful; vengeful; unforgiving

The Treaty of Versailles, which concluded World War I, was deliberately **vindictive**, imposing tremendous penalties on Germany.

virtuoso *n.* someone with masterly skills; expert musician

The British guitar virtuoso John Williams has entertained thousands of people during his long career.

Virtuoso is also the adjective.

Raymond is a virtuoso pianist.

visage *n.* countenance; appearance; aspect

The infant studied its mother's visage intently.

*viscous *adj.* thick, syrupy, and sticky

The maple syrup is so viscous we had trouble pouring it.

*vitiate *v.* to impair the quality of; corrupt morally; make inoperative

Unfortunately, one error in the study's methodology vitiates the entire body of work.

*vituperative *adj.* using or containing harsh, abusive censure

The young music critic's vituperative comments aroused the wrath of nearly every serious composer.

The verb is *vituperate.*

REVIEW 79

Matching
Match each word with its definition.

1. verbose	(A) thick, syrupy, and sticky
2. vertigo	(B) to impair the quality of
3. vexation	(C) spiteful; vengeful
4. viable	(D) countenance; appearance
5. vindictive	(E) practicable; capable of developing
6. virtuoso	(F) wordy
7. visage	(G) someone with masterly skills
8. viscous	(H) using or containing abusive censure
9. vitiate	(I) dizziness
10. vituperative	(J) irritation; annoyance

Fill-ins

Choose the best word to fill in the blank in each sentence.

verbose	vertigo	vexations	viable	vindictive
virtuoso	visage	viscous	vitiated	vituperative

1. The judge cautioned the attorney not to use his summing up as an opportunity to make _____ remarks about imperfections in the criminal justice system.
2. Heathcliff, the protagonist of *Wuthering Heights*, is _____ in seeking revenge against those he believes have harmed him.
3. Many people experience _____ when they stand near the edge of a cliff.
4. Sergei Rachmaninoff, a distinguished Russian-born composer, was also a _____ pianist who is famous for his interpretations of late romantic composers.
5. On the night before the battle, the soldier had a dream in which he saw the smiling _____ of his beloved mother.
6. The candidate's advisor warned her not to make her acceptance speech _____ .
7. The engineer designed the motor to be lubricated with very _____ oil.
8. The congressional committee is trying to work out a _____ plan to give every American access to affordable, high-quality medical care.
9. The effectiveness of the new government will probably be _____ by factors beyond its control.
10. Returning home after the war, the soldier reflected that the _____ of daily civilian life would seem like nothing compared to the suffering he had endured as a conscript on the front line.

Sense or Nonsense

Indicate whether each sentence makes good sense or not.
Put S (SENSE) if it does, and put N (NONSENSE) if it does not.

1. The verbose speaker kept digressing to tell anecdotes about her life. _____
2. The government is studying the plan to provide universal health care to see whether it is economically viable. _____
3. According to the English professor, virtuosos of the novel form include Nathaniel Hawthorne, Henry James, Willa Cather, and Joseph Conrad. _____

4. The children enjoyed their visage to their uncle's house during the summer vacation. _____

5. Attacks of vertigo can be a symptom of a serious underlying malady. _____

UNIT 80

vivisection *n.* dissection, surgery, or painful experiments performed on a living animal for the purpose of scientific research

The book Animal Rights *by the philosopher Tom Regan contains a long discussion of* **vivisection.**

vogue *n.* prevailing fashion or practice

Although protectionist policies are not in **vogue** *today, great capitalist democracies, such as Great Britain and the United States, flourished for long periods of their histories under protectionist trade policies that were nearly mercantilist—policies that imposed high tariffs on many foreign goods to promote domestic production.*

*volatile *adj.* tending to vary frequently; fickle

Volatility is the noun.

Some contemporary economists believe that advances in the understanding of the business cycle virtually preclude a recurrence of the crash of 1929, because governments can take steps to forestall depression. However, others worry that new factors are developing that are, to a significant extent, beyond the control of governments: notably, the ability of investors to quickly switch capital into and out of markets, a situation that could lead to **volatility** *in prices and destabilize markets.*

vortex *n.* whirlpool; whirlwind; center of turbulence

Inexorably, the country was drawn into the **vortex** *of war.*

warranted *adj.* justified

The book argues that a new investigation into Marilyn Monroe's death is **warranted** *by new evidence released by the FBI under the Freedom of Information Act.*

Warrant is a verb meaning to attest to the accuracy or quality; justify; grant authorization

Throughout most of America, procedures in criminal law cases are essentially the same: The government, through a prosecutor, presents its case against a suspect to a grand jury, which decides if there is sufficient evidence to **warrant** *a full trial.*

wary *adj.* careful; cautious

> *According to psychologists, human beings are naturally **wary** of strangers.*

welter *v.* to wallow or roll; toss about; be in turmoil

> *The pigs **weltered** about happily in the mud.*

whimsical *adj.* fanciful; unpredictable

> *Many children appreciate Dr. Seuss' **whimsical** stories.*

The noun *whimsy* means a playful or fanciful idea.

> *Despite its rigorous and systematic methodology, there is still considerable room in science for imagination and even **whimsy**.*

wistful *adj.* vaguely longing; sadly thoughtful

> *The poem casts a **wistful** look back at a way of life that has vanished forever.*

zealot *n.* one who is fanatically devoted to a cause

> *The Crusades of the eleventh to thirteenth centuries were conceived of by Christian **zealots** as a way to drive the Islamic interlopers from the Holy Land.*

Zealotry is a noun meaning fanaticism.

> *The fact that the judicial branch is relatively undemocratic compared to the other two branches of government is justified by some theorists of democracy on the grounds that it serves as a check not only on the legislative branch and executive branch, but also on democratic **zealotry**.*

The adjective *zealous* means enthusiastically devoted to a cause.

> *It is heretical to suggest to a **zealous** capitalist that free enterprise is not the only conceivable realistic economic system.*

REVIEW 80

Matching
Match each word with its definition.

1. vivisection	(A) tending to vary frequently
2. vogue	(B) dissection performed on a living animal for scientific research
3. volatile	(C) fanciful
4. vortex	(D) one who is fanatically devoted to a cause
5. warranted	(E) whirlpool; center of turbulence
6. wary	(F) to wallow or roll; be in turmoil
7. welter	(G) prevailing fashion
8. whimsical	(H) careful; cautious
9. wistful	(I) sadly thoughtful
10. zealot	(J) justified

Fill-ins
Choose the best word to fill in the blank in each sentence.

vivisections	vogue	volatile	vortex	warranted
wary	welter	whimsical	wistful	zealot

1. Brad is such a party _____ that he has never even considered voting for a candidate who does not belong to his party.
2. Joan's friend said that she should be _____ of the man loitering around campus.
3. Lost in the _____ of conflicting information was the fact that there was no decisive proof of the theory's validity.
4. In James Boswell's *Life of Johnson* (1775), Samuel Johnson comments that the American colonists are "a race of convicts;" Boswell, however, expresses a contrary view: "I had now formed a clear and settled opinion, that the people of America were well _____ to resist a claim that their fellow subjects in the mother country should have the entire command of their fortunes, by taxing them without their consent."
5. Militant feminism reached its zenith in the 1960s, and since then a less confrontational approach to asserting women's rights has been in _____ .
6. Steve advised his friend not to invest in the stock market until it became less _____ .

7. The animal rights group organized a protest against the
   _____ being performed in the university biology laboratory.
8. The Swiss painter Paul Klee is famous for his humorous, personal,
   and often _____ paintings.
9. All of the people visiting the war memorial had _____ looks
   on their faces.
10. The young people of the country were drawn steadily into the
    _____ of revolutionary activity.

Sense or Nonsense
Indicate whether each sentence makes good sense or not.
Put S (SENSE) if it does, and put N (NONSENSE) if it does not.

1. Mini-skirts were in vogue in the 1960s. _____
2. The panel is considering the legal and moral implications of
   vivisection. _____
3. The coach decided that his team's excellent performance in the
   game warranted a day off practice. _____
4. The psychologist excels in helping patients learn to understand
   their volatile emotions. _____
5. The English novelist Evelyn Waugh was a practicing Roman
   Catholic, though hardly a zealot. _____

Review:
300 High-Frequency
GRE Words

Matching
Match each word with its definition.

Part A

1. aberrant	(A) causing quarrels
2. aesthetics	(B) known only to a few
3. anomaly	(C) intentionally use vague language
4. arcane	(D) the conception of what is beautiful
5. bombastic	(E) pertaining to people
6. contentious	(F) attacking cherished traditions
7. demotic	(G) deviating from what is normal
8. disparage	(H) using inflated language
9. equivocate	(I) belittle
10. iconoclastic	(J) irregularity

Matching
Match each word with its definition.

Part B

11. immutable	(A) talkative
12. implacable	(B) using few words
13. intractable	(C) disgrace
14. juxtapose	(D) incapable of being pleased
15. laconic	(E) too helpful
16. laudable	(F) transparent
17. loquacious	(G) not easily managed
18. officious	(H) praiseworthy
19. opprobrium	(I) unchangeable
20. pellucid	(J) place side by side

Matching
Match each word with its definition.

Part C

21. plethora   (A) wordy
22. prevaricate   (B) excess
23. propitiate   (C) inactive
24. quiescent   (D) resisting control
25. reprobate   (E) evade the truth
26. salubrious   (F) not inclined to speak much
27. taciturn   (G) morally unprincipled person
28. recalcitrant   (H) containing harsh censure
29. verbose   (I) appease
30. vituperative   (J) healthful

Sense or Nonsense
Indicate whether each sentence makes good sense or not.
Put S (SENSE) if it does, and put N (NONSENSE) if it does not.

31. Perhaps because it had become too insular in its outlook, the monarchy obdurately refused to heed growing calls for liberalization. ____
32. An example of Earth's suitability for life is the vapid combination of temperature and pressure that allows large quantities of water to remain in the liquid phase. ____
33. Historians agree that the executive branch of government claimed more power for itself largely in response to the exigencies of the modern world. ____
34. A collective endeavor requires some degree of apathy because in order to work together people must to some extent sacrifice self-interest. ____
35. Aesop's fables are fatuous, teaching profound moral lessons through symbolism. ____
36. Studies of various types of psychotherapy in use show that they do not vary appreciably in their efficacy as measured by empirically verifiable means. ____
37. The existence of planets in other star systems is deduced from indirect evidence gathered from meticulous research on the effects of these planets on their sun's orbit. ____
38. In the view of some legal experts, if every individual acted according to his or her conscience the polity would break down into anarchy. ____
39. Defenders of intelligence tests say that they measure a quality, which although elusive, is none the less real, because scores on intelligence tests belie academic and career success. ____

40. Human behavior can be regarded as a result of the interaction between instincts, on the one hand, and, on the other hand, the effects of socialization and individual turgidity. ____

Fill-ins
Choose the best word to fill in the blank in each sentence.

41. _____ a list of phobias is a good way to learn some Latin and Greek roots; for example, *agora* in Greek means "marketplace," giving us *agoraphobia*—fear of public places.
    Ⓐ Burnishing
    Ⓑ Exacting
    Ⓒ Dissembling
    Ⓓ Perusing
    Ⓔ Diffusing

42. The _____ librarian merely raised her eyebrows when a fire broke out in the reference section.
    Ⓐ effete
    Ⓑ heterodox
    Ⓒ phlegmatic
    Ⓓ pedantic
    Ⓔ ambivalent

43. Many pacifists believe that because people are adept at rationalizing violence _____ by the state, warfare will not end until it is deemed an unacceptable option for pursuing national policy.
    Ⓐ sanctioned
    Ⓑ repudiated
    Ⓒ feigned
    Ⓓ apprised
    Ⓔ vitiated

44. Although most Americans were reluctant to enter World War II, many were persuaded that "fortress America"—a bulwark against antidemocratic forces—would become _____ if Germany triumphed in Europe and Japan dominated Asia.
    Ⓐ refractory
    Ⓑ untenable
    Ⓒ incompatible
    Ⓓ perfidious
    Ⓔ pervasive

45. Some third world leaders argue that the West, given its advanced development, can afford to give precedence to political rights, but that poor countries must be _____ and give priority to economic rights such as the right to eat and have a job, even if this means circumscribing political freedom.
   Ⓐ whimsical
   Ⓑ magnanimous
   Ⓒ abstemious
   Ⓓ pragmatic
   Ⓔ diffident

46. At one extreme of poetic form is the sonnet, a poem of fourteen lines demanding _____ rigorous _____ governing meter and form, while at the other extreme is free verse, which is composed of variable, unrhymed lines that have no fixed metrical pattern.
   Ⓐ concurrence with..platitudes
   Ⓑ adherence to..conventions
   Ⓒ conformity with..discrepancies
   Ⓓ deference to..anomalies
   Ⓔ approbation of..stigmas

47. There is an ongoing debate about whether watching violent programs on television makes people more violent, or whether it actually purges, or at least _____, the violent tendencies already _____ in people; unfortunately, there is no conclusive evidence yet for either view.
   Ⓐ tempers..inherent
   Ⓑ mitigates..discordant
   Ⓒ reprises..innate
   Ⓓ inculcates..pernicious
   Ⓔ avers..oblique

48. Some observers worry that the trend toward globalization may perpetuate poverty in developing countries and _____ the _____ between the rich and poor nations.
   Ⓐ aggrandize...transgressions
   Ⓑ assuage..discrepancy
   Ⓒ palliate..divergence
   Ⓓ exacerbate..disparity
   Ⓔ corroborate...propriety

49. An argument can appear plausible due to the author's ability to embellish a(n) _____ argument so that its _____ reasoning is concealed beneath a beguiling exterior.
    (A) tenuous..specious
    (B) doctrinaire..convoluted
    (C) disingenuous..rarefied
    (D) desultory..meretricious
    (E) inchoate..lucid

50. The remarkable conductivity of fiber-optic cables has _____ the need for expensive repeaters to boost signals that in _____ cable become _____ over long distances.
    (A) precipitated..analogous..amalgamated
    (B) exacerbated..pristine..mitigated
    (C) proscribed..recondite..ameliorated
    (D) subsumed..ordinary..occluded
    (E) obviated..conventional..attenuated

End of Review

REVIEW: 300 HIGH-FREQUENCY GRE WORDS ANSWERS

1. G	11. I	21. B	31. S	41. D
2. D	12. D	22. E	32. N	42. C
3. J	13. G	23. I	33. S	43. A
4. B	14. J	24. C	34. N	44. B
5. H	15. B	25. G	35. N	45. D
6. A	16. H	26. J	36. S	46. B
7. E	17. A	27. F	37. S	47. A
8. I	18. E	28. D	38. S	48. D
9. C	19. C	29. A	39. N	49. A
10. F	20. F	30. H	40. N	50. E

Review:
Essential Words for the GRE

Matching
Match each word with its definition.

Part A

1. desuetude
2. extraneous
3. bifurcate
4. fulminate
5. continence
6. extemporaneous
7. accretion
8. centrifugal
9. grouse
10. centripetal

(A) growth in size
(B) unrehearsed
(C) self-control
(D) divide into two parts
(E) complain
(F) moving away from the center
(G) denounce
(H) state of disuse
(I) moving toward the center
(J) not essential

Matching
Match each word with its definition.

Part B

11. impervious
12. labile
13. affinity
14. plethora
15. implacable
16. vitiate
17. disingenuous
18. pique
19. subsume
20. vacillate

(A) fleeting feeling of hurt pride
(B) not candid
(C) impossible to appease
(D) to waver; oscillate
(E) fondness; similarity
(F) overabundance
(G) likely to change
(H) incapable of being affected
(I) to include; incorporate
(J) to impair the quality of

Sense or Nonsense

Indicate whether each sentence makes good sense or not.
Put S (SENSE) if it does, and put N (NONSENSE) if it does not.

21. Artwork of the classical period can seem austere to the uninitiated, but to the discerning audience it is satisfying to have feelings expressed in this form because they are transmuted in the crucible of art into a more stygian form. _____

22. Although he is remembered chiefly as a novelist, D.H. Lawrence also had an enervation for writing verse. _____

23. In his poetry and novels, writer Thomas Hardy often portrayed a contumacious God who interfered almost maliciously in human affairs. _____

24. The nineteenth-century British satirist Thomas Love Peacock lampooned the metaphysical speculation of thinkers like Samuel Taylor Coleridge as pretentious and limpid. _____

25. Skeptics believe that the Green Revolution can only mitigate the effects of a rapidly increasing demand for food, and that in the long run starvation will reappear when pestilence and other disasters decrease food supplies. _____

26. The scientist is in an ethical quandary about whether he should repudiate his past involvement in developing a weapon of mass destruction. _____

27. In 1787, when the U.S. Constitution was being framed, it was proposed that slavery be abolished, but opponents of the measure forced a compromise whereby slavery would not be prescribed until early in the next century. _____

28. Evolution is a process that results in the overall improvement of life; paradoxically, however, that process of improvement is driven by aberrations in the process of DNA's self-replication. _____

29. In the so-called "clockwork universe" of the Deists, God is relegated to the role of a "clockmaker" who creates the cosmos and then withdraws to allow man autonomous action. _____

30. In his argument against conscription, Joseph conceded that there might be rarefied situations in which it is justified, but warned that allowing it in these cases might be a step down the slippery slope to totalitarianism. _____

Fill-ins

Choose the best word or set of words to fill in the blanks in each sentence.

31. The Hubble Space Telescope—in orbit around Earth to offer observations not _____ by Earth's atmosphere—has been a boon to astronomers; it is one of the finest astronomical instruments ever developed, greatly expanding man's gaze into space.

    Ⓐ attenuated
    Ⓑ mitigated
    Ⓒ imploded
    Ⓓ subsumed
    Ⓔ intimated

32. The literary critic Susan Sontag uttered a famous _____ dictum: "Taste has no system and no proofs"—by which she meant that artistic taste is subjective, since there are no unbiased criteria for assessing art.

    Ⓐ desultory
    Ⓑ aesthetic
    Ⓒ existential
    Ⓓ linguistic
    Ⓔ capricious

33. _____ of primitivism is that there is no progress in art, and thus the art of so-called "primitive" cultures is as _____ as that of so-called "high" civilization.

    Ⓐ An exigency..plastic
    Ⓑ A precept..felicitous
    Ⓒ A credo..gauche
    Ⓓ A supposition..whimsical
    Ⓔ A tenet..evocative

34. In 1787, when the United States Constitution was written, it was proposed that slavery be abolished, but opponents of the measure forced a compromise whereby slavery would not be _____ until early in the next century.

Ⓐ admonished
Ⓑ emulated
Ⓒ proscribed
Ⓓ interpolated
Ⓔ obviated

35. The following _____ , called Olber's paradox, long puzzled astronomers: If the universe is infinite in extent and age, and filled with stars, why is the sky dark at night?

Ⓐ apothegm
Ⓑ stricture
Ⓒ valedictory
Ⓓ conundrum
Ⓔ vendetta

36. _____ was an academic discipline at many universities in the early twentieth century, and was supported by such _____ figures as Winston Churchill and George Bernard Shaw until it became closely associated with abuses of the Nazis of the 1940s in Germany, who carried out atrocities such as the extermination of undersized population groups.

Ⓐ Epistemology..impassive
Ⓑ Eugenics..redoubtable
Ⓒ Necromancy..discerning
Ⓓ Hieroglyphics..beneficent
Ⓔ Cartography..avuncular

37. _____ generally believe that determinism is incompatible with human dignity, and _____ attempts to limit man's freedom.

Ⓐ Libertines..aver
Ⓑ Existentialists..disparage
Ⓒ Neophytes..repudiate
Ⓓ Conscripts..aggrandize
Ⓔ Anarchists..admonish

38. Scholars are sometimes tempted into _____ off the main topic to discuss esoteric areas of interest to them, but which are regarded by many readers as _____ display of _____ .

    (A) diatribes..a formidable..miscellany
    (B) soliloquies..a megalomaniacal..propriety
    (C) digressions..a pedantic..erudition
    (D) homilies..an egotistical..sagacity
    (E) expositions..a bombastic..chivalry

39. When the word "gay" began to be widely adopted to refer to homosexuals, some commentators, presumably unaware of the word's complex history and long association with homosexuality, _____ it as a _____ with connotations of merriment that was being foisted by homosexuals on the heterosexual majority.

    (A) defamed..tautology
    (B) denigrated..syllogism
    (C) derided..euphemism
    (D) disparaged..neologism
    (E) maligned..mnemonic

40. _____ student of literature remembers that literary terms are notoriously _____ in that their meanings are ever shifting depending on the premises of the writer using them and the nature of the work under discussion.

    (A) A jejune..inevitably
    (B) A craven..poignantly
    (C) A judicious..impetuously
    (D) An astute..querulously
    (E) A sagacious..plastic

41. The fact that social welfare programs existed only in embryonic form during the Great Depression _____ the effects of that depression because there was virtually no mechanism for coping with sudden and _____ unemployment.

    (A) negated..perennial
    (B) forestalled..precipitate
    (C) alleviated..ineluctable
    (D) exacerbated..pervasive
    (E) impeded..substantive

42. _____ believe that because people are _____ agents, they should not allow themselves to be circumscribed by the restrictions of the state.

   Ⓐ Misanthropes..covert

   Ⓑ Mavericks..complaisant

   Ⓒ Iconoclasts..viable

   Ⓓ Zealots..guileless

   Ⓔ Anarchists..autonomous

43. Because it is very quickly destroyed by ordinary matter, antimatter has _____ existence in our locality of the universe.

   Ⓐ a derivative

   Ⓑ an intangible

   Ⓒ a viable

   Ⓓ an ephemeral

   Ⓔ a poignant

44. To make your writing _____, it is a good idea to read what you have written from a reader's perspective, looking for any language that is _____ .

   Ⓐ execrable..bombastic

   Ⓑ banal..convoluted

   Ⓒ pellucid..equivocal

   Ⓓ discordant..tangential

   Ⓔ amenable..disjointed

45. Modern _____ uses _____ techniques involving methodologies such as photogrammetry, which utilizes photographs taken from airplanes and satellites to measure topography with extreme accuracy.

   Ⓐ meteorology..salutary

   Ⓑ paleontology..hermetic

   Ⓒ entomology..audacious

   Ⓓ ornithology..recondite

   Ⓔ cartography..esoteric

46. The _____, "Women are more intelligent than men" needs to be _____, because not all women are smarter than all men.

   Ⓐ axiom..jibed
   Ⓑ stricture..refuted
   Ⓒ extrapolation..queried
   Ⓓ contention..qualified
   Ⓔ credo..vitiated

47. The concept of the biosphere has helped to _____ the idea of life on earth as a fragile and interdependent system that humanity disrupts at its peril.

   Ⓐ supplant
   Ⓑ bifurcate
   Ⓒ burnish
   Ⓓ disseminate
   Ⓔ amalgamate

48. It seems likely that herd mentality plays a part in depressions; as an economy slumps, some people panic, others _____ this panic, and something akin to mass hysteria ensues.

   Ⓐ arrest
   Ⓑ foreswear
   Ⓒ impede
   Ⓓ subsume
   Ⓔ emulate

49. In burning fossil fuels so _____ , humanity is squandering a legacy from _____ times.

   Ⓐ ostentatiously..indeterminate
   Ⓑ presumptuously..antediluvian
   Ⓒ precipitously..sidereal
   Ⓓ prodigally..primordial
   Ⓔ abstemiously..anachronistic

50. Because of its political problems and _____ inflation for long periods after World War II, some economists have cited Argentina as a developed country that was nearly _____ to the rank of an underdeveloped country.

Ⓐ insuperable..divested
Ⓑ intractable..relegated
Ⓒ ineluctable..accrued
Ⓓ implacable..goaded
Ⓔ nugatory..interpolated

End of Review

REVIEW: ESSENTIAL WORDS FOR THE GRE ANSWERS

1. H	11. H	21. N	31. A	41. D
2. J	12. G	22. N	32. B	42. E
3. D	13. E	23. N	33. E	43. D
4. G	14. F	24. N	34. C	44. C
5. C	15. C	25. S	35. D	45. E
6. B	16. J	26. S	36. B	46. D
7. A	17. B	27. N	37. B	47. D
8. F	18. A	28. S	38. C	48. E
9. E	19. I	29. S	39. C	49. D
10. I	20. D	30. N	40. E	50. B

300 High-Frequency Word Roots

800 Essential Roots and Prefixes

1,500 English Derivatives

MASTERING HIGH-FREQUENCY WORD ROOTS TO FURTHER EXPAND YOUR VOCABULARY

You have learned 800 very important words. You now have a good vocabulary for the GRE. However, no book could possibly teach every single word that might appear on the test. What is the most efficient way to learn even more words?

The answer—as was already mentioned in the introduction—is to learn important root words and build up your knowledge of advanced words based on these roots.

This section teaches you 300 high-frequency roots and prefixes, as well as 1,500 words derived from them. Learning these roots will give you a solid understanding of the building blocks of English words. It will also reinforce your learning of many of the words covered earlier in the book. Most importantly, it will give you the tools to decipher tens of thousands of the sort of academic words that appear in high-level reading material—and therefore could be included on the GRE.

HOW ROOTS WORK—AND HOW THEY CAN WORK FOR YOU

Most English words were created from Anglo-Saxon, Greek, Latin, French, Italian, and German roots and stems, and certain affixes—word elements that are affixed to words as prefixes or suffixes to refine the meaning or change a word's grammatical form. Of the more than one million words in English, approximately 60 percent come from Latin and Greek roots. This means that knowledge of Latin and Greek roots that frequently appear in English words will help you to gain a better understanding of the origin and meaning of many words. For example, in Unit 30 you learned that the word *exacerbate* means "to aggravate; make worse," but do you know the origin of this word? *Exacerbate* was formed from a combination of the following: *ex* (an intensive prefix) + the Latin root *acer* (harsh, bitter), and the suffix *ate* (make, do). You also learned the word *aberrant*, which means "deviating from the expected or normal course." It is from *ab* (away from) + *errare* (to stray). Therefore, if you knew the meaning of the root *err* (to stray), and all of the suffixes attached to that root, such as *or* (a quality or condition), *ous* (full of), and *ant* (state of being), would you be able to decipher the meanings (or at least part of the meaning) of the following words? Try it: **err error errant erratic erroneous**

You would be correct if you said:

err means to make a mistake
an *error* is a mistake
errant means mistaken, or straying from the proper course
erratic means deviating from the customary course
erroneous means mistaken

Let's expand on this exercise to demonstrate how you can put roots to work to help decode very advanced words. The following ten words were created from one or more Latin and Greek roots and certain common suffixes:

acuminate ergatocracy orthotropism neonate noctilucent osseous paleography sacrosanct sequatious somniloquy

Write down what you think are the meanings of each word. If you do not know the exact definition, jot down your best guess. Then check to see if your answers are correct, or at least partially correct. Give yourself 10 points for each completely correct answer and 5 points for each partially correct answer. Here are the correct definitions:

acuminate = make sharp; taper to a point
ergatocracy = government by workers
orthotropism = vertical growth
neonate = newborn child
noctilucent = shining at night
osseous = bony; composed of, or containing bone
paleography = study of ancient writings
sacrosanct = extremely sacred; inviolable
sequatious = disposed to follow another
somniloquy = the act of talking in one's sleep

Total your score. If your score is below 50 percent, your root skills for the GRE are low and you will benefit tremendously from an intensive study of the major roots and prefixes that are listed in *300 High-Frequency Word Roots*. If your score is between 50 percent and 80 percent, you are strongly advised to review these Greek and Latin roots for a superior score on the GRE.

So, exactly how were the words in our exercise formed from Greek and Latin roots?

acuminate is from *acu* (sharp) + *ate* (verb suffix meaning make)

ergatocracy is from *erg* (work) + *cracy* (government)

orthotropism is from *ortho* (straight, upright, correct) + *tropo* (turning, change)

neonate is from *neo* (new) + *natur* (born)

noctilucent is from *nocti* (night) + *luc* (light, shine)

osseous is from *oss* (bone) + suffix ending *ous* (full of; characterized by)

paleography is from *paleo* (ancient) + *graph* (write)

sacrosanct is from *sacrum* (religious rite) + *sanctus* (to consecrate)

sequatious is from *sequi* (follow) + suffix ending *ous* (full of; characterized by)

somniloquy is from *somni* (sleep) + *loqui* (speak)

You may say that it is very unlikely you will have to know words like *orthotropism* or *sequatious*. This may be true if you become a plumber. However, if you do a postgraduate degree and go onto a career in academia or a professional career in medicine, law, and other fields you will be seeing *plenty* of such words. After you complete this unit, you will be able to attack words like this that you do not know, and steadily keep expanding your vocabulary.

Of course, your learning of roots should not stop here. You should keep adding new roots to your knowledge. You can do this by regularly consulting a dictionary. When you meet a word you don't know and you cannot decipher it, look it up. The dictionary will give you the word's etymology (origin and history). Make sure to use a good dictionary such as the *American Heritage College Dictionary* or *Merriam-Webster's Collegiate Dictionary*. Let's take an example to show how it works. Below is reproduced part of the entry for the word "aberration" from the *American Heritage College Dictionary*, fourth edition. The etymology is given at the end of the entry in brackets [   ].

[Lat. *aberratio, aberration-*, diversion < *aberratus*, p. part. of aberrare, to go astray: *ab-*, away from; see AB- + *errare*, to stray.]

Now let's begin our study of *300 High-Frequency Word Roots*. Major roots and prefixes appear as headings in each "Root Roundup" on the following pages, and there is a list of common suffixes provided at the end of the section. After mastering all the words and roots in each "Root Roundup," do the "Root Work" exercise to make sure you have learned everything. Comprehensive "Root Roundup" reviews are provided after every five units.

ROOT ROUNDUP 1

- **A/AN** (WITHOUT, ABSENSE OF, NOT) *Greek*
  atheist = person who does not believe in the existence of a god
  agnostic = person who is doubtful about something
  anarchy = absence of political authority
  anemia = deficiency in the part of the blood that carries oxygen
  anachronism = something out of the proper time

- **AB/ABS** (FROM, AWAY, OFF) *Latin*
  abduct = carry away by force; kidnap
  aberrant = deviating away from the expected or normal course
  abrade = wear away by friction; erode
  abdicate = formally relinquish power or responsibility
  abstinence = refraining from something

- **ACER/ACID/ACRI** (HARSH, BITTER, SOUR) *Latin*
  acrid = sharp or bitter to the taste or smell; sharp in language
    or tone
  acrimonious = bitter and sharp in language and tone
  acerbate = annoy
  acerbity = sourness or bitterness of taste, character, or tone
  ex**acer**bate = increase bitterness; make worse

- **ACT/AG** (DRIVE, DO, LEAD, ACT, MOVE) *Latin*
  active = being in physical motion
  actuate = put into motion; activate
  agenda = list or program of things to be done
  agency = condition of being in action
  agitation = act of causing to move with violent force

- **ACU** (SHARP) *Latin*
  acumen = keenness of judgment
  acuminate = tapering to a point; make sharp; taper
  acupuncture = therapeutic technique that uses needles to relieve
    pain
  aculeate = having a stinger; having sharp prickles
  acuity = sharpness of perception or vision

Root Work 1

Match each word with its definition.

1. agency	(A) formally relinquish power
2. exacerbate	(B) sharpness of vision
3. actuate	(C) deficiency in the blood
4. abstinence	(D) increase bitterness
5. anarchy	(E) condition of being in action
6. acuity	(F) make sharp; taper
7. abdicate	(G) sharp or bitter to the taste or smell
8. anemia	(H) absence of political authority
9. acrid	(I) put into motion
10. acuminate	(J) refraining from something

ROOT ROUNDUP 2

- **AD** (TO, TOWARD) **AC/AF/AG/AL/AN/AP/AR/AS/AT** before consonants *Latin*
  accord = cause to agree; bring into harmony
  acquiesce = consent quietly to something
  advent = arrival or coming
  aggregate = amounting to a whole; total
  appease = bring peace or calm to; to soothe

- **AEV/EV** (AGE, ERA) *Latin*
  prim**ev**al = belonging to the earliest age
  medi**ev**al = belonging to the Middle Ages
  medi**ev**alism = devotion to the ideas of the Middle Ages
  co**ev**al = existing during the same era
  long**ev**ity = long life; long duration

- **AGOG** (LEADER) *Greek*
  ped**agog**ue = teacher; a dogmatic teacher
  syn**agog**ue = place of meeting for worship in the Jewish faith
  emmen**agog**ue = agent that induces menstrual flow
  an**agog**y = mystical interpretation that detects allusions to the afterlife
  hypn**agog**ic = inducing sleep

- **AGR** (FIELD) *Latin*
  agribusiness = farming done as a large-scale business
  agriculture = farming
  agrarian = relating to farming or rural matters
  agritourism = form of tourism that lets people experience life on a farm
  agronomy = application of science to farming

- **ALI** (ANOTHER) *Latin*
  alien = characteristic of another place or society; strange
  alienation = emotional isolation or disassociation
  in**ali**enable = not capable of being surrendered
  alibi = fact of absence from the scene of a crime
  alienage = official status as an alien

Root Work 2
Match each word with its definition.

1. agrarian	(A) application of science to farming
2. primeval	(B) from another place or society
3. inalienable	(C) existing during the same era
4. pedagogue	(D) relating to farming
5. agronomy	(E) inducing sleep
6. appease	(F) belonging to the earliest age
7. coeval	(G) arrival or coming
8. advent	(H) bring peace or calm to
9. hypnagogic	(I) teacher; dogmatic leader
10. alien	(J) not capable of being surrendered

ROOT ROUNDUP 3

- **ALIM** (SUPPORT, NOURISH, CHERISH) *Latin*
  aliment = something that nourishes
  alimony = allowance for support to a divorced person by the former chief provider
  alible = nourishing
  alimentary = concerned with nutrition or food
  alimentation = giving or receiving of nourishment

- **ALTER** (OTHER) *Latin*
  alter = change; modify; become different
  alternate = proceed by turns
  alternative = one of two mutually exclusive possibilities
  alter ego = second self or another side of oneself
  altercate = argue vehemently

- **ALT** (HIGH, DEEP) *Latin*
  altar = elevated structure before which religious ceremonies are performed
  ex**alt**ation = condition of being raised up in rank
  altimeter = instrument that measures elevation
  altiplano = high plateau
  altitude = height of something above a certain reference level

- **AM** (LOVE, LIKING) *Latin*
  amiable = friendly; likeable
  en**am**ored = captivated
  amicable = friendly
  amity = friendship
  amatory = inclined toward love

- **AMB/AMBUL** (TO GO, TO WALK) *Latin*
  ambulate = walk from place to place
  amble = walk slowly
  ambulance = vehicle to transport injured people
  per**ambul**ate = walk about
  ambulatory = capable of walking

Root Work 3
Match each word with its definition.

  1. perambulate
  2. alter ego
  3. amatory
  4. alter
  5. amicable
  6. altiplano
  7. alimentary
  8. exaltation
  9. amble
 10. alible

(A) walk slowly
(B) friendly
(C) become different
(D) nourishing
(E) high plateau
(F) walk about
(G) another side of oneself
(H) concerned with nutrition
(I) being raised up in rank
(J) inclined toward love

ROOT ROUNDUP 4

- **AMBI** (AROUND, ON BOTH SIDES) *Latin*
  ambient = surrounding
  ambidextrous = able to use both hands well
  ambivalent = having conflicting feelings
  ambiguous = doubtful or unclear
  ambiversion = personality trait that combines both introversion and
    extroversion

- **AMPH/AMPHI** (AROUND, DOUBLE, ON BOTH SIDES) *Greek*
  amphibian = animal that can live both on land and in water
  amphora = two-handled Greek or Roman jar
  amphitheater = round structure with levels of seats rising upward
    from central area
  amphidiploid = having a diploid set of chromosomes from each parent
  amphibolous = having a grammatical structure that allows two
    interpretations

- **ANIM** (LIFE, BREATH, SPIRIT) *Latin*
  animal = multicellular organism of the kingdom Animalia
  animation = enthusiasm; excitement
  animism = belief that individual spirits inhabit natural phenomena
  animosity = hostility; hatred
  in**anim**ate = not exhibiting life

- **ANNU/ANNI/ENNI** (YEARLY) *Latin*
  annuity = yearly income payment
  anniversary = yearly recurring date of an event that occurred in
    the past
  bi**enni**al = happening every two years
  per**enni**al = lasting throughout the year or for several years
  mill**enni**um = thousand-year period

- **ANT/ANTE** (BEFORE) *Latin*
  antecedent = something that comes before
  antediluvian = extremely old; happening before the Flood
  antedate = come before in time
  anterior = placed before; earlier
  antler = bony growth on the head of a deer

Root Work 4
Match each word with its definition.

1. inanimate	(A) enthusiasm
2. ambiguous	(B) having conflicting feelings
3. antediluvian	(C) yearly income payment
4. animation	(D) animal able to live on land or in water
5. millennium	(E) not exhibiting life
6. amphibian	(F) doubtful; unclear
7. ambivalent	(G) something coming before
8. amphora	(H) two-handled Greek or Roman jar
9. annuity	(I) thousand-year period
10. antecedent	(J) extremely old

ROOT ROUNDUP 5

- **ANT/ANTI** (AGAINST, OPPOSITE) *Greek*
  antibiotic = substance that can kill microorganisms
  antiseptic = substance that can kill disease-causing organisms
  antipathy = dislike
  antithesis = opposite of
  antagonistic = hostile

ANTHROP (MANKIND, HUMAN BEING) *Greek*
anthropic = related to the human race
anthropoid = resembling human beings
anthropology = study of man
mis**anthrop**y = hatred of humanity
anthropocentric = regarding human beings as the center of the
   universe

ANTIQU (OLD, ANCIENT) *Latin*
antiquated = too old to be useful or fashionable
antique = belonging to an earlier period
antiquity = ancient times; an object from ancient times
antiquarian = relating to the study of antiquities
antiquate = make old-fashioned or obsolete

APPELL (NAME, CALL UPON) *Latin*
appellation = name or title
appellative = relating to the assignment of names
appeal = earnest or urgent request
appellant = relating to an appeal
appellate = having the power to hear court appeals

APT/EPT (SKILL, ABILITY) *Latin*
in**ept** = not suitable; having a lack of judgment or reason
apt = exactly suitable
un**apt** = not suitable
ad**apt** = make suitable to a specific situation
aptitude = inherent ability; a talent

Root Work 5
Match each word with its definition.

1. antiquated
2. misanthropy
3. inept
4. antithesis
5. appellative
6. anthropic
7. appellation
8. antipathy
9. apt
10. antique

(A) exactly suitable
(B) name or title
(C) hatred of humanity
(D) relating to the assignment of names
(E) dislike
(F) not suitable; lacking judgment
(G) belonging to an earlier period
(H) related to the human race
(I) too old to be useful
(J) the opposite of

ROOT ROUNDUP REVIEW 1–5

Match It
Match each of the following roots to its meaning.

1. ANTHROP ___	(A) harsh, bitter, sour
2. ACER/ACID/ACRI ___	(B) skill, ability
3. ACT/AG ___	(C) leader
4. AMBI ___	(D) to, toward
5. ANTE ___	(E) other
6. A/AD ___	(F) human being
7. ALTER ___	(G) around, on both sides
8. AP/EPT ___	(H) love, liking
9. AM ___	(I) drive, do, lead, act, move
10. AGOG ___	(J) before

Fill-ins
Fill in the blanks with the word that fits the definition.

aliment	anarchy	annuity	acumen	pedagogue
unapt	antiquate	agrarian	inanimate	perambulate

1. teacher; a dogmatic teacher _____
2. walk about _____
3. make old-fashioned or obsolete _____
4. something that nourishes _____
5. not exhibiting life _____
6. absence of political authority _____
7. not suitable _____
8. yearly income payment _____
9. relating to farming or rural matters _____
10. keenness of judgment _____

True or False
If the statement is correct, put (T) True; if it is incorrect, put (F) False.

1. An anachronism is something that is in tune with the times. _____
2. Things that are coeval are equally evil. _____
3. An altimeter is an instrument that measures elevation. _____
4. An amphora is a Greek or Roman jar with two handles. _____
5. Antagonistic people do not usually display hostility. _____

ROOT ROUNDUP 6

- **AQU/AQUA** (WATER) *Latin*
  aquarium = tank for holding fish and sea plants
  aqueduct = large pipe or canal that carries water to large communities
  aquatic = relating to things that occur in or on water: aquatic plants
  or sports
  sub**aqu**eous = created or existing under water
  aquifer = underground rock formation that bears water; where water
  flows underground

- **ARCH** (FIRST, CHIEF, RULE, SUPERIOR) *Greek*
  archangel = chief angel
  archaic = out of date
  patri**arch**y = family or community governed by men
  archeology = study of material evidence of past human life
  archetype = original model after which others are patterned

- **ARM/ARMA** (WEAPONS) *Latin*
  armistice = truce; temporary stop to fighting
  armada = fleet of warships
  dis**arma**ment = reduction of a nation's weapons and military forces
  armor = covering that protects one's body against weapons
  armadillo = burrowing mammal that has armorlike long plates

- **ART** (ART) *Latin*
  artisan = craftsperson
  artifact = object made by human craft
  art nouveau = late nineteenth-century style of art
  artificial = made by human action
  artifice = artful expedient

- **ASTR/ASTER** (STAR) *Greek*
  asterisk = the sign *
  astral = relating to stars
  astronaut = person who travels in space
  astrology = study of the influence of the stars and planets on
  human beings
  astronomy = scientific study of the stars and other bodies in the
  universe

Root Work 6
Match each word with its definition.

1. aqueduct   (A) craftsperson
2. patriarchy   (B) fleet of warships
3. archetype   (C) existing underwater
4. artisan   (D) community or family governed by men
5. armada   (E) scientific study of the stars and other bodies in the universe
6. astronomy   (F) reduction of a nation's weapons and military forces
7. subaqueous   (G) object made by human craft
8. astral   (H) relating to the stars
9. disarmament   (I) original model after which others are patterned
10. artifact   (J) canal that carries water to communities

ROOT ROUNDUP 7

- **AUD/AUDI/AUS** (BOLD, DARING, LISTEN, HEAR) *Latin*
  auditorium = part of a theater where the audience sits
  audible = capable of being heard
  audacious = bold, daring
  audacity = fearless, daring, and adventurousness
  auscultation = listening to the heart or other organs

- **AUG/AUX** (INCREASE) *Latin*
  augment = make greater
  in**aug**urate = begin or start officially
  august = dignified; awe-inspiring
  augur = foretell
  auxiliary = supplementary

- **AUTO** (SELF) *Greek*
  automatic = self-acting or self-regulating
  autograph = person's signature
  autonomic = occurring involuntarily
  autonomous = self-governing
  autobiography = self-written account of one's own life

- **BE** (THOROUGLY, OVER) *Old English*
  befuddled = confused; perplexed
  beguile = delude; deceive by guile
  besmirched = stained; soiled
  bedecked = adorned in a showy manner
  bedizen = dress in a showy manner

• **BEL/BELL** (WAR) *Latin*
re**bel** = carry out armed resistance to the government
bellicose = aggressive; warlike
belligerent = hostile; tending to fight
ante**bell**um = existing before a war
post**bell**um = existing after a war

Root Work 7

Match each word with its definition.

1. autonomic   (A) make greater
2. august   (B) existing before a war
3. audacious   (C) self-governing
4. antebellum   (D) confused; perplexed
5. auscultation   (E) hostile; tending to fight
6. bedizen   (F) bold; daring
7. befuddled   (G) occurring involuntarily
8. autonomous   (H) ornament or dress in a showy manner
9. belligerent   (I) dignified; awe-inspiring
10. augment   (J) listening to the heart or other organs

ROOT ROUNDUP 8

• **BEN/BON** (WELL, GOOD, FAVORABLE) *Latin*
beneficent = kindly; doing good
benediction = blessing
benevolent = generous; charitable
benign = harmless; kind
bonanza = large amount

• **BI** (TWO, TWICE, DOUBLE) *Latin*
bicycle = light-framed vehicle mounted on two wheels
biannual = happening twice each year
bifurcate = divide into two parts
bicuspid = having two points
bivalve = having a shell composed of two valves

BIO (LIFE) *Greek*
biologist = scientist who studies life
biosphere = part of the Earth's surface and atmosphere in which life
    exists
bionics = science concerned with applying biological systems to
    engineering problems
biotic = produced by living organisms
sym**bio**tic = relating to a relationship of mutual benefit or dependence

- **BREV** (SHORT) *Latin*
  ab**brev**iate = make shorter
  ab**brev**iation = act or product of shortening
  brevity = state of briefness in duration
  breve = symbol over a vowel to indicate a short sound
  breviary = book containing hymns and prayers for canonical hours

- **CAP/CAPT/CEPT/CIP** (HOLD, SEIZE, TAKE) *Latin*
  capable = having ability or capacity
  inter**cept** = interrupt the course of
  captious = faultfinding; intending to entrap, as in an argument
  pre**cept** = principle that prescribes a course of action
  capture = take captive; to seize

Root Work 8
Match each word with its definition.

1. biotic	(A) interrupt the course of
2. capture	(B) happening twice a year
3. bicuspid	(C) shortness in duration
4. breve	(D) harmless; kind
5. biannual	(E) produced by living organisms
6. intercept	(F) having two points
7. benign	(G) symbol over a vowel that indicates a short sound
8. biosphere	(H) generous; charitable
9. benevolent	(I) part of the Earth's surface and atmosphere in which life exists
10. brevity	(J) seize

ROOT ROUNDUP 9

- **CAP/CAPIT** (HEAD) *Latin*
  per **capit**a = per unit of population
  capitol = building in which a state legislature meets
  de**capit**ate = behead
  capitulate = surrender
  captain = someone who commands others

- **CARD/CORD** (HEART) *Latin*
  cardiac = relating to the heart
  cardiology = branch of medicine concerned with the heart
  cordial = warm and sincere
  con**cord** = harmony; agreement
  dis**cord**ant = disagreeable in sound; conflicting

- **CARN** (FLESH, BODY) *Latin*
  carnal = of the flesh or body
  carnation = perennial plant with showy flowers
  carnivore = animal or plant that feeds on flesh
  in**carn**ate = give bodily form to
  carnage = massive slaughter, as in war

- **CATA** (DOWN, DOWNWARD) *Greek*
  catalyst = something causing change
  cataract = high waterfall; a great downpour
  catapult = ancient military machine for hurling missiles
  cataclysm = violent upheaval
  catastrophic = relating to a great calamity

- **CED/CEED/CESS** (YIELD, SURRENDER, MOVE, GO) *Latin*
  cede = surrender; yield
  ac**ced**e = agree to
  pre**ced**e = go before
  ante**ced**ent = something that comes before
  in**cess**ant = never ceasing

Root Work 9

Match each word with its definition.

1. concord	(A) warm and sincere
2. incarnate	(B) animal or plant that feeds on flesh
3. captain	(C) high waterfall; great downpour
4. antecedent	(D) relating to a great calamity
5. cordial	(E) surrender; yield
6. cataract	(F) something that comes before
7. decapitate	(G) harmony; agreement
8. catastrophic	(H) behead
9. cede	(I) someone who commands others
10. carnivore	(J) give bodily form to

ROOT ROUNDUP 10

- **CELER** (SWIFT) *Latin*
  ac**celer**ate = increase speed
  ac**celer**ant = substance used as a catalyst
  celerity = swiftness; speed
  de**celer**ation = decrease the velocity of
  ac**celer**ando = musical direction for a dual quickening in time

- **CENTR** (CENTER) *Latin*
  con**centr**ic = having a common center
  centrifugal = moving or directed away from a center
  centripetal = moving or directed toward a center
  con**centr**ate = direct toward a center
  centric = situated near or at the center of something

- **CENT** (HUNDRED) *Latin*
  centimeter = unit of length equal to one hundredth of a meter
  centenary = relating to a 100-year period
  centenarian = one who is 100 years old or more
  century = period of 100 years
  centennial = relating to a period of 100 years; occurring every
      100 years

- **CERN** (PERCEIVE) *Latin*
  con**cern** = regard for or interest in
  dis**cern** = perceive; detect
  dis**cern**ing = showing good judgment; perceptive
  indis**cern**ible = difficult to perceive
  uncon**cern**edly = in a way that is unworried

- **CERT** (CERTAIN) *Latin*
  certify = confirm formally as genuine
  certificate = document confirming the truth of something
  certainty = state or fact of being certain
  certitude = state of being certain; sureness of occurrence
  as**cert**ain = discover with certainty

Root Work 10
Match each word with its definition.

1. centrifugal	(A) moving toward a center
2. certitude	(B) swiftness; speed
3. centennial	(C) substance used as a catalyst
4. centenarian	(D) discover with certainty
5. indiscernible	(E) relating to a period of 100 years
6. celerity	(F) showing good judgment; perceptive
7. discerning	(G) moving away from a center
8. accelerant	(H) difficult to perceive
9. centripetal	(I) state of being certain; sureness of occurrence
10. ascertain	(J) someone 100 years old or more

ROOT ROUNDUP REVIEW 6–10

Match It
Match each of the following roots to its meaning.

1. ASTR/ASTER ___	(A) short
2. ARM/ARMA ___	(B) flesh, body
3. AUG/AUS ___	(C) weapons
4. BE ___	(D) swift
5. BIO ___	(E) down
6. BREV ___	(F) perceive
7. CARN ___	(G) thoroughly, over
8. CATA ___	(H) star
9. CELER ___	(I) increase
10. CERN ___	(J) life

Fill-ins
Fill in the blanks with the word that fits the definition.

benediction	augur	symbiotic	archaic	captious
catapult	incessant	centripetal	centrifugal	subaqueous

1. relating to a relationship of mutual benefit or dependence
_____

2. foretell _____
3. created or existing underwater _____
4. out of date _____
5. never ceasing _____
6. moving away from a center _____
7. a blessing _____
8. an ancient military machine for hurling missiles _____
9. moving toward a center _____
10. faultfinding; intending to entrap, as in argument _____

True or False
If the statement is correct, put (T) True; if it is incorrect, put (F) False.

1. Antebellum refers to a period after a war. _____
2. Archeology is the study of the influence of stars and planets on human life. _____
3. Auscultation means speaking clearly and fluently. _____
4. A patriarchy is a family or community governed by men. _____
5. Centennial relates to a period of 1,000 years. _____

ROOT ROUNDUP 11

- **CHRON** (TIME, A LONG TIME) *Greek*
  chronic = constant; prolonged
  chronicle = record of historical events
  chronometer = instrument that measures time
  ana**chron**ism = something out of the proper time
  chronology = arrangement in order of occurrence

- **CID/CIS** (CUT, KILL) *Latin*
  homi**cid**e = killing of one person by another
  s**cis**sors = cutting instrument with two blades
  exor**cis**e = expel evil spirits
  ex**cis**ion = remove by cutting
  abs**cis**sion = natural separation of flowers, leaves, etc. from plants

- **CIRCU/CIRCUM** (AROUND) *Latin*
  circumvent = avoid; get around
  circumflex = curving around
  circuitous = taking a roundabout course
  circumlocution = indirect way of saying something
  circumscribe = limit

- **CIT/CITAT** (CALL, START) *Latin*
  cite = mention as illustration or proof; to quote as an example
  citable = able to be brought forward as support or proof
  citation = the act of citing; a quotation
  re**cit**e = say aloud before an audience something rehearsed
  re**cit**ative = having the character of a recital

- **CIVI** (CITIZEN) *Latin*
  civil = relating to a citizen or citizens; of ordinary citizens or ordinary community life
  civic = relating to a city, a citizen, or citizenship
  civilize = raise from barbarism to civilization; educate in matters of culture
  civilian = citizen who is not an acting member of the military or police
  civility = courteous behavior

Root Work 11
Match each word with its definition.

1. excision	(A) constant; prolonged
2. circumflex	(B) relating to a city or a citizen
3. cite	(C) say aloud before an audience something rehearsed
4. anachronism	(D) natural separation of flowers and leaves from plants
5. recite	(E) mention as an illustration
6. civic	(F) avoid; get around
7. abscission	(G) citizen who is not a member of the military
8. civilian	(H) curving around
9. chronic	(I) something out of the proper time
10. circumvent	(J) remove by cutting

ROOT ROUNDUP 12

- **CLAM/CLAIM** (CALL OUT, SHOUT) *Latin*
  ex**claim** = cry out suddenly; utter vehemently
  ex**clam**ation = an abrupt forceful utterance; an outcry
  clamor = a loud outcry
  re**claim** = demand the return of something
  ac**clam**ation = shout of enthusiastic approval

- **CLEMEN** (MILD, KIND, MERCIFUL) *Latin*
  clemency = disposition to show mercy; merciful act; mildness
  clement = inclined to be merciful; mild
  in**clemen**t = stormy; showing no mercy
  in**clemen**cy = state of showing no mercy
  in**clemen**tly = in a way that shows no mercy

- **CLAUD/CLAUS/CLOS/CLUD/CLUS** (SHUT, CLOSE) *Latin*
  clause = a stipulation or provision in a document
  ex**clud**e = keep out; reject; put out
  se**clus**ion = isolation; solitude
  re**clus**e = person who lives in seclusion
  oc**clud**e = cause to become closed; obstruct

- **CLI/CLIN/CLIV** (LEANING, INCLINED, SLOPED) *Latin*
  climax = point of greatest intensity in an ascending progression
  in**clin**ation = a tendency toward a certain condition
  disin**clin**ation = lack of inclination; reluctance
  syn**clin**al = sloping downward from opposite directions and meeting in a common point
  pro**cliv**ity = tendency; inclination

- **CO/COL/COM/CON/COR** (TOGETHER, WITH) *Latin*
  coherent = understandable; sticking together
  collaborate = work together
  communication = exchange of thoughts and information
  conformity = harmony; agreement
  corroborate = confirm

Root Work 12
Match each word with its definition.

1. collaborate	(A)	person who lives in seclusion
2. clamor	(B)	shout of enthusiastic approval
3. occlude	(C)	inclined to be merciful
4. conformity	(D)	harmony; agreement
5. acclamation	(E)	work together
6. disinclination	(F)	cause to become closed
7. clement	(G)	tendency; inclination
8. inclement	(H)	lack of inclination
9. proclivity	(I)	loud outcry
10. recluse	(J)	stormy; showing no mercy

ROOT ROUNDUP 13

- **COD** (BOOK) *Latin*
  code = systematic, comprehensive collection of laws; system of symbols used for sending messages that require secrecy
  de**cod**e = convert from code into text
  codify = reduce to a code
  codex = manuscript volume of a classic work
  codicil = an appendix to a will

- **COGNI/GNO** (LEARN, KNOW) *Latin/Greek*
  cognition = mental process by which knowledge is acquired
  in**cogni**to = in disguise; concealing one's identity
  dia**gno**sis = process of determining the nature and cause of a disease
  pro**gno**sticate = predict on the basis of present conditions
  a**gno**sia = loss of the ability to interpret sensory stimuli

- **CONTRA/CONTRO** (AGAINST, OPPOSITE) *Latin*
  contradict = speak against
  contrary = opposed
  contravene = act contrary to; to violate
  contraindicate = indicate the inadvisability of the use of a medicine
  controversy = dispute between sides holding opposing views

- **CORP** (BODY) *Latin*
  corpse = a dead body
  corpulent = excessively fat
  corporeal = concerned with the body
  corpus = a large collection of writings
  in**corp**orate = unite one thing with something else already in
  existence

- **COSM** (UNIVERSE) *Greek*
  cosmic = relating to the universe; infinite; vast
  micro**cosm** = a small system having analogies to a larger system
  cosmology = study of the physical universe
  cosmos = the universe as a harmonious whole
  cosmopolitan = common to or having elements from all over the
  world

Root Work 13
Match each word with its definition.

1. cognition   (A) manuscript volume of a classic work
2. contradict   (B) concerned with the body
3. codex   (C) study of the physical universe
4. cosmos   (D) mental process by which knowledge
                        is acquired
5. corporeal   (E) speak against
6. code   (F) predict on the basis of present conditions
7. contravene   (G) the universe as a harmonious whole
8. cosmology   (H) act contrary to
9. corpus   (I) systematic, comprehensive collection of laws
10. prognosticate   (J) a large collection of writings

ROOT ROUNDUP 14

- **CRACY/CRAT** (GOVERNMENT, RULE, STRENGTH) *Greek*
  aristo**cracy** = hereditary ruling class
  bureau**cracy** = administration of a government or a large complex
  pluto**cracy** = society ruled by the wealthy
  theo**cracy** = government by priests
  techno**crat** = strong believer in technology

- **CREA** (BRING FORTH, CREATE) *Latin*
  create = bring into being
  creature = something created; a living being
  re**crea**te = give fresh life to; refresh mentally or physically
  pro**crea**tion = the conceiving of offspring; producing or creating
  mis**crea**te = make or shape badly

- **CRED** (BELIEVE, TRUST) *Latin*
  credo = statement of belief or principle; creed
  credentials = evidence concerning one's right to confidence or authority
  credible = believable; plausible
  credence = acceptance of something as true
  in**cred**ulous = skeptical; doubtful

- **CRE/CRESC/CRET/CRU** (RISE, GROW) *Latin*
  ac**cru**e = increase; come about as a result of growth
  crescent = increasing; waxing, as the moon
  crescendo = in music, a gradual increase in the volume or intensity of sound
  in**cre**ment = something added; process of increasing
  in**cresc**ent = waxing; growing; showing a surface that is ever larger and lighted

- **CRIT** (SEPARATE, JUDGE) *Greek*
  critical = inclined to judge severely; characterized by careful judgment
  criterion = a standard on which a judgment can be made
  hypo**crit**ical = professing beliefs that one does not possess; false
  criticism = a critical comment or judgment
  critique = a critical review or commentary

Root Work 14
Match each word with its definition.

1. technocrat	(A) believable; plausible
2. incredulous	(B) producing or creating
3. accrue	(C) government by priests
4. miscreate	(D) waxing; growing
5. critical	(E) standard on which a judgment can be made
6. procreation	(F) strong believer in technology
7. criterion	(G) increase; come about as a result of growth
8. increscent	(H) inclined to judge severely
9. theocracy	(I) make or shape badly
10. credible	(J) skeptical; doubtful

ROOT ROUNDUP 15

- **COUR/CUR** (RUN, COURSE) *Latin*
  con**cur**rence = agreement in opinion; simultaneous occurrence
  courier = a messenger
  curriculum = the courses offered by an educational institution
  pre**cur**sor = a forerunner or predecessor
  current = a steady, smooth, onward movement

- **CUR/CURA** (CARE) *Latin*
  curator = someone who oversees a museum collection
  curé = a parish priest
  curette = surgical instrument that removes growths from a body cavity
  curative = tending to cure
  curate = a cleric who is in charge of a parish

- **CYCL/CYCLO** (CIRCLE, WHEEL, CYCLE) *Greek*
  cyclical = characterized by cycles; moving in cycles
  cyclosis = rotary motion of protoplasm within a cell
  cycloid = resembling a circle
  Cyclops = in Greek mythology, any of a race of one-eyed giants
  cyclothymia = affective disorder characterized by alternating periods
    of depression and elation

- **DE** (INTENSIVE PREFIX; FROM, DOWN, AWAY, AGAINST,
    THOROUGHLY) *Latin*
  demolish = tear down completely
  deplore = disapprove of; regret
  deride = mock
  denounce = condemn
  deprecate = belittle; express disapproval

- **DEC/DECA** (TEN) *Greek*
  Decalogue = the Ten Commandments
  decimate = destroy a large part of; inflict great destruction on
  decade = a period of ten years
  decahedron = a polyhedron with ten faces
  decapod = a crustacean having ten legs

Root Work 15
Match each word with its definition.

1. deride	(A) tear down completely
2. decahedron	(B) crustacean having ten legs
3. curative	(C) one who oversees a museum collection
4. cyclical	(D) forerunner
5. precursor	(E) resembling a circle
6. concurrence	(F) simultaneous occurrence
7. decapod	(G) mock
8. cycloid	(H) characterized by cycles
9. curator	(I) polyhedron with ten faces
10. demolish	(J) tending to cure

ROOT ROUNDUP REVIEW 11–15

Match It
Match each of the following roots to its meaning.

1. CID/CIS ___		(A)	body
2. CIRCU/CIRCUM ___		(B)	call out, shout
3. CLAM/CLAIM ___		(C)	believe, trust
4. CLEMEN ___		(D)	book, writing
5. COD ___		(E)	run, course
6. CORP ___		(F)	mild, kind, merciful
7. CRED ___		(G)	cut, kill
8. CRIT ___		(H)	from, down, away, against, thoroughly
9. COUR/CUR ___		(I)	around
10. DE ___		(J)	separate, judge

Fill-ins
Fill in the blanks with the word that fits the definition.

criterion	synclinal	cosmopolitan	civil	coherent
corpulent	cyclothymia	miscreate	deprecate	cite

1. relating to a citizen or citizens; of ordinary citizens or ordinary community life _____
2. common to or having elements from all over the world _____
3. sticking together; understandable _____
4. mention as illustration or proof; to quote as an example _____
5. a standard on which a judgment can be made _____
6. excessively fat _____
7. make or shape badly _____
8. belittle; to express disapproval _____
9. sloping downward from opposite directions and meeting in a common point _____
10. an affective disorder characterized by alternating periods of depression and elation _____

True or False

If the statement is correct, put (T) True; if it is incorrect, put (F) False.

1. A chronometer is an instrument that measures wind speed. _____
2. A proclivity is a tendency or inclination. _____
3. To prognosticate is to predict based on present conditions. _____
4. Something increscent is growing or showing a surface that is ever larger and lighted. _____
5. Decahedrons are polyhedrons with nine faces. _____

ROOT ROUNDUP 16

- **DEI/DIV** (GOD) *Latin*
  divine = having the nature of a god
  divinity = the state of being divine
  deify = raise to the condition of a god
  deism = belief that a God has created the universe, but exerts no control or influence on it
  deific = making divine; characterized by a godlike nature

- **DEMI** (PARTLY) *Latin*
  demigod = the male offspring of a god and a mortal; a minor god
  demimonde = a group whose respectability is questionable
  demirelief = structural relief having modeled forms projecting halfway from a background
  demirep = person whose reputation is doubtful
  demitasse = a small cup of espresso

- **DEM** (COMMON PEOPLE) *Greek*
  demographic = related to population balance
  epi**dem**ic = a widespread disease that affects many people at the same time
  pan**dem**ic = spread over a whole area or country
  demagogue = leader who appeals to emotion or prejudice
  democratic = of or for the people; popular

- **DERM** (SKIN) *Greek*
  dermatology = branch of medicine concerned with pathology of the skin
  dermatitis = inflammation of the skin
  epi**derm**is = the outer layer of the skin
  taxi**derm**ist = one who works in the art of stuffing and mounting skins of dead animals
  pachy**derm** = a thick-skinned hoofed animal like the elephant or hippopotamus

- **DI** (TWO, DOUBLE) *Greek*
  diphase = having two phases
  dichotomy = division into two usually contradictory parts
  dilemma = situation necessitating a choice between two unsatisfactory
    options
  dibromide = chemical compound having two bromine atoms
  dihedral = two-sided

Root Work 16
Match each word with its definition.

1. demigod	(A) leader who appeals to emotion or prejudice
2. pachyderm	(B) one who works stuffing and mounting dead animal skin
3. deific	(C) chemical compound having two bromine atoms
4. diphase	(D) minor god
5. taxidermist	(E) person whose reputation is doubtful
6. demirep	(F) raise to the condition of a god
7. deify	(G) making divine; having a godlike nature
8. demagogue	(H) spread over a whole area or country
9. pandemic	(I) thick-skinned hoofed animal
10. dibromide	(J) having two phases

ROOT ROUNDUP 17

- **DIA** (ACROSS, THROUGH, BETWEEN) *Greek*
  diagram = drawing that explains the relationship between parts of
    a whole
  diachronic = concerned with phenomena as they change through
    time
  diatribe = an abusive denunciation
  dialogue = a conversation between two or more people
  diaphanous = so fine as to be almost transparent or translucent

- **DIC/DICT** (SAY, SPEAK, PRONOUNCE) *Latin*
  e**dict** = a formal command
  bene**dict**ion = blessing
  in**dict** = charge with a crime
  male**dict**ion = curse
  dictum = authoritarian statement

- **DIF/DIS** (APART, AWAY, NOT) *Latin*
  diffuse = spread out
  disparity = difference
  dissuade = to persuade someone to alter intentions
  dispassionate = impartial; unaffected by emotion
  disseminate = to spread; scatter

- **DON** (GIVE) *Latin*
  donation = the act of giving to a cause or charity
  donor = one who contributes a donation to a cause or charity
  donee = one who receives a gift
  donary = a votive offering; a gift
  donatio mortis causa = gift by reason of death

- **DOC/DOCT** (TEACH, PROVE) *Latin*
  doctrinaire = relating to a person who cannot compromise about
    points of a theory or doctrine
  docent = lecturer
  doctrine = principle or system presented for acceptance or belief
  in**doct**rinate = instruct in a body of principles
  docile = willing to be taught; yielding to supervision

Root Work 17
Match each word with its definition.

1. dispassionate
2. dictum
3. donatio mortis causa
4. malediction
5. donary
6. diaphanous
7. diffuse
8. docent

9. dialogue
10. docile

(A) conversation between two or more people
(B) lecturer
(C) spread out
(D) authoritarian statement
(E) willing to be taught
(F) gift by reason of death
(G) unaffected by emotion
(H) so fine as to be almost transparent or translucent
(I) curse
(J) a gift; a votive offering

ROOT ROUNDUP 18

- **DOG/DOX** (OPINION, BELIEF, PRAISE) *Greek*
  dogmatic = characterized by an authoritarian assertion of unproved principles
  ortho**dox** = adhering to what is commonly accepted or traditional
  para**dox** = self-contradictory assertion based on valid deduction from acceptable premises
  hetero**dox** = not in agreement with accepted beliefs
  doxology = an expression of praise to God

- **DOM/DOMIN** (MASTER, LORD) *Latin*
  dominate = control by authority or power
  dominion = control; sovereignty
  pre**domin**ant = having greatest authority, influence, or force
  domination = control or power over another
  in**dom**itable = unconquerable; not able to be subdued

- **DORM** (SLEEP) *Latin*
  dormant = inactive; asleep
  dormitory = room used for sleeping quarters for many people
  dormient = sleeping; dormant; latent
  dormitive = causing sleep
  dormouse = a squirrel-like rodent

- **DROM/DROME** (RUN, STEP, ARENA) *Greek*
  dromedary = one-humped camel
  aero**drome** = an airport; military air base
  hippo**drome** = arena for equestrian shows
  dromond = a medieval sailing ship
  cata**drom**ous = inhabiting fresh water but migrating to the ocean to breed

- **DUC/DUCT** (LEAD, PULL) *Latin*
  in**duc**e = bring about
  se**duc**e = lead away from duty or proper conduct
  ab**duc**t = carry off by force
  via**duct** = series of arches used to carry a road over a valley or other roads
  ductile = easily drawn into wire; easily molded

Root Work 18
Match each word with its definition.

1. indomitable	(A) control; sovereignty
2. dormitive	(B) not in agreement with accepted beliefs
3. dromond	(C) arena for equestrian shows
4. doxology	(D) asleep; inactive
5. ductile	(E) lead away from duty or proper conduct
6. dominion	(F) unconquerable
7. hippodrome	(G) medieval sailing ship
8. seduce	(H) expression of praise to God
9. heterodox	(I) causing sleep
10. dormant	(J) easily molded

ROOT ROUNDUP 19

- **DUPL** (DOUBLE, TWO) *Latin*
  duplicity = double-dealing; being twofold; deceptiveness
  duplex = twofold; double
  duplicate = identically copied from an original
  duplicator = machine that copies printed material
  duple = consisting of two; double

- **DUR** (HARD, LASTING) *Latin*
  durable = able to withstand wear and tear
  duration = persistence in time; a period of existence
  en**dur**e = carry on through hardships; bear tolerantly
  duress = constraint by threat; forcible confinement
  ob**dur**ate = hardened; hardhearted; inflexible

- **DYN/DYNAM** (POWER, ENERGY) *Greek*
  dynamite = a class of powerful explosives
  dynamo = a generator that produces current; an energetic person
  dynasty = succession of rulers from the same line
  dynamic = marked by intensity and vigor
  hetero**dyn**e = having alternating currents with two different
    frequencies

- **DYS** (BAD, IMPAIRED, ABNORMAL) *Greek*
  dysfunctional = functioning abnormally
  dyslexia = learning disorder causing impairment of the ability
    to read
  dystopia = an imaginary place in which life is bad
  dysentery = disorder of the lower intestinal tract
  dyspepsia = indigestion

- **E/EX** (INTENSIVE PREFIX; APART, ABOVE, AWAY, BEYOND, FROM, OUT) *Latin*
  emit = send out
  enervate = weaken
  extricate = free from
  exhale = breathe out
  exotic = unusual

Root Work 19
Match each word with its definition.

1. dynasty	(A) imaginary place where life is bad
2. obdurate	(B) being twofold; deceptiveness
3. emit	(C) energetic person
4. endure	(D) hardhearted
5. dystopia	(E) breathe out
6. duplicity	(F) succession of rulers from the same line
7. dysentery	(G) consisting of two
8. exhale	(H) disorder of lower intestinal tract
9. dynamo	(I) send out
10. duple	(J) carry on through hardships

ROOT ROUNDUP 20

- **ECTO** (OUTSIDE, EXTERNAL) *Greek*
  ectogenous = able to develop outside a host
  ectoplasm = outer part of the cytoplasm of a cell
  ectopic pregnancy = development of an ovum outside the uterus
  ectoderm = outermost germ layer of an embryo
  ectopia = abnormal location of an organ or body part

- **EGO** (I, SELF) *Latin*
  egocentric = self-centered
  egomania = extreme egocentrism
  egotistical = excessively self-centered
  egoist = person devoted to his or her own interests
  super **ego** = the part of the mind that opposes the desires of the id (the subconscious source of instinctual impulses)

ENDO (WITHIN, INSIDE) *Greek*
endomorph = a mineral enclosed inside another mineral
endogenous = growing from within; produced inside an organism
endoscope = instrument for viewing the inside of an organ of
  the body
endobiotic = living as a parasite within a host
endocardial = relating to a membrane that lines the heart's interior

EPI (UPON, OVER, NEAR) *Greek*
epidermis = outer layer of skin covering the dermis
epidemic = widely prevalent
epigeal = living in or near the surface of the ground
epitaph = inscription on a tombstone
epicenter = point in the Earth directly above the center of an
  earthquake

EQU (EQUAL) *Latin*
equator = imaginary circle around the Earth, which is equidistant
  from the poles
equation = statement asserting the equality of two mathematical
  expressions
equivocal = ambiguous; misleading
equanimity = composure
in**equ**ity = unfairness

Root Work 20
Match each word with its definition.

1. egoist	(A) able to develop outside a host
2. ectoderm	(B) instrument to look inside an organ of the body
3. epigeal	(C) excessively self-centered
4. endobiotic	(D) composure
5. epitaph	(E) inscription on a tombstone
6. ectogenous	(F) unfairness
7. equanimity	(G) outermost germ layer of an embryo
8. inequity	(H) living near the surface of the ground
9. egotistical	(I) living as a parasite within a host
10. endoscope	(J) person devoted to his or her own interests

ROOT ROUNDUP REVIEW 16–20

Match It
Match each of the following roots to its meaning.

1. DEI/DIV ___
2. DEMI ___
3. DON ___
4. DOC/DOCT ___
5. DOM/DOMIN ___

6. DORM ___
7. DYN/DYNAM ___
8. ENDO ___
9. EGO ___
10. E/EX ___

(A) teach, prove
(B) power, energy
(C) sleep
(D) within
(E) apart, above, beyond, from, intensive prefix
(F) I, self
(G) God
(H) give
(I) master, lord
(J) partly

Fill-ins
Fill in the blanks with the word that fits the definition.

dichotomy	obdurate	malediction	duple	ductile
inequity	pandemic	dermatitis	epigeal	
donatio mortis causa				

1. spread over an entire area _____
2. consisting of two _____
3. hardened; inflexible; hardhearted _____
4. gift by reason of death _____
5. unfairness _____
6. division into two usually contradictory parts _____
7. living near or in the surface of the ground _____
8. easily molded _____
9. inflammation of the skin _____
10. curse _____

True or False
If the statement is correct, put (T) True; if it is incorrect, put (F) False.

1. A taxidermist is a thick-skinned hoofed animal. _____
2. Diachronic means concerned with phenomena of a particular time. _____
3. An ectoderm is the outermost germ layer of an embryo. _____
4. Doxology is adherence to unorthodox beliefs. _____
5. A dystopia is an imaginary place in which life is bad. _____

ROOT ROUNDUP 21

ERG (WORK) *Greek*
ergatocracy = government by workers
ergonomics = science of the design of equipment for maximizing productivity
erg = a unit of work
ergograph = instrument for measuring work capacity of a muscle while contracting
syn**erg**ic = working together

ERR (WANDER, MISTAKE) *Latin*
errant = mistaken; straying from the proper course
erratic = lacking regularity; deviating from the customary course
erroneous = mistaken
err = make a mistake
erratum = mistake in writing or printing

ETH/ETHOS (CHARACTER) *Greek*
ethos = character peculiar to a person, people, or culture
bio**eth**ics = study of ethical implications of scientific discoveries, as in genetic engineering
ethic = set of principles of correct conduct; system of moral values
ethics = rules that govern conduct of people or members of a profession
ethology = the study of human ethos

EU (GOOD, WELL) *Greek*
eulogy = high praise
euphemism = use of inoffensive language in place of unpleasant language
eugenics = a philosophy that advocates the improvement of human traits through various means
euphoria = feeling of extreme happiness
euphony = pleasant and harmonious sound

EXTRA/EXTRO (BESIDES, BEYOND, OUTSIDE OF, MORE) *Latin*
extraordinary = beyond the ordinary
extracurricular = outside of the regular curriculum
extraterrestrial = outside Earth
extraneous = not essential
extroversion = behavior directed outside one's self

Root Work 21

Match each word with its definition.

1. euphony	(A) character peculiar to a person or people
2. erratic	(B) high praise
3. ethos	(C) working together
4. erg	(D) set of principles of correct conduct
5. ethic	(E) deviating from the customary course
6. erroneous	(F) outside Earth
7. extraterrestrial	(G) a unit of work
8. eulogy	(H) harmonious sound
9. synergic	(I) mistaken
10. extraneous	(J) not essential

ROOT ROUNDUP 22

- **FAC/FIC/FEC** (DO, MAKE) *Latin*
  bene**fic**ent = performing acts of kindness
  manu**fac**ture = make or process
  con**fec**tion = act of making a sweet preparation; a sweet preparation
  sapori**fic** = something that produces sleep
  facile = done with little effort; easy

- **FALL/FALS** (DECEPTIVE/FALSE/ERRONEOUS) *Latin*
  false = untrue; mistaken; wrong; misleading
  fallacious = based on a false idea or fact; misleading
  falsify = state untruthfully; misrepresent
  fallible = capable of making an error
  in**fall**ible = incapable of making a mistake

- **FED** (LEAGUE, PACT) *Latin*
  federal = related to a system of government in which power is
    divided between a central government and constituent states
  federation = the act of joining into a league or federal union; a
    federal group of states
  federacy = an alliance; a confederacy
  federative = forming, belonging to, or having the nature of a
    federation
  con**fed**erate = a member of a league; an ally

- **FER** (BEAR, CARRY) *Latin*
  coni**fer**ous = pertaining to needle-leaved cone-bearing trees such
    as pines or firs
  aqui**fer** = stratum of permeable rock that bears water
  pesti**fer**ous = bearing moral contagion; pestilent; deadly
  voci**fer**ous = loud, vocal, and noisy
  spori**fer**ous = producing spores

- **FID** (FAITH, TRUST) *Latin*
  con**fid**e = tell in confidence
  fidelity = loyalty; exact correspondence
  con**fid**ence = trust or faith in someone or something
  per**fid**ious = faithless; disloyal; untrustworthy
  con**fid**ante = a person to whom one's private affairs or thoughts are
    disclosed

Root Work 22
Match each word with its definition.

1. fidelity	(A) loud, vocal, and noisy
2. facile	(B) based on a false idea
3. vociferous	(C) loyalty
4. beneficent	(D) done with little effort
5. federation	(E) pertaining to cone-bearing trees
6. fallacious	(F) a federal group of states
7. federacy	(G) performing acts of kindness
8. coniferous	(H) deliberate breach of trust
9. infallible	(I) an alliance
10. perfidy	(J) incapable of making a mistake

ROOT ROUNDUP 23

- **FIN** (END) *Latin*
  finite = limited; impermanent
  finale = concluding part of a musical composition
  de**fin**itive = conclusive; authoritative; precisely defined
  fin de siècle = end of a century
  ad in**fin**itum = forever; again and again

- **FLECT/FLEX** (BEND) *Latin*
  flexible = capable of being bent
  re**flex** = bent or thrown back; reflected
  re**flect**ion = the act of bending back or throwing back from a surface
  de**flect** = turn aside; bend; deviate
  circum**flex** = curving around

- **FLU/FLUCT/FLUX** (FLOW) *Latin*
  fluctuate = vary irregularly; rise and fall in waves
  in**flu**ent = flowing into
  con**flu**ence = a flowing together; a juncture of two or more streams
  flux = flowing; a continuous moving
  re**flux** = a flowing back; an ebbing

- **FORT** (BRAVE, STRONG, CHANCE) *Latin*
  fortify = strengthen; reinforce
  forte = a person's strong point
  fortitude = quality that enables a person to face pain and suffering with courage
  fortuitous = occurring by chance
  fortress = a large military stronghold

- **FRAC/FRAG** (BREAK) *Latin*
  fractional = very small; being in fractions or pieces
  re**frac**t = deflect sound or light
  in**fring**e = transgress; violate
  fractious = unruly; rebellious
  fragmentary = consisting of small disconnected parts

Root Work 23

Match each word with its definition.

1. fortuitous	(A) curving around
2. definitive	(B) a person's strong point
3. fractious	(C) a flowing together
4. confluence	(D) conclusive
5. forte	(E) deflect sound or light
6. circumflex	(F) end of a century
7. deflect	(G) occurring by chance
8. refract	(H) rise and fall in waves
9. fluctuate	(I) unruly; rebellious
10. fin de siècle	(J) turn aside; bend

ROOT ROUNDUP 24

- **FRAT** (BROTHER) *Latin*
  fraternity = a social organization of men students
  con**frat**ernity = an association of persons united in a common purpose
  fraternal = brotherly
  fraternize = mingle on friendly terms
  fratricide = the killing of one's brother or sister

- **FUNC** (PERFORM, DISCHARGE) *Latin*
  function = assigned duty or activity
  de**func**t = no longer existing
  per**func**tory = performed really as a duty; superficial
  functionary = someone who performs a particular function
  mal**func**tion = failure to work

- **GAM** (MARRIAGE) *Greek*
  poly**gam**ous = having more than one wife or husband at a time
  endo**gam**y = marriage within a particular group
  exo**gam**y = marriage outside a social unit
  gamic = requiring fertilization to reproduce
  mono**gam**ous = relating to marriage to one person at a time

- **GEN** (BIRTH, CLASS, DESCENT, RACE, GENERATE) *Latin*
  en**gen**der = cause, produce
  genesis = beginning; origin
  genetics = branch of biology that deals with heredity
  gentry = people of standing; class of people just below nobility
  genre = type, class; distinct literary or artistic category

- **GEO** (EARTH) *Greek*
  geology = science that studies the structure and composition of
    the Earth
  geography = science that studies the Earth and the distribution of
    life on it
  geocentric = having the Earth as center
  geothermal = produced by the heat in the Earth's interior
  geophysics = the physics of the Earth

Root Work 24
Match each word with its definition.

1. polygamy	(A)	cause; produce
2. fratricide	(B)	relating to marriage to one person at a time
3. defunct	(C)	type; class
4. geothermal	(D)	no longer existing
5. fraternal	(E)	the physics of the Earth
6. monogamous	(F)	killing of one's brother or sister
7. engender	(G)	produced by heat in the Earth's interior
8. genre	(H)	performed really as a duty
9. geophysics	(I)	having more than one wife or husband at a time
10. perfunctory	(J)	brotherly

ROOT ROUNDUP 25

- **GLOSS/GLOT** (LANGUAGE, TONGUE) *Latin*
  glossa = the tongue
  poly**glot** = speaker of many languages
  glossolalia = fabricated and meaningless speech associated with
    trance states

glossary = list of words and their meanings, usually at the back of a book

glottis = opening between the vocal chords and the larynx

- **GRAD/GRESS** (STEP) *Latin*
  re**gress** = move backward; revert to an earlier state
  pro**gress**ive = going step-by-step; favoring progress
  e**gress** = an exit
  in**gress** = an entrance
  graduate = advance to a new level of skill or achievement

- **GRAPH/GRAM** (WRITE, DRAW, RECORD) *Greek*
  graphology = study of handwriting, particularly for the purpose of character analysis
  bio**graph**ical = relating to facts and events of a person's life
  gramophone = a record player
  epi**gram** = short and witty saying
  grammar = the system of rules of a language

- **GRAT** (PLEASING) *Latin*
  gratify = please
  gratitude = thankfulness
  gratuitous = free; voluntary
  persona non **grat**a = a person who is not acceptable or welcome
  ex **grat**ia = done voluntarily, out of kindness or grace

- **GRAV/GRIEV** (SERIOUS, HEAVY, HARMFUL) *Latin*
  gravity = seriousness
  grave = requiring serious thought
  gravitas = seriousness in demeanor or treatment
  grievous = causing grief or pain
  ag**griev**ed = afflicted; distressed

Root Work 25
Match each word with its definition.

1. epigram	(A) please
2. progressive	(B) entrance
3. polyglot	(C) free; voluntary
4. gratify	(D) the tongue
5. gravity	(E) afflicted; distressed
6. ingress	(F) short and witty saying
7. aggrieved	(G) study of handwriting
8. graphology	(H) speaker of many languages
9. glossa	(I) going step-by-step
10. gratuitous	(J) seriousness

ROOT ROUNDUP REVIEW 21–25

Match It
Match each of the following roots to its meaning.

1. ERR ___   (A) league, pact
2. EU ___   (B) earth
3. FER ___   (C) language, tongue
4. FED ___   (D) flow
5. FLECT/FLEX ___   (E) pleasing
6. FLU/FLUCT/FLUX ___   (F) good, well
7. FRAT ___   (G) bear, carry
8. GEO ___   (H) brother
9. GRAT ___   (I) wander, mistake
0. GLOSS/GLOT ___   (J) bend

Fill-ins
Fill in the blanks with the word that fits the definition.

genre	gravitas	soporific	egress	perfidious
extraneous	fractious	perfunctory	euphony	fin de siècle

1. seriousness in demeanor _____
2. faithless; disloyal; untrustworthy _____
3. unruly; rebellious _____
4. type; class _____
5. performed really as a duty _____
6. pleasant and harmonious sound _____
7. an exit _____
8. end of a century _____
9. not essential _____
10. producing sleep _____

True or False
If the statement is correct, put (T) True; if it is incorrect, put (F) False.

1. Endogamy refers to marriage outside a particular group. _____
2. Something fallacious is based on a false idea or fact. _____
3. An erg is a mistake in writing or printing. _____
4. Fortitude enables one to face pain and suffering with courage. _____
5. Ethos is a feeling of extreme happiness. _____

ROOT ROUNDUP 26

- **GREG** (FLOCK, HERD) *Latin*
  ag**greg**ate = collective mass or sum; total
  con**greg**ation = a gathering
  gregarious = sociable
  gregarine = various parasitic protozoans in the digestive tracts of invertebrates
  se**greg**ate = separate from a main body or group

- **GYN** (WOMAN) *Greek*
  miso**gyn**ist = one who hates women
  gynecology = branch of medicine dealing with women's health care
  gynarchy = government by women
  gynophobia = fear of women
  gynecoid = characteristic of a woman

- **HELIO** (SUN) *Greek*
  heliocentric = having the Sun as a center
  heliolatry = Sun worship
  heliotaxis = an organism's movement in response to the Sun's light
  heliotrope = kind of plant that turns toward the Sun
  heliotherapy = therapy based on exposure to sunlight

- **HEMO** (BLOOD) *Greek*
  hemorrhage = heavy bleeding
  hemoglobin = respiratory pigment in red blood cells
  hemophilia = blood coagulation disorder
  hemoptysis = the expectoration of blood
  hemophobia = fear of blood

- **HERB** (VEGETATION) *Latin*
  herbal = relating to or containing herbs
  herbicide = chemical that destroys plants or weeds
  herbaceous = characteristic of an herb
  herbivorous = feeding mainly on plants
  herbalism = herbal medicine

Root Work 26

Match each word with its definition.

1. herbaceous		(A)	blood coagulation disorder
2. hemophobia		(B)	kind of plant that turns toward the Sun
3. aggregate		(C)	characteristic of a herb
4. heliotrope		(D)	collective mass or sum
5. gregarious		(E)	an organism's movement in response to the Sun's light
6. gynarchy		(F)	feeding mainly on plants
7. hemophilia		(G)	sociable
8. herbivorous		(H)	fear of blood
9. heliotaxis		(I)	characteristic of a woman
10. gynecoid		(J)	government by women

ROOT ROUNDUP 27

HETERO (DIFFERENT, MIXED, UNLIKE) *Greek*
heterosexual = sexually oriented to persons of the opposite sex
heterodox = unorthodox, not widely accepted
heterogeneous = composed of unlike parts, different, diverse
heterodyne = having alternating currents of two different frequencies producing two new ones
heterochromatic = characterized by different colors

HOMO (SAME, ALIKE) *Greek*
homologous = similar in value or function
homonym = word identical in pronunciation and sometimes spelling to one or more other words but different in meaning
homogeneous = composed of identical parts; uniform in composition
homocentric = having the same center
homogenize = make uniform in consistency

HOM/HOMO/HUMAN (MAN, HUMANITY) *Latin*
humane = characterized by kindness or compassion
humanity = humans as a group
humanism = system of thought focusing on humans, their values, and capacities
humanitarian = relating to the promotion of human welfare
hominoid = belonging to the family *Hominidae*, which includes apes and man

HYDR/HYDRA/HYDRO (WATER) *Greek*
hydroelectric = producing electricity through action of falling water
hydroponics = science of growing plants in water reinforced with nutrients

hydrant = large pipe for drawing water
de**hydr**ate = remove water from
hydrophyte = a water plant

- **HYPER** (ABOVE, EXCESSIVE, OVER) *Greek*
  hyperbole = purposeful exaggeration for effect
  hyperactive = excessively active
  hypertension = high blood pressure
  hypercritical = excessively critical
  hyperventilate = to breathe abnormally fast

Root Work 27
Match each word with its definition.

1. homologous
2. dehydrate
3. heterodox
4. heterochromatic
5. hyperbole
6. humane
7. hydroponics
8. humanity
9. hyperventilate
10. homogeneous

(A) characterized by kindness or compassion
(B) composed of identical parts
(C) breathe abnormally fast
(D) characterized by different colors
(E) remove water from
(F) similar in value or function
(G) purposeful exaggeration for effect
(H) not widely accepted
(I) science of growing plants in water reinforced with nutrients
(J) humans as a group

ROOT ROUNDUP 28

- **HYPO** (BENEATH, LOWER, UNDER) *Greek*
  hypothetical = based on assumptions or hypotheses
  hypothermia = abnormally low body temperature
  hypoglycemia = abnormally low glucose level in the blood
  hypochondria = unfounded belief that one is likely to become ill
  hypoplasia = arrested development of an organ

- **IG/IL/IM/IN/IR** (CAUSATIVE PREFIX; NOT, WITHOUT) *Latin*
  ignominious = disgraceful and dishonorable
  impecunious = poor; having no money
  impoverish = make poor or bankrupt
  intractable = not easily managed
  irrelevant = not applicable; unrelated

- **IN** (INTENSIVE PREFIX; IN, ON, UPON, NOT) *Latin*
  incite = arouse to action
  incarnate = having bodily form
  indigenous = native, occurring naturally in an area

inclusive = tending to include all
incongruity = state of not fitting

- **INTER** (AMONG, BETWEEN, WITHIN, MUTUAL) *Latin*
  intervene = come between
  interpose = insert; intervene
  interregnum= interval between reigns
  intersperse = distribute among; mix with
  internecine = deadly to both sides

- **INTRA/INTRO** (INTO, INWARD, WITHIN) *Latin*
  intraocular = occurring within the eyeball
  intravenous = within a vein
  intramural = within an institution such as a school
  introvert = someone given to self-analysis
  introspective = contemplating one's own thoughts and feelings

Root Work 28
Match each word with its definition.

1. incongruous
2. interregnum
3. irrelevant
4. introspective
5. indigenous
6. hypothermia
7. intramural
8. hypochondria
9. interpose
10. intractable

(A) within an institution
(B) occurring naturally in an area
(C) not easily managed
(D) not fitting
(E) not applicable; unrelated
(F) unfounded belief that one is likely to become ill
(G) contemplating one's own thoughts and feelings
(H) insert; intervene
(I) abnormally low body temperature
(J) interval between reigns

ROOT ROUNDUP 29

- **JAC/JACT/JECT** (THROW, FLING) *Latin*
  re**ject** = refuse to accept or consider; deny
  e**ject** = throw out
  tra**ject**ory = path taken by a projectile
  inter**ject** = interpose; insert
  e**jac**ulate = eject abruptly

- **JUR/JUS/JUD** (SWEAR, LAW, JUDGE, JUST) *Latin*
  judicious = wise; sound in judgment
  per**jur**e = tell a lie under oath
  jurisdiction = power to interpret and apply law; control
  jurisprudence = philosophy of law
  justice = quality of being honorable and fair

- **LECT/LEG/LIG** (READ, CHOOSE) *Latin*
  legible = readable
  se**lect** = make a choice
  lector = someone who reads scriptural passages in a church service
  e**lect**ion = ability to make a choice
  predi**lect**ion = preference; liking

- **LEG** (LAW) *Latin*
  legacy = a gift made by a will
  il**leg**al = prohibited by law
  legalese = abstruse vocabulary of the legal profession
  legitimate = in accordance with established standards; genuine; reasonable
  legislation = laws, decrees, mandates

- **LEV** (LIGHT) *Latin*
  levity = light manner or attitude
  levitate = rise in the air or cause to rise
  lever = a means of accomplishing something
  al**lev**iate = relieve; improve partially
  leverage = power to act effectively

Root Work 29
Match each word with its definition.

1. legitimate	(A)	laws, decrees, mandates
2. jurisprudence	(B)	to relieve, improve partially
3. legislation	(C)	tell a lie under oath
4. levity	(D)	readable
5. perjure	(E)	preference, liking
6. legible	(F)	throw out
7. eject	(G)	in accordance with established standards
8. trajectory	(H)	path taken by a projectile
9. alleviate	(I)	light manner or attitude
10. predilection	(J)	philosophy of law

ROOT ROUNDUP 30

- **LEX** (WORD) *Greek*
  lexicon = dictionary; list of words
  lexicography = process of compiling a dictionary
  lexis = vocabulary; set of words in a language
  lexical = relating to the words of a language
  lexeme = basic unit of the lexicon of a language

- **LIBER** (FREE) *Latin*
  liberal = tolerant, broad-minded; generous, lavish
  liberation = freedom, emancipation
  libertine = one without moral restraint
  il**liber**al = bigoted; narrow-minded
  libertarian = one who believes in unrestricted freedom

- **LIBRAR/LIBR** (BOOK) *Latin*
  library = place where books are kept; collection of books
  librarianship = specialization in library work
  libel = defamatory statement; act of writing something that smears a
    person's character
  libretto = text of a dramatic musical work
  librettist = author of a libretto

- **LITER** (LETTER) *Latin*
  literati = scholarly or learned persons
  literature = a body of written works
  il**liter**ate = unable to read and write
  literation = letter for letter
  literal = limited to the most obvious meaning of a word; word
    for word

- **LOC/LOG/LOQU** (WORD, SPEAK, TALK) *Latin*
  loquacious = talkative
  col**loqu**ial = typical of informal speech
  soli**loqu**y = literary or dramatic speech by one character, not
    addressed to others
  circum**locu**tion = indirect way of saying something
  epi**log**ue = short speech at the end of a play

Root Work 30
Match each word with its definition.

1. lexis	(A) talkative
2. literate	(B) indirect way of saying something
3. libertarian	(C) word for word
4. loquacious	(D) tolerant; broadminded
5. lexicon	(E) believer in unrestricted freedom
6. libretto	(F) able to read and write
7. circumlocution	(G) list of words
8. libel	(H) writing something to smear a character
9. literal	(I) vocabulary
10. liberal	(J) text of a musical work

ROOT ROUNDUP REVIEW 26–30

Match It
Match each of the following roots to its meaning.

1. HERB ___	(A) free
2. HEMO ___	(B) law
3. HETERO ___	(C) same, alike
4. HOMO ___	(D) into, inward, within
5. IN ___	(E) light
6. INTRA/INTRO ___	(F) blood
7. LEG ___	(G) in, on, upon, not, intensive prefix
8. LEV ___	(H) letter
9. LIBER ___	(I) vegetation
10. LITER ___	(J) different, mixed, unlike

Fill-ins
Fill in the blanks with the word that fits the definition.

internecine	literati	hominoid	impecunious	hyperbole
lector	lexical	misogynist	jurisprudence	hemoptysis

1. relating to the words of a language _____
2. expectoration of blood _____
3. one who reads scriptural passages in a church service

   _____
4. purposeful exaggeration for effect _____
5. scholarly or learned persons _____
6. deadly to both sides _____
7. philosophy of law _____
8. hater of women _____
9. having no money _____
10. belonging to the family that includes apes and man

   _____

True or False
If the statement is correct, put (T) True; if it is incorrect, put (F) False.

1. A homonym is a word identical in pronunciation and sometimes spelling to one or more other words but different in meaning. _____
2. Hypothermia is an abnormally high body temperature. _____

3. Heliotaxis refers to an organism's movement in response to the Sun's light. _____
4. Circumlocution is an extremely direct way of saying something. _____
5. To interject is to throw out or delete. _____

ROOT ROUNDUP 31

LUC/LUM/LUS (LIGHT) *Latin*
lucid = bright; clear; intelligible
trans**luc**ent = partially transparent
e**luc**idation = clarification
pel**luc**id = transparent; translucent; easily understood
luminous = bright; brilliant; glowing

• **LUD** (PLAY, GAME) *Latin*
al**lud**e = make an indirect reference to
ludicrous = laughable; ridiculous
pre**lud**e = an introductory performance preceding the principal matter
inter**lud**e = an entertainment between acts of a play
e**lud**e = evade

• **MACRO** (LARGE, LONG) *Greek*
macrocosm = the universe
macroeconomics = study of the overall workings of the economy
macroscopic = large enough to be seen with the naked eye
macronutrient = an element needed in large proportion for a plant's growth
macrocyte = an abnormally large red blood cell

• **MAGN** (GREAT) *Latin*
magnify = enlarge
magna cum laude = with high honors
magnate = powerful person
magnitude = extent; greatness of size
magnanimity = generosity; nobility

• **MAL** (BAD) *Latin*
malign = speak evil of
malaise = feeling of discomfort; general sense of depression
malicious = full of animosity and hatred
malefactor = doer of evil
malfeasance = misconduct

Root Work 31
Match each word with its definition.

1. pellucid	(A) large enough to be seen with the naked eye
2. elucidation	(B) powerful person
3. macroscopic	(C) the universe
4. malfeasance	(D) evade
5. magnate	(E) clarification
6. malefactor	(F) make an indirect reference to
7. allude	(G) misconduct
8. macrocosm	(H) transparent; translucent
9. magnanimous	(I) generous; noble
10. elude	(J) doer of evil

ROOT ROUNDUP 32

- **MAN** (HAND) *Latin*
  emancipate = liberate
  manipulate = operate or control by the hands
  manubrium = a body part that is shaped like a handle
  maniable = easy to handle; flexible
  quadru**man**us = having four feet with the first digits being opposable

- **MAND** (ORDER) *Latin*
  mandate = authoritative order or instruction
  mandatory = commanded by authority
  com**mand**ment = a command
  mandamus = an order issued by a superior court to a lower court
  repri**mand** = a strong formal rebuke

- **MANIA** (OBSESSION) *Greek*
  mania = mental disorder characterized by excessive gaiety; wild
  enthusiasm
  maniac = someone who has excessive enthusiasm for something; an
  insane person
  megalo**mania** = delusions of power or importance
  maniacal = characterized by excessive enthusiasm; marked by
  insanity
  manic-depressive = affective disorder marked by alternating periods
  of mania and depression

- **MAR/MARI** (SEA) *Latin*
  maritime = relating to the sea
  marine = native to the sea; relating to the sea
  marina = a boat basin for small boats
  aqua**mari**ne = pale blue to light greenish blue
  sub**mari**ne = undersea

- **MATER/MATR** (MOTHER) *Latin*
  maternal = relating to or characteristic of a mother
  matron = a mother of mature age and social position
  matrix = the womb
  matrilineal = tracing ancestry through the mother's line
  matriarchy = a family or community governed by women

Root Work 32
Match each word with its definition.

1. reprimand	(A) characterized by excessive enthusiasm
2. matriarchy	(B) body part shaped like a handle
3. submarine	(C) easy to handle
4. mandate	(D) community governed by women
5. mania	(E) undersea
6. maritime	(F) wild enthusiasm
7. matrilineal	(G) an authoritative order
8. maniable	(H) tracing ancestry through the mother's line
9. manubrium	(I) relating to the sea
10. maniacal	(J) a strong formal rebuke

ROOT ROUNDUP 33

- **MEGA** (GREAT, LARGE) *Greek*
  megaphone = device used to amplify the voice
  megalomania = delusions of power or importance
  megalith = huge stone used in prehistoric structures
  megalopolis = vast city
  megalophonous = having a loud voice

- **META** (CHANGE, AT A LATER TIME, BEYOND) *Greek*
  metaphor = figure of speech that compares two different things
  metamorphosis = change, transformation
  metaplasia = change of one kind of tissue into another kind
  metanoia = spiritual conversion
  metaphysical = pertaining to speculative philosophy

- **METER/METR** (MEASURE) *Greek*
  baro**meter** = instrument used in weather forecasting for measuring
    atmospheric pressure
  peri**meter** = the outer limits of an area
  micro**meter** = device that measures small distances or objects
  am**meter** = instrument that measures electric current in amperes
  metrology = study of weights and measures

- **MICRO** (SMALL) *Greek*
  microbiota = the microscopic life of an area

micrology = excessive devotion to small details
microclimate = the climate of a small area
microcosm = a small system having analogies to a larger system; small world
microdont = having small teeth

- **MIN** (SMALL) *Latin*
di**min**ution = lessening; reduction
di**min**utive = small
minute = very small
minutia = petty details
minuscule = very small

Root Work 33
Match each word with its definition.

1. microcosm	(A) huge stone used in prehistoric structures
2. megalomania	(B) very small
3. metamorphosis	(C) study of weights and measures
4. micrometer	(D) spiritual conversion
5. metanoia	(E) device that measures small distances or objects
6. minuscule	(F) having small teeth
7. microdont	(G) small world
8. metrology	(H) delusions of importance or power
9. megalith	(I) petty details
10. minutia	(J) transformation

ROOT ROUNDUP 34

- **MIS** (HATRED, BAD, IMPROPER, WRONG) *Greek*
misconstrue = misunderstand
misapprehension = a misunderstanding
misnomer = incorrect name
misanthropy = hatred of humanity
misogynist = hater of women

- **MISS/MIT** (MOVE, SEND) *Latin*
trans**mit** = send from one place to another; cause to spread
re**mit**tance = something sent as payment
missive = a letter
dis**miss** = put away from consideration; reject
mittimus = writ that commits one to prison

- **MOB/MOT/MOV** (MOVE) *Latin*
  im**mob**ile = fixed; motionless
  mobility = state of being capable of moving
  auto**mob**ile = passenger vehicle having four wheels and an engine
  e**mot**ive = appealing to or expressing emotion
  movie = sequence of images on a screen so rapid that they create
     the illusion of movement

- **MONO** (ONE, SINGLE) *Greek*
  monogamy = marriage to one person at a time
  monologue = speech performed by one actor
  monocline = in geology, a single upward fold
  monochromatic = having one color
  monolithic = constituting a single, unified whole

- **MON/MONIT** (WARN) *Latin*
  monitor = maintain continuous observation of
  ad**mon**ish = caution or reprimand
  ad**monit**ion = mild reproof
  pre**monit**ion = forewarning; presentiment
  re**mon**strate = object or protest

Root Work 34
Match each word with its definition.

1. premonition	(A)	speech performed by one actor
2. misogynist	(B)	something sent as payment
3. movie	(C)	exciting emotion
4. misnomer	(D)	a letter
5. monologue	(E)	incorrect name
6. monochromatic	(F)	images on a screen that give the illusion of movement
7. missive	(G)	forewarning
8. emotive	(H)	caution
9. remittance	(I)	hater of women
10. admonish	(J)	having one color

ROOT ROUNDUP 35

- **MORI/MORT** (DEATH) *Latin*
  moribund = dying
  mortorio = sculpture of the dead Christ
  im**mort**al = not subject to death; everlasting
  mortification = shame or humiliation
  mortician = undertaker

- **MORPH** (FORM, SHAPE) *Greek*
  morphous = having definite form
  a**morph**ous = lacking definite form
  morphometry = measurement of form
  anthropo**morph**ic = attributing human qualities to nonhumans
  morphology = the form and structure of an organism

- **MULTI** (MANY) *Latin*
  multipara = mother of two or more children
  multifaceted = made up of many parts
  multifarious = diverse
  multiplicity = state of being numerous
  multeity = state of being many

- **MUT** (CHANGE) *Latin*
  mutative = in grammar, expressing change of state or place
  mutation = significant genetic change
  trans**mut**ation = change in appearance, shape, or nature
  im**mut**able = unchangeable
  mutable = changeable

- **NAS/NAT** (BIRTH, BE FROM, SPRING FORTH) *Latin*
  nationality = state of belonging to a particular nation by birth or
    by naturalization
  nativity = place or circumstances of birth
  natal = relating to birth
  native = an original inhabitant of a particular place
  nascent = starting to develop, coming into existence

Root Work 35
Match each word with its definition.

1. multifarious
2. natal
3. nascent
4. moribund
5. immutable
6. morphous
7. morphology
8. mortician
9. mutation
10. multipara

(A) having definite form
(B) significant genetic change
(C) mother of two or more children
(D) undertaker
(E) the form and structure of an organism
(F) dying
(G) diverse
(H) unchangeable
(I) starting to develop; come into existence
(J) relating to birth

ROOT ROUNDUP REVIEW 31–35

Match It
Match each of the following roots to its meaning.

1. LUD ___	(A) sea
2. MAGN ___	(B) small
3. MANIA ___	(C) one, single
4. MAR/MARI ___	(D) great
5. METER/METRE ___	(E) change
6. MICRO ___	(F) death
7. MON/MONIT ___	(G) play
8. MONO ___	(H) obsession
9. MORI/MORT ___	(I) warn
10. MUT ___	(J) measure

Fill-ins
Fill in the blanks with the word that fits the definition.

mandamus	**morphology**	**matrilineal**	**missive**	**diminution**
nascent	**misogynist**	**macrocosm**	**metanoia**	**malfeasance**

1. a letter _____
2. starting to develop _____
3. lessening; reduction _____
4. misconduct _____
5. hater of women _____
6. tracing ancestry through the mother's line _____
7. the form and structure of an organism _____
8. an order issued by a superior court to a lower court

   _____
9. spiritual conversion _____
10. the universe _____

True or False
If the statement is correct, put (T) True; if it is incorrect, put (F) False.

1. Pellucid means cloudy, vague, or unintelligible. _____
2. Manubrium refers to a body part that is shaped like an egg. _____
3. A person's nativity refers to his or her place of birth. _____
4. Metrology means urban planning. _____
5. In geology, a monocline is a single upward fold. _____

ROOT ROUNDUP 36

- **NAV** (SHIP) *Latin*
  naval = relating to ships or shipping
  navigation = theory and practice of charting a ship's course
  navarch = commander of a fleet
  naviform = boat-shaped
  circum**nav**igate = to go completely around

- **NEC/NIC/NOC/NOX** (KILL, DEATH, HARM) *Latin*
  inter**nec**ine = deadly to both sides
  per**nic**ious = very harmful
  nocent = causing injury
  in**noc**uous = not harmful
  noxious = injurious to health

- **NECRO** (DEAD, CORPSE) *Greek*
  necromancy = divination through communicating with spirits
  necrophobia = fear of dead bodies
  necrotype = extinct species
  necrophilia = intercourse with dead bodies
  necromorphous = feigning death

- **NEG** (NO) *Latin*
  negate = nullify; cancel out
  negative = indicating opposition
  re**neg**e = go back on one's word
  negligent = careless; inattentive
  negligible = not worth considering

- **NEO** (NEW, RECENT) *Greek*
  neologism = new word or expression; an existing word or expression used in a new way
  neophyte = novice, beginner
  neonate = newborn child
  neoplasia = formation of new tissue
  neolithic = New Stone Age; period in the development of technology at end of the Stone Age

Root Work 36
Match each word with its definition.

1. necrotype   (A) boat-shaped
2. negligible   (B) deadly to both sides
3. navarch   (C) nullify
4. pernicious   (D) fear of dead bodies
5. neonate   (E) novice
6. necrophobia   (F) commander of a fleet
7. neophyte   (G) newborn child
8. internecine   (H) very harmful
9. naviform   (I) not worth considering
10. negate   (J) extinct species

ROOT ROUNDUP 37

- **NEUR** (NERVE) *Greek*
  neurology = study of the nerves and the brain
  neurosis = disorder of the nervous system
  neuroid = nervelike
  neurergic = pertaining to nerve action
  neuralgia = pain along nerve

- **NEUT/NEUTR** (NOT EITHER) *Latin*
  neutral = belonging to neither side in a war or controversy
  neutralize = make neutral; counterbalance the effect of
  neutrality = state of being neutral
  neutron = an electrically neutral subatomic particle
  neuter = neither masculine nor feminine

- **NOCT/NOX** (NIGHT) *Latin*
  nocturnal = pertaining to night; active at night
  equi**nox** = either of two times in a year when the Sun crosses the celestial equator
  noctambulant = walking in one's sleep
  noctivagant = wandering around at night
  noctilucous = shining at night

- **NOM/NOMEN/NYM** (NAME) *Latin, Greek*
  nominal = existing in name only
  nom de guerre = war name; pseudonym
  mis**nom**er = incorrect name
  ig**nom**inious = disgraceful and dishonorable
  nomenclature = terms used in a particular science or discipline

- **NON** (NOT) *Latin*
  nonplussed = bewildered
  nonchalant = casual, unconcerned
  non licet = not lawful
  non sequitur = conclusion not following from apparent evidence
  nondescript = lacking interesting or distinctive qualities; dull

Root Work 37
Match each word with its definition.

1. noctambulant	(A)	counterbalance the effect of
2. misnomer	(B)	shining at night
3. nonplussed	(C)	pain along nerve
4. neuroid	(D)	not lawful
5. nom de guerre	(E)	neither masculine nor feminine
6. neuralgia	(F)	nervelike
7. non licet	(G)	incorrect name
8. noctilucous	(H)	walking in one's sleep
9. neuter	(I)	bewildered
10. neutralize	(J)	war name

ROOT ROUNDUP 38

- **NOV** (NEW) *Latin*
  re**nov**ate = restore to an earlier condition
  novice = apprentice, beginner
  novel = new or original
  novitiate = state of being a beginner or novice
  in**nov**ation = something newly introduced

- **NUM** (NUMBER) *Latin*
  numismatics = coin collecting
  numeral = a symbol that represents a number
  numerate = count
  e**num**erate = count off; list
  numerology = study of mystical meanings in numbers

- **OB/OC/OF/OP** (AGAINST) *Latin*
  obdurate = stubborn
  occlude = shut; block
  obliterate = destroy completely
  opprobrious = disgraceful; contemptuous
  obfuscate = obscure; confuse

- **OLIG** (FEW, LITTLE) *Greek*
  oligopoly = situation with only a few sellers so that action by any
    one of them will affect price
  oligarchy = government by only a few
  oligodontous = having few teeth
  oligophagous = eating only a few kinds of food
  oligosyllable = a word with only a few syllables

- **OMNI** (ALL, EVERY) *Latin*
  omnipotent = having unlimited power
  omnivorous = eating everything; absorbing everything
  omnipresent = present everywhere
  omniscient = having infinite knowledge
  omneity = state of including all things

Root Work 38
Match each word with its definition.

1. obdurate	(A) shut; block
2. novice	(B) coin collecting
3. oligarchy	(C) eating everything
4. innovation	(D) stubborn
5. oligodontous	(E) study of mystical meanings in numbers
6. occlude	(F) state of including all things
7. omnivorous	(G) something newly introduced
8. numerology	(H) government by only a few
9. omneity	(I) having few teeth
10. numismatics	(J) beginner

ROOT ROUNDUP 39

- **OPER** (WORK) *Latin*
  opera = musical work
  opere citato = already mentioned in the work
  operon = a group of genes that operate as a unit
  operative = functioning; working
  operose = working hard

- **OPTI/OPTO** (EYE, VISION) *Latin*
  optimistic = looking on the positive side
  optician = someone who makes eyeglasses
  optometry = measuring and testing of vision
  optogram = an image fixed on the retina
  optical = of or relating to sight

- **ORTHO** (STRAIGHT, CORRECT) *Latin*
  orthodox = traditional; conservative
  orthopraxy = correct action
  orthodontics = correction of irregularity of teeth
  orthognathism = condition of having straight jaws
  orthopedic = correcting physical deformities

- **OS/OSS/OST/OSTEO** (BONE) *Latin, Greek*
  osseous = bony
  ossify = turn into bone
  osteitis = bone inflammation
  ostosis = formation of bone
  osteoma = bone tumor

- **PAL/PALEO** (ANCIENT) *Greek*
  paleontology = study of past geological eras through fossil remains
  paleoethnic = relating to the earliest races of man
  paleography = study of ancient writings
  paleology = study of antiquities
  paleogenetic = of past origin

Root Work 39
Match each word with its definition.

1. optician
2. paleogenetic
3. orthopraxy
4. operon
5. paleography
6. optometry
7. ostosis
8. orthodontics
9. operative
10. osseous

(A) bony
(B) correction of teeth irregularity
(C) functioning
(D) bone formation
(E) study of ancient writings
(F) testing of vision
(G) correct action
(H) group of genes operating as a unit
(I) of past origin
(J) maker of eyeglasses

ROOT ROUNDUP 40

- **PAC** (PEACE) *Latin*
  pact = a treaty
  pacifist = person opposed to war or violence between nations
  pacify = to restore calm, bring peace
  pacific = calm; peaceful
  pacification = appeasement

- **PAN** (ALL, EVERY) *Greek*
  panorama = broad view; comprehensive picture
  panacea = cure-all
  pantheon = all the gods of a people; group of highly regarded persons
  panoply = impressive array
  pandemic = spread over a whole area

- **PAR** (EQUAL) *Latin*
  parable = simple story that teaches a lesson
  parity = equality
  par = equality of status or value
  dis**par**ity = difference
  a**par**theid = a system of discrimination based on race that formerly
    existed in South Africa

- **PARA** (BEYOND, RELATED, ALONGSIDE) *Greek*
  paradigm = model; example; pattern
  paradisiacal = heavenly; wonderful
  paramount = supreme; primary
  paragon = model of excellence
  parasite = person or animal that lives at another's expense

- **PAS/PATH** (FEELING, DISEASE, SUFFERING) *Greek*
  a**path**y = indifference
  anti**path**y = dislike
  pathos = pity, compassion
  pathogen = agent that causes disease
  dis**pas**sionate = impartial; unaffected by emotion

Root Work 40
Match each word with its definition.

1. paradigm	(A) all the gods of a people
2. pantheon	(B) restore calm
3. paramount	(C) dislike
4. disparity	(D) comprehensive picture
5. pacify	(E) difference
6. pathos	(F) equality
7. panorama	(G) person opposed to war
8. antipathy	(H) supreme
9. parity	(I) model
10. pacifist	(J) pity; compassion

ROOT ROUNDUP REVIEW 36–40

Match It
Match each of the following roots to its meaning.

1. NECRO ___	(A) kill, death, harm
2. NEC/NIC/NOC/NOX ___	(B) against
3. NEUR ___	(C) peace
4. NOCT/NOX ___	(D) ancient
5. NOV ___	(E) nerve
6. OB/OC/OF/OP ___	(F) dead, corpse
7. OPER ___	(G) new
8. PAL/PALEO ___	(H) feeling, disease, suffering
9. PAC ___	(I) work
10. PAS/PATH ___	(J) night

Fill-ins
Fill in the blanks with the word that fits the definition.

paramount	**noctivagant**	**oligophagous**	**omniscient**	**navarch**
pernicious	**apartheid**	**ignominious**	**orthopraxy**	**osteoma**

1. correct action _____
2. disgraceful and dishonorable _____
3. supreme; primary _____
4. bone tumor_____
5. having infinite knowledge _____
6. commander of a fleet _____
7. wandering around at night _____
8. eating only a few kinds of food _____
9. a system of discrimination based on race that formerly existed in South Africa _____
10. very harmful _____

True or False
If the statement is correct, put (T) True; if it is incorrect, put (F) False.

1. To renege is to repeat an offer of negotiation. _____
2. A neologism can be an existing word or expression used in a new way. _____
3. A neutron is an electrically neutral subatomic particle. _____
4. Numerology is the study of mystical meanings in natural phenomena. _____
5. A non sequitor is a conclusion that follows from apparent evidence. _____

ROOT ROUNDUP 41

- **PATER/PATR** (FATHER) *Latin*
  paternity = fatherhood; descent from father's ancestors
  patronize = condescend to; disparage; buy from
  patronage = support of a sponsor or benefactor, as for a cause or an institution
  patricide = murder of one's father
  patrimony = inheritance or heritage derived from one's father

- **PED** (CHILD) *Greek*
  pedant = uninspired, boring academic who makes a display of his or her learning
  pedantic = showing off learning
  pedagogue = teacher
  pedodontics = dentistry dealing with the treatment of children's teeth
  encyclo**ped**ia = reference work that contains articles on a broad range of subjects

- **PED/POD** (FOOT) *Greek*
  pediform = shaped like a foot
  pedestrian = commonplace
  pedate = having feet
  pedometer = a device that measures distance by the number of steps of a walker
  podiatry = the diagnosis and treatment of diseases of the foot

- **PEL/PULS** (DRIVE, URGE) *Latin*
  pulse = a regular or rhythmical beating
  pulsate = beat; to vibrate
  re**pel**lant = something that repels or drives back
  re**puls**e = drive back; repel
  pro**pel**lant = something that provides thrust

- **PER** (THROUGH, COMPLETELY) *Latin*
  peregrinate = wander through
  percutaneous = effecting something through the skin
  permeable = penetrable
  pervasive = spread throughout every part
  permeate = diffuse through

Root Work 41
Match each word with its definition.

1. pedate	(A)	fatherhood
2. pedodontics	(B)	murder of one's father
3. repellant	(C)	something that provides thrust
4. patricide	(D)	dentistry dealing with children's teeth
5. propellant	(E)	shaped like a foot
6. pedantic	(F)	having feet
7. peregrinate	(G)	something that drives back
8. paternity	(H)	diffuse through
9. permeate	(I)	showing off learning
10. pediform	(J)	wander through

ROOT ROUNDUP 42

- **PERI** (AROUND, NEAR) *Greek*
  periosteal = around a bone
  peripatetic = moving about or from place to place
  perihelion = the point in orbit nearest the Sun
  perigee = the point in orbit nearest Earth
  periphrasis = circumlocution

- **PET** (SEEK, REQUEST, ASSAIL) *Latin*
  petition = a request to a superior authority
  com**pet**ition = the act of striving against others to attain a goal
  petulant = contemptuous; peevish
  re**pet**itive = given to the act of repeating
  petitio principli = begging the question

- **PHIL** (LOVE, FONDNESS, PREFERENCE) *Greek*
  philanthropist = lover of mankind; doer of good
  techno**phil**e = lover of technology
  philogynist = lover of women
  philhelline = lover of things Greek
  philtre = love potion

- **PHOBOS** (FEAR) *Greek*
  phobia = abnormal, irrational fear of a situation or thing
  arachno**phob**ia = abnormal fear of spiders
  agora**phob**ia = fear of places that are public or open
  claustro**phob**ic = fear of being in enclosed spaces
  hydro**phob**ia = fear of water

- **PHON** (SOUND, VOICE) *Greek*
  micro**phon**e = an instrument that changes sound waves into
    electric current
  phonogram = a symbol that represents sound
  phonic = relating to sound
  phonetics = study of speech sounds
  caco**phon**y = jarring, unpleasant noise

Root Work 42
Match each word with its definition.

1. petition	(A)	lover of mankind
2. philtre	(B)	begging the question
3. perihelion	(C)	moving about
4. hydrophobia	(D)	relating to sound
5. cacophony	(E)	request to a superior authority
6. peripatetic	(F)	love potion
7. phonic	(G)	the point in orbit nearest the Sun
8. petitio principli	(H)	fear of water
9. philanthropist	(I)	fear of places that are public or open
10. agoraphobia	(J)	unpleasant, jarring sound

ROOT ROUNDUP 43

- **PHOS/PHOT** (LIGHT) *Greek*
  photosensitive = sensitive to light or radiant energy
  photograph = an image recorded by a camera and reproduced on
    a photosensitive surface
  phototaxis = growth directed by light
  photophile = loving light
  photometry = measurement of the properties of light

- **PHYS/PHYSIO** (NATURE) *Greek*
  physiology = the function of a living organism
  physical = relating to the body
  physiolatry = worship of nature
  physiocracy = government that is in accord with the operation of
    natural laws
  physiognomy = divination of character from a person's face

- **PICT** (PAINT) *Latin*
  picture = an image rendered on a flat surface
  de**pict** = represent in a picture
  pictograph = a picture that represents a word or idea
  picturesque = of a picture; quaintly attractive
  pictorial = relating to or composed of pictures

- **PLAC** (PLEASE) *Latin*
  placid = calm
  placate = lessen another's anger; pacify
  im**plac**able = inflexible, incapable of being appeased
  com**plac**ent = self-satisfied
  placebo = something given to please or quiet

- **POLI** (CITY, STATE, CITIZEN) *Greek*
  politics = the art of governing a state and the control of its affairs
  metro**poli**tan = relating to a major city
  cosmo**poli**tan = common to the whole world
  political = relating to the affairs of the state
  polity = political organization of a state

Root Work 43
Match each word with its definition.

1. implacable	(A) something given to please
2. physiology	(B) growth directed by light
3. metropolitan	(C) worship of nature
4. polity	(D) incapable of being appeased
5. phototaxis	(E) functions of a living organism
6. depict	(F) of a picture
7. placebo	(G) loving light
8. physiolatry	(H) relating to a major city
9. picturesque	(I) represent in a picture
10. photophile	(J) political organization of a state

ROOT ROUNDUP 44

- **POLY** (MANY) *Greek*
  polyphony = use of one symbol for many sounds
  polymorphic = having many forms
  polyglot = speaker of many languages
  polygamy = having more than one wife or husband at a time
  polytheist = one who believes in more than one god

- **PON/POS** (PUT, PLACE) *Latin*
  com**pos**e = constitute or form
  com**pon**ent = an element or ingredient
  com**pos**ite = made up of components
  op**pos**e = place so as to be opposite something else
  re**pos**e = place; to lay down

- **POPUL** (THE PEOPLE) *Latin*
  populate = supply with inhabitants; people
  popular = reflecting the taste of the people at large
  populace = the masses
  population = all of the people who inhabit an area
  populous = containing many inhabitants

- **PORT** (CARRY, GATE) *Latin*
  portage = the act of transporting or carrying
  portal = an entrance or gate
  portable = able to be carried easily
  de**port** = expel from a country
  portfolio = case to carry papers

- **POST** (AFTER, BEHIND) *Latin*
  posterity = future generations; all of a person's descendants
  posterior = bottom, rear
  postdiluvian = after the flood
  posthumous = after a person's death
  post factum = after the event

Root Work 44
Match each word with its definition.

1. repose	(A) future generations
2. posterity	(B) having many forms
3. populace	(C) people
4. polytheist	(D) after the event
5. portal	(E) entrance or gate
6. populate	(F) place; to lay down
7. oppose	(G) place so as to be opposite something else
8. portfolio	(H) one who believes in more than one god
9. polymorphic	(I) case to carry papers
10. post factum	(J) the masses

ROOT ROUNDUP 45

- **PRE** (BEFORE, EARLIER) *Latin*
  prenatal = before birth
  preclude = make impossible in advance
  premise = proposition upon which an argument is based
  precept = principle; law
  precedent = a model for something that follows

- **PREHEND/PREHENS** (SEIZE, GRASP) *Latin*
  re**prehend** = censure; reprove
  com**prehend** = take in the meaning; to grasp
  ap**prehens**ion = act of seizing; understanding
  prehensile = able to grasp
  prehension = act of grasping

- **PRIM** (BEFORE, FIRST) *Latin*
  prima facie = at first sight; on the face of it
  primapara = a woman having her first child
  primeval = ancient, primitive
  primordial = original, existing from the beginning
  primogeniture = state of being the eldest child

- **PRO** (IN FAVOR OF) *Latin*
  pro re nata = for an emergency (for the thing born)
  proponent = a supporter
  prodigy = highly gifted child; marvel
  propensity = inclination, tendency
  proclivity = tendency, inclination

- **PROTO** (FIRST, EARLIEST) *Greek*
  protogenic = formed at the beginning
  prototype = an original model
  protomorphic = primitive
  protoplast = an original ancestor
  protolithic = relating to the first Stone Age

Root Work 45
Match each word with its definition.

1.	prehension	(A)	a supporter
2.	primordial	(B)	at first sight
3.	precedent	(C)	highly gifted child
4.	protoplast	(D)	original ancestor
5.	prima facie	(E)	able to grasp
6.	prodigy	(F)	a model for something that follows
7.	proponent	(G)	act of grasping
8.	protogenic	(H)	original
9.	prenatal	(I)	formed at the beginning
10.	prehensile	(J)	before birth

ROOT ROUNDUP REVIEW 41–45

Match It
Match each of the following roots to its meaning.

1. PATER ___	(A) seek, request, assail
2. PEL/PULS ___	(B) put, place
3. PET ___	(C) father
4. PHIL ___	(D) in favor of
5. PHOS/PHOT ___	(E) city, state, citizen
6. POLI ___	(F) before, first
7. PON/POS ___	(G) drive, urge
8. POPUL ___	(H) light
9. PRIM ___	(I) love, fondness, preference
10. PRO ___	(J) the people

Fill-ins
Fill in the blanks with the word that fits the definition.

pedagogue	prehensile	placate	depict	percutaneous
protogenic	cacophony	portage	postdiluvian	agoraphobia

1. able to grasp _____
2. represent in a picture_____
3. fear of places that are open or public _____
4. teacher _____
5. formed at the beginning _____
6. affecting something through the skin _____
7. after the flood _____
8. lessen another's anger in; pacify _____
9. jarring, unpleasant noise _____
10. act of transporting or carrying _____

True or False
If the statement is correct, put (T) True; if it is incorrect, put (F) False.

1. The perigee is the point in orbit farthest from Earth. _____
2. A physiocracy is a government that is in accord with the operation of natural laws. _____
3. Pro re nata means for an emergency. _____
4. Polyphony refers to the use of one symbol for many sounds. _____
5. A pedometer is a device that measures distance by the number of steps of a walker. _____

ROOT ROUNDUP 46

- **PSEUDO** (FALSE) *Greek*
  pseudonym = pen name; fictitious or borrowed name
  pseudopsia = an optical illusion
  pseudodox = false doctrine
  pseudomorph = false or irregular form
  pseudocyesis = false pregnancy

- **PSYCH** (MIND) *Greek*
  psyche = the mind
  psychic = perceptive of nonmaterial, spiritual forces; originating in the mind
  psychiatrist = a doctor who treats disorders of the mind
  psychedelic = mind-expanding
  psychology = study of the mind

- **PUB** (THE PUBLIC) *Latin*
  public = concerning the community or the people
  re**pub**lic = a political order in which a body of citizens has supreme power
  publication = communication of information to the public
  publicity = act of communicating information to attract public interest
  publish = announce; bring to the attention of the public

- **PUNCT** (POINT, PRICK) *Latin*
  punctilious = strictly attentive to small details of form in conduct
  punctilio = a fine point of etiquette
  punctual = prompt
  puncture = a hole made by a sharp object
  punctate = like a point; ending in a point

- **PUT/PUTAT** (THINK, CALCULATE) *Latin*
  putative = supposed
  re**put**e = consider; suppose
  re**put**ed = supposed to be such
  re**put**ation = state of being held in high esteem
  com**put**e = determine an amount or number

Root Work 46
Match each word with its definition.

1. psychic	(A) concerning the people
2. punctate	(B) the mind
3. compute	(C) bring to the attention of the public
4. public	(D) fine point of etiquette
5. putative	(E) an optical illusion
6. pseudodox	(F) determine an amount
7. punctilio	(G) false doctrine
8. psyche	(H) supposed
9. publish	(I) originating in the mind
10. pseudopsia	(J) like a point

ROOT ROUNDUP 47

- **QUER/QUES/QUIR/QUIS** (ASK/SEEK) *Latin*
  query = a question
  in**ques**t = an investigation; court or legal proceeding
  in**quis**ition = an investigation; act of inquiring
  in**quir**er = one who asks a question
  re**quis**ite = required

- **RE** (BACK AGAIN, REPEAT) *Latin*
  recant = retract a statement or opinion
  rebut = refute by evidence or argument
  retract = withdraw; take back
  recurrence = repetition
  redundant = exceeding what is necessary; unnecessarily repetitive

- **RECT** (STRAIGHT) *Latin*
  erect = fix in an upright position
  erectile = able to be raised to an upright position
  rectitude = moral uprightness
  rectilinear = bounded by straight lines
  recto = right-hand page of a book

- **RECT/REG/REGN** (RULE, GOVERN) *Latin*
  rector = an Anglican cleric in charge of a parish
  cor**rect** = remove the errors from; punish for the purpose of
    improving
  regime = a government in power
  regulation = a law to govern conduct
  regular = conforming with fixed procedure or discipline

- **RETRO** (BACKWARD)   *Latin*
  retrospect = review or contemplation of the past
  retrograde = having a backward motion or direction
  retroactive = applying to an earlier time
  retroject = throw back
  retrovirus = a virus that synthesizes DNA from RNA instead of the
    reverse

Root Work 47
Match each word with its definition.

1. retrograde		(A)	applying to an earlier time
2. redundant		(B)	a question
3. rectitude		(C)	right-hand page of a book
4. query		(D)	having a backward motion
5. recto		(E)	law to govern conduct
6. retroactive		(F)	government in power
7. regulation		(G)	required
8. regime		(H)	unnecessarily repetitive
9. requisite		(I)	moral uprightness
10. retract		(J)	take back

ROOT ROUNDUP 48

- **RID/RIS** (LAUGH) *Latin*
  de**rid**e = mock
  ridicule = words that evoke contemptuous laughter at a person
  de**ris**ion = ridicule
  ridiculous = deserving ridicule; absurd
  ridibund = easily moved to laughter

- **ROG/ROGAT** (ASK) *Latin*
  inter**rog**atory = asking a question
  pre**rog**ative = a special right or privilege
  rogatory = requesting information
  rogation = solemn prayer
  de**rog**atory = disparaging; belittling

- **SACR/SANCT** (SACRED, HOLY) *Latin*
  sanctuary = haven, retreat
  sanctify = set apart as holy; consecrate
  sanction = approval; ratification; permission
  sacrosanct = extremely sacred; beyond criticism
  sanctimonious = pretending to be pious or righteous

- **SCI** (KNOW) *Latin*
  scibile = something that is possible to know
  sciolism = conceited and shallow knowledgeability
  con**sci**entious = careful and thorough; governed by conscience
  pre**sci**ent = having foresight
  ne**sci**ence = absence of knowledge; ignorance

- **SCOP** (EXAMINE, OBSERVE, WATCH) *Greek*
  scopic = visual
  tele**scop**e = device used to observe distant objects
  peri**scop**e = optical instrument used to see things from a position
    not in a direct line of sight
  micro**scop**ic = too small to be seen with the naked eye
  colono**scop**e = long, flexible instrument used to visually examine
    the colon

Root Work 48

Match each word with its definition.

1. prescient	(A) absence of knowledge
2. ridibund	(B) set apart as holy
3. sacrosanct	(C) mock
4. rogatory	(D) visual
5. telescope	(E) having foresight
6. interrogatory	(F) extremely sacred
7. nescience	(G) easily moved to laughter
8. deride	(H) device used to observe distant objects
9. sanctify	(I) asking a question
10. scopic	(J) requesting information

ROOT ROUNDUP 49

- **SCRIB/SCRIP** (WRITE) *Latin*
  a**scrib**e = attribute to a cause or source
  circum**scrib**e = limit; confine
  pre**scrib**e = set down a rule; recommend a treatment
  manu**scrip**t = a document written by hand
  nonde**scrip**t = lacking interesting or distinctive qualities; dull

- **SE** (AWAY, APART) *Latin*
  secede = withdraw from membership in an alliance
  select = pick out; choose
  seclusion = act of keeping apart from social contact
  seduce = lead away from accepted principles; attract
  secretive = not open or frank

- **SEC/SECT/SEGM** (CUT) *Latin*
  sectile = relating to a mineral that can be cut smoothly by a knife
  dis**sect** = cut apart
  inter**sect**ion = the process or result of cutting across or through
  secant = a straight line that intersects a curve at two or more points
  segmented = divided into parts

- **SECU/SEQU** (FOLLOW) *Latin*
  pro**secu**tor = one who initiates a civil or criminal court action
  sequel = something that follows
  incon**sequ**ential = insignificant; unimportant
  ob**sequ**ious = overly submissive
  sequatious = disposed to follow another

- **SEMI** (HALF, PARTLY) *Latin*
  semiterrestrial = partially living on land
  semiannual = occurring twice a year
  semiaquatic = not entirely adapted for living in water
  semicircle = half of a circle
  semitaur = in mythology, a creature that is half-man and half-bull

Root Work 49
Match each word with its definition:

1. secede	(A) act of keeping apart from social contact
2. obsequious	(B) a document written by hand
3. sectile	(C) something that follows
4. sequel	(D) cut apart
5. manuscript	(E) withdraw from membership in an alliance
6. semitaur	(F) half-man and half-bull
7. seclusion	(G) set down a rule
8. semiaquatic	(H) not entirely adapted for living in water
9. dissect	(I) overly submissive
10. prescribe	(J) relating to a mineral that can be cut smoothly by a knife

ROOT ROUNDUP 50

- **SENS/SENT** (FEEL, BE AWARE) *Latin*
  sensate = perceived by the senses
  in**sens**ible = unconscious; unresponsive
  sentiment = a view based on emotion rather than reason
  sentient = aware, conscious, able to perceive
  sentisection = vivisection performed without the use of anesthesia

- **SOL** (SUN) *Latin*
  solarium = room exposed to sunlight
  solarize = expose to sunlight
  solstice = point or time when the Sun is furthest from the Equator
  soliterraneous = relating to the meteorological effect of Sun
  and Earth
  solarimeter = device that measures the flux of the Sun's radiation

- **SOLV/SOLU** (FREE, LOOSEN, DISSOLVE) *Latin*
  dis**solv**e = make something pass into solution; melt; dispel
  soluble = able to be dissolved; possible to solve
  solute = a substance dissolved in another one
  dis**solu**tion = disintegration; debauchery
  irre**solu**te = undecided

- **SOMN** (SLEEP) *Latin*
  somnambulance = walking in one's sleep
  somniloquence = talking in one's sleep
  in**somn**ia = inability to fall asleep or remain asleep
  somnolent = sleepy
  somniferous = inducing sleep

- **SOPH** (WISE, SKILLFUL, SHREWD) *Greek*
  sophist = one who is skilled in deceptive argumentation
  sophistry = plausible but misleading argumentation
  sophisticate = make more worldly; refine
  sophomoric = showing lack of judgment and immaturity
  philo**soph**y = love of wisdom

Root Work 50
Match each word with its definition.

1. solarium	(A) able to perceive
2. somniferous	(B) able to be dissolved or solved
3. philosophy	(C) inducing sleep
4. dissolution	(D) point when the Sun is furthest from the Equator
5. sentiment	(E) sleepy
6. soluble	(F) disintegration; debauchery
7. somnolent	(G) refine; make more worldly
8. sophisticate	(H) a view based on emotion
9. solstice	(I) room exposed to sunlight
10. sentient	(J) love of wisdom

ROOT REVIEW 46–50

Match It
Match each of the following roots to its meaning.

1. PSYCH ___	(A) sacred, holy
2. PUB ___	(B) backward
3. RECT ___	(C) know
4. RETRO ___	(D) free, loosen, dissolve
5. SCI ___	(E) the public
6. SACR/SANCT ___	(F) follow
7. SE ___	(G) straight
8. SECU/SEQU ___	(H) feel, be aware
9. SENS/SENT ___	(I) mind
10. SOLV/SOLUT ___	(J) away, apart

Fill-ins
Fill in the blanks with the word that fits the definition.

retrospect	secant	punctilio	ridibund	pseudodox
somniloquence	sophistry	sequacious	recant	rogation

1. easily moved to laughter _____
2. plausible but misleading argumentation _____
3. contemplation of the past _____
4. straight line that intersects a curve at two or more points

   _____
5. talking in one's sleep _____
6. false doctrine _____
7. retract a statement or opinion _____
8. solemn prayer _____
9. a fine point of etiquette _____
10. disposed to follow another _____

True or False
If the statement is correct, put (T) True; if it is incorrect, put (F) False.

1. A punctilious person is inattentive to small details of form in conduct. _____
2. Rectilinear means bounded by straight lines. _____
3. Sectile relates to a mineral that can be cut smoothly by a knife. _____
4. A semitaur is a mythological creature that is half-man and half-lion. _____
5. Soliterraneous refers to the meteorological effect of Moon and Earth. _____

ROOT ROUNDUP 51

- **SPEC/SPECT/SPIC** (SEE, LOOK AT) *Latin*
  specimen = a representative of a class or whole; a sample
  specter = an apparition
  speculate = take something as true based on insufficient evidence
  retro**spect**ive = review of the past
  per**spic**acious = shrewd, astute, keen-witted

- **SPIR** (BREATH, ENERGY, ANIMATION) *Latin*
  re**spir**ation = breathing
  a**spir**ation = expulsion of breath in speaking
  spirit = animating force within living things
  spirited = animated; courageous
  spirograph = device that records the movements of breathing

- **STAS/STAT** (STAND, BEING IN A PLACE, POSITION) *Greek*
  stationary = not moving
  static = having no motion; fixed; stationary
  state = condition of being
  status = position or standing in relation to that of others
  status quo = existing state of affairs

- **STRICT/STRING** (TIGHT, DRAWN TOGETHER) *Latin*
  re**strict** = keep within limits
  stricture = a limit or restriction
  stringent = imposing rigorous standards; constricted; tight
  strict = precise; within narrow limits; rigorous in discipline
  con**strict** = squeeze or compress; restrict the scope of

- **STRUCT** (BUILD) *Latin*
  de**struct**ion = act of destroying
  structure = something built
  con**struct** = build
  in**struct**ion = act of methodically providing with knowledge
  inde**struct**ible = impossible to destroy

Root Work 51
Match each word with its definition.

1. spirited	(A) impossible to destroy
2. stricture	(B) existing state of affairs
3. retrospective	(C) limit or restriction
4. stringent	(D) device that records the movements of breathing
5. constrict	(E) restrict the scope of
6. status quo	(F) review of the past
7. spirograph	(G) fixed; stationary
8. indestructible	(H) imposing rigorous standards; constricted
9. static	(I) an apparition
10. specter	(J) animated

ROOT ROUNDUP 52

- **SUB/SUC/SUF/SUG/SUP/SUS** (BELOW, UNDER, LESS) *Latin*
  subtle = hard to detect or describe
  subterfuge = trick or tactic used to avoid something
  subsume = include; incorporate
  suppress = put down by force; restrain
  suspend = defer, interrupt; dangle, hang

- **SUPER/SUR** (OVER, ABOVE) *Latin*
  superior = higher than another in rank or authority
  supersede = take the place of
  in**super**able = insurmountable, unconquerable
  supernal = celestial; heavenly
  surtax = additional tax

- **SYL/SYM/SYN/SYS** (TOGETHER, WITH) *Greek*
  syllogism = argument with a conclusion deduced from two premises
  synchronous = occurring at the same time; moving at the same rate
  syndicate = association of people who undertake a duty or transact business
  synthesis = blend, combination
  system = group of interrelated elements that form a whole

- **TACT/TANG** (TOUCH) *Latin*
  con**tact** = a coming together or touching
  tactile = relating to the sense of touch
  tactus = sense of touch
  tangible = able to be touched
  tangent = digression, diversion

- **TELE** (DISTANCE, FAR) *Greek*
  telemeter = an instrument that measures distance
  telemetry = science of transmitting data from someplace remote to a
    distant receiving station
  telecommunication = science of communicating over distances by
    electronic transmission
  teleseism = tremor from a distant earthquake
  telephony = sound transmission between distant stations

Root Work 52

Match each word with its definition.

1. suspend	(A) a blend
2. supernal	(B) sense of touch
3. suppress	(C) heavenly
4. tactus	(D) interrupt; dangle
5. synchronous	(E) able to be touched
6. teleseism	(F) insurmountable
7. synthesis	(G) instrument that measures distance
8. telemeter	(H) put down by force
9. tangible	(I) tremor from a distant earthquake
10. insuperable	(J) occurring at the same time

ROOT ROUNDUP 53

- **TEMPOR** (TIME) *Latin*
  con**tempor**ary = belonging to the same time period
  temporal = related to time
  temporize = act evasively to gain time, avoid an argument, or
    postpone a decision
  ex**tempor**aneous = unrehearsed
  temporality = being bounded in time

- **TEN/TAIN** (HOLD) *Latin*
  de**tain** = delay; keep from proceeding
  per**tain** = relate to
  tenacious = stubborn, holding firm
  con**ten**t = something that is contained
  tenure = a period during which something is held

- **TEND/TENS/TENT** (STRETCH, STRIVE) *Latin*
  tension = act of stretching tight
  con**tend** = strive in opposition; to struggle
  con**tent**ion = act of striving in controversy
  tense = tightly stretched
  tensor = a muscle that stretches a body part

- **TERM** (END, LIMIT) *Latin*
  terminal = concluding, final; fatal
  mid**term** = middle of an academic term
  terminate = end
  in**term**inable = endless
  termless = having no limits; unending

- **TERR** (LAND, THE EARTH) *Latin*
  terraqueous = consisting of land and water
  terraceous = earthen
  terrestrial = earthly
  terra firma = dry land
  terra incognita = unknown land

Root Work 53
Match each word with its definition.

1. interminable	(A)	earthen
2. terminal	(B)	act evasively to gain time
3. tensor	(C)	stubborn; holding firm
4. contend	(D)	consisting of land and water
5. temporal	(E)	endless
6. tenacious	(F)	a muscle that stretches a body part
7. detain	(G)	final
8. terraqueous	(H)	strive in opposition
9. temporize	(I)	related to time
10. terraceous	(J)	delay

ROOT ROUNDUP 54

- **TERTI** (THIRD) *Latin*
  tertial = relating to the third row of flight feathers on the basal
    section of a bird's wing
  tertian = recurring after three days
  tertiary = third in degree or rank
  tertium quid = a third thing of indeterminate character
  tertiary color = a color that results from mixing two secondary colors

- **THE/THEI/THEO** (GOD) *Greek*
  a**the**ist = person who does not believe in the existence of God
  theocracy = government by priests representing a god
  theology = study of God and religion
  apo**theo**sis = glorification; glorified ideal
  theogamy = marriage of gods

THERAP (ATTEND, TREAT) *Greek*
therapy = treatment of illness
therapeutic = having healing powers
therapist = specialist in a particular therapy
bio**therap**y = treatment of disease with preparations synthesized
  from living organisms
physio**therap**y = treatment of physical injury with therapeutic
  exercise

THERM/THERMO (WARM, HOT) *Greek*
thermochemistry = the chemistry of heat
thermal = relating to, or caused by heat
thermoduric = able to survive high temperatures
thermodynamic = resulting from heat conversion
thermolabile = subject to change or destruction by heating

TOM/TOME/TOMY (CUT, SECTION) *Greek*
tome = one book in a work of many volumes
derma**tome** = instrument used to cut slices of the skin in skin grafts
micro**tome** = instrument that cuts specimens into slices for
  examination with microscopes
gastro**tom**y = surgical incision into the stomach
vasec**tomy** = surgical removal of a duct that carries semen

Root Work 54
Match each word with its definition.

1. tertian	(A) marriage of gods
2. therapy	(B) surgical incision into the stomach
3. thermoduric	(C) having healing powers
4. apotheosis	(D) recurring after three days
5. thermal	(E) one book in a work of many volumes
6. tertium quid	(F) caused by heat
7. gastrotomy	(G) glorified ideal
8. therapeutic	(H) able to survive high temperatures
9. tome	(I) a third thing of an indeterminate character
10. theogamy	(J) treatment of illness

ROOT ROUNDUP 55

TOP/TOPO (PLACE, REGION) *Greek*
topography = the configuration of a land surface
topology = regional anatomy
toponym = the name of a place
topophobia = fear of certain places
topos = a traditional theme

- **TORS/TORT/TORQU** (TWIST, TURN) *Latin*
  re**tort** = quick caustic reply that turns the first speaker's words to one's own advantage
  torsion = act of twisting or turning
  con**tort** = twist out of shape
  torque = turning or twisting force
  tortuous = winding; twisting; circuitous

- **TRACT** (DRAG, PULL) *Latin*
  at**tract** = cause to draw near
  tractor = vehicle for pulling machinery
  tractable = easy to manage or control; easy to manipulate; easily remedied
  in**tract**able = not easily managed
  pro**tract** = draw out; prolong

- **TRAN/TRANS** (ACROSS, THROUGH) *Latin*
  transcend = rise above, go beyond
  transmute = change in appearance, shape or nature
  transgression = the exceeding of a limit or boundary
  translucent = clear; lucid
  transmogrify = change into a different shape or form

- **TREM/TREMU** (TREMBLE, SHAKE) *Latin*
  tremendous = enormous; able to make one tremble
  tremulous = marked by shaking or trembling
  tremble = shake involuntarily; quake; feel fear
  tremor = a shaking movement; a trembling or quivering
  tremolo = a quivering effect produced by quickly repeating a single tone

Root Work 55
Match each word with its definition.

1. tortuous	(A)	turning or twisting force
2. attract	(B)	name of a place
3. topophobia	(C)	go beyond
4. protract	(D)	change in appearance or nature
5. transmute	(E)	cause to draw near
6. torque	(F)	winding; twisting
7. tremulous	(G)	fear of certain places
8. toponym	(H)	a shaking movement
9. tremor	(I)	marked by trembling
10. transcend	(J)	draw out; prolong

ROOT ROUNDUP REVIEW 51–55

Match It

Match each of the following roots to its meaning.

1. SPIR ___	(A) far
2. STRUCT ___	(B) end, limit
3. TACT/TANG ___	(C) place, region
4. TELE ___	(D) attend, treat
5. TEMPOR ___	(E) warm, hot
6. TERM ___	(F) build
7. THERAP ___	(G) touch
8. THERM/THERMO ___	(H) time
9. TOP/TOPO ___	(I) drag, pull
10. TRACT ___	(J) breath, energy, animation

Fill-ins

Fill in the blanks with the word that fits the definition.

supernal	tenacious	theogamy	synchronous	stricture
thermoduric	toponym	torque	status quo	contention

1. marriage of gods _____
2. act of striving in controversy _____
3. able to survive high temperatures _____
4. existing state of affairs_____
5. stubborn, holding firm _____
6. occurring at the same time; moving at the same rate

   _____
7. twisting or turning force _____
8. celestial; heavenly _____
9. a limit or restriction _____
10. name of a place _____

True or False

If the statement is correct, put (T) True; if it is incorrect, put (F) False.

1. To transmogrify is to change into a different shape or form. _____
2. To subsume is to regard something as assumed. _____
3. A spirograph is an instrument used to measure wind direction. _____
4. Tertial refers to the second row of flight feathers on the basal section of a bird's wing. _____
5. A tremolo is a quivering effect produced by quickly repeating a single tone. _____

ROOT ROUNDUP 56

- **TURB** (SPINNING, CONFUSION, DISTURBANCE) *Greek*
  turbid = in a state of turmoil
  turbine = machine that converts the energy of moving fluid to rotary mechanical power
  turbojet = jet engine with a turbine-driven compressor
  turbulent = violently agitated
  dis**turb**ance = a commotion

- **TYP/TYPE** (TYPE) *Greek*
  typal = relating to or serving as a type
  typical = conforming to a type
  typify = represent as a typical example of; symbolize
  typology = the study or classification of types
  stereo**typ**e = a formulaic conception or image

- **ULTRA** (BEYOND, EXCESSIVE, ON THE OTHER SIDE OF) *Latin*
  ultrasonic = relating to acoustic frequencies above the ear's audible range
  ultramodern = extremely modern in style or ideas
  ultraconservative = conservative to an extreme
  ultranationalism = extreme nationalism
  ultramundane = extending beyond the world or the universe

- **UN** (INTENSIVE PREFIX; NOT, REVERSE, UNDO, REMOVE) *Latin*
  unfeigned = not feigned; not made up; genuine; real
  untenable = not viable; indefensible
  unyielding = firm, resolute
  unequivocal = absolute, certain
  unfetter = free from restraints; liberate

- **UNI** (ONE) *Latin*
  unique = one of a kind
  universal = characterizing or affecting all; present everywhere
  unipolar = having a single magnetic or electric pole
  unicorn = mythological creature, usually represented as a horse, with a single horn projecting from its forehead
  unanimity = state of total agreement or unity

Root Work 56
Match each word with its definition.

1. unfeigned	(A) a commotion
2. unipolar	(B) extending beyond the world or universe
3. unanimity	(C) in a state of turmoil
4. typify	(D) not made up; genuine
5. turbid	(E) serving as a type
6. ultramodern	(F) not viable
7. typal	(G) state of total agreement
8. untenable	(H) represent as an example
9. disturbance	(I) extremely modern in ideas or style
10. ultramundane	(J) having a single magnetic or electric pole

ROOT ROUNDUP 57

- **URB** (CITY) *Latin*
  urban = related to a city
  sub**urb** = residential area outlying a city
  urbane = refined, sophisticated, suave
  urbanite = city dweller
  urbanologist = specialist in city life

- **US/UT** (USE/USEFUL) *Latin*
  usage = act of using
  usurp = seize by force
  usury = lending money at exorbitant rates
  utilitarian = concerned with usefulness rather than beauty
  utile = useful

- **VAC/VACA/VACU** (EMPTY) *Latin*
  vacate = empty of occupants
  vacuum = space empty of matter
  vacuous = empty; void; lacking intelligence; purposeless
  vacuity = emptiness of mind; lack of ideas
  vacuole = small cavity in cell cytoplasm

- **VEH/VECT** (CARRY) *Latin*
  vehicular = relating to vehicles
  vehemently = vigorously; energetically
  vector = a course or direction
  vectoring = guiding by radio communication according to vectors
  con**vect**ion = transmission

- **VEN/VENT** (COME) *Latin*
  in**vent** = produce or contrive by ingenuity
  pre**vent**ion = act of impeding; a hindrance
  con**vent**ional = customary
  circum**vent** = avoid
  contra**ven**e = act contrary to; to violate

Root Work 57
Match each word with its definition.

1. vacuity	(A) act of using
2. urbanite	(B) vigorously
3. conventional	(C) concerned with usefulness rather than beauty
4. usage	(D) city dweller
5. vehemently	(E) small cavity in cell cytoplasm
6. utilitarian	(F) avoid
7. convection	(G) specialist in city life
8. urbanologist	(H) customary
9. circumvent	(I) emptiness of mind; lack of ideas
10. vacuole	(J) transmission

ROOT ROUNDUP 58

- **VER/VERAC/VERI** (TRUE) *Latin*
  veritable = real; genuine
  verity = truthfulness
  a**ver** = to affirm; declare to be true
  veracity = accuracy, truthfulness
  verisimilitude = quality of appearing true or real

- **VERB** (WORD) *Latin*
  verbatim = corresponding word for word
  verbal = associated with words
  pro**verb**ial = widely referred to
  verbiage = an excess of words; wordiness
  verbose = wordy; long-winded

- **VERS/VERT** (TURN, CHANGE) *Latin*
  versatile = adaptable, all-purpose
  re**vers**ion = return to an earlier stage
  a**vert** = turn away; prevent
  extro**vert** = person whose psychological energy is directed outward toward other people
  vertigo = dizziness

- **VIA** (WAY, ROAD) *Latin*
  via = by way of
  via media = middle way or course
  viaduct = series of spans that carry a road over another road or
     a valley
  viatical = relating to a road or traveling
  viaticum = traveling provisions

- **VICT/VINC/VANQ** (CONQUER) *Latin*
  victor = one who defeats an adversary
  victory = defeat of an enemy; triumph
  e**vict** = force out; expel
  in**vinc**ible = impossible to overcome or defeat
  vanquish = conquer in battle; subjugate

Root Work 58
Match each word with its definition.

1.	verbose	(A)	an excess of words
2.	aver	(B)	turn away; prevent
3.	via media	(C)	relating to a road or traveling
4.	verisimilitude	(D)	declare to be true
5.	vanquish	(E)	adaptable
6.	avert	(F)	wordy; long-winded
7.	viatical	(G)	conquer in battle; subjugate
8.	verbiage	(H)	the middle way or course
9.	invincible	(I)	quality of appearing true or real
10.	versatile	(J)	impossible to defeat

ROOT ROUNDUP 59

- **VID/VIS** (SEE, LOOK) *Latin*
  video = relating to televised images
  visible = perceptible to the eye
  super**vis**or = one who is in charge
  vista = a distant view or prospect
  visage = appearance; aspect; countenance

- **VIR** (MAN) *Latin*
  virile = having the characteristics of an adult male
  virulent = very harmful; poisonous; hostile
  virago = woman who is noisy and scolding, or domineering
  virility = manly characteristic; potency
  virilism = male sexual characteristics in a female

- **VIT** (LIFE) *Latin*
  vital = characteristic of or relating to life
  vitalize = endow with life; invigorate
  curriculum **vit**ae = summary of a person's education and
    professional life
  vitamin = organic substance needed for normal growth and
    body activity
  vitality = capacity to live and grow

- **VIV/VIVA** (ALIVE, LIVELY, ANIMATED) *Latin*
  sur**viv**e = remain alive
  vivacious = lively
  con**viv**iality = sociable; merry
  vivarium = enclosure where living things are raised for observation
    and research
  vivisection = the practice of cutting into or otherwise injuring living
    animals, especially for the purpose of scientific research

- **VOC/VOKE** (CALL) *Latin*
  ad**voc**ate = recommend; to plead for
  equi**voc**al = ambiguous; misleading
  irre**voc**able = conclusive, irreversible
  vociferous = loud, vocal, and noisy
  e**voke** = to produce a reaction

Root Work 59
Match each word with its definition.

1. virulent	(A)	capacity to live and grow
2. conviviality	(B)	appearance; countenance
3. vista	(C)	endow with life
4. advocate	(D)	having the characteristics of an adult male
5. vitalize	(E)	a distant view
6. virile	(F)	loud, vocal, and noisy
7. vociferous	(G)	lively
8. vitality	(H)	very harmful; poisonous
9. visage	(I)	plead for
10. vivacious	(J)	sociable; merry

ROOT ROUNDUP 60

- **VOL/VOLI** (WISH, CHOICE) *Latin*
  voluntary = done of one's own free will
  volition = act of making a conscious choice
  bene**vol**ent = characterized by doing good

male**vol**ent = showing ill will; wishing harm to others
volitive = relating to the will; expressing a wish

• **VOLV/VOLU** (ROLL, TURN) *Latin*
e**volu**tion = changing of a thing into a more complex or better form
de**volv**e = pass on or transfer to another
re**volu**tion = a turning around an axis
volution = a turn or twist around a center
volvulus = abnormal twisting of the intestine

• **VOR/VORAC** (DEVOUR, GREEDY) *Latin*
voracious = having an insatiable appetite; ravenous
voracity = condition of being eager to consume great amounts of
food
carni**vor**e = flesh-eating animal
herbi**vor**e = animal that feeds mainly on plants
omni**vor**ous = eating both animals and plants

• **XEN/XENO** (STRANGER, FOREIGNER) *Greek*
xenophobe = person who is afraid of strangers or foreigners
xenophile = one who is attracted to foreigners
xenobiotic = foreign to living organisms
xenocryst = foreign crystal in an igneous rock
xenogenesis = production of children that are very different from
either parent

• **ZO/ZOO** (ANIMAL) *Greek*
zoology = study of the structure and classification of animals
zoolatry = animal worship
zoogenic = produced by animals
zoonosis = animal disease that can be transmitted to human beings
zoophilia = affection for animals

Root Work 60
Match each word with its definition.

1. volvulus
2. malevolent
3. herbivore
4. xenobiotic
5. revolution
6. zoogenic
7. xenophile
8. volitive
9. zoolatry
10. voracious

(A) foreign to living organisms
(B) relating to the will
(C) animal worship
(D) a turning around an axis
(E) abnormal twisting of the intestine
(F) wishing harm to others
(G) ravenous
(H) animal that feeds on plants
(I) produced by animals
(J) one who is attracted to foreigners

ROOT ROUNDUP REVIEW 56–60

Match It
Match each of the following roots to its meaning.

1. TURB ___	(A) life
2. UNI ___	(B) word
3. VEH/VECT ___	(C) one
4. VEN/VENT ___	(D) conquer
5. VERB ___	(E) devour, greedy
6. VICT/VINC/VANQ ___	(F) carry
7. VIT/VITA ___	(G) spinning, confusion, disturbance
8. VOC/VOKE ___	(H) stranger, foreigner
9. VOR/VORAC ___	(I) come
10. XEN/XENO ___	(J) call

Fill-ins
Fill in the blanks with the word that fits the definition.

invincible	**vacuous**	**virago**	**convection**	**ultramundane**
usurp	**urbane**	**unfeigned**	**viatical**	**curriculum vitae**

1. extending beyond the world or the universe _____
2. empty; void _____
3. impossible to defeat or overcome _____
4. sophisticated; refined; suave _____
5. woman who is domineering _____
6. not made up; genuine; real _____
7. relating to a road or traveling _____
8. seize by force _____
9. summary of a person's education and professional life

   _____
10. transmission _____

True or False
If the statement is correct, put (T) True; if it is incorrect, put (F) False.

1. Unanimity is a state of total chaos. _____
2. A utilitarian is concerned with aesthetics rather than usefulness. _____
3. The quality of appearing real or true is verisimilitude. _____
4. Xenogenesis is the production of children that are very similar to one parent. _____
5. Zoophilia is an abnormal fear of animals. _____

Common Suffixes

Below is a list of common suffixes with examples of how they are added to roots:

able, ible   capable of, subject to, prone to; worthy of, deserving of (*impeccable, incorrigible, irrefutable, mutable, feasible, affable, gullible, laudable, reprehensible, culpable*)

ac   relating to; person affected with (*ammoniac, celiac, maniac, cardiac, hypochondriac*)

age   relationship; condition; action or result; place (*parentage, bondage, carnage, anchorage*)

al   of, pertaining to; the act of (*logical, ephemeral, equivocal, glacial, peripheral, polemical, prodigal, provincial, rhetorical, satirical, superficial, terrestrial, whimsical, denial, rehearsal*)

an, ian   belonging to, related to, characteristic of, resembling, one that is (*Canadian, Freudian, reptilian, civilian, antediluvian, subterranean, authoritarian, partisan, artisan*)

ance, ence   action or process; state of being (*emergence, dependence, arrogance, compliance, vigilance, exuberance, impudence, nonchalance, opulence, quiescence, reticence*)

ant, ent   causing or performing something; state of being; one who does or undergoes (*document, flagrant, ardent, benevolent, indifferent, inherent, munificent, strident, virulent, contestant, pedant*)

ar, ary   relating to; connected to (*solar, polar, jocular, arbitrary, exemplary, mercenary, centenary*)

ate   act upon; having; characterized by (*obliterate, mitigate, deprecate, emulate, debilitate, extricate, facilitate, instigate, perpetuate, truncate; placate; intimidate, repudiate, ornate, innate, articulate*)

cy   state of being; quality (*ascendancy, bankruptcy, lunacy, dependency, complacency*)

dom   domain; rank; state of being; collective office (*fiefdom, boredom, martyrdom, officialdom*)

eer, er, or   person who does something (*auctioneer, engineer, contender, director, executor, orator*)

ery   a place for; the act of; state of; qualities of (*bakery, bribery, chicanery, slavery, snobbery*)

escent   becoming; beginning to be; characterized by (*crescent, nascent, evanescent, phosphorescent*)

ferous   producing; carrying (*coniferous, vociferous, aquiferous, calciferous, carboniferous*)

fic   making; causing (*terrific, horrific, beatific, prolific, soporific, benefic, malefic*)

fy   make; cause to become (*falsify, magnify, exemplify, ratify, rectify, personify, purify, mortify*)

ia   abnormal condition; relating to (*anorexia, toxemia, septicemia, memorabilia, personalia*)

ial   relating to; characterized by (*colloquial, glacial, terrestrial, inconsequential, superficial, cordial*)

ic   having to do with; one characterized by (*cosmic, hedonistic, caustic, aesthetic, altruistic, archaic, ascetic, bombastic, cryptic, dogmatic, eclectic, ironic, soporific, sporadic, lunatic, heretic*)

ide   group of related chemical compounds; binary compound; chemical element with properties that are similar to another (*diglyceride, monosaccharide, sodium chloride, potassium bromide, boride*)

il, ile   pertaining to; capable of being (*puerile, ductile, infantile, senile, servile, tensile, versatile*)

ine   having the nature of; relating to; resembling; made of; chemical substance (*divine, feline, marine, leonine, saturnine, opaline, crystalline, tourmaline, incarnadine, gasoline*)

ion, tion, ation   state or condition; the result of (*criterion, oblivion, limitation, adulation, affirmation, apprehension, aversion, conviction, degradation, disinclination, innovation, sanction, seclusion*)

ise, ize   make; become like (*surmise, maximize, scrutinize, vaporize, hypothesize, cauterize*)

ism   belief; doctrine; devotion to; act of (*ethnocentrism, egotism, fanaticism, criticism, witticism*)

ist   one who does something; one who believes or adheres to; an expert (*opportunist, cartoonist, ventriloquist, altruist, pacifist, nihilist, prohibitionist, linguist, geologist, psychiatrist, scientist*)

ite   make, do; inhabitant or native of; descendant of; adherent of (*ignite, Israelite, Luddite*)

itis inflammatory disease (*dermatitis, phlebitis, appendicitis, tendonitis, osteoarthritis*)

ity, ty state of; quality (*animosity, paucity, reality, uniformity, similarity, enmity, duplicity, depravity, insularity, notoriety, novelty, integrity, virility, tenacity, veracity*)

ive tending toward an action; belonging, quality of (*argumentative, introspective, collective, comprehensive, derivative, elusive, exhaustive, furtive, inclusive*)

let small one; small object worn on the body (*eaglet, islet, piglet, ringlet, amulet, rivulet, pamphlet*)

logy, ology expression; theory; science or study of (*eulogy, phraseology, ideology, geology*)

ly like; to the extent of, recurring at specified intervals; in a specified way (*miserly; daily, slowly*)

ment an act; state; means (*entertainment, admonishment, abatement, detachment, instrument*)

oid resembling; relating to (*android, humanoid, planetoid, asteroid, spheroid, paranoid*)

or a person or thing that does something; a quality or condition (*inspector, progenitor, incisor*)

ory relating to; characterized by; a place used for (*obligatory, conciliatory, cursory, observatory*)

ose full of; characterized by; a form of sugar (*verbose, lachrymose, jocose, sucrose, dextrose*)

osis condition; disease (*apotheosis, metamorphosis, morphosis, apoptosis, neurosis, psychosis*)

ous full of, characterized by (*assiduous, autonomous, capricious, contentious, erroneous, fastidious, gregarious, ingenious, innocuous, nefarious, pretentious, querulous, raucous, scrupulous*)

tude state of (*magnitude, solitude, solicitude, verisimilitude, lassitude, pulchritude, turpitude*)

Posttest

It's time to put your new knowledge of words and roots to the test. If you studied carefully and did the exercises diligently, you should see a significant improvement in your score compared to your score on the Pretest. Good luck!

Fill in the blank in each sentence by selecting *two* answer choices that fit the overall meaning of the sentence and produce completed sentences that are equivalent in meaning. Answers that are not fully correct will receive no credit.

1. The advent of immunization helped to _____ the spread of many communicable diseases, but more stringent public health standards probably were the major cause of their diminution.

   A precipitate
   B forestall
   C enhance
   D reprise
   E prevent
   F augment

2. The bourgeoisie is often _____ as conformist and materialistic, but they played an important role in the emergence of democracy in Europe.

   A abjured strongly
   B mocked harshly
   C lauded openly
   D lampooned
   E patronized widely
   F averred

3. As a scientist, Sigmund Freud believed that nothing happens
_____ and that all behavior is governed by laws.

   A capriciously

   B jocularly

   C latently

   D myopically

   E unpredictably

   F morbidly

4. Opponents of didacticism argue that writers should be free to write
as they want, exploring human nature unfettered by the expecta-
tions of society and unafraid of the _____ of conservative
readers and critics.

   A contempt

   B clichés

   C opprobrium

   D chagrin

   E puissance

   F mettle

**Fill in the blank in each sentence below by selecting *one* entry
from the corresponding column of choices in the way that best
completes the text.**

5. In his book *Knowledge and Wisdom,* the distinguished twentieth-
century philosopher Bertrand Russell said, "Although our age
far surpasses all previous ages in knowledge, there has been no
_____ increase in wisdom."

correlative
articulate
analogous
prodigious
imminent

6. The phrase "true fact" may prompt one to _____ whether a fact can be untrue.

gainsay
foreswear
jibe
query
juxtapose

7. The statement "Men can run faster than women" is not true because it is an overgeneralization since some women can run faster than some men. The statement could be made valid by _____ it: "Many men can run faster than many women."

substantiating
rescinding
sanctioning
distilling
qualifying

Fill in all of the blanks in the sentences by selecting *one* entry from the corresponding column of choices in the way that best completes the text. Answers that are not fully correct will not receive any credit.

8. The English expert regards concern about slight redundancies as (i) _____ and senseless (ii) _____ .

Blank (i)	Blank (ii)
meretricious	metaphysics
pedantic	argot
fractious	quibbling

9. The field of parapsychology is a (i) _____ one, with some experimenters reporting relatively small but statistically significant extrasensory perception phenomena, whereas other experimenters have been unable to replicate these results and thus (ii) _____ them.

Blank (i)	Blank (ii)
nascent	refute
moribund	corroborate
controversial	abjure

10. Until his death in 2004 John Mack, who was a professor of psychiatry at Harvard Medical School, had a reputation as (i) _____ investigator who believed that many scientists are reluctant to investigate reports of humans being abducted by aliens because such events are incompatible with the prevailing western materialist and (ii) _____ worldview.

Blank (i)	Blank (ii)
an iconoclastic	salacious
a saturnine	anthropocentric
a garrulous	egotistical

11. Countries with strong elements of communism have existed in history, but modern communism formed in response to the rise of capitalism and industrialization, which created a new class of people living and working in (i) _____ poverty of a type (ii) _____ in history.

Blank (i)	Blank (ii)
demotic	tangential
complaisant	unprecedented
abject	problematic

12. Literary critics are sometimes (i) _____ as parasites of art, but it can be argued that they serve the (ii) _____ function of distinguishing literary works that are (iii) _____ from ones that are to become central components of culture.

Blank (i)	Blank (ii)	Blank (iii)
mollified	indispensible	implausible
maligned	tacit	nugatory
rhapsodized	innocuous	ephemeral

13. The (i) _____ tradition in America has its roots in the Christian churches, such as the Quakers and Brethren, whose (ii) _____ holds that war is a transgression of Christian principles, and that men should practice conscientious objection and refuse (iii) _____ .

Blank (i)	Blank (ii)	Blank (iii)
sartorial	treatise	reparations
platonic	dogma	minutia
pacifist	tautology	conscription

14. In Africa, the European colonial powers often imposed borders (i) _____ , and so when colonies later achieved autonomy, they found themselves to be nations that were (ii) _____ and thus difficult to govern due to (iii) _____ disputes.

Blank (i)	Blank (ii)	Blank (iii)
arbitrarily	defunct	internecine
warily	democratic	international
equably	heterogeneous	mundane

Read the passages below, and then answer the questions that follow them based on the information in the passages themselves and in any introductory material or notes. The correct answer may be either stated or merely suggested in the passages.

"You cannot plumb the depths of the human heart, nor find what a man is thinking; how do you expect to search out God, who made all these things, and find out his mind or comprehend his thoughts?"

—*Apocrypha*, Judith 8:14

Experience has repeatedly confirmed that well-known maxim of Bacon's, that "a little philosophy inclineth man's mind to atheism, but depth in philosophy bringeth men's minds about to religion." In every age the most comprehensive thinkers have found in the
(5) religion of their time and country something they could accept, interpreting and illustrating that religion so as to give it depth and universal application. Even the heretics and atheists, if they have had profundity, turn out after a while to be forerunners of some new orthodoxy.
(10) What they rebel against is a religion alien to their nature; they are atheists only by accident, and relatively to a convention which inwardly offends them, but they yearn mightily in their own souls after the religious acceptance of a world interpreted in their own fashion. So it appears in the end that their atheism and loud pro-
(15) testation were in fact the hastier part of their thought, since what emboldened them to deny the poor world's faith was that they were too impatient to understand it. Indeed, the enlightenment common to young wits and worm-eaten old satirists, who plume themselves on detecting the scientific ineptitude of religion—something which
(20) the blindest half see—is not nearly enlightened enough; it points to notorious fact incompatible with religious tenets literally taken, but it leaves unexplored the habits of thought from which those tenets sprang; their original meaning, and their true function. Such studies would bring the skeptic face to face with the mystery
(25) and pathos of mortal existence. They would make him understand why religion is so profoundly moving and in a sense so profoundly just. There must needs be something humane and necessary in an influence that has become the most general sanction of virtue, the chief occasion for art and philosophy, and the source, perhaps, of
(30) the best human happiness.

—*Reason in Religion*, George Santayana

387

Select one answer choice for each of the following questions.

15. The phrase "the poor world's faith" (line 16) refers to

   Ⓐ the moribund belief systems of an earlier stage of history

   Ⓑ religions practiced in developing countries

   Ⓒ prevailing religious orthodoxy

   Ⓓ unfounded spiritual beliefs

   Ⓔ the need of indigent people to have faith that they will have a better life in the hereafter

16. The most accurate term to apply to the word "perhaps" as it is used in line 29 is

   Ⓐ irony

   Ⓑ tongue-in-cheek

   Ⓒ qualification

   Ⓓ hyperbole

   Ⓔ oxymoron

17. The phrase "the scientific ineptitude of religion" as it is used in line 19 refers to the

   Ⓐ failure of theologians to create a systematically structured belief system

   Ⓑ failure of religion to provide verifiable explanations for natural phenomena

   Ⓒ reluctance of orthodox religions to accept the discoveries of modern science

   Ⓓ disinclination of religious leaders to question church dogma

   Ⓔ inability of religion to provide a solid rational and empirical basis for its beliefs

In the following passage the author refers to articles by several scholars in two collections of papers on Mediterranean anthropology.

"Mediterranean honor," according to David Gilmore's introduction, "is a 'libidinized' social reputation; and it is this eroticized aspect of honor—albeit unconscious or implicit—that seems to make the Mediterranean variant distinctive." Again: "Mediter-
(5) ranean . . . unity is at least partly derived from the primordial values of honor and shame, and these values are deeply tied up with sexuality and power, with masculine and gender relations." Again: "If a gender-based honor-and-shame moral system defines a

Mediterranean World, then this category emerges not simply as an
(10) example of butterfly collecting, but as a mutually intelligible frame-
work of moral choices by which people communicate and gain an
identity both with and within the group." That same specification is
underlined in the collection's concluding essay by Stanley Brandes.
"It is this pervasive sexuality that is particularly characteristic of
(15) Mediterranean value systems, of Mediterranean codes of honor and
shame. In this, the codes may be distinguished from parallel moral
systems elsewhere, in Japan, for example."

In his 1977 survey of Mediterranean anthropology, John Davis
claims, "There are three main forms of stratification which have
(20) been observed in the Mediterranean: bureaucracy, class, and
honor. Each of them is related to the distribution of wealth, more
or less directly. They are, for the purpose of analysis, ideal types,
distinct elementary forms which, in substantive politics, are intertwined, mixed in varying degrees, variously important. Each is
(25) associated with an appropriate mode of political representation—
again, ideal types, elementary forms, which in the *hugger-mugger
of actual political activity have variable importance. These are:
insistence on citizen's rights; class struggle; patronage."

Those three stratification systems are exemplified very clearly in
(30) John G. Peristiany's essay. His fieldwork concentrated on the Greek
Cypriot mountain village of Alona in the middle 1950's. Stratification by bureaucracy and power is clear when the villager has to
approach a government civil servant and when "in the impersonal
interaction between citizen and civil servant the only claim upon
(35) the latter's *philotimo is that of his sectional interests, and these
call for the assertion of his administrative dignity, for arrogance
and the marking of social distance." Stratification by wealth and
class is clear "when the returned expatriate who had achieved success in a city environment wished to trade on this success as a
(40) means of achieving immediate recognition in the village . . . [and]
considered . . . further that his financial success raised him above
the confines of the village hierarchy." But neither of those other
stratifications is confused by the villagers with their own hierarchy
of honor and shame. Peristiany concludes by comparing honor and
(45) honesty:

"The punctiliousness of honor must be referred to the code of
an exclusive and *agonistic microsociety: that of honesty to an
inclusive, egalitarian macrosociety. Duty, in the first instance, is to
those with whom one shares honor. In the second, the un-Greek
(50) macrosociety, one's duty is to all fellow citizens or, even further,

*hugger-mugger: disorderly confusion
*philotimo: a Greek word meaning "love of honor"
*agonistic: combative

to all humans. . . . Honor is active. Here insecurity and the daily reevaluation of one's standing breed constant self-assertion and even heroism. The ideals of honesty and equality breed passive conformity and are more congenial to a conception of duty wide in
(55) its application, but more accommodating in its expectation."

—*The Historical Jesus, The Life of a Mediterranean Jewish Peasant,*
John Dominic Crossan

Select one answer choice for each of the following questions.

18. According to David Gilmore, honor and shame are

   Ⓐ analogous values
   Ⓑ anachronistic moral codes found only in Mediterranean culture
   Ⓒ original values of Mediterranean culture
   Ⓓ immutable values in all cultures studied by anthropologists
   Ⓔ perennial truths

19. The phrase "punctiliousness of honor" as it is used in line 46 most nearly refers to

   Ⓐ the uniqueness of the Mediterranean variant of honor
   Ⓑ the subjective nature of the concept of honor
   Ⓒ carefulness in observing rules governing honor
   Ⓓ the fact that honor is a universal concept found in all cultures
   Ⓔ the fact that the idea of honor is inextricably linked to the idea of honesty

Identify the sentence by writing its first three words and last three words on the line below.

Identify the sentence in which it is asserted that in the Mediterranean the moral code governing honesty is not as rigid as the moral code governing honor.

20. _____

End of Posttest

POSTTEST ANSWERS

1. B, E
2. B, D
3. A, E
4. A, C
5. correlative
6. query
7. qualifying
8. pedantic/quibbling
9. controversial/corroborate
10. an iconoclastic/anthropocentric
11. abject/unprecedented
12. maligned/indispensable/ephemeral
13. pacifist/dogma/conscription
14. arbitrarily/heterogeneous/internecine
15. C
16. C
17. E
18. C
19. C
20. "The ideals of . . . in its expectation." (lines 53–55)

YOUR POSTTEST SCORE

1–2   CORRECT ANSWERS: **VERY POOR**

3–5   CORRECT ANSWERS: **POOR**

6–9   CORRECT ANSWERS: **BELOW AVERAGE**

10–13   CORRECT ANSWERS: **AVERAGE**

14–16   CORRECT ANSWERS: **GOOD**

17–18   CORRECT ANSWERS: **VERY GOOD**

19–20   CORRECT ANSWERS: **EXCELLENT**

Answer Keys

ESSENTIAL WORDS FOR THE GRE

UNIT 1
Matching
1. G   2. C   3. J   4. B   5. F   6. A   7. I   8. E   9. H   10. D
Fill-ins
1. abdicated   2. aberrations   3. abeyance   4. abstemious   5. abate
6. abstinence   7. abject   8. abjured   9. abscission   10. absconded
Sense or Nonsense
1. S   2. S   3. N   4. N   5. S

UNIT 2
Matching
1. B   2. F   3. A   4. I   5. D   6. J   7. E   8. C   9. G   10. H
Fill-ins
1. affected   2. affinity   3. accretion   4. aesthetic   5. admonished
6. accrued   7. abysmal   8. adamant   9. adulterated   10. adjunct
Sense or Nonsense
1. S   2. N   3. S   4. N   5. N

UNIT 3
Matching
1. D   2. G   3. A   4. J   5. F   6. H   7. B   8. C   9. E   10. I
Fill-ins
1. allure   2. alacrity   3. alleviate   4. aggrandize   5. alchemy
6. ambiguous   7. aggregate   8. alloys   9. allay   10. amalgamate
Sense or Nonsense
1. N   2. S   3. N   4. N   5. S

UNIT 4
Matching
1. C   2. I   3. G   4. A   5. J   6. E   7. F   8. B   9. H   10. D
Fill-ins
1. ambivalent   2. anarchy   3. amulet   4. ambrosia   5. analgesic
6. analogy   7. ameliorate   8. amenable   9. anachronism   10. amenities
Sense or Nonsense
1. N   2. S   3. N   4. S   5. S

UNIT 5
Matching
1. G   2. I   3. C   4. B   5. E   6. A   7. H   8. F   9. J   10. D
Fill-ins
1. antecedents   2. antipathy   3. apathy   4. anomalous   5. appease
6. antediluvian   7. apothegms   8. anodyne   9. apogee   10. apex
Sense or Nonsense
1. N   2. S   3. N   4. N   5. S

UNIT 6
Matching
1. E   2. G   3. J   4. H   5. B   6. A   7. D   8. I   9. C   10. F
Fill-ins
1. apropos   2. apprised   3. arduous   4. ardor   5. archeology
6. appropriated   7. arabesque   8. appellation   9. apposite   10. approbation
Sense or Nonsense
1. S   2. N   3. S   4. S   5. N

UNIT 7
Matching
1. H   2. E   3. C   4. A   5. J   6. G   7. B   8. F   9. D   10. I
Fill-ins
1. artless   2. asperity   3. ascetic   4. astringent   5. artifact
6. arrest   7. assuage   8. assiduously   9. argot   10. aspersions
Sense or Nonsense
1. N   2. N   3. S   4. S   5. S

UNIT 8
Matching
1. H   2. B   3. J   4. E   5. A   6. G   7. C   8. I   9. D   10. F
Fill-ins
1. autonomous   2. austere   3. atavism   4. avuncular   5. avocation
6. asylum   7. audacious   8. avarice   9. avers   10. attenuate
Sense or Nonsense
1. N   2. S   3. S   4. S   5. N

UNIT 9
Matching
1. H   2. C   3. F   4. A   5. I   6. E   7. J   8. D   9. G   10. B
Fill-ins
1. bawdy   2. bard   3. axiomatic   4. belie   5. behemoths
6. banal   7. bedizen   8. beatification   9. bacchanalian   10. banter
Sense or Nonsense
1. N   2. S   3. S   4. N   5. S

UNIT 10
Matching
1. C   2. I   3. A   4. E   5. G   6. J   7. H   8. B   9. D   10. F
Fill-ins
1. blasé   2. bifurcation   3. beneficence   4. broached   5. bovine
6. blandishments   7. brazen   8. boorish   9. bombastic   10. bolstered
Sense or Nonsense
1. N   2. N   3. S   4. S   5. N

UNIT 11
Matching
1. F   2. H   3. A   4. B   5. I   6. C   7. G   8. J   9. D   10. E
Fill-ins
1. burgeoning   2. buttress   3. canard   4. bucolic   5. cadge
6. burnish   7. calumny   8. cacophonous   9. callous   10. canon
Sense or Nonsense
1. S   2. N   3. N   4. S   5. S

UNIT 12
Matching
1. D   2. I   3. B   4. J   5. A   6. E   7. G   8. C   9. F   10. H
Fill-ins
1. caste 2. cant 3. captious 4. capricious 5. cardinal
6. carnal 7. cartography 8. castigated 9. carping 10. cantankerous
Sense or Nonsense
1. N   2. S   3. N   4. S   5. N

UNIT 13
Matching
1. E   2. H   3. B   4. J   5. A   6. I   7. C   8. F   9. D   10. G
Fill-ins
1. championed 2. causal 3. categorical 4. catalysts 5. cataclysm
6. centripetal 7. centrifugal 8. celestial 9. caucus 10. caustic
Sense or Nonsense
1. S   2. S   3. N   4. S   5. N

UNIT 14
Matching
1. E   2. C   3. H   4. A   5. D   6. J   7. F   8. I   9. B   10. G
Fill-ins
1. chivalric 2. coagulates 3. clique 4. clamor 5. circuitous
6. churlish 7. chicanery 8. chastened 9. clairvoyant 10. cloistered
Sense or Nonsense
1. S   2. S   3. N   4. N   5. S

UNIT 15
Matching
1. B   2. H   3. A   4. J   5. C   6. E   7. I   8. F   9. D   10. G
Fill-ins
1. coda 2. complaisant 3. coalesced 4. commensurate 5. codification
6. compendium 7. complement 8. complacent 9. cognizant 10. collage
Sense or Nonsense
1. S   2. S   3. S   4. N   5. N

UNIT 16
Matching
1. B   2. I   3. A   4. G   5. D   6. J   7. E   8. C   9. H   10. F
Fill-ins
1. concomitant 2. compliant 3. conjugal 4. compunction 5. congenial
6. confounded 7. concocted 8. concave 9. condoned 10. conciliatory
Sense or Nonsense
1. N   2. S   3. S   4. S   5. S

UNIT 17
Matching
1. G   2. E   3. B   4. J   5. F   6. C   7. A   8. I   9. D   10. H
Fill-ins
1. contentious 2. contends 3. conscripted 4. conundrums 5. continence
6. connoisseur 7. contumacious 8. contiguous 9. consecrated 10. contrite
Sense or Nonsense
1. N   2. S   3. S   4. N   5. S

UNIT 18
Matching
1. F   2. D   3. B   4. J   5. A   6. G   7. H   8. E   9. C   10. I
Fill-ins
1. cosmology 2. conventions 3. convoluted 4. convex 5. convivial
6. copious 7. converges 8. covert 9. coquette 10. cornucopia
Sense or Nonsense
1. N   2. S   3. N   4. S   5. N

UNIT 19
Matching
1. D   2. H   3. A   4. E   5. I   6. C   7. B   8. G   9. J   10. F
Fill-ins
1. dearth 2. craven 3. cozens 4. daunting 5. credence
6. decorum 7. covets 8. credo 9. debauchery 10. defaming
Sense or Nonsense
1. S   2. N   3. S   4. S   5. S

UNIT 20
Matching
1. F   2. B   3. J   4. G   5. D   6. I   7. A   8. E   9. C   10. H
Fill-ins
1. denouement 2. demographic 3. denizens 4. defunct 5. delineated
6. demurred 7. demotic 8. default 9. deference 10. denigrated
Sense or Nonsense
1. N   2. S   3. N   4. S   5. S

UNIT 21
Matching
1. J   2. F   3. C   4. H   5. D   6. A   7. E   8. I   9. B   10. G
Fill-ins
1. dichotomy 2. diaphanous 3. desiccated 4. deterrent 5. derided
6. derivative 7. desultory 8. desuetude 9. diatribe 10. detraction
Sense or Nonsense
1. N   2. S   3. S   4. S   5. S

UNIT 22
Matching
1. F   2. B   3. D   4. H   5. A   6. J   7. C   8. G   9. I   10. E
Fill-ins
1. disabuse 2. discrepancy 3. dirge 4. digressions 5. discredited
6. discerning 7. diffidence 8. diffuse 9. discomfited 10. discordant
Sense or Nonsense
1. S   2. S   3. N   4. S   5. S

UNIT 23
Matching
1. I   2. F   3. H   4. B   5. A   6. J   7. D   8. C   9. G   10. E
Fill-ins
1. disinterested 2. disseminated 3. disjointed 4. disparate 5. discrete
6. dismissed 7. discretion 8. disingenuous 9. disparaged 10. dissembled
Sense or Nonsense
1. N   2. S   3. N   4. N   5. N

UNIT 24
Matching
1. I   2. C   3. J   4. E   5. B   6. G   7. F   8. D   9. H   10. A
Fill-ins
1. distill 2. dissolution 3. distended 4. dissonance 5. divested
6. dissidents 7. diverged 8. distrait 9. divulge 10. doctrinaire
Sense or Nonsense
1. N   2. N   3. S   4. S   5. S

UNIT 25
Matching
1. C   2. B   3. F   4. H   5. J   6. A   7. G   8. E   9. D   10. I
Fill-ins
1. eclectic 2. documented 3. duped 4. doggerel 5. effete
6. dogmatic 7. effervescent 8. dormant 9. dross 10. ebullient
Sense or Nonsense
1. N   2. S   3. S   4. S   5. N

UNIT 26
Matching
1. I   2. E   3. D   4. F   5. B   6. H   7. C   8. A   9. G   10. J
Fill-ins
1. elixirs 2. egoism 3. elicit 4. emaciated 5. egotistical
6. embellish 7. efficacious 8. effrontery 9. Elysian 10. elegy
Sense or Nonsense
1. N   2. N   3. N   4. S   5. S

UNIT 27
Matching
1. C   2. E   3. I   4. J   5. B   6. H   7. F   8. A   9. D   10. G
Fill-ins
1. emulated 2. enhance 3. empirical 4. enervating 5. enunciate
6. endemic 7. engendered 8. encomiums 9. emollient 10. entomologist
Sense or Nonsense
1. N   2. S   3. S   4. S   5. S

UNIT 28
Matching
1. H   2. B   3. D   4. J   5. E   6. F   7. I   8. C   9. G   10. A
Fill-ins
1. esoteric 2. ephemeral 3. equanimity 4. errant 5. erudition
6. epistemology 7. equivocate 8. essayed 9. equable 10. estimable
Sense or Nonsense
1. N   2. S   3. N   4. S   5. N

UNIT 29
Matching
1. C   2. A   3. G   4. I   5. B   6. F   7. D   8. H   9. J   10. E
Fill-ins
1. etymology 2. euphoria 3. evinces 4. etiology 5. eugenics
6. evocative 7. eulogy 8. ethnocentrism 9. euthanasia 10. euphemisms
Sense or Nonsense
1. S   2. N   3. S   4. N   5. S

UNIT 30
Matching
1. D   2. G   3. B   4. J   5. F   6. A   7. C   8. I   9. E   10. H
Fill-ins
1. exigency   2. exorcises   3. exacerbating   4. exacting   5. expatriate
6. exhorted   7. expatiate   8. execrable   9. existential   10. exculpated
Sense or Nonsense
1. N   2. S   3. S   4. N   5. N

UNIT 31
Matching
1. I   2. F   3. H   4. D   5. A   6. C   7. J   8. B   9. G   10. E
Fill-ins
1. facetious   2. explication   3. extraneous   4. expository   5. extant
6. extemporaneous   7. extirpate   8. extrinsic   9. expiate   10. extrapolating
Sense or Nonsense
1. N   2. N   3. S   4. S   5. S

UNIT 32
Matching
1. C   2. G   3. E   4. F   5. A   6. I   7. H   8. D   9. B   10. J
Fill-ins
1. fauna   2. fawning   3. feral   4. factotum   5. felicitous
6. fallacious   7. fervor   8. fatuous   9. facilitate   10. fallow
Sense or Nonsense
1. N   2. N   3. S   4. N   5. S

UNIT 33
Matching
1. I   2. F   3. C   4. E   5. A   6. H   7. B   8. D   9. J   10. G
Fill-ins
1. filibuster   2. fetid   3. fidelity   4. fiat   5. flag
6. fledgling   7. flora   8. fettered   9. finesse   10. fissures
Sense or Nonsense
1. N   2. S   3. S   4. S   5. S

UNIT 34
Matching
1. I   2. A   3. F   4. D   5. J   6. C   7. H   8. B   9. G   10. E
Fill-ins
1. flourishes   2. foundered   3. formidable   4. forswear   5. flux
6. forestall   7. foment   8. flouts   9. forbearance   10. florid
Sense or Nonsense
1. N   2. N   3. S   4. S   5. S

UNIT 35
Matching
1. I   2. E   3. A   4. F   5. C   6. J   7. G   8. B   9. H   10. D
Fill-ins
1. futile   2. fusion   3. fracas   4. frugality   5. froward
6. frieze   7. fulsome   8. fractious   9. fulminated   10. fresco
Sense or Nonsense
1. N   2. N   3. S   4. S   5. S

UNIT 36
Matching
1. C   2. F   3. D   4. I   5. H   6. J   7. G   8. B   9. E   10. A
Fill-ins
1. garrulous 2. gambol 3. geniality 4. glib 5. gerrymandering
6. goaded 7. gossamer 8. gauche 9. gouged 10. gainsay
Sense or Nonsense
1. N   2. N   3. N   4. S   5. N

UNIT 37
Matching
1. F   2. J   3. H   4. A   5. G   6. D   7. B   8. E   9. I   10. C
Fill-ins
1. grouse 2. gregarious 3. hallowed 4. gullible 5. grandiloquent
6. gustatory 7. guises 8. guileless 9. halcyon 10. harangue
Sense or Nonsense
1. N   2. S   3. S   4. S   5. N

UNIT 38
Matching
1. B   2. I   3. E   4. A   5. J   6. F   7. C   8. H   9. G   10. D
Fill-ins
1. homily 2. hermetic 3. heterodox 4. herbivorous 5. harrowing
6. homogeneous 7. hirsute 8. homeostatic 9. hieroglyphics 10. histrionic
Sense or Nonsense
1. N   2. S   3. N   4. N   5. S

UNIT 39
Matching
1. C   2. G   3. B   4. D   5. I   6. A   7. F   8. J   9. H   10. E
Fill-ins
1. hyperbole 2. impecunious 3. idolatry 4. imbroglio 5. impeded
6. immutable 7. igneous 8. iconoclastic 9. impassive 10. ideological
Sense or Nonsense
1. S   2. S   3. N   4. S   5. S

UNIT 40
Matching
1. F   2. J   3. H   4. B   5. I   6. A   7. E   8. D   9. C   10. G
Fill-ins
1. implausible 2. implacable 3. implicit 4. implosions 5. impinging
6. impermeable 7. impervious 8. imperturbable 9. impute 10. imprecations
Sense or Nonsense
1. S   2. S   3. S   4. N   5. S

UNIT 41
Matching
1. F   2. H   3. A   4. J   5. C   6. B   7. D   8. I   9. G   10. E
Fill-ins
1. inconsequential 2. indolent 3. incursions 4. incorporates 5. indeterminate
6. incongruous 7. inchoate 8. inadvertently 9. incarnate 10. indigent
Sense or Nonsense
1. S   2. S   3. S   4. N   5. S

UNIT 42
Matching
1. F   2. C   3. I   4. G   5. J   6. D   7. A   8. E   9. B   10. H
Fill-ins
1. insensible 2. insularity 3. insipid 4. ingenuous 5. inert
6. insinuating 7. insouciance 8. inherent 9. ineluctable 10. innocuous
Sense or Nonsense
1. N   2. N   3. N   4. N   5. S

UNIT 43
Matching
1. B   2. D   3. I   4. E   5. J   6. G   7. F   8. C   9. A   10. H
Fill-ins
1. intransigence 2. intimate 3. insuperable 4. interdicting 5. intangible
6. interpolated 7. internecine 8. introspection 9. interregnum 10. intractable
Sense or Nonsense
1. N   2. N   3. S   4. S   5. S

UNIT 44
Matching
1. D   2. B   3. E   4. A   5. J   6. F   7. H   8. I   9. G   10. C
Fill-ins
1. invective 2. irascible 3. invidious 4. itinerant 5. inveigh
6. inundated 7. inveterate 8. inured 9. irresolute 10. inveigle
Sense or Nonsense
1. N   2. S   3. S   4. N   5. S

UNIT 45
Matching
1. H   2. E   3. A   4. C   5. J   6. G   7. B   8. F   9. D   10. I
Fill-ins
1. juggernaut 2. junta 3. jocose 4. itinerary 5. labile
6. juxtaposed 7. jaundiced 8. kudos 9. laconic 10. jibe
Sense or Nonsense
1. N   2. N   3. S   4. S   5. S

UNIT 46
Matching
1. B   2. D   3. J   4. G   5. C   6. E   7. A   8. H   9. F   10. I
Fill-ins
1. levee 2. lambasted 3. lassitude 4. lauded 5. liberal
6. latent 7. lethargic 8. lascivious 9. levity 10. libertine
Sense or Nonsense
1. N   2. S   3. S   4. S   5. S

UNIT 47
Matching
1. B   2. F   3. D   4. A   5. J   6. G   7. H   8. C   9. I   10. E
Fill-ins
1. libido 2. literati 3. logs 4. loquacious 5. limpid
6. litany 7. litigation 8. limning 9. linguistics 10. Lilliputian
Sense or Nonsense
1. N   2. N   3. S   4. S   5. S

UNIT 48
Matching
1. G 2. B 3. A 4. J 5. I 6. D 7. F 8. C 9. H 10. E
Fill-ins
1. lucid 2. Machiavellian 3. luminous 4. maligned 5. lucre
6. magnanimity 7. lustrous 8. maelstrom 9. malingering 10. machinations
Sense or Nonsense
1. N 2. S 3. N 4. S 5. S

UNIT 49
Matching
1. H 2. A 3. E 4. B 5. J 6. D 7. I 8. G 9. C 10. F
Fill-ins
1. metaphysical 2. metamorphosed 3. mendicant 4. megalomania 5. malleable
6. mavericks 7. meretricious 8. mesmerized 9. mendacious 10. menagerie
Sense or Nonsense
1. N 2. N 3. S 4. N 5. S

UNIT 50
Matching
1. H 2. C 3. A 4. G 5. F 6. D 7. I 8. B 9. J 10. E
Fill-ins
1. mettle 2. meteorological 3. misanthropic 4. militates 5. meticulous
6. minatory 7. microcosm 8. mettlesome 9. minuscule 10. minutia
Sense or Nonsense
1. S 2. S 3. N 4. S 5. N

UNIT 51
Matching
1. E 2. B 3. F 4. I 5. G 6. C 7. J 8. A 9. D 10. H
Fill-ins
1. misogynist 2. mollify 3. monolithic 4. mnemonic 5. miscellany
6. morose 7. mitigate 8. modicum 9. miscreant 10. motley
Sense or Nonsense
1. N 2. S 3. S 4. S 5. S

UNIT 52
Matching
1. D 2. J 3. C 4. A 5. F 6. B 7. I 8. G 9. E 10. H
Fill-ins
1. negated 2. mundane 3. nonplussed 4. nostrums 5. nexus
6. neologisms 7. multifarious 8. nostalgia 9. neophyte 10. necromancy
Sense or Nonsense
1. S 2. S 3. N 4. S 5. N

UNIT 53
Matching
1. G 2. C 3. B 4. F 5. J 6. E 7. H 8. D 9. A 10. I
Fill-ins
1. obsequious 2. obviated 3. olfactory 4. officious 5. occult
6. occludes 7. obdurate 8. odyssey 9. nugatory 10. obsequies
Sense or Nonsense
1. N 2. S 3. S 4. N 5. S

UNIT 54
Matching
1. E   2. C   3. J   4. A   5. H   6. F   7. B   8. G   9. D   10. I
Fill-ins
1. paeans 2. oligarchy 3. oscillating 4. ornithologists 5. onerous
6. paleontologists 7. ostentatious 8. overweening 9. opprobrium 10. onomatopoeia
Sense or Nonsense
1. N   2. N   3. S   4. S   5. S

UNIT 55
Matching
1. H   2. J   3. G   4. B   5. D   6. A   7. I   8. C   9. F   10. E
Fill-ins
1. pathology 2. pellucid 3. pedantic 4. partisan 5. patois
6. pallid 7. penchant 8. paragons 9. panegyric 10. paucity
Sense or Nonsense
1. N   2. N   3. S   4. S   5. S

UNIT 56
Matching
1. F   2. I   3. G   4. D   5. J   6. B   7. C   8. A   9. E   10. H
Fill-ins
1. perigee 2. permeable 3. pervasive 4. perennial 5. perfidious
6. penury 7. perfunctory 8. peregrinations 9. perturbed 10. peremptory
Sense or Nonsense
1. N   2. N   3. S   4. S   5. S

UNIT 57
Matching
1. C   2. B   3. F   4. D   5. J   6. H   7. G   8. I   9. A   10. E
Fill-ins
1. placid 2. piety 3. plaintive 4. piqued 5. physiognomy
6. petulant 7. phoenix 8. placated 9. piquant 10. phlegmatic
Sense or Nonsense
1. N   2. S   3. S   4. N   5. S

UNIT 58
Matching
1. G   2. A   3. F   4. D   5. I   6. E   7. H   8. B   9. J   10. C
Fill-ins
1. plethora 2. porous 3. platonic 4. plumbed 5. platitudes
6. poseur 7. plutocracy 8. pragmatic 9. plasticity 10. plummet
Sense or Nonsense
1. S   2. N   3. S   4. S   5. S

UNIT 59
Matching
1. B   2. E   3. C   4. I   5. G   6. H   7. J   8. F   9. A   10. D
Fill-ins
1. precursor 2. precepts 3. prehensile 4. precarious 5. prattle
6. preamble 7. precipitated 8. preempted 9. precipitate 10. prated
Sense or Nonsense
1. S   2. S   3. N   4. S   5. S

UNIT 60
Matching
1. E   2. G   3. A   4. C   5. I   6. D   7. J   8. F   9. B   10. H
Fill-ins
1. preternatural 2. presage 3. premonition 4. primordial 5. prevaricating
6. pristine 7. problematic 8. prodigal 9. presumptuous 10. probity
Sense or Nonsense
1. N   2. N   3. N   4. S   5. S

UNIT 61
Matching
1. E   2. C   3. J   4. G   5. I   6. A   7. D   8. F   9. B   10. H
Fill-ins
1. proscribes 2. proliferating 3. punctilious 4. puissant 5. propriety
6. profound 7. propensity 8. propitiated 9. prohibitive 10. provident
Sense or Nonsense
1. S   2. N   3. S   4. S   5. S

UNIT 62
Matching
1. E   2. C   3. G   4. A   5. I   6. F   7. J   8. H   9. B   10. D
Fill-ins
1. quagmire 2. purported 3. pungent 4. quailed 5. qualms
6. query 7. qualified 8. pusillanimous 9. quibble 10. quiescent
Sense or Nonsense
1. S   2. S   3. N   4. S   5. S

UNIT 63
Matching
1. J   2. E   3. H   4. D   5. B   6. C   7. A   8. I   9. F   10. G
Fill-ins
1. recalcitrant 2. ramifications 3. rationale 4. raiment 5. rails
6. quorum 7. raconteur 8. rarefied 9. rebus 10. recant
Sense or Nonsense
1. N   2. N   3. S   4. S   5. S

UNIT 64
Matching
1. F   2. C   3. I   4. G   5. A   6. E   7. B   8. J   9. D   10. H
Fill-ins
1. regaled 2. refractory 3. relegated 4. reneged 5. refulgent
6. recluse 7. recondite 8. redoubtable 9. remonstrated 10. refute
Sense or Nonsense
1. N   2. S   3. S   4. S   5. N

UNIT 65
Matching
1. G   2. B   3. I   4. A   5. F   6. E   7. J   8. C   9. D   10. H
Fill-ins
1. reproached 2. resolved 3. repudiated 4. rescinded 5. resolution
6. reparations 7. reticent 8. repine 9. reprobate 10. reprise
Sense or Nonsense
1. S   2. S   3. S   4. S   5. N

UNIT 66
Matching
1. F   2. H   3. D   4. J   5. G   6. A   7. C   8. B   9. I   10. E
Fill-ins
1. revere   2. riposte   3. rue   4. ruse   5. sage
6. salacious   7. salubrious   8. salutary   9. rubric   10. rococo
Sense or Nonsense
1. S   2. N   3. S   4. S   5. S

UNIT 67
Matching
1. D   2. G   3. A   4. F   5. J   6. H   7. B   8. I   9. C   10. E
Fill-ins
1. savored   2. satiate   3. saturnine   4. saturated   5. sanctions
6. sartorial   7. satyr   8. schematic   9. secrete   10. sardonic
Sense or Nonsense
1. N   2. S   3. S   4. S   5. S

UNIT 68
Matching
1. C   2. G   3. J   4. E   5. A   6. F   7. I   8. B   9. D   10. H
Fill-ins
1. servile   2. sedition   3. sedulous   4. seismic   5. shards
6. sextant   7. sidereal   8. sentient   9. sensual   10. sensuous
Sense or Nonsense
1. S   2. N   3. S   4. S   5. S

UNIT 69
Matching
1. I   2. C   3. A   4. E   5. J   6. F   7. B   8. D   9. H   10. G
Fill-ins
1. sobriety   2. singular   3. solicitous   4. skeptic   5. similes
6. sinecure   7. sinuous   8. soliloquy   9. sodden   10. simian
Sense or Nonsense
1. S   2. S   3. S   4. S   5. N

UNIT 70
Matching
1. D   2. H   3. J   4. A   5. F   6. B   7. E   8. C   9. G   10. I
Fill-ins
1. specious   2. spendthrift   3. squalor   4. staccato   5. spectrum
6. sporadic   7. solvent   8. soporific   9. somatic   10. sordid
Sense or Nonsense
1. S   2. S   3. N   4. S   5. S

UNIT 71
Matching
1. I   2. H   3. J   4. A   5. D   6. F   7. B   8. G   9. C   10. E
Fill-ins
1. stipulate   2. stolid   3. striated   4. stratified   5. strident
6. stanch   7. stentorian   8. stint   9. strictures   10. stigma
Sense or Nonsense
1. S   2. S   3. S   4. N   5. S

UNIT 72
Matching
1. E   2. I   3. C   4. A   5. G   6. F   7. B   8. J   9. H   10. D
Fill-ins
1. stupefied 2. substantive 3. strutted 4. subsumes 5. stultifying
6. subversive 7. stygian 8. subpoenaed 9. subside 10. substantiate
Sense or Nonsense
1. S   2. N   3. S   4. N   5. S

UNIT 73
Matching
1. G   2. J   3. B   4. E   5. C   6. I   7. A   8. D   9. H   10. F
Fill-ins
1. superseded 2. sundry 3. supplicants 4. succor 5. supine
6. syllogism 7. supposition 8. suffrage 9. supplanted 10. suppliant
Sense or Nonsense
1. S   2. N   3. S   4. N   5. S

UNIT 74
Matching
1. F   2. B   3. H   4. I   5. E   6. G   7. A   8. J   9. D   10. C
Fill-ins
1. tacit 2. tangential 3. sylvan 4. taciturn 5. theocracy
6. talismans 7. tenet 8. taxonomy 9. tenuous 10. tautologies
Sense or Nonsense
1. N   2. S   3. S   4. S   5. S

UNIT 75
Matching
1. D   2. G   3. A   4. F   5. H   6. J   7. B   8. I   9. C   10. E
Fill-ins
1. timbre 2. thespians 3. touts 4. tractable 5. tirade
6. torpor 7. tortuous 8. torque 9. tome 10. toady
Sense or Nonsense
1. N   2. N   3. N   4. N   5. N

UNIT 76
Matching
1. H   2. D   3. B   4. G   5. E   6. A   7. J   8. C   9. F   10. I
Fill-ins
1. travails 2. truculence 3. transient 4. treatise 5. tremulous
6. translucent 7. transgressed 8. tryst 9. travesty 10. trepidation
Sense or Nonsense
1. S   2. S   3. S   4. N   5. S

UNIT 77
Matching
1. C   2. G   3. I   4. A   5. E   6. B   7. D   8. J   9. H   10. F
Fill-ins
1. unfeigned 2. untenable 3. usury 4. turgid 5. tumid
6. untoward 7. undulating 8. uncanny 9. tutelary 10. turbid
Sense or Nonsense
1. S   2. N   3. S   4. N   5. S

UNIT 78
Matching
1. C   2. J   3. H   4. F   5. B   6. D   7. A   8. I   9. G   10. E
Fill-ins
1. venerated 2. vapid 3. veracious 4. venal 5. valedictory
6. vendetta 7. vaunted 8. vacuous 9. variegated 10. vacillating
Sense or Nonsense
1. N   2. S   3. S   4. S   5. N

UNIT 79
Matching
1. F   2. I   3. J   4. E   5. C   6. G   7. D   8. A   9. B   10. H
Fill-ins
1. vituperative 2. vindictive 3. vertigo 4. virtuoso 5. visage
6. verbose 7. viscous 8. viable 9. vitiated 10. vexations
Sense or Nonsense
1. S   2. S   3. S   4. N   5. S

UNIT 80
Matching
1. B   2. G   3. A   4. E   5. J   6. H   7. F   8. C   9. I   10. D
Fill-ins
1. zealot 2. wary 3. welter 4. warranted 5. vogue
6. volatile 7. vivisections 8. whimsical 9. wistful 10. vortex
Sense or Nonsense
1. S   2. S   3. S   4. S   5. S

ROOT ROUNDUP

ROOT WORK 1
1. E   2. D   3. I   4. J   5. H   6. B   7. A   8. C   9. G   10. F

ROOT WORK 2
1. D   2. F   3. J   4. I   5. A   6. H   7. C   8. G   9. E   10. B

ROOT WORK 3
1. F   2. G   3. J   4. C   5. B   6. E   7. H   8. I   9. A   10. D

ROOT WORK 4
1. E   2. F   3. J   4. A   5. I   6. D   7. B   8. H   9. C   10. G

ROOT WORK 5
1. I   2. C   3. F   4. J   5. D   6. H   7. B   8. E   9. A   10. G

ROOT WORK 6
1. J   2. D   3. I   4. A   5. B   6. E   7. C   8. H   9. F   10. G

ROOT WORK 7
1. G   2. I   3. F   4. B   5. J   6. H   7. D   8. C   9. E   10. A

ROOT WORK 8
1. E   2. J   3. F   4. G   5. B   6. A   7. D   8. I   9. H   10. C

ROOT WORK 9
1. G   2. J   3. I   4. F   5. A   6. C   7. H   8. D   9. E   10. B

ROOT WORK 10
1. G   2. I   3. E   4. J   5. H   6. B   7. F   8. C   9. A   10. D

ROOT WORK 11
1. J   2. H   3. E   4. I   5. C   6. B   7. D   8. G   9. A   10. F

ROOT WORK 12
1. E   2. I   3. F   4. D   5. B   6. H   7. C   8. J   9. G   10. A

ROOT WORK 13
1. D   2. E   3. A   4. G   5. B   6. I   7. H   8. C   9. J   10. F

ROOT WORK 14
1. F   2. J   3. G   4. I   5. H   6. B   7. E   8. D   9. C   10. A

ROOT WORK 15
1. G   2. I   3. J   4. H   5. D   6. F   7. B   8. E   9. C   10. A

ROOT WORK 16
1. D   2. I   3. G   4. J   5. B   6. E   7. F   8. A   9. H   10. C

ROOT WORK 17
1. G   2. D   3. F   4. I   5. J   6. H   7. C   8. B   9. A   10. E

ROOT WORK 18
1. F   2. I   3. G   4. H   5. J   6. A   7. C   8. E   9. B   10. D

ROOT WORK 19
1. F   2. D   3. I   4. J   5. A   6. B   7. H   8. E   9. C   10. G

ROOT WORK 20
1. J   2. G   3. H   4. I   5. E   6. A   7. D   8. F   9. C   10. B

ROOT WORK 21
1. H   2. E   3. A   4. G   5. D   6. I   7. F   8. B   9. C   10. J

ROOT WORK 22
1. C   2. D   3. A   4. G   5. F   6. B   7. I   8. E   9. J   10. H

ROOT WORK 23
1. G   2. D   3. I   4. C   5. B   6. A   7. J   8. E   9. H   10. F

ROOT WORK 24
1. I   2. F   3. D   4. G   5. J   6. B   7. A   8. C   9. E   10. H

ROOT WORK 25
1. F   2. I   3. H   4. A   5. J   6. B   7. E   8. G   9. D   10. C

ROOT WORK 26
1. C   2. H   3. D   4. B   5. G   6. J   7. A   8. F   9. E   10. I

ROOT WORK 27
1. F 2. E 3. H 4. D 5. G 6. A 7. I 8. J 9. C 10. B

ROOT WORK 28
1. D 2. J 3. E 4. G 5. B 6. I 7. A 8. F 9. H 10. C

ROOT WORK 29
1. G 2. J 3. A 4. I 5. C 6. D 7. F 8. H 9. B 10. E

ROOT WORK 30
1. I 2. F 3. E 4. A 5. G 6. J 7. B 8. H 9. C 10. D

ROOT WORK 31
1. H 2. E 3. A 4. G 5. B 6. J 7. F 8. C 9. I 10. D

ROOT WORK 32
1. J 2. D 3. E 4. G 5. F 6. I 7. H 8. C 9. B 10. A

ROOT WORK 33
1. G 2. H 3. J 4. E 5. D 6. B 7. F 8. C 9. A 10. I

ROOT WORK 34
1. G 2. I 3. F 4. E 5. A 6. J 7. D 8. C 9. B 10. H

ROOT WORK 35
1. G 2. J 3. I 4. F 5. H 6. A 7. E 8. D 9. B 10. C

ROOT WORK 36
1. J 2. I 3. F 4. H 5. G 6. D 7. E 8. B 9. A 10. C

ROOT WORK 37
1. H 2. G 3. I 4. F 5. J 6. C 7. D 8. B 9. E 10. A

ROOT WORK 38
1. D 2. J 3. H 4. G 5. I 6. A 7. C 8. E 9. F 10. B

ROOT WORK 39
1. J 2. I 3. G 4. H 5. E 6. F 7. D 8. B 9. C 10. A

ROOT WORK 40
1. I 2. A 3. H 4. E 5. B 6. J 7. D 8. C 9. F 10. G

ROOT WORK 41
1. F 2. D 3. G 4. B 5. C 6. I 7. J 8. A 9. H 10. E

ROOT WORK 42
1. E 2. F 3. G 4. H 5. J 6. C 7. D 8. B 9. A 10. I

ROOT WORK 43
1. D 2. E 3. H 4. J 5. B 6. I 7. A 8. C 9. F 10. G

ROOT WORK 44
1. F   2. A   3. J   4. H   5. E   6. C   7. G   8. I   9. B   10. D

ROOT WORK 45
1. G   2. H   3. F   4. D   5. B   6. C   7. A   8. I   9. J   10. E

ROOT WORK 46
1. I   2. J   3. F   4. A   5. H   6. G   7. D   8. B   9. C   10. E

ROOT WORK 47
1. D   2. H   3. I   4. B   5. C   6. A   7. E   8. F   9. G   10. J

ROOT WORK 48
1. E   2. G   3. F   4. J   5. H   6. I   7. A   8. C   9. B   10. D

ROOT WORK 49
1. E   2. I   3. J   4. C   5. B   6. F   7. A   8. H   9. D   10. G

ROOT WORK 50
1. I   2. C   3. J   4. F   5. H   6. B   7. E   8. G   9. D   10. A

ROOT WORK 51
1. J   2. C   3. F   4. H   5. E   6. B   7. D   8. A   9. G   10. I

ROOT WORK 52
1. D   2. C   3. H   4. B   5. J   6. I   7. A   8. G   9. E   10. F

ROOT WORK 53
1. E   2. G   3. F   4. H   5. I   6. C   7. J   8. D   9. B   10. A

ROOT WORK 54
1. D   2. J   3. H   4. G   5. F   6. I   7. B   8. C   9. E   10. A

ROOT WORK 55
1. F   2. E   3. G   4. J   5. D   6. A   7. I   8. B   9. H   10. C

ROOT WORK 56
1. D   2. J   3. G   4. H   5. C   6. I   7. E   8. F   9. A   10. B

ROOT WORK 57
1. I   2. D   3. H   4. A   5. B   6. C   7. J   8. G   9. F   10. E

ROOT WORK 58
1. F   2. D   3. H   4. I   5. G   6. B   7. C   8. A   9. J   10. E

ROOT WORK 59
1. H   2. J   3. E   4. I   5. C   6. D   7. F   8. A   9. B   10. G

ROOT WORK 60
1. E   2. F   3. H   4. A   5. D   6. I   7. J   8. B   9. C   10. G

ROOT ROUNDUP REVIEW

ROOT ROUNDUP REVIEW 1–5
Match It
1. F   2. A   3. I   4. G   5. J   6. D   7. E   8. B   9. H   10. C
Fill-ins
1. pedagogue   2. perambulate   3. antiquate   4. aliment   5. inanimate
6. anarchy   7. unapt   8. annuity   9. agrarian   10. acumen
True or False
1. F   2. F   3. T   4. T   5. F

ROOT ROUNDUP REVIEW 6–10
Match It
1. H   2. C   3. I   4. G   5. J   6. A   7. B   8. E   9. D   10. F
Fill-ins
1. symbiotic   2. auger   3. subaqueous   4. archaic   5. incessant
6. centrifugal   7. benediction   8. catapult   9. centripetal   10. captious
True or False
1. F   2. F   3. F   4. T   5. F

ROOT ROUNDUP REVIEW 11–15
Match It
1. G   2. I   3. B   4. F   5. D   6. A   7. C   8. J   9. E   10. H
Fill-ins
1. civil   2. cosmopolitan   3. coherent   4. cite   5. criterion
6. corpulent   7. miscreate   8. deprecate   9. synclinal   10. cyclothymia
True or False
1. F   2. T   3. T   4. T   5. F

ROOT ROUNDUP REVIEW 16–20
Match It
1. G   2. J   3. H   4. A   5. I   6. C   7. B   8. D   9. F   10. E
Fill-ins
1. pandemic   2. duple   3. obdurate   4. donatio mortis causa   5. inequity
6. dichotomy   7. epigeal   8. ductile   9. dermatitis   10. malediction
True or False
1. F   2. F   3. T   4. F   5. T

ROOT ROUNDUP REVIEW 21–25
Match It
1. I   2. F   3. G   4. A   5. J   6. D   7. H   8. B   9. E   10. C
Fill-ins
1. gravitas   2. perfidious   3. fractious   4. genre   5. perfunctory
6. euphony   7. egress   8. fin de siècle   9. extraneous   10. soporific
True or False
1. F   2. T   3. F   4. T   5. F

ROOT ROUNDUP REVIEW 26–30
Match It
1. I   2. F   3. J   4. C   5. G   6. D   7. B   8. E   9. A   10. H
Fill-ins
1. lexical   2. hemoptysis   3. lector   4. hyperbole   5. literati
6. internecine   7. jurisprudence   8. misogynist   9. impecunious   10. hominoid
True or False
1. T   2. F   3. T   4. F   5. F

ROOT ROUNDUP REVIEW 31–35
Match It
1. G   2. D   3. H   4. A   5. J   6. B   7. I   8. C   9. F   10. E
Fill-ins
1. missive 2. nascent 3. diminution 4. malfeasance 5. misogynist
6. matrilineal 7. morphology 8. mandamus 9. metanoia 10. macrocosm
True or False
1. F   2. F   3. T   4. F   5. T

ROOT ROUNDUP REVIEW 36–40
Match It
1. F   2. A   3. E   4. J   5. G   6. B   7. I   8. D   9. C   10. H
Fill-ins
1. orthopraxy 2. ignominious 3. paramount 4. osteoma 5. omniscient
6. navarch 7. noctivagant 8. oligophagous 9. apartheid 10. pernicious
True or False
1. F   2. T   3. T   4. F   5. F

ROOT ROUNDUP REVIEW 41–45
Match It
1. C   2. G   3. A   4. I   5. H   6. E   7. B   8. J   9. F   10. D
Fill-ins
1. prehensile 2. depict 3. agoraphobia 4. pedagogue 5. protogenic
6. percutaneous 7. postdiluvian 8. placate 9. cacophony 10. portage
True or False
1. F   2. T   3. T   4. T   5. T

ROOT ROUNDUP REVIEW 46–50
Match It
1. I   2. E   3. G   4. B   5. C   6. A   7. J   8. F   9. H   10. D
Fill-ins
1. ridibund 2. sophistry 3. retrospect 4. secant 5. somniloquence
6. pseudodox 7. recant 8. rogation 9. punctilio 10. sequatious
True or False
1. F   2. T   3. T   4. F   5. F

ROOT ROUNDUP REVIEW 51–55
Match It
1. J   2. F   3. G   4. A   5. H   6. B   7. D   8. E   9. C   10. I
Fill-ins
1. theogamy 2. contention 3. thermoduric 4. status quo 5. tenacious
6. synchronous 7. torque 8. supernal 9. stricture 10. toponym
True or False
1. T   2. F   3. F   4. F   5. T

ROOT ROUNDUP REVIEW 56–60
Match It
1. G   2. C   3. F   4. I   5. B   6. D   7. A   8. J   9. E   10. H
Fill-ins
1. ultramundane 2. vacuous 3. invincible 4. urbane 5. virago
6. unfeigned 7. viatical 8. usurp 9. curriculum vitae 10. convection
True or False
1. F   2. F   3. T   4. F   5. F

Index